An Introduction to European Law

Third edition

Robert Schütze

D1639825

OXFORD
UNIVERSITY PRESS

Great Clarendon Street, Oxford, OX2 6DP,
United Kingdom

Oxford University Press is a department of the University of Oxford.
It furthers the University's objective of excellence in research, scholarship,
and education by publishing worldwide. Oxford is a registered trade mark of
Oxford University Press in the UK and in certain other countries

First Edition 2012
Second Edition 2015
Third Edition 2020

Impression: 3

Public sector information reproduced under Open Government Licence v3.0
(http://www.nationalarchives.gov.uk/doc/open-government-licence/open-government-licence.htm)

Published in the United States of America by Oxford University Press
198 Madison Avenue, New York, NY 10016, United States of America

British Library Cataloguing in Publication Data

Data available

Library of Congress Control Number: 2020936576

ISBN 978–0–19–885894–2

Printed in Great Britain by
Bell & Bain Ltd., Glasgow

In Memory of Boris Rotenberg:
Debater, Dreamer, Traveller

Summary Contents

Contents

Part II European Law: Enforcement

List of Illustrations

List of Tables

Acknowledgements

Thankful acknowledgements are made to Hart Publishing, Kluwer Law International, Cambridge University Press, and Sweet & Maxwell for their kind permission to incorporate sections from previously published material. Chapter 4 in particular represents a shortened and amended version of material originally published in R. Schütze, 'Three "Bills of Rights" for the European Union' (2011) 30 *Yearbook of European Law* 131. Figure 1.2 is adapted from 'A new push for European democracy' © European Union, 2019. Extracts from EUR-Lex are reproduced with permission of the European Union, in accordance with Creative Commons Attribution 4.0 International: https://creativecommons.org/licenses/by/4.0/. Every effort has been made to trace and contact copyright holders prior to publication. Where this has not been possible, if notified, the publisher will undertake to rectify any errors or omissions at the earliest opportunity.

In writing this small text, I am grateful to many a colleague and collaborator, and especially to Sinead Moloney, Valerie Appleby, and Amy Chard who have provided truly wonderful and professional support for, respectively, the first, second, and third editions of this book. The book is dedicated to an extraordinary friend from my 'EUI years': Boris Rotenberg, who died much too young.

Table of cases

1. European Court of Justice: cases (numerical)

2. European Court of Justice: cases (alphabetical)

3. General Court: cases (numerical)

4. Other jurisdictions: cases (alphabetical)

BVerfGE	*Bundesverfassungsgerichtsentscheidungen* (German Federal Constitutional Court Reports)
BvR	Case number of the *Bundesverfassungsgericht*
CCP	Common Commercial Policy
CEE	Charge having an Equivalent Effect
CMLR	Common Market Law Reports
Coreper	Committee of Permanent Representatives
DR	European Commission on Human Rights: Decisions and Reports
EC	European Community (Treaty)
ECHR	European Convention on Human Rights
ECJ	European Court of Justice
ECR	European Court Reports
ECSC	European Coal and Steel Community
EEA	European Economic Area
EEC	European Economic Community (Treaty)
EFTA	European Free Trade Association
EMU	European Monetary Union
EU (old)	European Union (Maastricht Treaty)
GATT	General Agreement on Tariffs and Trade
MEEQR	Measure having an Equivalent Effect to Quantitative Restrictions
MFN	Most Favoured Nation (principle)
OJ	Official Journal of the European Union
SEA	Single European Act
TEU	Treaty on European Union (post-Lisbon)
TFEU	Treaty on the Functioning of the European Union
US	United States
WTO	World Trade Organization

Introduction

The idea of European integration is as old as the European idea of the sovereign State.[1] Yet the spectacular rise of the latter overshadowed the idea of a European Union for centuries. Within the twentieth century, two ruinous world wars and the social forces of globalization have however increasingly discredited the idea of the sovereign State. The decline of the—isolated—State found expression in the spread of interstate cooperation. The various efforts at European cooperation after the Second World War indeed formed part of the transition from an international law of coexistence to an international law of cooperation.[2] Yet European 'integration' would go far beyond the traditional forms of international 'cooperation'.

The European Union was born in 1952 with the coming into being of the European Coal and Steel Community (ECSC). Its original members were six European States: Belgium, France, Germany, Italy, Luxembourg, and the Netherlands. The Community had been created to integrate only one industrial sector—coal and steel; but the very concept of *integration* indicated the general wish of the contracting States 'to break with the ordinary forms of international treaties and organizations'.[3] The 1957 Treaties of Rome subsequently created two additional Communities: the European Atomic Energy Community and the European (Economic) Community. These *three* Communities were partly 'merged' in 1967,[4] but continued to exist in relative independence. A first major treaty reform was effected in 1987 through the Single European Act. But a much bigger organizational leap was taken by the 1992 Maastricht Treaty. The latter integrated the three Communities into the (Maastricht) European Union.

---

[1] R. H. Foerster, *Die Idee Europa 1300–1946, Quellen zur Geschichte der politischen Einigung* (Deutscher Taschenbuchverlag, 1963).

[2] W. G. Friedmann, *The Changing Structure of International Law* (Stevens, 1964).

[3] For a detailed discussion of the negotiations leading up to the signature of the ECSC Treaty, see: H. Mosler, 'Der Vertrag über die Europäische Gemeinschaft für Kohle und Stahl' (1951/2) 14 *Zeitschrift für ausländisches öffentliches Recht und Völkerrecht* 24 (author's translation).

[4] This was achieved through the 1965 'Merger Treaty' (see Treaty establishing a Single Council and a Single Commission of the European Communities).

From 1992-2001, this European Union was under constant constitutional construction. Treaty amendment followed treaty amendment! And in an attempt to get away from the ever-repeating minor treaty amendments, a European Convention was tasked to prepare a major reform that would result in the 'Constitutional Treaty'. The 2004 Constitutional Treaty would have caused the biggest structural change in the history of the European Union. Yet the Treaty failed when Dutch and French referenda were lost. When the 2007 Reform (Lisbon) Treaty came into force on 1st December 2009, it was the conclusion of nearly two decades of reform effort. The Lisbon Treaty replicates nearly 90 per cent of the (failed) Constitutional Treaty and came into force on 1 December 2009. Despite its modest name, the Lisbon Treaty constituted a radical new chapter in the history of the European Union. For while it formally builds on one of the original founding Treaties and the 1992 Treaty on European Union (Table 0.1), it has nonetheless merged the old 'Community' legal

Table 0.1 European Treaties—chronology

Signed	Name	Published	Entry
1951	Treaty establishing the European Coal and Steel Community	Founding Treaty[5]	1952
1957	Treaty establishing the European (Economic) Community	Founding Treaty[6]	1958
1957	Treaty establishing the European Atomic Energy Community	Founding Treaty	1958
1965	Treaty establishing a Single Council and a Single Commission	[1967] OJ 152	1967
1986	Single European Act	[1987] OJ L169	1987
1992	Treaty on European Union	[1992] OJ C191[7]	1993
1997	Treaty of Amsterdam	[1997] OJ C340	1999
2001	Treaty of Nice	[2001] OJ C80	2003
2004	Treaty establishing a Constitution for Europe	[2004] OJ C310	Failed
2007	Treaty of Lisbon amending the Treaty on European Union and the Treaty establishing the European Community	[2007] OJ C306	2009

[5] The Treaty expired in 2002.

[6] For a consolidated version of the Treaty establishing the European Community, see [2002] OJ C325.

[7] For a consolidated version of the Treaty on European Union, see ibid.

order with the old 'Union' legal order. The textual foundations of the 'new' European Union are indeed dramatically different from anything that existed before the 2007 Reform Treaty.

What is the structure of the present European Union? The Union is based on two treaties: the Treaty on European Union (TEU) and the Treaty on the Functioning of the European Union (TFEU). The division into two EU Treaties thereby follows a functional criterion. The Treaty on European Union contains the *general* provisions defining the Union, while the Treaty on the Functioning of the European Union contains the specific provisions with regard to the Union institutions and policies. Depending on their length, the Treaties are divided into 'Parts', 'Titles', 'Chapters', 'Sections', and 'Articles'. Moreover, numerous Protocols and the 'Charter of Fundamental Rights' join the Treaties. According to Article 51 TEU, Protocols to the Treaties 'shall form an integral part thereof'; and the best way to make sense of them is to see them as legally binding 'footnotes' to a particular article or section of the Treaties. By contrast, the Charter is 'external' to the Treaties; yet it also has 'the same legal value as the Treaties'.[8] The structure of the Treaties is shown in Table 0.2.

Despite their impressive wordiness, the EU Treaties are designed to be 'framework treaties'. They are treaties whose substance is mainly made up from institutional provisions that are to provide the *framework* for subsequent

Table 0.2 Structure of the TEU and TFEU

EU Treaty		FEU Treaty	
Title I	Common Provisions	Part I	Principles
Title II	Democratic Principles	Part II	Citizenship (Non-Discrimination)
Title III	Institutions	Part III	Union (Internal) Policies
Title IV	Enhanced Cooperation	Part IV	Overseas Associations
Title V	External Action, and CFSP	Part V	External Action
Title VI	Final Provisions	Part VI	Institutions & Finances
		Part VII	General & Final Provisions
Protocols (37), **Charter of Fundamental Rights**			

[8] Art. 6(1) (new) TEU.

secondary law. The policy areas in which the Union can act are thereby set out in Parts III and V of the TFEU. The former sets out 24 *internal* policies,[9] while the latter lists a much smaller number of *external* areas of Union action. In order to legislate within one of these policy areas, the Union must have a legislative competence. These competences will generally be found in the specific policy title within Part III or V of the TFEU; and they will constitute the principal legislative fountain for a particular part of European Union law.

What is the structure of this book on European Union law? The book is divided into three parts, which correspond to the three themes of 'creation', 'enforcement', and 'substance' of European law (Figure 0.1).

Part I analyses the Union as an institutional 'creature', and considers the creation of European (secondary) law. It starts with an overview of the four major Union institutions: the European Parliament, the Council, the Commission, and the European Court in Chapter 1. Chapter 2 investigates how these institutions cooperate in the creation of European legislation. The Union cannot legislate in all areas of social life; and Chapters 3 and 4 look at two constitutional limits to all Union legislation. Based on the principle of conferral, the Union must act within the scope of competences conferred upon it by the Member States. The scope of these competences—and their nature—will be discussed in Chapter 3. The final Chapter 4 within this part analyses a second constitutional limit to the exercise of Union competences: European fundamental rights. These rights first emerged as general principles of Union law, but have now been codified in the Union's Charter of Fundamental Rights.

Part II concentrates on the 'enforcement' of European law in the courts. We shall see that European law establishes rights and obligations that directly affect individuals. The direct effect of European law in the national legal

Figure 0.1 Structure of the book

---

[9] See Table 3.1 in Chapter 3.

orders will be discussed in Chapter 5. Where a European norm is directly effective, it will also be supreme over national law. The 'primacy' of European law is the subject of Chapter 6. But how will individuals enforce their 'supreme' European rights? Chapters 7 and 8 look at the dual enforcement machinery within the Union legal order. Individuals will typically enforce their European rights in national courts. The Union legal order has thereby required national courts to provide effective remedies for the enforcement of European rights; and in order to assist national courts in the interpretation and application of European law, the Union envisages a preliminary reference procedure. The indirect enforcement of European law through the national courts is discussed in Chapter 7. It is complemented by the direct enforcement of European law in the European Courts, and Chapter 8 explores these direct actions.

Part III analyses the substantive heart of European law; that is: the law governing the internal market and European competition law. From the very beginning, *the* central economic task of the European Union was the creation of a 'common market'. The Rome Treaty had thereby not solely provided for a common market in goods. It equally required the abolition of obstacles to the free movement of persons, services, and capital. Europe's internal market was thus to comprise four fundamental freedoms. Two of these freedoms will be discussed in turn. The free movement of goods is the 'classic' freedom of the Union, and Chapters 9 and 10 explore two strategies of market integration—negative and positive integration—in this context. Chapter 11 subsequently examines the free movement of persons. The last chapter within this part provides a brief overview of EU competition law through the lens of Article 101 TFEU. European competition law is traditionally seen as a functional complement to the internal market. It was meant—primarily—to protect the internal market from *private* power.

This book is (relatively) short for a book on European law. But brevity is the spice of language; and in order to keep this book as spicy as possible, many selective choices had to be made. Inevitably, some aspects will not be covered, others only marginally. Nevertheless, this 'Introduction to European Law' will deal with all essential aspects of this complex legal subject. And by concentrating on the essence of the subject, the book aims to help to see the proverbial 'wood' instead of the trees. For these European trees are ever growing and multiplying, and it is no wonder that many a student might get lost in the legal undergrowth! But if there is a second wish which this 'Introduction to European Law' has, it is also to make the reader 'thirsty' for more.

Yet this thirst will have to be quenched by one of the larger generalist textbooks,[10] or one of the major textbooks dedicated to a specialized branch of European law.[11]

This third edition, finally, contains a special Epilogue at the end of the book that tries to summarize the past, present, and future of the British exit ('Brexit') from the European Union. Since the last edition, the withdrawal of the United Kingdom surely constitutes the most dramatic development for the Union—even if its ultimate effects on the Union and on European law remain as uncertain as the future relationship between the United Kingdom and the European Union.

---

[10] For an overview of the main general textbooks in English, see Appendix I.

[11] European law is traditionally divided into three major branches: European *constitutional* law (see T. Hartley, *The Foundations of European Union Law* (Oxford University Press, 2014) and R. Schütze, *European Constitutional Law* (Oxford University Press, 2021)); European *internal market* law (see C. Barnard, *The Substantive Law of the EU* (Oxford University Press, 2019) and F. Weiss and C. Kaupa, *European Union Internal Market Law* (Cambridge University Press, 2014)); and European *competition* law (see A. Ezrachi, *EU Competition Law* (Hart, 2018) and A. Jones et al., *EU Competition Law* (Oxford University Press, 2019)). In addition to these three principal branches, the last two decades have seen the emergence of many smaller branches, such as European *external relations* law (see P. Eeckhout, *EU External Relations Law* (Oxford University Press, 2011) and P. Koutrakos, *EU International Relations Law* (Hart, 2015)) and European *environmental* law (see S. Kingston et al., *European Environmental Law* (Cambridge University Press, 2017) and L. Krämer, *EU Environmental Law* (Sweet & Maxwell, 2016)).

Part I

European Law: Creation

This Part analyses the Union as an institutional 'creature', and it equally considers the creation of European (secondary) law. It starts in Chapter 1 with an overview of the four major Union institutions: the European Parliament, the Council, the Commission, and the European Court. Chapter 2 investigates how these institutions cooperate in the creation of European legislation. The Union cannot legislate in all areas of social life; and Chapters 3 and 4 look at two constitutional limits to all Union legislation. Based on the principle of conferral, the Union must act within the scope of competences conferred upon it by the Member States. The scope of these competences—and their nature—will be discussed in Chapter 3. Chapter 4 finally analyses a second constitutional limit to the exercise of Union competences: European fundamental rights. These rights first emerged as general principles of Union law, but have now been codified in the Union's Charter of Fundamental Rights.

1

Union Institutions

Introduction

The creation of governmental institutions is *the* central task of all constitutions. Each political community needs institutions to govern its society; as each society needs common rules and a method for their making, execution, and adjudication. The European Treaties establish a number of European institutions to make, execute, and adjudicate European law. The Union's institutions and their core tasks are defined in Title III of the TEU. The central provision here is Article 13 TEU, which states:

> The Union shall have an institutional framework which shall aim to promote its values, advance its objectives, serve its interests, those of its citizens and those of the Member States, and ensure the consistency, effectiveness and continuity of its policies and actions.
>   The Union's institutions shall be:
>
> – the European Parliament,
> – the European Council,
> – the Council,
> – the European Commission (hereinafter referred to as 'the Commission'),
> – the Court of Justice of the European Union,
> – the European Central Bank,
> – the Court of Auditors.[1]

The provision lists seven governmental institutions of the European Union. They constitute the core players in the Union legal order.[2] What strikes the attentive eye first is the number of institutions: unlike a classic tripartite institutional structure, the Union offers more than twice that number. Parliaments and courts are thereby typically found in national legal orders. The two institutions that do not—at first sight—seem to directly correspond to 'national' institutions are the (European) Council and the Commission. The name 'Council' represents a reminder of the 'international' origins of the European Union, but such institutions can equally be found in the governmental structure of federal States. It will be harder to find the name 'Commission' among the public institutions of States, where the executive is typically referred to as the 'government'. By contrast, central banks and courts of auditors again exist in many national legal orders.

---

[1]   Art. 13(1) TEU. Paragraph 2 adds: 'Each institution shall act within the limits of the powers conferred on it in the Treaties, and in conformity with the procedures, conditions and objectives set out in them. The institutions shall practise mutual sincere cooperation.'

[2]   While the Treaties set up seven 'institutions', they do acknowledge the existence of other 'bodies'. First, according to Art. 13(4) TEU, the Parliament, the Council, and the Commission 'shall be assisted by an Economic and Social Committee and a Committee of the Regions acting in an advisory capacity'. The composition and powers of the 'Economic and Social Committee' are set out in Arts 301–4 TFEU. The composition and powers of the 'Committee of the Regions' are defined by Arts 305–7 TFEU. In addition to the Union's 'Advisory Bodies', the EU Treaties also acknowledge the existence of a 'European Investment Bank' (Arts 308–9 TFEU).

Table 1.1 Treaty provisions on EU institutions

TEU—Title III		TFEU—Part VI—Title I—Chapter 1	
Article 13	Institutional Framework	Section 1	European Parliament (Arts 223–34)
Article 14	European Parliament	Section 2	European Council (Arts 235–6)
Article 15	European Council	Section 3	Council (Arts 237–43)
Article 16	Council	Section 4	Commission (Arts 244–50)
Article 17	Commission	Section 5	Court of Justice (Arts 251–81)
Article 18	High Representative for Foreign Affairs	Section 6	European Central Bank (Arts 282–4)
Article 19	Court of Justice	Section 7	Court of Auditors (Arts 285–7)

Protocol (No. 3): Statute of the Court of Justice
Protocol (No. 4): Statute of the ESCB and the ECB
Protocol (No. 6): Location of the Seats of the Institutions etc.

Where do the Treaties define the Union institutions? The provisions dealing with the Union institutions are split between the Treaty on European Union and the Treaty on the Functioning of the European Union (Table 1.1).

The four sections of this chapter will concentrate on the classic four Union institutions: the Parliament, the Council, the Commission, and the Court.[3]

1. The European Parliament

Despite its formal place in the Treaties, the European Parliament has never been the Union's 'first' institution. For a long time it followed, in rank, behind the Council and the Commission. Parliament's original powers were indeed minimal. It was an auxiliary organ that was to assist the institutional duopoly of Council and Commission. This minimal role gradually increased from the 1970s onwards. Today the Parliament constitutes—with the Council—a chamber of the Union legislature.

Directly elected by the European citizens,[4] Parliament constitutes not only the most democratic institution; in the light of its elective 'appointment', it is also the most supranational institution of the European Union.

---

[3] For an analysis of the three other Union institutions, see R. Schütze, *European Union Law* (Cambridge University Press, 2018), chs 5 and 6.

[4] Art. 10(2) TEU: 'Citizens are directly represented at Union level in the European Parliament.'

This section will discuss two aspects of the European Parliament. First, we shall explore its formation through European elections. A second subsection provides an overview of Parliament's powers in the various governmental functions of the Union.

(a) Formation: Electing Parliament

When the European Union was born, the European Treaties envisaged that its Parliament was to be composed of 'representatives of the peoples of the States'.[5] This characterization corresponded to its formation because the European Parliament was not directly elected. It was to 'consist of delegates who shall be designated by the respective Parliaments from among their members in accordance with the procedure laid down by each Member State'.[6] European parliamentarians were thus—delegated—*national* parliamentarians. This formation method brought Parliament close to an (international) 'assembly'. The founding Treaties had nonetheless already breached the classic international law logic in two ways. First, they had abandoned the idea of a sovereign equality between the Member States by recognizing different sizes for national parliamentary delegations.[7] Second, and more importantly, the Treaties already envisaged that the European Parliament would eventually be formed through 'elections by direct universal suffrage in accordance with a uniform procedure in all Member States'.[8]

When did the transformation of the European Parliament from an assembly of national parliamentarians into a directly elected Parliament take place? It took two decades before the Union's 1976 'Election Act' was adopted.[9] And ever since the first parliamentary elections in 1979, the European Parliament ceased to be composed of 'representatives of the peoples of the States'. It constituted henceforth the representative of all European citizens. The Treaties have—belatedly—recognized this dramatic constitutional change. For they now characterize the European Parliament as being 'composed of representatives of the Union's citizens'.[10]

---

[5] Ex-Art. 137 EEC.   [6] Ex-Art. 138 EEC.

[7] Originally, the EEC Treaty granted 36 delegates to Germany, France, and Italy; 14 delegates to Belgium and the Netherlands; and six delegates to Luxembourg.

[8] Ex-Art. 138(3) EEC.

[9] Act concerning the Election of the Members of the European Parliament by direct universal Suffrage. The Act was adopted in 1976 ([1976] OJ L278/5).

[10] Art. 14(2) TEU.

What is the size and composition of the European Parliament? How are elections conducted? The Treaties stipulate the following on the size and composition of the European Parliament:

> The European Parliament shall be composed of representatives of the Union's citizens. They shall not exceed seven hundred and fifty in number, plus the President. Representation of citizens shall be degressively proportional, with a minimum threshold of six members per Member State. No Member State shall be allocated more than ninety-six seats.
>
> The European Council shall adopt by unanimity, on the initiative of the European Parliament and with its consent, a decision establishing the composition of the European Parliament, respecting the principles referred to in the first subparagraph.[11]

The European Parliament thus has a (potential) maximum size of 751 members. While relatively big in comparison with the (American) House of Representatives, it is not much bigger than the German Parliament.[12] Yet it is not the Treaties themselves but the European Council that decides on its actual size and composition.[13] The distribution of seats must, however, be 'degressively proportional' within a range spanning from six to 96 seats. For the 2019–24 parliamentary term, the European Council has recently taken a formal decision on the size and allocation of national 'quotas'.[14] Following the British withdrawal from the European Union,[15] the size of the current European Parliament is now set at 705 members; and the concrete distribution of seats among Member States can be seen in Table 1.2.

What does 'degressively proportional' here mean? The national quotas for European parliamentary seats constitute a compromise between the democratic principle and the federal principle. For while the democratic principle demands that each citizen in the Union has equal voting power ('one person, one vote'), the federal principle insists on the political existence of States. The result of this compromise was the rejection of a *purely* proportional distribution, in which some Member States would have no seats at all, in favour of a

---

[11] Ibid.

[12] To compare: the (American) House of Representatives has 435 seats, while the German Parliament presently has over 700 members.

[13] This had been different prior to the 2007 reforms brought by the Lisbon Treaty.

[14] European Council Decision 2018/937 establishing the composition of the European Parliament, [2018] OJ L165 1/1.

[15] For a brief overview of the British exit ('Brexit') from the European Union, see the new Epilogue chapter at the end of the book.

Table 1.2 Distribution of seats in the European Parliament (Member States)

Member State (seats) out of 705		
Belgium (21)	France (79)	Netherlands (29)
Bulgaria (17)	Ireland (13)	Austria (19)
Croatia (12)	Italy (76)	Poland (52)
Czech Republic (21)	Cyprus (6)	Portugal (21)
Denmark (14)	Latvia (8)	Romania (33)
Germany (96)	Lithuania (11)	Slovenia (8)
Estonia (7)	Luxembourg (6)	Slovakia (14)
Greece (21)	Hungary (21)	Finland (14)
Spain (59)	Malta (6)	Sweden (21)

degressively proportional system. The degressive element within that system unfortunately means that a Luxembourg citizen has ten times more voting power than, say, a French or German citizen.

How are the *individual* members of Parliament elected? The Treaties solely provide us with the most general of rules: 'The members of the European Parliament shall be elected for a term of five years by direct universal suffrage in a free and secret ballot.'[16] More precise rules are set out in the (amended) 1976 Election Act. Article 1 of the Act commands that the elections must be conducted 'on the basis of proportional representation'.[17] This outlawed the traditionally British election method of first-past-the-post.[18] The specifics of the election procedure are, however, principally left to the Member States.[19] European parliamentary elections thus still do not follow 'a uniform electoral procedure in all Member States', but are rather conducted 'in accordance with principles common to all Member States'.[20]

---

[16] Art. 14(3) TEU.   [17] Art. 1(1) and (3) of the 1976 Election Act (n. 9).

[18] This condition had not been part of the original 1976 Election Act, but was added through a 2002 amendment. This amendment was considered necessary as, hitherto, the British majority voting system 'could alone alter the entire political balance in the European Parliament' (F. Jacobs et al., *The European Parliament* (Harper Publishing, 2005), 17). The best example of this distorting effect was the 1979 election to the European Parliament in which the British Conservatives won 60 out of 78 seats with merely 50 per cent of the vote (ibid.).

[19] Art. 8 of the 1976 Election Act: 'Subject to the provisions of this Act, the electoral procedure shall be governed in each Member State by its national provisions.' Under the Act, Member States are free to decide whether to establish national or local constituencies for elections to the European Parliament (ibid., Art. 2), and whether to set a minimum threshold for the allocation of seats (ibid., Art. 3).

[20] Both alternatives are provided for in Art. 223(1) TFEU.

The Treaties nonetheless insist on one common constitutional rule: 'every citizen of the Union residing in a Member State of which he is not a national shall have the right to vote and to stand as a candidate in elections to the European Parliament in the Member State in which he resides, under the same conditions as nationals of that State.'[21]

(b) Parliamentary Powers

When the 1951 ECSC Treaty set up the European Parliament, its sole function was to exercise 'supervisory powers'.[22] Parliament was here a passive onlooker at the decision-making process within the first Community. The 1957 EEC Treaty expanded Parliament's functions to 'advisory and supervisory powers'.[23] This recognized the active power of Parliament to be consulted on Commission proposals before their adoption by the Council.[24] After more than 60 years of evolution and numerous amendments, the Treaty on European Union today defines the powers of the European Parliament in Article 14 TEU as follows:

> The European Parliament shall, jointly with the Council, exercise legislative and budgetary functions. It shall exercise functions of political control and consultation as laid down in the Treaties. It shall elect the President of the Commission.[25]

This definition distinguishes between four types of powers: legislative and budgetary powers as well as supervisory and elective powers.

(i) Legislative Powers

The European Parliament's primary power lies in the making of European laws. In the recent past, it has evolved into a 'legislative powerhouse'.[26]

Its participation in the legislative process may thereby take place at two moments in time. Parliament may informally propose new legislation.[27]

---

[21] Art. 22(2) TFEU.

[22] Ex-Art. 20 ECSC.   [23] Ex-Art. 137 EEC.

[24] *Roquette Frères v Council* (*Isoglucose*), Case 138/79 [1980] ECR 3333.

[25] Art. 14(1) TEU.

[26] M. Kohler, 'European Governance and the European Parliament: From Talking Shop to Legislative Powerhouse' (2014) 52 *Journal of Common Market Studies* 600.

[27] Art. 225 TFEU: 'The European Parliament may, acting by a majority of its component Members, request the Commission to submit any appropriate proposal on matters on which it considers that a Union act is required for the purpose of implementing the Treaties. If the Commission does not submit a proposal, it shall inform the European Parliament of the reasons.'

However, it is not—unlike many national parliaments—entitled to formally propose bills. The task of making legislative proposals is, with minor exceptions, a constitutional prerogative of the Commission.[28]

The principal legislative involvement of Parliament starts therefore later, namely after the Commission has submitted a proposal to the European legislature. Like other legal orders, the European legal order acknowledges a number of different legislative procedures. The Treaties now textually distinguish between the 'ordinary' legislative procedure and a number of 'special' legislative procedures. The former is defined as 'the joint adoption by the European Parliament and the Council' on a proposal from the Commission.[29] Special legislative procedures cover various degrees of parliamentary participation. Importantly, the Parliament's 'legislative' powers may also extend to the external relations sphere. These various procedures will be discussed in Chapter 2.

(ii) Budgetary Powers

Parliaments have historically been involved in the adoption of national budgets. For they were seen as legitimating the *raising* of revenue. In the words of the American colonists: 'No taxation, without representation.' In the European Union, this picture is somewhat inverted. For since Union revenue is fixed by the Member States,[30] the European Parliament's budgetary powers have not focused on the income side but on the expenditure side. Its powers have consequently been described as the 'reverse of those traditionally exercised by parliaments'.[31]

(iii) Supervisory Powers

A third parliamentary power is that of holding the executive to account. Parliamentary supervisory powers typically involve the power to debate, question, and investigate.

A soft parliamentary power is the power to *debate*. To that effect, the European Parliament is entitled to receive the 'general report on the activities of the Union' from the Commission,[32] which it 'shall discuss in open session'.[33] And as regards the European Council, the Treaties require its President to 'present a report to the European Parliament after each of the meetings of the European Council'.[34]

---

[28] On this power, see Chapter 2, Section 1(a).   [29] Art. 289(1) TFEU.
[30] See Art. 311 TFEU on the 'Union's own resources'.
[31] D. Judge and D. Earnshaw, *The European Parliament* (Palgrave, 2008), 198.
[32] Art. 249(2) TFEU.   [33] Art. 233 TFEU.   [34] Art. 15(6)(d) TEU.

The power to *question* the European executive is formally enshrined only for the Commission: 'The Commission shall reply orally or in writing to questions put to it by the European Parliament or by its Members.'[35] However, both the European Council and the Council have confirmed their willingness to be questioned by Parliament.[36] Early on, Parliament introduced the institution of 'Question Time'—modelled on the procedure within the British Parliament.[37]

Parliament also enjoys the formal power to *investigate*. It is constitutionally entitled to set up temporary Committees of Inquiry to investigate alleged contraventions or maladministration in the implementation of European law.[38] These (temporary) committees complement Parliament's standing committees. They have been used, inter alia, to investigate the (mis)handling of the BSE crisis.

Finally, European citizens have the general right to 'petition' the European Parliament.[39] And according to a Scandinavian constitutional tradition, the European Parliament will also elect an 'ombudsman'. The European Ombudsman 'shall be empowered to receive complaints' from any citizen or Union resident 'concerning instances of maladministration in the activities of the Union institutions, bodies or agencies'. S/he 'shall conduct inquiries' on the basis of complaints addressed to her or him directly or through a member of the European Parliament.[40]

(iv) Elective Powers

Modern constitutionalism distinguishes between 'presidential' and 'parliamentary' systems. Within the former, the executive is independent from Parliament, whereas in the latter the executive is elected by Parliament. The European constitutional order sits somewhere 'in between'. Its executive was for a long time selected without any parliamentary involvement. However, as

---

[35] Art. 230 TFEU, second indent.

[36] The Council accepted this political obligation in 1973; see Jacobs et al., *The European Parliament* (n. 18), 284.

[37] For acceptance of that obligation by the Commission, see Framework Agreement on Relations between the European Parliament and the European Commission, [2010] OJ L304/47, para. 46.

[38] Art. 226(1) TFEU. For a good overview of the history of these committees, see M. Shackleton, 'The European Parliament's New Committees of Inquiry: Tiger or Paper Tiger?' (1998) 36 *Journal of Common Market Studies* 115.

[39] According to Art. 227 TFEU, any citizen or Union resident has the right to petition the European Parliament 'on any matter which comes within the Union's fields of activity and which affects him, her or it directly'. See also Art. 20(2)(d) TFEU.

[40] Art. 228 TFEU.

regards the Commission, the European Parliament has increasingly come to be involved in the appointment process. Today, Article 17 TEU describes the involvement of the European Parliament in the appointment of the Commission as follows:

> Taking into account the elections to the European Parliament and after having held the appropriate consultations, the European Council, acting by a qualified majority, shall propose to the European Parliament a candidate for President of the Commission. This candidate shall be elected by the European Parliament by a majority of its component members . . . The Council, by common accord with the President-elect, shall adopt the list of the other persons whom it proposes for appointment as members of the Commission. They shall be selected, on the basis of the suggestions made by Member States . . . The President, the High Representative of the Union for Foreign Affairs and Security Policy and the other members of the Commission shall be subject as a body to a vote of consent by the European Parliament. On the basis of this consent the Commission shall be appointed by the European Council, acting by a qualified majority.[41]

The appointment of the European executive thus requires dual parliamentary consent. First, Parliament must 'elect' the President of the Commission. Second, it must also confirm the Commission as a collective body as a whole. (The European Parliament does not consequently have the power to confirm each and every Commissioner.[42]) In the light of this elective power given to Parliament, one is justified in characterizing the Union's governmental system as a 'semi-parliamentary democracy'.[43]

Once appointed, the Commission continues to 'be responsible to the European Parliament'.[44] Where its trust is lost, Parliament may vote on a motion of censure. If this vote of mistrust is carried, the Commission must resign as a body. The motion of collective censure here mirrors Parliament's appointment power, which is also focused on the Commission *as a collective body*. This blunt 'nuclear option' has never been used.[45] However, unlike

[41] Art. 17(7) TEU.

[42] However, Parliament may request each nominated Commissioner to appear before Parliament and to 'present' his or her views. This practice thus comes close to 'confirmation hearings' (Judge and Earnshaw, *The European Parliament* (n. 31), 205).

[43] P. Dann, 'European Parliament and Executive Federalism: Approaching a Parliament in a Semi-Parliamentary Democracy' (2003) 9 *European Law Journal* 549.

[44] Art. 17(8) TEU.

[45] Once, however, the European Parliament came close to using this power when in 1999 it decided to censure the Santer Commission. However, that Commission chose collectively to resign instead.

the appointment power, Parliament has been able to sharpen its tools of censure significantly by concluding a political agreement with the Commission. Accordingly, if Parliament expresses lack of confidence in an *individual* member of the Commission, the President of the Commission 'shall either require the resignation of that Member' or, after 'serious' consideration, explain the refusal to do so before Parliament.[46]

Parliament is also involved in the appointment of other European officers. This holds true for the Court of Auditors,[47] the European Central Bank,[48] and the European Ombudsman.[49] However, it is not involved in the appointment of judges to the Court of Justice of the European Union.

2. The Council of Ministers

The EEC Treaty had originally charged the Council of Ministers with the task 'to ensure that the objectives set out in this Treaty are attained'.[50] This task involved the exercise of legislative as well as executive functions. And while other institutions would also be involved in these functions, the Council was to be the central institution.

This has—over time—dramatically changed with the rise of two rival institutions. On one side, the ascendancy of the European Parliament has limited the Council's legislative role within the Union. On the other side, the rise of the *European* Council has restricted the Council's executive powers. (Importantly, the European Council is not identical with the Council. It constitutes a separate Union institution composed of the heads of State or government of the Member States.[51]) Today, the Council is best characterized as the 'federal' chamber within the Union legislature. It is the organ in which national governments meet.

What is the composition of this States' chamber, and what is its internal structure? How will the Council decide—by unanimity or qualified majority? And what are the powers enjoyed by the Council? This second section addresses these questions in four subsections.

---

[46] Framework Agreement (n. 37), para. 5. However, this rule had been contested by the Council; see Council Statement concerning the Framework Agreement on Relations between the European Parliament and the Commission, [2010] OJ C287/1.

[47] Art. 286(2) TFEU.   [48] Art. 283(2) TFEU.   [49] Art. 228(2) TFEU.

[50] Art. 145 EEC.

[51] Art. 15(2) TEU. For an analysis of the European Council, see Schütze, *European Union Law* (n. 3), ch. 5, section 3.

(a) Composition and Configurations

Within the European Union, the Council is the institution of the Member States. Its intergovernmental character lies in its composition. The Treaty on European Union defines it as follows:

> The Council shall consist of a representative of each Member State at ministerial level, who may commit the government of the Member State in question and cast its vote.[52]

Within the Council, each national minister thus represents the interests of 'his' or 'her' Member State. These interests may vary depending on the subject matter decided in the Council. And, indeed, depending on the subject matter at issue, there are different Council configurations.[53] And for each configuration, a different national minister will be representing 'his' State. While there is thus—legally—but one single Council, there are—politically—ten different Councils. The existing Council configurations are shown in Table 1.3.

What is the mandate of each Council configuration? The Treaties only define the tasks of the first two Council configurations.[54] The 'General Affairs Council' is charged to 'ensure consistency in the work of the different Council configurations' below.[55] The 'Foreign Affairs Council', on the other hand,

Table 1.3 Council configurations

Council Configurations
1   General Affairs
2   Foreign Affairs
3   Economic and Financial Affairs
4   Justice and Home Affairs
5   Employment, Social Policy, Health and Consumer Affairs
6   Competitiveness (Internal Market, Industry, Research and Space)
7   Transport, Telecommunications and Energy
8   Agriculture and Fisheries
9   Environment
10   Education, Youth, Culture and Sport

[52] Art. 16(2) TEU.

[53] Art. 16(6) TEU: 'The Council shall meet in different configurations, the list of which shall be adopted in accordance with Article 236 of the Treaty on the Functioning of the European Union.'

[54] Art. 16(6) TEU.   [55] Ibid.

is required to 'elaborate the Union's external action on the basis of strategic guidelines laid down by the European Council and ensure that the Union's action is consistent'.[56] The thematic scope and functional tasks of the remaining Council configurations are constitutionally open. They will generally deal with the subjects falling within their thematic ambit.

(b) Internal Structure and Organs

The Council has developed committees to assist it. From the very beginning, a committee composed of representatives of the Member States would support the Council.[57] That committee was made permanent under the 1957 EEC Treaty. The resultant 'Committee of *Permanent* Representatives' became known under its French acronym: 'Coreper'. The Permanent Representative is the ambassador of a Member State at the European Union. S/he is based in the national 'Permanent Representation to the European Union'. Coreper has two parts: Coreper II represents the meeting of the ambassadors, while Coreper I—against all intuition—represents the meetings of their deputies. Both parts correspond to particular Council configurations. Coreper II prepares the first four Council configurations—the more important political decisions; whereas Coreper I prepares the more technical remainder.

The function of Coreper is vaguely defined in the Treaties: 'A Committee of Permanent Representatives of the Governments of the Member States shall be responsible for preparing the work of the Council'.[58] This abstract definition has been—somewhat—specified in the following way: 'All items on the agenda for a Council meeting shall be examined in advance by Coreper unless the latter decides otherwise. Coreper shall endeavour to reach agreement at its level to be submitted to the Council for adoption'.[59] In order to achieve that task, Coreper has set up 'working parties' below it. (These working parties are composed of national civil servants operating on instructions from national ministries.) Where Coreper reaches agreement, the point will be classed as an 'A item' that will be rubber-stamped by the Council. Where it fails to agree in advance, a 'B item' will need to be expressly discussed by the ministers in the Council. But, importantly, even for 'A items' Coreper is not formally entitled to take decisions itself. It merely 'prepares' and facilitates formal decision-making in the Council.

---

[56] Ibid.
[57] The Committee beneath the ECSC Council was called 'Commission de Coordination du Conseil des Ministres' (Cocor). Its members did not permanently reside in Brussels.
[58] Art. 16(7) TEU and Art. 240(1) TFEU. See also Art. 19 of the Council Rules of Procedure.
[59] Art. 19(2) Council Rules of Procedure.

(c) Decision-Making and Voting

The Council will—physically—meet in Brussels to decide. The meetings are divided into two parts: one dealing with legislative activities, the other with non-legislative activities. When discussing legislation, the Council must meet in public.[60] The Commission will attend Council meetings.[61] However, it is not a formal member of the Council and is thus not entitled to vote. The quorum within the Council is as low as it is theoretical: a majority of the members of the Council are required to enable the Council to vote.[62]

Decision-making in the Council will take place in two principal forms: *unanimity* voting and *majority* voting. Unanimity voting requires the consent of all national ministers and is provided in the Treaties for sensitive political questions.[63] Formal majority voting, however, represents the constitutional norm. The Treaties here distinguish between a *simple* and a *qualified* majority. 'Where it is required to act by a simple majority, the Council shall act by a majority of its component members.'[64] This form of majority vote is rare.[65] The constitutional default is indeed the qualified majority: 'The Council shall act by a qualified majority except where the Treaties provide otherwise.'[66]

What constitutes a qualified majority of Member States in the Council? This has been one of the most controversial constitutional questions in the European Union. From the very beginning, the Treaties had instituted a system of *weighted votes*. Member States would thus not be 'sovereign equals' in the Council, but would possess a number of votes that correlated with the size of their population. Table 1.4 shows the traditional but now abolished system of weighted votes.

The weighting of votes was to some extent 'degressively proportional'. The voting ratio between the biggest and the smallest State was ten to one—a ratio that is roughly similar to the degressively proportional system for the European Parliament. However, the voting system also represented a system of symbolic compromises. For example, the four biggest Member States were

---

[60] Art. 16(8) TEU.

[61] According to Art. 5(2) Council Rules of Procedure, the Council may, however, decide to deliberate without the Commission.

[62] Ibid., Art. 11(4).

[63] Important examples of sensitive political issues still requiring unanimity are foreign affairs (see Art. 31 TEU), and 'the harmonisation of legislation concerning turnover taxes, excise duties and other forms of indirect taxation' (see Art. 113 TFEU).

[64] Art. 238(1) TFEU.

[65] E.g. Art. 150 TFEU. Most matters that allow for a simple majority are (internal) procedural or institutional matters.

[66] Art. 16(3) TEU.

Table 1.4 Weighted votes system within the Council

Member States: Votes	
Germany, France, Italy, United Kingdom	29
Spain, Poland	27
Romania	14
Netherlands	13
Belgium, Czech Republic, Greece, Hungary, Portugal	12
Austria, Bulgaria, Sweden	10
Croatia, Denmark, Ireland, Lithuania, Slovakia, Finland	7
Cyprus, Estonia, Latvia, Luxembourg, Slovenia	4
Malta	3
Qualified Majority: 260/352	

all given the same number of votes—despite Germany's significantly greater demographic magnitude.[67]

In the past, this system of weighted votes had been attacked from two sides: from the smaller Member States as well as the bigger Member States. The smaller Member States claimed that it favoured the bigger Member States and therefore insisted that the 260 votes must be cast by a majority of the States. The bigger Member States, by contrast, have complained that the weighting unduly favoured smaller Member States and have insisted on the political safeguard that the 260 votes cast in the Council correspond to 62 per cent of the total population of the Union. With these two qualifications taken into account, the 'old' decision-making in the Council therefore traditionally demanded a *triple* majority: a *majority* of the weighted votes had to be cast by a *majority* of the Member States representing a *majority* of the Union population.

This triple majority system governed decision-making in the Union until 1 November 2014. From that date, however, a completely new system of voting applies in the Council. This revolutionary change is set out in Article 16(4) TEU, which states:

As from 1 November 2014, a qualified majority shall be defined as at least 55% of the members of the Council, comprising at least fifteen of them and representing Member States comprising at least 65% of the population of the Union.

---

[67] The German population exceeds that of France—the second most populous State of the Union—by about 15 million people.

A blocking minority must include at least four Council members, failing which the qualified majority shall be deemed attained.[68]

This new Lisbon voting arrangement abolished the old system of weighted votes in favour of a system that grants each State a single vote. In a Union of 27 States, 55 per cent of the Council members correspond to 15 States. But this majority is again qualified from two sides. The bigger Member States have insisted on a high population majority behind the State majority. The population threshold of 65 per cent of the Union population would theoretically mean that any three of the four biggest States of the Union could block a Council decision (see Table 1.5). The smaller Member States have thus insisted on a qualification of the second majority. A qualified majority will be 'deemed attained' where fewer than four States try to block a Council decision.

The new Lisbon system of qualified majority voting was designed to replace the complex triple majority system with a simpler double majority. And yet the Member States—always fearful of abrupt changes—have agreed on a

Table 1.5 Member State population sizes

Member State	Population (x 1,000)	*(Potential) Blocking Minority*	*(Potential) Population Majority*
Germany	80,523.7		
France	65,633.2		
Italy	59,685.2		
Spain	46,704.3		
Poland	38,533.3		
Romania	20,057.5		
Netherlands	16,779.6		
Belgium	11,161.6		
European Union (65%)	287,197.6		
European Union (35%)	154,644.8		

[68] The Treaty recognizes an express exception to this in Art. 238(2) TFEU which states: 'By way of derogation from Article 16(4) of the Treaty on European Union, as from 1 November 2014 and subject to the provisions laid down in the Protocol on transitional provisions, where the Council does not act on a proposal from the Commission or from the High Representative of the Union for Foreign Affairs and Security Policy, the qualified majority shall be defined as at least 72 % of the members of the Council, representing Member States comprising at least 65 % of the population of the Union.'

small number of constitutional compromises that cushion the new system of qualified majority voting. The most important one here is the 'Ioannina Compromise'.[69] The latter was envisaged in a 'Declaration on Article 16(4)',[70] and is now codified in a Council Decision.[71] According to the Ioannina Compromise, the Council is under an obligation—despite the formal existence of the double majority in Article 16(4) TEU—to continue deliberations, where one-quarter of the States or States representing one-fifth of the Union population oppose a decision.[72] The Council is here under the procedural duty to 'do all in its power' to reach—within a reasonable time—'a satisfactory solution' to address the concerns of the blocking Member States.[73]

(d) Functions and Powers

The Treaties summarize the functions and powers of the Council as follows:

> The Council shall, jointly with the European Parliament, exercise legislative and budgetary functions. It shall carry out policy-making and coordinating functions as laid down in the Treaties.[74]

Let us look at each of these four functions. First, the Council has traditionally been at the core of the Union's legislative function. Prior to the rise of the European Parliament, the Council was indeed *the* Union 'legislator'. The Council is however today only a *co*-legislator; that is: a branch of the bicameral Union legislature.[75] And like Parliament, it must exercise its legislative powers in public.[76] Second, Council and Parliament also share in the exercise of the budgetary function. What about the policy-making function? In this—third—respect, the *European* Council has overtaken the Council. The former now decides on the Union's general policy choices, and the role of the Council has consequently been limited to specific policy choices that implement the general ones. Fourth, the Council has significant coordinating functions

---

[69] The compromise was negotiated by the Member States' foreign ministers in Ioannina (Greece)—from where it takes its name. The compromise was designed to smooth the transition from the Union of 12 to a Union of 15 Member States.

[70] Declaration (No. 7) on Art. 16(4) is attached to the Treaties and contains a draft Council Decision.

[71] The Council formally adopted the decision in 2007 (see Council Decision 2009/857, [2009] OJ L314/73).

[72] Ibid., Art. 4.   [73] Ibid., Art. 5.   [74] Art. 16(1) TEU.

[75] On this point, see Chapter 2, Section 1(a).   [76] Art. 16(8) TEU.

within the European Union. Thus, in the context of general economic policy, the Member States are required to 'regard their economic policies as a matter of common concern and shall coordinate them within the Council'.[77] This idea of an 'open method of coordination' has experienced a renaissance in the last decade.[78]

3. The Commission

The technocratic character of the early European Union expressed itself in the name of a third institution: the Commission. The Commission originally constituted the centre of the European Coal and Steel Community, where it was 'to ensure that the objectives set out in [that] Treaty [were] attained'.[79] In the European Union, the role of the Commission was however gradually 'marginalized' by the Parliament and the Council. With these two institutions constituting the Union legislature, the Commission is today firmly located in the executive branch. In guiding the European Union, it—partly—acts like the Union's 'government'. This third section analyses the composition of the Commission first, before exploring the relationship between the Commission President and her college. A final subsection looks at the functions and powers of the Commission.

(a) Composition and Election

The Commission consists of one national from each Member State.[80] Its members are chosen 'on the ground of their general competence and European commitment from persons whose independence is beyond doubt'.[81]

---

[77] Art. 121(1) TFEU.

[78] On the 'open method of coordination', see G. de Búrca, 'The Constitutional Challenge of New Governance in the European Union' (2003) 28 *European Law Review* 814.

[79] Ex-Art. 8 ECSC.

[80] Art. 17(4) TEU. The Lisbon Treaty textually limited this principle in a temporal sense: it would theoretically only apply from the date of entry into force of the Treaty of Lisbon to 31 October 2014. Thereafter, Art. 17(5) TEU states: 'As from 1 November 2014, the Commission shall consist of a number of members, including its President and the High Representative of the Union for Foreign Affairs and Security Policy, corresponding to two thirds of the number of Member States, unless the European Council, acting unanimously, decides to alter this number.' This provision had been a centrepiece of the Lisbon Treaty, as it was designed to increase the effectiveness of the Commission by decreasing its membership. However, after the failure of the first Irish referendum on the Lisbon Treaty, the European Council decided to abandon this constitutional reform in order to please the Irish electorate; see Presidency Conclusions of 11–12 December 2008 (Doc. 17271/1/08 Rev 1).

[81] Art. 17(3) TEU.

The Commission's term of office is five years.[82] During this term, it must be *completely independent*. Its members 'shall neither seek nor take instructions from any Government or other institution, body, office or entity'.[83] The Member States are under a duty to respect this independence.[84] Breach of the duty of independence may lead to a Commissioner being 'compulsorily retired'.[85]

How is the Commission selected? Originally, the Commission was 'appointed'. The appointment procedure has subsequently given way to an election procedure. This election procedure has two stages. In a first stage, the President of the Commission will be elected. The President will have been nominated by the European Council '[t]aking into account the elections to the European Parliament'; that is: the latter's political composition.[86] The nominated candidate, ideally the 'lead candidate' of the biggest political party, must then be 'elected' by the European Parliament. If not confirmed by Parliament, a new candidate needs to be found by the European Council.[87] Today's Commission President can be seen in Figure 1.1.

Figure 1.1 Commission President: Ursula von der Leyen

---

[82] Ibid.   [83] Ibid.   [84] Art. 245 TFEU, first indent.

[85] Art. 245 TFEU, second indent. See also Art. 247 TFEU: 'If any Member of the Commission no longer fulfils the conditions required for the performance of his duties or if he has been guilty of serious misconduct, the Court of Justice may, on application by the Council acting by a simple majority or the Commission, compulsorily retire him.' On the replacement procedure, see Art. 246 TFEU.

[86] The term of the Commission runs in parallel with that of the Parliament.

[87] Art. 17(7) TEU, first indent.

After the election of the Commission President begins the second stage of the selection process of the Commission. In accord with the President-elect, the Council will adopt a list of candidate Commissioners on the basis of suggestions made by the Member States.[88] Once this list is agreed, the proposed Commission is then subjected 'as a body to a vote of consent by the European Parliament', and on the basis of this election, the Commission shall be appointed by the European Council.[89] Through this complex and compound selection process, the Commission's democratic legitimacy derives partly from the Member States, and partly from the European Parliament.

(b) The President and 'Her' College

The Commission President helps in the selection of 'his' or 'her' institution. This position as the 'Chief' Commissioner *above* her college is clearly established by the Treaties.[90] 'The Members of the Commission shall carry out the duties devolved upon them by the President *under [her] authority*.'[91] In the light of this political authority, the Commission is typically named after its President.[92]

The powers of the President are identified in Article 17(6) TEU, which reads:

The President of the Commission shall:

(a) lay down guidelines within which the Commission is to work;
(b) decide on the internal organization of the Commission, ensuring that it acts consistently, efficiently and as a collegiate body;
(c) appoint Vice-Presidents, other than the High Representative of the Union for Foreign Affairs and Security Policy, from among the members of the Commission.

A member of the Commission shall resign if the President so requests. The High Representative of the Union for Foreign Affairs and Security Policy shall resign, in accordance with the procedure set out in Article 18(1), if the President so requests.

---

[88] Art. 17(7) TEU, second indent.   [89] Art. 17(7) TFEU, third indent.

[90] N. Nugent, *The European Commission* (Palgrave, 2000), 68: 'The Commission President used to be thought of as *primus inter pares* in the College. Now, however, he is very much *primus*.'

[91] Art. 248 TFEU (emphasis added).

[92] E.g. the last Commission was called the 'Juncker Commission', while the current Commission is called the 'von der Leyen Commission'.

The three powers of the President mentioned above are formidable. First, s/he can lay down the political direction of the Commission in the form of strategic guidelines. Second, the President is entitled to decide on the internal organization of the Commission.[93] In the words of the Treaties: '[T]he responsibilities incumbent upon the Commission shall be structured and allocated among its members by its President'. The President is authorized to 'reshuffle the allocation of those responsibilities during the Commission's term of office',[94] and may even ask a Commissioner to resign. Third, the President can appoint Vice-Presidents from 'within' the Commission. Finally, there is a fourth power not expressly mentioned in Article 17(6) TEU: 'The President shall represent the Commission'.[95]

What are the 'ministerial' responsibilities into which the present Commission is structured? Due to the requirement of one Commissioner per Member State, the 'von der Leyen Commission' had to divide the tasks of the European Union into 26 (!) 'portfolios'. Reflecting the priorities of the current President, they are as set out in Figure 1.2.

Each Commissioner is thereby responsible for his or her portfolio, and will be assisted in this by the Commissioner's own cabinet.[96] However, an organizational novelty since the 2014 Commission has been the idea of 'Project Groups'—combining various portfolios under the authority of a Vice-President of the Commission. The aim behind this administrative grouping seems to be the desire to set policy priorities from the very start, and to create more cohesion between various ministerial portfolios.[97]

---

[93] Due to its dual constitutional role, some special rules apply to the High Representative of the Union. For whereas the Treaties determine the latter's role within the Commission, the President will not be able *unilaterally* to ask for her resignation. See Art. 18(4) TEU: 'The High Representative shall be one of the Vice-Presidents of the Commission. He shall ensure the consistency of the Union's external action. He shall be responsible within the Commission for responsibilities incumbent on it in external relations and for coordinating other aspects of the Union's external action'. On the role of the High Representative, see Schütze, *European Union Law* (n. 3), ch. 5, section 4(b)(cc).

[94] Art. 248 TFEU.   [95] Art. 3(5) Commission Rules of Procedure.

[96] Art. 19(1) Commission Rules of Procedure: 'Members of the Commission shall have their own cabinet to assist them in their work and in preparing Commission decisions. The rules governing the composition and operation of the cabinets shall be laid down by the President'.

[97] The 'Project Groups' currently suggested are: 'European Green Deal', 'Promoting our European Way of Life', 'A Europe Fit for the Digital Age', 'An Economy that Works for People', 'A New Push for European Democracy', and 'A Stronger Europe in the World'. For an excellent analysis, see R. Böttner, 'The Size and Structure of the European Commission: Legal Issues Surrounding Project Teams and a (future) reduced College' (2018) 14 *European Constitutional Law Review* 37.

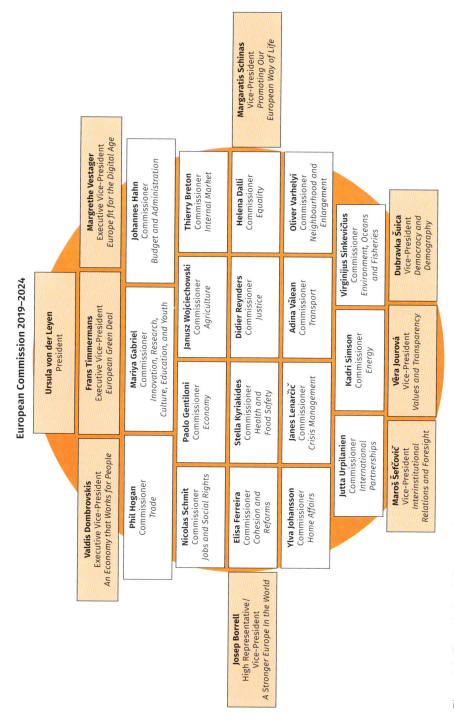

Figure 1.2 Commission College: people and portfolios

(c) Functions and Powers

What are the functions and corresponding powers of the Commission in the governmental structure of the European Union? The Treaties provide a concise constitutional overview of its tasks in Article 17 TEU:

> The Commission shall promote the general interest of the Union and take appropriate initiatives to that end. It shall ensure the application of the Treaties, and of measures adopted by the institutions pursuant to them. It shall oversee the application of Union law under the control of the Court of Justice of the European Union. It shall execute the budget and manage programmes. It shall exercise coordinating, executive and management functions, as laid down in the Treaties. With the exception of the common foreign and security policy, and other cases provided for in the Treaties, it shall ensure the Union's external representation. It shall initiate the Union's annual and multiannual programming with a view to achieving interinstitutional agreements.[98]

The provision distinguishes six different functions. The first three functions constitute the Commission's core functions.

First, the Commission is tasked to '*promote* the general interests of the Union' through initiatives. It is thus to act as a 'motor' of European integration. In order to fulfil this—governmental—function, the Commission is given the (almost) exclusive right to formally propose legislative bills:

> Union acts may only be adopted on the basis of a Commission proposal, except where the Treaties provide otherwise.[99]

The Commission's prerogative to propose legislation is a fundamental characteristic of the European constitutional order. The right of initiative extends

---

[98] Art. 17(1) TEU.

[99] Art. 17(2) TEU. The European Parliament may, however, 'informally' suggest legislative initiatives to the Commission; and there is even the possibility for European citizens to suggest legislative initiatives to the Commission. For an analysis of the so-called 'European Citizens' Initiative', see A. Karatzia, 'The European Citizens' Initiative and the EU Institutional Balance: On Realism and the Possibilities of Affecting EU Lawmaking' (2017) 54 *Common Market Law Review* 177.

to (multi)annual programming of the Union,[100] and embraces the power to make proposals for law reform.[101]

The second function of the Commission is to '*ensure* the application' of the Treaties. This function covers a number of powers—legislative and executive in nature. The Commission may thus be entitled to apply the Treaties by adopting secondary legislation. These acts may be adopted directly under the Treaties;[102] or, under powers delegated to the Commission from the Union legislature.[103] In some areas the Commission may also be granted the executive power to apply the Treaties itself. The direct enforcement of European law can best be seen in the context of European competition law,[104] where the Commission enjoys significant powers to fine—private or public—wrongdoers. These administrative penalties sanction the non-application of European law.

The third function of the Commission is to act as guardian of the Union. It shall thus '*oversee* the application' of European law. The Treaties indeed grant the Commission significant powers to act as 'police' and 'prosecutor' of the Union. The policing of European law involves the power to monitor and to investigate infringements of European law. The powers are—again—best defined in the context of European competition law.[105] Where an infringement of European law has been identified, the Commission may bring the matter before the Court of Justice. The Treaties thus give the Commission the power to bring infringement proceedings against Member States,[106] and other Union institutions.[107]

---

[100] Under Art. 314(2) TFEU, the Commission is entitled to propose the draft budget: 'The Commission shall submit a proposal containing the draft budget to the European Parliament and to the Council not later than 1 September of the year preceding that in which the budget is to be implemented.'

[101] This is normally done through 'White Papers' or 'Green Papers'. For a famous 'White Paper', see EU Commission, Completing the Internal Market: White Paper from the Commission to the European Council (COM(85) 310). For a famous 'Green Paper', see EU Commission, Damages Actions for Breach of the EC Antitrust Rules (COM(2005) 672).

[102] See Art. 106(3) TFEU: 'The Commission shall ensure the application of the provisions of this Article and shall, where necessary, address appropriate directives or decisions to Member States.'

[103] On delegated legislation, see Schütze, *European Union Law* (n. 3), ch. 9, section 2.

[104] See Art. 105(1) TFEU: '[T]he Commission shall ensure the application of the principles laid down in Articles 101 and 102. On application by a Member State or on its own initiative, and in cooperation with the competent authorities in the Member States, which shall give it their assistance, the Commission shall investigate cases of suspected infringement of these principles. If it finds that there has been an infringement, it shall propose appropriate measures to bring it to an end.'

[105] See Regulation 1/2003 on the implementation of the rules on competition laid down in Articles [101] and [102] of the Treaty, [2003] OJ L1/1, Chapter V: 'Powers of Investigation'.

[106] Art. 258 TFEU. For an extensive discussion of this, see Chapter 8, Section 1.

[107] On this point, see Chapter 8, Sections 2–4.

4. The Court of Justice of the European Union

'Tucked away in the fairyland Duchy of Luxembourg',[108] and housed in its 'palace', lies the Court of Justice of the European Union. The Court constitutes the judicial branch of the European Union. It is not a 'real' court but an institution that is composed of various courts that are generically referred to as the 'Court of Justice of the European Union'. This generic roof includes the 'Court of Justice', the 'General Court', and any 'specialized courts' established within the Union legal order.[109] The Court's task is to 'ensure that in the interpretation and application of the Treaties the law is observed'.[110]

This fourth section starts by analysing the Union's judicial architecture, before surveying the judicial powers of the Court of Justice of the European Union.

(a) Judicial Architecture: the European Court System

When the European Union was born, its judicial branch consisted of a single court only: the 'Court of Justice'. The (then) Court was a 'one-stop shop'. All judicial affairs of the Union would need to pass through its corridors.

With its workload having risen to dizzying heights, the Court pressed the Member States to provide for a judicial 'assistant'; and the Member States agreed to create a second court in the Single European Act. The latter granted the Council the power to 'attach to the Court of Justice a court with jurisdiction to hear and determine [cases] at first instance', that was 'subject to a right of appeal to the Court of Justice'.[111] Thanks to this definition, the newly created court was baptized the 'Court of First Instance'.[112] With the Lisbon Treaty, the Court has been renamed the 'General Court'. The reason for this change of name lies in the fact that the Court is no longer confined to first instance cases. Instead, '[t]he General Court shall have jurisdiction to hear and determine actions or proceedings brought against decisions of the specialized courts'.[113]

---

[108] E. Stein, 'Lawyers, Judges, and the Making of a Transnational Constitution' (1981) 75 *American Journal of International Law* 1.

[109] Art. 19(1) TEU.   [110] Ibid.   [111] Art. 11(1) Single European Act.

[112] The Court was set up by Council Decision 88/591 establishing a Court of First Instance of the European Communities, [1988] OJ L319/1.

[113] Art. 256(2) TFEU.

Figure 1.3 Structure of the Court of Justice of the European Union

What are the 'specialized courts' in the European Union? The Union had for about a decade one specialized court: the 'Civil Service Tribunal'.[114] The latter has, however, recently been abolished. But even in the absence of any existing 'specialized court' at the moment, the Court of Justice of the European Union formally has a three-tiered system of courts.[115] The architecture of the Union's judicial branch can be seen in Figure 1.3.

The highest and most important court here is undoubtedly the (European) 'Court of Justice' (ECJ). It consist of one judge per Member State. Judges are nevertheless not representatives of their Member State, and must be completely independent. Their term of appointment is for six years—a relatively short term for judges—that can be renewed.

The Court, as a formal institution, decides as a collective body that has its own President. In theory, the principle of collegiality should mean that the Court of Justice only decides in plenary session; that is: as a 'full court' of all judges. However, from the very beginning the Court was entitled to set up 'chambers'. This organizational device allows the Court to 'multiply' into a variety of 'miniature' courts that enjoy all the powers of the full Court. The division into chambers allows the Court to spread its workload.

The Court is often assisted by an 'Advocate General'.[116] Advocates General are appointed as officers of the Court, but their duty is not to 'judge'. The

---

[114] Council Decision 2004/752 establishing the European Union Civil Service Tribunal, [2004] OJ L333/7. See also N. Lavranos, 'The New Specialised Courts within the European Judicial System' (2005) 30 *European Law Review* 261.

[115] In terms of the European Union's judicial reports, there are thus three different prefixes before a case. Cases before the Court of Justice are C-Cases, cases before the General Court are T-Cases (as the French name for the General Court is 'Tribunal'), and cases before the Civil Service Tribunal were F-Cases (stemming from the French 'fonction publique' for civil service).

[116] Art. 19(2) TEU.

Treaties define their function as follows: 'It shall be the duty of the Advocate General, acting with complete impartiality and independence, to make, in open court, reasoned submissions[.]'[117] According to this definition, an Advocate General is thus neither advocate nor general. S/he is an independent advisor to the Court, who produces an 'opinion' that is not legally binding on the Court.[118] The opinion is designed to inform the Court of ways to decide a case and, in this respect, the Advocate General should act like an academic *amicus curiae*.

(b) Jurisdiction and Judicial Powers

The traditional role of courts in modern societies is to act as independent adjudicators between competing interests. Their jurisdiction may be compulsory, or not. The jurisdiction of the Court of Justice of the European Union is compulsory 'within the limits of the powers conferred on it in the Treaties'.[119] While compulsory, the Court's jurisdiction is thus limited. Based on the principle of conferral, the Court has no 'inherent' jurisdiction.[120] The functions and powers of the Court are classified in Article 19(3) TEU:

> The Court of Justice of the European Union shall, in accordance with the Treaties:
>
> (a) rule on actions brought by a Member State, an institution or a natural or legal person;
> (b) give preliminary rulings, at the request of courts or tribunals of the Member States, on the interpretation of Union law or the validity of acts adopted by the institutions;
> (c) rule in other cases provided for in the Treaties.

The provision classifies the Court's judicial tasks by distinguishing between direct and indirect actions. The former are brought directly before the European Court. The latter arrive at the Court indirectly through preliminary references from national courts. The powers of the Court under the preliminary reference procedure are set out in a single article.[121] By contrast, there exist a number of direct actions set out in the Treaty on the Functioning of

---

[117] Art. 252(2) TFEU.

[118] Famous examples, where the Court went against the Advocate General are *Van Gend en Loos v Netherlands Inland Revenue Administration*, Case 26/62 [1963] ECR 1; as well as *Unión de Pequeños Agricultores (UPA) v Council*, Case C-50/00P [2002] ECR I-6677.

[119] Art. 13(2) TEU.   [120] On the principle of conferral, see Chapter 3.

[121] Art. 267 TFEU. The provision is analysed in Chapter 7, Sections 3 and 4.

the European Union. The TFEU distinguishes between enforcement actions brought by the Commission or a Member State,[122] judicial review proceedings for actions and inactions of the Union institutions,[123] damages actions for the (non-)contractual liability of the Union,[124] as well as a few minor jurisdictional heads.[125]

In the light of its broad jurisdiction, the Court of Justice of the European Union can be characterized as a 'constitutional', 'administrative', and an 'international' court as well as an 'industrial tribunal'. Its jurisdiction includes public and private matters; and the number of cases decided every year is staggering.

Conclusion

This chapter analysed the governmental structure of the European Union. The Union has seven 'institutions'—four of which were discussed in some detail in this chapter, namely: the European Parliament, the Council of Ministers, the Commission, and the Court of Justice of the European Union. Each of these institutions is characterized by its distinct composition and its decision-making mode. Importantly, the Union is not based on a strict separation of functions between its institutions but follows a 'checks and balances' version of the separation-of-powers principle.[126] This means that various Union institutions share in the exercise of various governmental functions. This institutional power-sharing can clearly be seen with regard to the legislative function, which will be discussed in the next chapter.

---

[122]   Arts 258–60 TFEU. The provisions are analysed in Chapter 8, Section 1.

[123]   Arts 263–6 TFEU. The provisions are analysed in Chapter 8, Sections 2 and 3.

[124]   Arts 268 and 340 TFEU. The provisions are analysed in Chapter 8, Section 4.

[125]   Arts 269–74 TFEU.

[126]   For a discussion of this point, see R. Schütze, *European Union Law* (n. 3), ch. 5, section 1.

2

Union Legislation

Introduction

Each society needs common rules and mechanisms for their production. Legislation here refers to the making of laws (*legis*). But what is legislation? American constitutionalism defines legislation as an act adopted by 'Congress'. Behind this bicameral legislator stands a legislative procedure. This legal procedure links the House of Representatives and the Senate. German constitutionalism also adopts such a procedural definition of legislative power. However, unlike many national legal orders, the EU Treaties expressly distinguish two types of legislative procedures: an ordinary legislative procedure and special legislative procedures. Article 289 TFEU here states:

1. The ordinary legislative procedure shall consist in the joint adoption by the Turopean Parliament and the Council of a regulation, directive or decision on a proposal from the Commission. This procedure is defined in Article 294.

2. In the specific cases provided for by the Treaties, the adoption of a regulation, directive or decision by the European Parliament with the participation of the Council, or by the latter with the participation of the European Parliament, shall constitute a special legislative procedure.[1]

European 'legislation' is thus—formally—defined as an act adopted by the bicameral Union legislator: the Parliament and the Council. According to the *ordinary* legislative procedure, the Parliament and the Council act as co-legislators with *symmetric* procedural rights. European legislation is here seen as the product of a 'joint adoption' by both institutions.

But the Treaties also recognize *special* legislative procedures (Figure 2.1). The defining characteristic of these special procedures is that they abandon the institutional equality between the Parliament and the Council. Logically, then, Article 289(2) TFEU recognizes two variants. In the first variant, the European Parliament acts as the dominant institution, with the mere 'participation' of the Council in the form of 'consent'.[2] The second variant inverts this relationship. The Council is here the dominant institution, with the Parliament either participating through its 'consent',[3] or in the form of 'consultation'.[4]

Having analysed the various Union institutions in Chapter 1, this chapter explores their interaction in the creation of European (secondary) law. Sections 1 and 2 respectively discuss the ordinary and special legislative procedures in more detail. Section 3 looks at the principle of subsidiarity—an

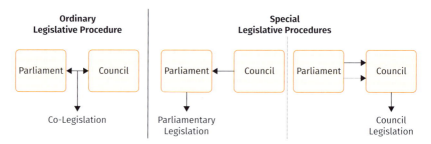

Figure 2.1 Structure of the Union legislator

[1] Art. 289(1) and (2) TFEU.

[2] See Arts 223(2), 226, and 228 TFEU. The procedure for the adoption of the Union budget is laid down in Art. 314 TFEU and will not be discussed here.

[3] See Arts 19(1), 25, 86(1), 223(1), 311, 312, and 352 TFEU.

[4] See Arts 21(3), 22(1), 22(2), 23, 64(3), 77(3), 81(3), 87(3), 89, 113, 115, 118, 126, 127(6), 153(2), 182(4), 192(2), 203, 262, 308, 311, and 349 TFEU.

EU constitutional principle that was designed to prevent the Union legislator from exercising its competences where the Member States would be able to achieve the desirable social aim themselves. Within the Union legal order, this principle has been primarily understood as a procedural safeguard that—indirectly—involves the national parliaments prior to the adoption of a legislative act. Finally, Section 4 looks at the procedure for the conclusion of international agreements. These agreements, while not formally concluded under a legislative procedure, nonetheless constitute a rich (external) source of European secondary law.

1. The 'Ordinary' Legislative Procedure

(a) Constitutional Theory: Formal Text

The ordinary legislative procedure has seven stages. Article 294 TFEU defines five stages (Figure 2.2); two additional stages are set out in Article 297 TFEU.

Proposal stage. Under the ordinary legislative procedure, the Commission enjoys—with minor exceptions—the exclusive right to submit a legislative proposal.[5] This (executive) prerogative guarantees a significant agenda-setting power to the Commission. The Treaties—partly—protect this power from 'external' interferences by insisting that any amendment by the Council requires unanimity in the Council—an extremely high decisional hurdle.[6]

First reading. The Commission proposal goes to the European Parliament. The Parliament will act by a majority of the votes cast;[7] that is: the majority of physically present parliamentarians. It can reject the proposal,[8] approve it, or—as a middle path—amend it. The bill then moves to the Council, which must act by a qualified majority of its members.[9] Where the Council agrees with Parliament's position, the bill is adopted at the first reading. Where it disagrees, the Council is called on to provide its own position and communicate it, with reasons, to Parliament.

---

[5] Art. 294(2) TFEU. On this core Commission function, see Chapter 1, Section 3(c).

[6] Art. 293(1) TFEU.

[7] Art. 294(3) TFEU is silent on the voting regime within Parliament, and therefore Art. 231 TFEU applies: 'Save as otherwise provided in the Treaties, the European Parliament shall act by a majority of the votes cast. The rules of procedure shall determine the quorum.'

[8] This option is not expressly recognized in the text of Art. 294(3) TFEU, but it is indirectly recognized in Rule 60 of the Parliament's Rules of Procedure.

[9] Art. 294(4) and (5) TFEU are silent on the voting regime, and therefore Art. 16(4) TEU applies: 'The Council shall act by a qualified majority except where the Treaties provide otherwise.'

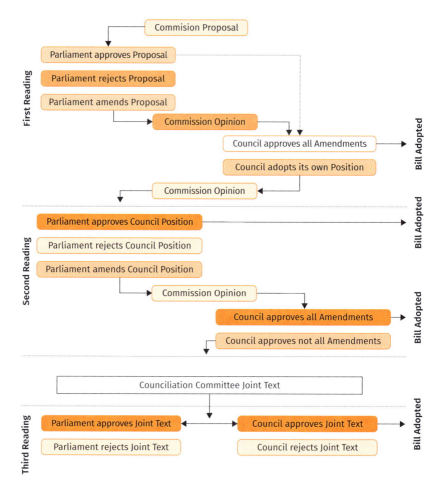

Figure 2.2 Ordinary legislative procedure under Article 294

Second reading. The (amended) bill lies for the second time in Parliament's court; and Parliament has three choices as to what to do with it. Parliament may positively approve the Council's position by a majority of the votes cast;[10] or reject it by a majority of its component members.[11] Approval is thus easier than rejection. (This tendency is reinforced by assimilating passivity to approval.[12]) However, Parliament has a third choice: it may propose, by a majority of its component members, amendments to the Council position.[13]

---

[10] Art. 294(7)(a) TFEU.   [11] Art. 294(7)(b) TFEU.
[12] According to Art. 294(7)(a) TFEU, second alternative, where the Parliament does not act within three months, 'the act shall be deemed to have been adopted in the wording which corresponds to the position of the Council'.
[13] Art. 294(7)(c) TFEU.

The amended bill will be forwarded to the Council (and to the Commission which must deliver an opinion on the amendments). The bill is thus back in the Council's court, and the Council has two options. Where it approves all (!) of Parliament's amendments, the legislative act is adopted.[14] The Council thereby acts by a qualified majority (unless the Commission disagrees with any of the amendments suggested by the Council or the Parliament).[15] But where the Council cannot approve all of Parliament's amendments, the bill enters into the conciliation stage.[16]

Conciliation stage. This stage presents the last chance to rescue the legislative bill. As agreement within the 'formal' legislature has proved impossible, the Union legal order 'delegates' the power to draft a 'joint text' to a committee. This committee is called the 'Conciliation Committee'.[17] The mandate of the Committee is restricted to reaching agreement on a joint text 'on the basis of the positions of the European Parliament and the Council at second reading'.[18] The Committee is composed of members representing the Council,[19] and an equal number of members representing the European Parliament.[20] (The Commission will take part 'in' the committee, but is not a part 'of' the Committee. Its function is to act as a catalyst for conciliation.[21]) The Committee thus represents a 'miniature legislature'; and like its constitutional model, the Committee co-decides by a qualified majority of the Council representatives, and a majority of the representatives sent by Parliament. Where the Committee does not adopt a joint text, the legislative bill has failed. Where the Committee has managed to approve a joint text, the latter returns to the 'formal' Union legislator for a third reading.

---

[14] Art. 294(8)(a) TFEU.   [15] Art. 294(9) TFEU.   [16] Art. 294(8)(b) TFEU.

[17] The Conciliation Committee is not a standing committee, but an ad hoc committee that 'is constituted separately for each legislative proposal requiring conciliation' (European Parliament, 'Codecision and Conciliation' at www.europarl.europa.eu/code/information/guide_en.pdf, 15).

[18] Art. 294(10) TFEU. However, the Court of Justice has been flexible and allowed the Conciliation Committee to find a joint text that goes beyond the common position after the second reading (see *The Queen on the Application of International Air Transport Association et al. v Department of Transport*, Case C-344/04 [2006] ECR I-403).

[19] The Permanent Representative or his Deputy will typically represent the national ministers in the Council.

[20] The parliamentary delegation must reflect the political composition of the formal Parliament. It will normally include the three Vice-Presidents responsible for conciliation, the Rapporteur, and Chair of the responsible parliamentary committee.

[21] Art. 294(11) TFEU. Formally, it will be the Commissioner responsible for the subject matter of the legislative bill who will take part in the Conciliation Committee.

Third reading. The 'formal' Union legislature must positively approve the joint text (without the power of amending it). The Parliament needs to endorse the joint text by a majority of the votes cast, whereas the Council must confirm the text by a qualified majority. Where one of the two chambers disagrees with the proposal made by the Conciliation Committee, the bill finally flounders. Where both chambers approve the text, the bill is adopted and only needs to be 'signed' and 'published'.

Signing and publication. The last two stages before a bill becomes law are set out in Article 297 TFEU which states: 'Legislative acts adopted under the ordinary legislative procedure shall be signed by the President of the European Parliament and by the President of the Council'; and they shall subsequently 'be published in the Official Journal of the European Union'.[22] The publication requirement is a fundamental element of modern societies governed by the rule of law. Only 'public' legislative acts will have the force of law. The Union legal order also requires that all legislative acts 'shall state the reasons on which they are based and shall refer to any proposals, initiatives, recommendations, request or opinions required by the Treaties'.[23] This formal 'duty to state reasons' can be judicially reviewed, and represents a hallmark of legislative rationality.

(b) Constitutional Practice: Informal Trilogues

Constitutional texts often only provide a stylized sketch of the formal relations between institutions. And this formal picture will need to be coloured and revised by informal constitutional practices. This is very much the case for the constitutional text governing the ordinary legislative procedure. The rudimentary status of the constitutional text is indeed recognized by the Treaties themselves.[24]

The primary expression of these informal institutional arrangements are tripartite meetings called 'trilogues'. They combine the representatives of the three institutions involved in the legislative process—that is: Parliament, Council, and Commission—in 'informal' negotiations.

---

[22] Art. 297(1) TFEU. For legislation, this will be the 'L' Series.

[23] Art. 296 TFEU, second indent.

[24] Art. 295 TFEU states: 'The European Parliament, the Council and the Commission shall consult each other and by common agreement make arrangements for their cooperation. To that end, they may, in compliance with the Treaties, conclude interinstitutional agreements which may be of a binding nature.'

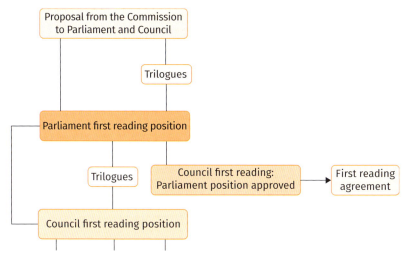

Figure 2.3 Trilogues during the first reading

What is the task of institutional trilogues? The trilogue system is designed to create informal bridges during the formal co-decision procedure that open up 'possibilities for agreements at first and second reading stages, as well as contributing to the preparation of the work of the Conciliation Committee'.[25] Trilogues may thus be held 'at all stages of the [ordinary legislative] procedure'.[26] However, they are particularly important and successful during the first reading (see Figure 2.3).

The strategy of using trilogues has proved extremely successful. It has indeed become so successful that the ordinary legislative procedure has '*de facto* become a single-reading legislative procedure'.[27] And yet, there are serious constitutional problems. For informal trilogues should not be allowed to short-circuit the formal legislative procedure. Were this to happen, democratic deliberation within a fairly representative European Parliament would be replaced by the informal government of a small number of members of the three institutions (see Figure 2.4). Representative democracy is here severely curtailed in the interest of efficiency. The democratic deficit of the Union here lies less in the *formal* structure of the Union legislator, but more in its *informal* bypassing.

---

[25] 'Joint Declaration on Practical Arrangements for the Codecision Procedure', [2007] OJ C145/5, para. 7.

[26] Ibid., para. 8.

[27] C. Roederer-Rynning and J. Greenwood, 'The Culture of Trilogues' (2015) 22 *Journal of European Public Policy* 1148. Within the last parliamentary terms, more than four-fifths of all legislative acts were agreed at first reading with less than 5 per cent ever reaching the third reading.

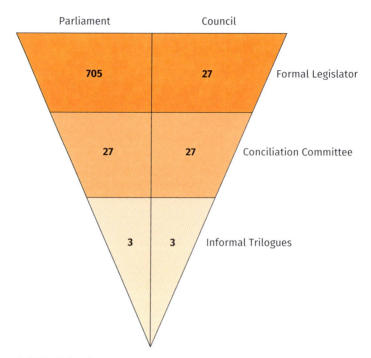

Figure 2.4 Declining democratic representation

2. The 'Special' Legislative Procedures

There is no specific definition of what constitutes a 'special' legislative procedure in the Treaty section on procedures. They are thus defined in each specific
legislative competence. The Treaties here recognize three special legislative
procedures. Unlike the ordinary procedure, Union legislation will thereby not
be the result of a 'joint adoption' of the European Parliament and the Council.
It will be adopted by *one* of the two institutions. In the first variant of Article
289(2) TFEU, this will be the Parliament; yet the Treaties generally require
the 'consent' of the Council. In the second variant of Article 289(2) TFEU, the
Council will adopt the legislative act; yet the Treaties require either the 'consent' or 'consultation' of the Parliament. The first two special procedures may
be characterized as the 'consent procedure', while the third special procedure
can be referred to as the 'consultation procedure'.

What are the characteristics of the 'consent procedure' and the 'consultation procedure'? The former requires one institution to consent to the legislative bill of the other. Consent is less than co-decision, for only the dominant
institution will be able to determine the substantive content of the bill. The

non-dominant institution will be forced to 'take it or leave it'. But this veto power is still—much—stronger than mere consultation. For while the Court has recognized that consultation is 'an essential factor in the institutional balance intended by the Treaty',[28] consultation is nonetheless a mere 'formality'.[29] The formal obligation to consult will *not* mean that the adopting institution must take into account the substantive views of the other.[30] The latter must just be 'heard'—but nothing more.

3. The Principle of Subsidiarity

Subsidiarity—the quality of being 'subsidiary'—derives from *subsidium*. The Latin concept evolved in the military context. It represented an 'assistance' or 'aid' that stayed in the background. Figuratively, an entity is subsidiary where it provides a 'subsidy'—an assistance of subordinate or secondary importance. In political philosophy, the principle of subsidiarity came to represent the idea 'that a central authority should have a subsidiary function, performing only those tasks which cannot be performed effectively at a more immediate or local level'.[31] The principle thus has a positive and a negative aspect.[32] It positively encourages 'large associations' to assist smaller ones, where they need help; and it negatively discourages 'to assign to a greater and higher association what lesser and subordinate organizations can do'. It is this dual character that has given the principle of subsidiarity its 'Janus-like' character.[33]

When did the subsidiarity principle become a constitutional principle of the European Union? The principle of subsidiarity surfaced in 1975,[34] but

---

[28] *Roquette Frères v Council (Isoglucose)*, Case 138/79 [1980] ECR 3333, para. 33.

[29] The 'formality' still requires that the Council has to wait until Parliament has provided its opinion (see ibid., para. 34): 'In that respect it is pertinent to point out that observance of that requirement implies that the Parliament has expressed its opinion. It is impossible to take the view that the requirement is satisfied by the Council's simply asking for the opinion.' On this point, see also *Parliament v Council*, Case C-65/93 [1995] ECR I-643; however, this case also established implied limitations on Parliament's prerogative (ibid., paras 27–8).

[30] This was confirmed in *Parliament v Council*, Case C-417/93 [1995] ECR I-1185, esp. paras 10 and 11.

[31] See *Oxford English Dictionary*: 'subsidiary' and 'subsidiarity'.

[32] C. Calliess, *Subsidiaritäts- und Solidaritätsprinzip in der Europäischen Union* (Nomos, 1999), 26.

[33] V. Constantinesco, 'Who's Afraid of Subsidiarity?' (1991) 11 *Yearbook of European Law* 33 at 35.

[34] For a detailed textual genealogy of the subsidiarity principle in the European legal order, see R. Schütze, *From Dual to Cooperative Federalism: The Changing Structure of European Law* (Oxford University Press, 2009), 247 et seq.

it would only find official expression in the context of the Union's environmental policy after the Single European Act (1986).[35] The Maastricht Treaty on European Union (1992) finally lifted the subsidiarity principle beyond its environmental confines. It became a general constitutional principle of the European Union. Today, the Treaty on European Union defines it in Article 5, whose third paragraph states:

> Under the principle of subsidiarity, in areas which do not fall within its exclusive competence, the Union shall act only if and in so far as the objectives of the proposed action cannot be sufficiently achieved by the Member States, either at central level or at regional and local level, but can rather, by reason of the scale or effects of the proposed action, be better achieved at Union level.

This definition clarifies that subsidiarity is only to apply within the sphere of the Union's non-exclusive powers—to be discussed later in Chapter 3.[36]

The Treaty definition of subsidiarity thereby builds on *two* tests. The first may be called the *national insufficiency test*. The Union can only act where the objectives of the proposed action could not be sufficiently achieved by the Member States (centrally or regionally). This appears to be an absolute standard. By contrast, a second test is a *comparative efficiency test*. The Union should not act unless it can *better* achieve the objectives of the proposed action. This appears to be a relative standard. The question that therefore arises is this: will the combination of these two tests mean that the Union would not be entitled to act where it is—in relative terms—better able to tackle a social problem, but where the Member States could—in absolute terms—still achieve the desired result?

This is indeed not the only textual problem with Article 5(3). For the formulation 'if and in so far' potentially offered *two* versions of the subsidiarity principle. The first version concentrates on the 'if' question by asking *whether* the Union should act. This has been defined as the principle of subsidiarity *in a strict sense*. The second version concentrates on the 'in so far' question by asking *how* the Union should act. This has been referred to as the principle of subsidiarity *in a wide sense*.[37]

---

[35] The (then) newly inserted ex-Art. 130r(4) EEC restricted Community environmental legislation to those actions whose objectives could 'be attained better at Community level than at the level of the individual Member States'.

[36] On the different EU competence types, see Chapter 3, Section 4.

[37] K. Lenaerts, 'The Principle of Subsidiarity and the Environment in the European Union: Keeping the Balance of Federalism' (1994) 17 *Fordham International Law Journal* 846 at 875.

The wording of Article 5(3) TEU is thus a terrible textual failure. Too many political cooks seem to have spoiled the legal broth! In the past three decades, two—parallel—approaches therefore evolved to give meaning to the subsidiarity principle. The first approach concentrates on its political and procedural dimension. The second approach focuses on subsidiarity as an objective judicial standard.

(a) Subsidiarity as a Political Safeguard

Despite its literary presence,[38] the principle of subsidiarity has remained a subsidiary principle of European constitutionalism. The reason for its shadowy existence has been its lack of conceptual contours. If subsidiarity was everything to everyone, how should the Union apply it?

To limit this semantic uncertainty, the Member States have tried to 'proceduralize' the principle. This attempt to develop subsidiarity into a political safeguard of federalism can be seen in Protocol (No. 2) 'On the Application of the Principles of Subsidiarity and Proportionality'. Importantly, the Protocol only applies to 'draft legislative acts';[39] that is: acts to be adopted under the ordinary or a special legislative procedure.

The Protocol thereby aims to establish 'a system of monitoring' the application of subsidiarity. Each Union institution is called upon to ensure constant respect for the principle.[40] And this means, in particular, that they must forward draft legislative acts to national parliaments.[41] These draft legislative acts must 'be justified' with regard to the principle of subsidiarity (and proportionality).[42] This procedural duty to provide reasons is defined as follows:

> Any draft legislative act should contain a detailed statement making it possible to appraise compliance with the principles of subsidiarity and proportionality. This statement should contain some assessment of the proposal's financial impact and, in the case of a directive, of its implications for the rules to be put in place by Member States, including, where necessary, the regional legislation. The reasons for concluding that a Union objective can be better achieved at Union level shall

---

[38]   From the—abundant—literature, see G. Berman, 'Taking Subsidiarity Seriously: Federalism in the European Community and the United States' (1994) 94 *Columbia Law Review* 331; D. Z. Cass, 'The Word that Saves Maastricht? The Principle of Subsidiarity and the Division of Powers within the European Community' (1992) 29 *Common Market Law Review* 1107; Constantinesco, 'Who's Afraid' (n. 33).

[39]   Art. 3 of the Protocol.   [40]   Ibid., Art. 1.   [41]   Ibid., Art. 4.   [42]   Ibid., Art. 5.

be substantiated by qualitative and, wherever possible, quantitative indicators. Draft legislative acts shall take account of the need for any burden, whether financial or administrative, falling upon the Union, national governments, regional or local authorities, economic operators and citizens, to be minimised and commensurate with the objective to be achieved.[43]

How is this duty enforced? One solution here points to the European Court;[44] yet, the Protocol famously develops a second solution: the active involvement of national parliaments in the legislative procedure of the European Union.[45] It was hoped that this idea would kill two birds with one stone. The procedural involvement of national parliaments promised to strengthen the federal *and* the democratic safeguards within Europe.

But if national parliaments are to be the Union's 'watchdogs of subsidiarity',[46] would they enjoy a veto right (hard legislative solution) or only a monitoring right (soft legislative solution)? According to the Subsidiarity Protocol, each national parliament may within eight weeks produce a reasoned opinion stating why it considers that a European legislative draft does not comply with the principle of subsidiarity.[47] Each Parliament will thereby have two votes.[48] Where the negative votes amount to one-third of all the votes allocated to the national parliaments, the European Union draft 'must be reviewed'. This is called the 'yellow card' mechanism, since the Union legislator 'may decide to maintain, amend or withdraw the draft'.[49]

---

[43]   Ibid.

[44]   Ibid., Art. 8: 'The Court of Justice of the European Union shall have jurisdiction in actions on grounds of infringement of the principle of subsidiarity by a legislative act, brought in accordance with the rules laid down in Article 263 of the Treaty on the Functioning of the European Union by Member States, or notified by them in accordance with their legal order on behalf of their national Parliament or a chamber thereof.' For a discussion of the Court's deferential stance, see Section 3(b) below.

[45]   This function is acknowledged in Art. 12(b) TEU, which requests national parliaments to contribute to the good functioning of the Union 'by seeing to it that the principle of subsidiarity is respected in accordance with the procedures provided for in the Protocol on the application of the principles of subsidiarity and proportionality'.

[46]   I. Cooper, 'The Watchdogs of Subsidiarity: National Parliaments and the Logic of Arguing in the EU' (2006) 44 *Journal of Common Market Studies* 281.

[47]   Art. 6 Protocol (No. 2) 'On the Application of the Principles of Subsidiarity and Proportionality'.

[48]   Ibid., Art. 7(1).

[49]   Ibid., Art. 7(2). For an analysis of the first activation of the yellow card mechanism, see F. Fabbrini and K. Granat, '"Yellow Card, but no Foul": The Role of the National Parliaments under the Subsidiarity Protocol and the Commission Proposal for an EU Regulation on the Right to Strike' (2013) 50 *Common Market Law Review* 115.

The yellow card mechanism is slightly strengthened in relation to proposals under the *ordinary* legislative procedure; albeit, here, only a majority of the votes allocated to the national parliaments will trigger it.[50] Under this 'orange card' mechanism, the Commission's justification for maintaining the proposal, as well as the reasoned opinions of the national parliaments, will be submitted to the Union legislator. And the Union legislator will have to consider whether the proposal is compatible with the principle of subsidiarity. Where one of its chambers finds that the proposal violates the principle of subsidiarity, the proposal is rejected.[51]

How successful has the yellow card mechanism been? In the light of having been activated only three times, critics have pointed to a number of practical inadequacies in the existing procedure; and calls for a 'red card' mechanism have therefore been made.[52] These—tempting—calls should nevertheless be resisted. For 'to give national parliaments what would amount to a veto over proposals would be incompatible with the Commission's constitutionally protected independence'.[53] And 'a veto power vested in national Parliaments would distort the proper distribution of power and responsibility in the EU's complex but remarkably successful system of transnational governance by conceding too much to State control'.[54] Viewed in this light, the rejection of the red-card solution is to be welcomed. The yellow card solution will indeed better allow national parliaments to channel their scrutiny to where it can be most useful and effective: on their respective national governments.

(b) Subsidiarity as a Judicial Safeguard

After a first subsidiarity review at the political level, a second review lies with the EU judiciary. The European Court of Justice must, most importantly, verify whether the EU legislature has complied with the *substantive conditions* set

---

[50] Ibid., Art. 7(3).

[51] Ibid., Art. 7(3)(b): 'if, by a majority of 55% of the members of the Council or a majority of the votes cast in the European Parliament, the legislator is of the opinion that the proposal is not compatible with the principle of subsidiarity, the legislative proposal shall not be given further consideration.'

[52] Most famously, this idea was championed by David Cameron in his attempt to renegotiate the British 'deal' with the European Union prior to the Brexit referendum. For a brief analysis, see http://blogs.lse.ac.uk/europpblog/2016/06/13/how-the-red-card-system-could-increase-the-power-of-national-parliaments-within-the-eu/.

[53] A. Dashwood, 'The Relationship between the Member States and the European Union/ Community' (2004) 41 *Common Market Law Review* 355 at 369.

[54] S. Weatherill, 'Using National Parliaments to Improve Scrutiny of the Limits of EU Action' (2003) 28 *European Law Review* 909 at 912.

out in Article 5(3) TEU. How has the Court defined the relationship between the national insufficiency test and the comparative efficiency test? And has the Court favoured the restrictive or the wide meaning of subsidiarity?

There are surprisingly few judgments that address the principle of subsidiarity. In *United Kingdom v Council* (*Working Time Directive*),[55] for example, the United Kingdom had applied for the annulment of the Working Time Directive. The applicant had claimed that:

> [T]he [Union] legislature neither fully considered nor adequately demonstrated whether there were transnational aspects which could not be satisfactorily regulated by national measures, whether such measures would conflict with the requirements of the [Treaties] or significantly damage the interests of Member States or, finally, whether action at [European] level would provide clear benefits compared with action at national level . . . [The principle of subsidiarity would] not allow the adoption of a directive in such wide and prescriptive terms as the contested directive, given that the extent and the nature of legislative regulation of working time vary very widely between Member States.[56]

How did the Court respond? The Court offered an interpretation of subsidiarity that has structured its judicial vision of the principle ever since. It held:

> Once the [Union legislature] has found that it is necessary to improve the existing level of protection as regards the health and safety of workers and to harmonize the conditions in this area while maintaining the improvements made, achievement of that objective through the imposition of minimum requirements necessarily presupposes [Union]-wide action, which otherwise, as in this case, leaves the enactment of the detailed implementing provisions required largely to the Member States. The argument that the [Union legislature] could not properly adopt measures as general and mandatory as those forming the subject-matter of the directive will be examined below in the context of the plea alleging infringement of the principle of proportionality.[57]

This judicial passage contained two fundamental choices. First, the Court assumed that where the Union legislature had decided to 'harmonize' national laws, that objective necessarily presupposed Union legislation. This view answers the national insufficiency test with a mistaken tautology: only the Union can harmonize laws, and therefore the Member States already fail the first test!

---

[55] *United Kingdom v Council*, Case C-84/94 [1996] ECR I-5755.   [56] Ibid., para. 46.
[57] Ibid., para. 47.

But assuming the 'whether' of European action had been affirmatively established, could the Union go 'as far' as it had? This was the second crucial choice of the Court. It decided against the idea of subsidiarity in a wider sense. For instead of analysing the intensity of the European law under Article 5(3) TEU, it chose to review it under the auspices of the principle of proportionality under Article 5(4) TEU. And it is there that the Court made a third important choice. In analysing the proportionality of the Union law, it ruled that 'the [Union] must be allowed a wide discretion in an area which, as here, involves the legislature in making social policy choices and requires it to carry out complex assessments'. Judicial review would therefore be limited to examining 'whether it has been vitiated by *manifest error or misuse of powers, or whether the institution concerned has manifestly exceeded the limits of its discretion*'.[58] The Court would thus apply a *low* degree of judicial scrutiny.

Choices one and three have been confirmed in subsequent jurisprudence. By concentrating on the national insufficiency test, the Court has thus short-circuited the comparative efficiency test.[59] It has not searched for qualitative or quantitative benefits of Union laws,[60] but confirmed its manifest error test—thus leaving subsidiarity to the political safeguards of federalism. This is reflected in the low justificatory standard imposed on the Union legislator.[61] By contrast, as regards the second choice, the Court has remained ambivalent. While in some cases it has incorporated the intensity question

---

[58] Ibid., para. 58 (emphasis added).

[59] See *The Queen v Secretary of State for Health, ex parte British American Tobacco (Investments) Ltd and Imperial Tobacco Ltd*, Case C-491/01 [2002] ECR I-11453, paras 181–3: '[T]he Directive's objective is to eliminate the barriers raised by the differences which still exist between the Member States' laws, regulations and administrative provisions on the manufacture, presentation and sale of tobacco products, while ensuring a high level of health protection, in accordance with Article [114(3) TFEU]. Such an objective cannot be sufficiently achieved by the Member States individually and calls for action at [European] level, as demonstrated by the multifarious development of national laws in this case.'

[60] See Art. 5 Protocol (No. 2) 'On the Application of the Principles of Subsidiarity and Proportionality'.

[61] See *Netherlands v Parliament*, Case C-377/98 [2001] ECR I-7079, para. 33: 'Compliance with the principle of subsidiarity is necessarily implicit in the fifth, sixth and seventh recitals of the preamble to the Directive, which state that, in the absence of action at [European] level, the development of the laws and practices of the different Member States impedes the proper functioning of the internal market. It thus appears that the Directive states sufficient reasons on that point.'

into its subsidiarity analysis,[62] other jurisprudence has kept the subsidiarity and the proportionality principles at arm's length.[63]

What is the better option here? It has been argued that subsidiarity should best be understood 'in a wider sense'.[64] For it is indeed impossible to reduce subsidiarity to 'whether' the Union should exercise one of its competences. The distinction between 'competence' and 'subsidiarity'—between Article 5(2) and (3) TEU—will only make sense if the subsidiarity principle concentrates on the 'whether' of *the specific act at issue*. But the 'whether' and the 'how' of the specific action are inherently tied together. The principle of subsidiarity will thus ask *whether* the Union legislator has *unnecessarily* restricted national autonomy.

4. Excursus: The (Ordinary) Treaty-Making Procedure

Whenever it legislates, the Union adopts rules for its own legal order. Yet in today's global world, many laws originate in international agreements or international organizations. International agreements concluded by the Union have indeed come to constitute a rich source of European law.

But how are its international agreements concluded? The 'ordinary' treaty-making procedure is found in Article 218 TFEU (Figure 2.5).[65] The central institution within this procedure is the Council—not just as *primus inter pares* with Parliament, but simply as *primus*. Article 218 acknowledges the central role of the Council in all stages of the procedure:

> The Council shall authorize the opening of negotiations, adopt negotiating directives, authorize the signing of agreements and conclude them.[66]

---

[62]   In *The Queen v Secretary of State for Health*, Case C-491/01 (n. 59), the Court identified the 'intensity of the action undertaken by the [Union]' with the principle of subsidiarity and not the principle of proportionality (ibid., para. 184). This acceptance of subsidiarity *sensu lato* can also be seen at work in *Arcor v Germany*, Case C-55/06 [2008] ECR I-2931, where the Court identified the principle of subsidiarity with the idea that 'the Member States retain the possibility to establish specific rules on the field in question' (ibid., para. 144).

[63]   See *United Kingdom v Council* (*Working Time Directive*), Case C-84/94 (n. 55).

[64]   Schütze, *From Dual to Cooperative Federalism* (n. 34), 263 et seq.

[65]   Two special procedures are found in Arts 207 and 219 TFEU. The former deals with trade agreements within the context of the Union's common commercial policy. The latter expresses a derogation from the 'ordinary' procedure for 'formal agreements on an exchange-rate system for the euro in relation to the currencies of third states' (see Art. 219(1) TFEU).

[66]   Art. 218(2) TFEU.

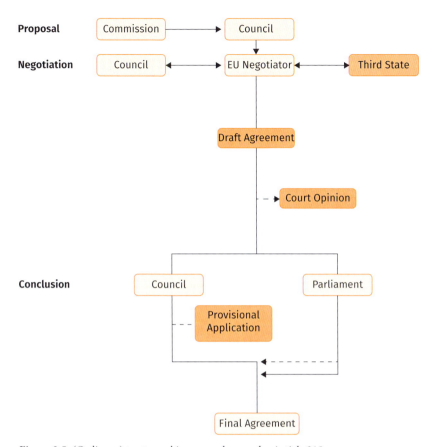

Figure 2.5 (Ordinary) treaty-making procedure under Article 218

The Council here acts by a qualified majority, except in four situations. It must get the consent of all national ministers: when the agreement deals with an area for which unanimity is required; for all association agreements; for all economic cooperation agreements with States that are candidates for Union accession; as well as in respect of the Union's accession agreement to the European Convention on Human Rights (ECHR).[67]

Having recognized the primary role of the Council, Article 218 then defines the secondary roles of the other EU institutions in the various procedural stages of treaty-making. The provision distinguishes between the 'initiation' and 'negotiation' of the agreement, its 'signing' and 'conclusion'; and it also provides special rules for its modification and suspension. Exceptionally, the Union can even become a party to an international agreement without having

[67] Art. 218(8) TFEU.

concluded it. This—rare—phenomenon occurs where the Union 'inherits' international agreements from its Member States through the doctrine of functional succession.

(a) Initiation and Negotiation

Who can propose an international agreement that the Union should conclude? Under Article 218(3), the Commission holds the exclusive right to make recommendations for agreements that principally deal with matters that do not fall within the Common Foreign and Security Policy (CFSP). By contrast, as regards subject matter that exclusively or principally falls into the CFSP, it is the High Representative who will submit recommendations to the Council. For matters falling partly within the CFSP and partly outside it, there is also the possibility of 'joint proposals'.[68]

Acting on the recommendation, the Council may decide to open negotiations and nominate the Union negotiator 'depending on the subject matter of the agreement envisaged'.[69] This formulation is ambivalent. Textually, the phrase suggests a liberal meaning. The Council can—but need not necessarily—appoint the Commission as Union negotiator for an agreement. According to this reading, the Commission will not automatically enjoy a prerogative to be the Union's negotiator. However, a systematic reading of the phrase leads to a different meaning. For if read in the light of the jurisdictional division between the Commission and the High Representative at the recommendation stage, the Commission should be constitutionally entitled to be the Union negotiator for all Union agreements that 'exclusively or principally' fall into the Treaty on the Functioning of the European Union.[70]

The Council will be able to address directives to the Union negotiator and subject its powers to consultation with a special committee. Where the Commission is chosen as Union negotiator, it thus not only needs to be 'authorized' by the Council but will also conduct the negotiations under the control of the Council. The Commission's powers are here between 'autonomous' and 'delegated' powers. The lower degree of institutional autonomy is justified by the fact that third parties are involved. (For the subsequent rejection of a draft agreement by the Council may have 'external' negative repercussions.) On the other hand, the existence of a Council committee checking on the Union negotiator creates, to some extent, a 'two-front war'. For the Union negotiator

---

[68] See Arts 22(2) and 30(1) TEU.   [69] Art. 218(3) TFEU.

[70] In this sense, see also P. Eeckhout, *EU External Relations Law* (Oxford University Press, 2011), 196.

has not only to negotiate externally with the third party, but it also needs to deal internally with the Council.

What about the European Parliament? Parliament is not formally involved in the negotiation. However, Article 218(10) constitutionalizes its right to be informed during all stages of the procedure. And this right has the potential of becoming an informal political safeguard that anticipates the interests of Parliament at the negotiation stage.[71]

Finally, any Union institution and the Member States are entitled to challenge the 'constitutionality' of a draft agreement *prior* to its conclusion. This judicial safeguard can be found in Article 218(11), which creates the jurisdiction of the Court for an 'Opinion'.[72] Where this 'Opinion' leads to a finding that the envisaged agreement is not compatible with the Treaties, the agreement may not enter into force—unless the EU Treaties themselves are amended.[73] The possibility of an *ex ante* 'review' of a draft agreement contrasts with the Court's ordinary *ex post* review powers.[74] This exception is—again—justified by the fact that third party rights under international law are involved. Indeed, it is a rule of international law that, once an agreement is validly concluded under international law, a contracting party generally cannot subsequently invoke internal constitutional problems to deny its binding effect.[75] *Ex post* review of an international agreement will thus be too late to negate the external effects of an international agreement.

(b) Signing and Conclusion

The Council must sign and conclude the agreement following the proposal by the Union negotiator.[76]

---

[71] See Framework Agreement on Relations between the European Parliament and the European Commission, [2010] OJ L304/47, especially Annex III. According to para. 3 of the Annex, '[t]he Commission shall take due account of Parliament's comments throughout the negotiations'.

[72] Art. 218(11) TFEU.

[73] This happened, e.g., with regard to the European Convention on Human Rights in 1996; see *Opinion 2/94 (Accession to the ECHR I)* [1996] ECR I-1759. Prior to the Lisbon Treaty, accession to the Convention was thus unconstitutional. The Lisbon Treaty has amended the original Treaties, which now contain an express competence to accede to the ECHR in Art. 6(2) TEU.

[74] On (*ex post*) judicial review in the Union legal order, see Chapter 8, Section 3.

[75] See Art. 46 Vienna Convention on the Law of Treaties: '(1) A State may not invoke the fact that its consent to be bound by a treaty has been expressed in violation of a provision of its internal law regarding competence to conclude treaties as invalidating its consent unless that violation was manifest and concerned a rule of its internal law of fundamental importance. (2) A violation is manifest if it would be objectively evident to any State conducting itself in the matter in accordance with normal practice and in good faith.'

[76] Art. 218(5) and (6) TFEU. The conclusion will usually be done by means of a Council Decision.

Yet, importantly, prior to the formal conclusion of the agreement, the European Parliament must be actively involved (except where the agreement exclusively relates to the CFSP). Article 218(6) here distinguishes between two principal forms of parliamentary participation in the conclusion procedure: *consultation* and *consent*. The former is the residual category and applies to all agreements that do not require consent. The types of agreements where the Council needs to obtain parliamentary consent are thereby enumerated in the form of five situations individually listed under Article 218(6)(a), namely: (i) association agreements; (ii) the agreement on Union accession to the European Convention on Human Rights; (iii) agreements establishing a specific institutional framework; (iv) agreements with important budgetary implications for the Union; (v) agreements covering fields to which either the ordinary legislative procedure applies, or the special legislative procedure where consent by the European Parliament is required.

The first, second, and third categories may be explained by the constitutional idea of 'political treaties'.[77] For fundamental political choices, Parliament—the representative of the European citizens—must give its democratic consent. The fourth category represents a constitutional reflex that protects the special role the European Parliament enjoys in establishing the Union budget.[78] The fifth category makes profound sense from the perspective of procedural parallelism. Under paragraph 6(a)(v), Parliament is entitled to veto 'agreements covering fields' that internally require parliamentary co-decision or consent.

The parallelism between the internal and external spheres is not, however, complete: indeed, Parliament will *not* enjoy the power of co-conclusion in areas in which the ordinary legislative procedure applies. Its internal power of co-decision is here reduced to a mere power of consent. It must 'take or leave' the negotiated international agreement. This structural 'democratic deficit' in the procedural regime for international agreements is not a *sui generis* characteristic of the European Union, but can be found in other constitutional orders of the world.[79] It is generally justified by reference to the 'exceptional' nature of foreign affairs and, in particular, their 'volatile' and 'secretive' nature.

---

[77] R. Jennings and S. Watts (eds), *Oppenheim's International Law* (Oxford University Press, 2008), 211.

[78] For an extensive discussion of this category, see *Parliament v Council* (*Mauritania Fisheries Agreement*), Case 189/97 [1999] ECR I-4741.

[79] E.g. in the United States. For a comparison between the EU and the US in this context, see R. Schütze, 'The "Treaty Power" and Parliamentary Democracy: Comparative Perspectives' in *Foreign Affairs and the EU Constitution* (Cambridge University Press, 2014), ch. 11.

(c) Modification and Suspension (Termination)

Article 218(7) deals with *modifications* of international agreements that have been successfully concluded. The Council may 'authorize the negotiator to approve on the Union's behalf modifications to the agreement where it provides for them to be adopted by a simplified procedure or by a body set up by the agreement'. In the absence of such a specific authorization for a simplified revision procedure, the ordinary treaty-making procedure will however apply. This follows from a constitutional principle called *actus contrarius*. In order to modify an act or international agreement, the same procedure needs to be followed that led to the conclusion of the international agreement in the first place.

Article 218(9) deals with the *suspension* of an international agreement. The provision specifies that the Commission (or the High Representative) may propose to the Council the suspension of the agreement. And while the provision does not expressly refer to the jurisdictional division between the two actors, as mentioned in Article 218(3) for the proposal stage, we should assume that this rule would apply analogously. Parliament is not expressly mentioned and will thus only have to be informed of the Council decision. This truncated procedure allows the Union quickly to decide on the (temporary) suspension of an agreement. However, this 'executive' decision without parliamentary consent distorts to some extent the institutional balance in the external relations field.

How are Union agreements *terminated?* Unfortunately, Article 218 does not expressly set out a procedural regime for the termination of a Union agreement. Two views are possible. The first view is again based on the idea of *actus contrarius*: the termination of an agreement would need to follow the very same procedure for its conclusion. This procedural parallelism has been contested by reference to the common constitutional traditions of the Union's Member States, which leave the termination decision principally in the hands of the executive.[80] A second view therefore reverts to the suspension procedure applied analogously.

(d) Union Succession to Member State Agreements

Can the Union be bound by agreements that it has not formally concluded? The counterintuitive answer is indeed 'yes': under European law, the Union

---

[80] C. Tomuschat, 'Artikel 300 EG' in H. von der Groeben and J. Schwarze (eds), *Kommentar zum Vertrag über die Europäische Union und zur Gründung der Europäischen Gemeinschaft* (Nomos, 2004), Vol. IV, para. 61.

can be bound by agreements of its Member States where the Union has succeeded the latter.[81]

The doctrine of Union succession to international agreements of the Member States is thereby a doctrine of *functional* succession.[82] It is not based on a transfer of territory, but on a transfer of *functions*. The European Court announced this European doctrine in relation to the General Agreement on Tariffs and Trade in *International Fruit*.[83] Formally, the Union was not a party to the international treaty, but the Court nonetheless found as follows:

> [I]n so far as under the [European] Treat[ies] the [Union] has *assumed the powers previously exercised by Member* States in the area covered by the General Agreement, the provisions of that agreement have the effect of binding the [Union].[84]

Functional succession here emanated from the exclusive nature of the Union's powers. Since the Union had exclusively assumed the 'functions' previously exercised by the Member States in this area, it was entitled and obliged to also assume their international obligations.

For a long time after *International Fruit*, the succession doctrine remained quiet. But in the last decade it has experienced a constitutional revival. This allowed the Court better to define the doctrine's contours. Three principles have thereby traditionally applied to functional succession in the European legal order. First, for the succession doctrine to come into operation *all* the Member States must be parties to an international treaty.[85] Second, *when* the international treaty is concluded is irrelevant. It will thus not matter whether the international treaty was concluded before or after the creation of the European Community in 1958.[86] Third, the Union will only succeed to international treaties where there is a '*full transfer of the powers* previously exercised

---

[81] For an overview, see R. Schütze, 'The "Succession Doctrine" and the European Union' in *Foreign Affairs and the EU Constitution* (n. 79), ch. 3.

[82] See P. Pescatore, *L'ordre juridique des Communautés Européennes* (Presse universitaire de Liège, 1975), 147–8 (author's translation): '[B]y taking over, by virtue of the Treaties, certain competences and certain powers previously exercised by the Member States, the [Union] equally had to assume the international obligations that controlled the exercise of these competences and powers[.]'

[83] *International Fruit Company NV v Produktschap voor Groenten en Fruit*, Joined Cases 21–4/72 [1972] ECR 1219.

[84] Ibid., paras 14–18 (emphasis added).

[85] *Commune de Mesquer v Total*, Case C-188/07 [2008] ECR I-4501.

[86] *Intertanko and others v Secretary of State for Transport*, Case 308/06 [2008] ECR I-4057.

by the Member States'.[87] The Union will thus not succeed to all international agreements concluded by all the Member States, only to those where it has assumed an exclusive competence.

Would the European succession doctrine thereby be confined to the sphere of the Union's *constitutionally* exclusive powers; or would *legislative* exclusivity generated by Article 3(2) TFEU be sufficient?[88] The Court has shown a preference for a succession doctrine that includes legislative exclusivity. In *Bogiatzi*,[89] the Court indeed found that a 'full transfer' could take place where Union legislation completely pre-empted the Member States from the substantive scope of the international treaty.

Conclusion

Who is the Union legislator? The Union legislator is a compound legislator that combines various institutions through a procedure. For the Union legal order, there exist one 'ordinary' and three 'special' legislative procedures. All four procedures combine the European Parliament and the Council, yet only under the ordinary legislative procedure do both enjoy symmetric constitutional rights.

Ordinary legislation must be adopted following a complex formal procedure that may, in the most extreme situation, comprise three readings. In the past, the Union has nonetheless tried to adopt legislation after its first reading. In order to achieve this result, it has used informal trilogues between the Parliament, the Council, and the Commission. But while these trilogues have been very successful, they do contain the danger of short-circuiting the democratic representation underpinning the ordinary legislative procedure.

The Union legislator is—generally—a subsidiary legislator. For the exercise of its non-exclusive competences is restricted by the principle of subsidiarity. The latter grants a constitutional advantage to national legislation; and in order to protect that constitutional advantage, the Union has pursued two mechanisms. The first mechanism concentrates on the procedural involvement of national parliaments in the (political) principle of subsidiarity.

---

[87]   Ibid., para. 4 (emphasis added).

[88]   On the idea of legislative exclusivity, see Chapter 3, Section 4(a).

[89]   *Bogiatzi v Deutscher Luftpool and others*, Case C-301/08 [2009] ECR I-10185.

The second mechanism focuses on judicial limits imposed by the (legal) principle of subsidiarity.

A final section within the chapter explored the (ordinary) treaty-making procedure. The negotiation of international treaties is thereby left in the hands of the Commission (and the High Representative). The conclusion of the agreement, by contrast, is the task of the Council. However, Parliament will need to give its consent on a wide range of agreements; yet, as we saw earlier, the external powers of the Parliament are here more limited than its internal powers.

3

Union Competences

Introduction

When a sovereign parliament legislates, it need not 'justify' its acts. It is considered to enjoy a competence to do all things.[1] This 'omnipotence' is seen as inherent in the idea of a 'sovereign' State. The European Union is however neither 'sovereign' nor a 'State'. Its powers are *not inherent* powers. They must be *conferred* on it by the Member States in the European Treaties.

---

[1] For the classic British legal order, see A. V. Dicey, *Introduction to the Study of the Law of the Constitution* (Liberty Fund, 1982), 37–8: 'The principle of Parliamentary sovereignty means neither more nor less than this, namely that Parliament thus defined has, under the English constitution, the right to make or unmake any law whatever: and, further, that no person or body is recognized by the law of England as having a right to override or set aside the legislation of Parliament.'

This constitutional principle is called the 'principle of conferral'. The Treaty on European Union defines it as follows:

> Under the principle of conferral, the Union shall act only within the limits of the competences conferred upon it by the Member States in the Treaties to attain the objectives set out therein. Competences not conferred upon the Union in the Treaties remain with the Member States.[2]

The Treaties employ the notion of competence in various provisions. But sadly, there is no positive definition of the concept. So what is a legislative competence? The best definition is this: a legislative competence is the *material field* within which an authority is entitled to legislate.

What are these material fields in which the Union is entitled to legislate? The Treaties do *not* enumerate the Union's competences in a single list. Instead, the EU Treaties pursue a different technique: they attribute legislative competence for each and every Union activity in the respective Treaty title dealing with that activity. Each policy area contains a provision—sometimes more than one—on which Union legislation can be based. The various 'Union policies and internal actions' are set out in Part III of the TFEU (Table 3.1).[3]

The Treaties here present a picture of thematically limited competences in distinct policy areas. This picture is however—partly—misleading. Three legal developments have significantly undermined the principle of conferral in the past; and these three developments have led to widespread accusations that the European Union's competences are 'unlimited'. What are they? First, there has been a rise of teleological interpretation, which will be discussed in Section 1. The Union's competences are here interpreted in such a way that they potentially 'spill over' into other policy areas. This 'spillover' effect can be particularly observed with regard to a second development: the rise of the Union's general competences. For in addition to its specific competences in specific areas, the Union enjoys two very general legislative competences that horizontally cut across the various policy titles within the Treaties. These two competences are Articles 114 and 352 TFEU and will be discussed in Section 2. Lastly, there is a third development that would qualify the principle of conferral significantly: the doctrine of implied external powers, which will be analysed in Section 3.

---

[2] Art. 5(2) TEU.

[3] And yet, there exist some legal bases outside Part III of the TFEU, such as Art. 352 TFEU—the Union's most famous legal base.

Table 3.1 Union policies and internal actions

Part III TFEU – Union Policies and Internal Actions			
Title I	The Internal Market	Title XIII	Culture
Title II	Free Movement of Goods	Title XIV	Public Health
Title III	Agriculture and Fisheries	Title XV	Consumer Protection
Title IV	Free Movement of Persons, Services and Capital	Title XVI	Trans-European Networks
		Title XVII	Industry
Title V	Area of Freedom, Security and Justice	Title XVIII	Economic, Social and Territorial Cohesion
Title VI	Transport	Title XIX	Research and Technological Development and Space
Title VII	Common Rules on Competition, Taxation and Approximation of Laws	Title XX	Environment
		Title XXI	Energy
		Title XXII	Tourism
Title VIII	Economic and Monetary Policy	Title XXIII	Civil Protection
		Title XXIV	Administrative Cooperation
Title IX	Employment		
Title X	Social Policy		
Title XI	The European Social Fund		
Title XII	Education, Vocational Training, Youth and Sport		

Article 192	Title XX – Environment
The European Parliament and the Council, acting in accordance with the ordinary legislative procedure … shall decide what action is to be taken by the Union in order to achieve the objectives referred to in Article 191.	Article 191 Aims and Objectives
	Article 192 Legislative Competence
	Article 193 Powers of the Member States

Importantly, not all Union competences thereby allow the Union to act to the same degree. Indeed, depending on the type of competence involved, the Union may or may not be permitted to interfere with national choices. What types of competences are thus recognized by the Treaties? Different competence categories were originally 'discovered' by the European Court of Justice, and the EU Treaties have today codified them. These competence categories will be discussed in Section 4.

1. Union Competences: Teleological Interpretation

The Union must act 'within the limits of the competences conferred upon it *by the Member States*'.[4] Did this mean that the Member States would be able to determine the scope of the Union's competences? A *strict* principle of conferral would indeed deny the Union the power autonomously to interpret its competences. But this solution encounters serious practical problems: how

---

[4] Art. 5(2) TEU (emphasis added).

is the Union to work if every legislative bill would need to gain the consent of every national parliament? Classic international organizations solve this dilemma between theory and practice by insisting that the interpretation of international treaties must be in line with the clear intentions of the Member States.[5] Legal competences will thus be interpreted restrictively. This restrictive interpretation is designed to preserve the sovereign rights of the States by preserving the historical meaning of the founding treaty.

By contrast, a *soft* principle of conferral allows for the teleological interpretation of competences. Instead of looking at the historical will of the founders, teleological interpretation asks what is the purpose—or *telos*—of a rule. It thus looks behind the legal text in search of a legal solution to a social problem that may not have been anticipated when the text was drafted. Teleological interpretation can therefore constitute a 'small' amendment of the original rule. It is potentially a method of incremental change that complements the—rare—qualitative changes following 'big' Treaty amendments.

Has the Union been able autonomously to interpret the scope of its competences, and if so how? After a brief period of following international law logic,[6] the Union embraced the constitutional technique of teleological interpretation. This technique can be seen in relation to the interpretation of the Union's *competences*, as well as in relation to the interpretation of European *legislation*.

The first situation is famously illustrated in the controversy surrounding the adoption of the (first) Working Time Directive.[7] The Directive had been based on a provision within Title X on 'Social Policy'. That provision allowed the Union to 'encourage improvements, especially in the working environment, as regards the health and safety of workers'.[8] Would this competence entitle the Union to adopt legislation on the general organization of working time?[9]

---

[5]   In international law, this principle is called the '*in dubio mitius*' principle. In case of doubt, the 'milder' interpretation should be preferred.

[6]   See *Federation Charbonnière de Belgique v High Authority of the European Coal and Steel Community*, Case 8/55 [1954–6] ECR 245.

[7]   *United Kingdom of Great Britain and Northern Ireland v Council*, Case C-84/94 [1996] ECR I-5755.

[8]   Ex-Art. 118a(1) EEC. This competence is today Art. 153(1)(a) TFEU, which allows the Union to support and implement the activities of the Member States as regards the 'improvement in particular of the working environment to protect workers' health and safety'.

[9]   Section II of Directive 93/104 regulated minimum rest periods. Member States were obliged to introduce national laws to ensure that every worker is entitled to a minimum daily rest period of 11 consecutive hours per 24-hour period (ibid., Art. 3) and to a rest break where the working day is longer than six hours (ibid., Art. 4). Art. 5 granted a minimum uninterrupted rest period of 24 hours in each seven-day period and determined that this period should in principle include Sunday. Art. 6 established a maximum weekly working time of 48 hours; and finally, the Directive established four weeks' paid annual leave (ibid., Art. 7).

The United Kingdom strongly contested this teleological reading. It claimed that there was no thematic link to health and safety, and that the Union legislator had therefore acted *ultra vires*. The Court, however, backed up the Union legislator. Its teleological reasoning was as follows:

> There is nothing in the wording of Article [153 TFEU] to indicate that the concepts of 'working environment', 'safety' and 'health' as used in that provision should, in the absence of other indications, be interpreted restrictively, and not as embracing all factors, physical or otherwise, capable of affecting the health and safety of the worker in his working environment, including in particular certain aspects of the organization of working time.[10]

A famous exception aside,[11] the European Court has indeed accepted almost all teleological interpretations of Union competences by the Union legislator in the past.

But more than that, the Court itself interprets Union legislation in a teleological manner. The classic case in this context is *Casagrande*.[12] In order to facilitate the free movement of persons in the internal market, the Union had adopted legislation designed to abolish discrimination between workers of different Member States as regards employment, remuneration, and other conditions of work.[13] And to facilitate the integration of the worker and his or her family into the host state, the relevant Union legislation contained the following provision:

> The children of a national of a Member State who is or has been employed in the territory of another Member State *shall be admitted* to that State's general educational, apprenticeship and vocational training courses under the same conditions as the nationals of that State, if such children are residing in its territory. Member States shall encourage all efforts to enable such children to attend these courses under the best possible conditions.[14]

Would this provision entitle the son of an Italian worker employed in Germany to receive an educational grant for his or her studies? Literally interpreted,

---

[10] *United Kingdom v Council*, Case C-84/94 (n. 7), para. 15.

[11] *Germany v Parliament and Council (Tobacco Advertising)*, Case C-376/98 [2000] ECR I-8419. This exception will be discussed later in Section 2(a).

[12] *Casagrande v Landeshauptstadt München*, Case 9/74 [1974] ECR 773.

[13] Regulation 1612/68 on freedom of movement for workers within the Community, [1968] OJ (Special English Edition) 475.

[14] Ibid., Art. 12 (emphasis added).

the provision exclusively covers the 'admission' of workers' children to the educational system of the host State. But the Court favoured a teleological interpretation that would maximize the 'useful effect' (*effet utile*) behind the Union legislation. And since the purpose of the provision was 'to ensure that the children may take advantage on an equal footing of the educational and training facilities available', it followed that the provision referred '*not only to rules relating to admission*, but also to general measures intended to facilitate educational attendance'.[15] Thus, despite the fact that the (then) Treaties did not confer an express competence in educational matters on the Union, the Court considered that national educational grants fell within the scope of European legislation. The teleological interpretation of Union legislation had thus 'spilled over' into a sphere that the Member States had believed to have remained within their exclusive competences.

2. General Competences of the Union

In principle, the European Treaties grant a specific competence to legislate within each policy area. For example, we find the Union's competence on environmental protection in the Treaty's title dedicated to the environment (see again Table 3.1). Yet in addition to these specific competences, the Union legislator also enjoys two general competences. These competences are not specific to a policy area but *horizontally* cut through the Union's sectoral policies. They have even been used—or some might say abused—to develop policies not expressly mentioned in the Treaties. The two 'bad boys' in that context are Articles 114 and Article 352 TFEU. The former represents the Union's 'internal market competence'; the latter constitutes its 'residual competence'.

(a) The Internal Market Competence: Article 114

On the basis of Article 114 TFEU, the European Union is entitled to adopt measures for the approximation of national laws 'which have as their object the establishment and functioning of the internal market'.

What is the scope of Article 114? In the past, the Union legislator has given an extremely wide interpretation to this general competence. Its potentially unlimited scope is illustrated by *Spain v Council*.[16] The Court here permitted

---

[15] *Casagrande v Landeshauptstadt München*, Case 9/74 (n. 12) paras 8–9 (emphasis added).
[16] *Spain v Council*, Case C-350/92 [1995] ECR I-1985.

the Union legislator to act under its internal market competence so as '*to prevent the heterogeneous development of national laws*'.[17] This teleological interpretation would allow the Union to harmonize national laws to prevent *future* obstacles to trade or a *potential* fragmentation of the internal market.

For a long time, the scope of the Union's internal market competence thus appeared devoid of constitutional boundaries. Yet the existence of constitutional limits was famously confirmed in *Germany v Parliament and Council* (*Tobacco Advertising*).[18] The bone of contention here was a European law that banned the advertising and sponsorship of tobacco products.[19] Could a prohibition or ban be based on the Union's internal market competence? Germany objected to the idea and argued that the Union's internal market competence could only be used to promote trade within the internal market; and this was not so, where Union legislation limited rather than facilitated trade—such as a prohibition of tobacco advertising.[20] The Court accepted—to the surprise of many—the argument. And it therefore annulled, for the first time in its history, European legislation on the ground that it went beyond the Union's internal market power. Emphatically, the Court pointed out that Article 114 could not grant the Union an unlimited power to regulate the internal market:

> To construe that article as meaning that it vests in the [Union] legislature a general power to regulate the internal market would not only be contrary to the express wording of the provisions cited above but would also be incompatible with the principle embodied in Article [5 TEU] that the powers of the [Union] are limited to those specifically conferred on it. Moreover, a measure adopted on the basis of Article [114] of the [TFEU] must genuinely have as its object the improvement of the conditions for the establishment and functioning of the internal market. If a mere finding of disparities between national rules and of the abstract risk of obstacles to the exercise of fundamental freedoms or of distortions of competition liable to result therefrom were sufficient to justify the choice of Article [114] as a legal basis, judicial review of compliance with the proper legal basis might be rendered nugatory.[21]

---

[17] Ibid., para. 35 (emphasis added).

[18] *Germany v Parliament and Council* (*Tobacco Advertising*), Case C-376/98 (n. 11).

[19] Directive 98/43/EC on the approximation of the laws, regulations and administrative provisions of the Member States relating to the advertising and sponsorship of tobacco products, [1998] OJ L213/9.

[20] Germany had pointed out that the sole form of advertising allowed under the Directive was advertising at the point of sale, which only accounted for 2 per cent of the tobacco industry's advertising expenditure (*Tobacco Advertising* (n. 11), para. 24).

[21] Ibid., paras 83–4.

With *Tobacco Advertising*, the Court has come to rhetorically insist on *three* constitutional limits to the Union's internal market power. First, the European law must *harmonize* national laws. Thus Union legislation 'which leaves unchanged the different national laws already in existence, cannot be regarded as aiming to approximate the laws of the Member States'.[22] Second, a simple disparity in national laws will not be enough to trigger the Union's general competence. The disparity must give rise to obstacles in trade or appreciable distortions in competition. Thus, while Article 114 can be used to 'harmonize' *future* disparities in national laws, it must be 'likely' that the divergent development of national laws will lead to obstacles in trade.[23] Third, the Union legislation must actually contribute to the elimination of obstacles to free movement or distortions of competition.[24]

These three constitutional limits to the Union's 'internal market' competence have been confirmed *in abstracto*;[25] yet subsequent jurisprudence has led to fresh accusations that Article 114 grants the Union an (almost) unlimited competence. The competence has thus recently been used to abolish roaming charges when mobile telephones are used abroad. It has also been used to require tobacco manufacturers to have 65 per cent of the external surface of each cigarette packet covered by health warnings.[26]

(b) The Residual Competence: Article 352

Article 352 TFEU constitutes the most general competence within the EU Treaties. It states:

> If action by the Union should prove necessary, within the framework of the policies defined in the Treaties, to attain one of the objectives set out in the Treaties, and the Treaties have not provided the necessary powers, the Council, acting unanimously on a proposal from the Commission and after obtaining the consent of the European Parliament, shall adopt the appropriate measures.

The legislative competence under Article 352 may be used in two ways. First, it can be employed in a policy title in which the Union is already given a

---

[22] *Parliament and Council*, Case C-436/03 [2006] ECR I-3733, para. 44.

[23] *Germany v Parliament and Council (Tobacco Advertising)*, Case C-376/98 (n. 11), para. 86.

[24] *British American Tobacco*, Case C-491/01 [2002] ECR I-11453, para. 60.

[25] On this point, see *Germany v Parliament and Council (Tobacco Advertising II)*, Case C-380/03 [2006] ECR I-11573.

[26] The directive concerned was unsuccessfully challenged in *Philip Morris Brands and others v Secretary of State for Health*, Case C-547/14, EU:C:2016:325.

Figure 3.1 General and special competences

specific competence, but where the latter is deemed insufficient to achieve a specific objective. Second, the residual competence can be used to develop a policy area that has no specific title within the Treaties (see Figure 3.1).

The textbook illustration for the second—and more dangerous—use of Article 352 is provided by the development of a Union environmental policy *prior* to it becoming an express Union competence (through the Single European Act). For, stimulated by the political enthusiasm to 'create' such a European policy in 1972, the Commission and the Council indeed developed such a policy *without* a specific competence title offered by the EU Treaties. The Member States themselves here called on the Union institutions to make the widest possible use of all provisions of the Treaties, especially Article 352.[27] This indirect development of a EU environmental competence in the following years was indeed impressive.[28] It was only sidelined when the Union finally received an express competence in environmental matters in 1987.

Are there conceptual limits to Article 352? The provision expressly establishes two textual limitations. First, '[m]easures based on this Article shall not entail harmonization of Member States' laws or regulations in cases where the

---

[27] European Council, *First Summit Conference of the Enlarged Community*; Bulletin of the European Communities, EC 10-1972, 9 at 23.

[28] Prior to the entry into force of the Single European Act (SEA), a significant number of environment-related measures were adopted on the basis of Arts 115 and 352, thus 'laying the foundation for the formation of a very specific [Union] environmental policy' (see F. Tschofen, 'Article 235 of the Treaty Establishing the European Economic Community: Potential Conflicts between the Dynamics of Lawmaking in the Community and National Constitutional Principles' (1991) 12 *Michigan Journal of International Law* 471 at 477).

Treaties exclude such harmonization.'[29] This precludes the use of the Union's residual competence in specific policy areas in which the Union is limited to merely 'complementing' national action.[30] Second, Article 352 'cannot serve as a basis for attaining objectives pertaining to the common foreign and security policy'.[31] This codifies past jurisprudence,[32] and is designed to protect the constitutional boundary drawn between the Treaty on European Union and the Treaty on the Functioning of the European Union.[33]

In addition to these two express constitutional boundaries, the European Court has also recognized an *implied* limitation to the Union's residual competence. While accepting that Article 352 could be used for 'small' amendments to the Treaties, the Court has insisted that it could not be used to effect 'qualitative leaps' that constitute big changes to the constitutional identity of the European Union.[34] This was confirmed in *Opinion 2/94*.[35] The European Court had been requested to preview the Union's power to accede to the European Convention on Human Rights—at a time when there was no express power to do so in the Treaties.[36] The Court here characterized the relationship between the Union's residual competence and the principle of conferral as follows:

> Article [352] is designed to fill the gap where no specific provisions of the Treaty confer on the [Union] institutions express or implied powers to act, if such powers appear none the less to be necessary to enable the [Union] to carry out its functions with a view to attaining one of the objectives laid down by the Treaty. That provision, being an integral part of an institutional system based on the principle of conferred powers, cannot serve as a basis for widening the scope of [Union] powers *beyond the general framework* created by the provisions of the Treaty as a whole and, in particular, by those that define the *tasks* and the *activities* of the [Union]. On any view, Article [352] cannot be used as a basis for the adoption of provisions whose effect would, in substance, be to amend the Treaty without following the procedure which it provides for that purpose.[37]

---

[29]   Art. 352(3) TFEU.

[30]   On 'complementary' competences in the Union legal order that exclude all harmonization, see Section 4(d).

[31]   Art. 352(4) TFEU.

[32]   See *Kadi v Council and Commission*, Case C-402/05P [2008] ECR I-6351, paras 198–9.

[33]   See Art. 40 TEU, second indent.

[34]   A. Tizzano, 'The Powers of the Community' in Commission (ed.), *Thirty Years of Community Law* (Office for Official Publications of the EC, 1981), 43.

[35]   *Opinion 2/94 (Accession to the ECHR I)* [1996] ECR I-1759.

[36]   After the Lisbon Treaty, the Union is now given the express competence to accede to the Convention (see Art. 6(2) TEU). On this point, see Chapter 4, Section 4.

[37]   *Opinion 2/94*, paras 29–30 (emphasis added).

The general framework of the Treaty was here defined as an outer jurisdictional boundary within which any legislative activity of the Union had to take place. The judicial reasoning in the second part of the judgment was then as follows. The Court found that the accession of the Union to the ECHR would have '*fundamental institutional implications* for the [Union] and for the Member States'; and since accession 'would be of *constitutional significance*', it would 'go beyond the scope of Article [352]'.[38]

Despite these—express and implied—conceptual limits, Article 352 has in the past been (almost) boundless. With the European Court granting the Union legislature (almost) complete freedom to interpret the scope of this competence, the only 'real' limit to Article 352 seems to lie in a political safeguard: unanimous voting in the Council. Yet even this political limit has increasingly come to be seen as insufficient. Fearful that a national minister would 'go native' when voting in Brussels, some Member States have thus established prior parliamentary authorization mechanisms for the use of Article 352.

3. The Doctrine of Implied (External) Powers

The European Treaties do acknowledge the international personality of the European Union,[39] which means that the Union can engage in the conclusion of international agreements. But what are the Union's treaty-making competences? The powers of the Union are enumerated powers; and under the 1957 EEC Treaty, these treaty-making powers were originally confined to two areas only.[40] This—very—restrictive attribution of treaty-making competence to the Union was designed to protect a status quo in which the Member States were to remain the dominant protagonists on the international relations scene. This picture has changed dramatically since 1958. In the past six decades, the European Court has led—and won—a remarkable campaign to expand the Union's treaty-making powers.[41]

---

[38] Ibid., para. 35.

[39] Art. 47 TEU: 'The Union shall have legal personality.'

[40] In what are today Arts 207 and 217 TFEU.

[41] R. Schütze, 'Parallel External Powers in the European Union: From "Cubist" Perspectives Towards "Naturalist" Constitutional Principles?' in *Foreign Affairs and the EU Constitution* (Cambridge University Press, 2014), ch. 7.

(a) *ERTA* and the Doctrine of Parallel Powers

The battle over the Union's external competences began with *ERTA*.[42] The European Road Transport Agreement (ERTA) had been drafted to harmonize certain social aspects of international road transport and involved a number of Member States as potential signatories. The negotiations were conducted without the formal involvement of the Union. The Commission felt excluded from its role as Europe's external broker and eventually brought the matter before the European Court. There, the Commission argued that the Union competence under its transport policy included a treaty-making power (and that this power had become exclusive after the adoption of Union legislation).[43]

With regard to the scope of the Union's external powers, the Commission specifically argued that Article 91 TFEU 'conferred on the [Union] powers defined in wide terms with a view to implementing the common transport policy [which] must apply to external relations just as much as to domestic measures.'[44] This wide teleological interpretation of the wording of the Union's transport competence was justified, for 'the full effect of this provision would be jeopardized if the powers which it confers, particularly that of laying down "any appropriate provisions", within the meaning of subparagraph (1) [d] of the article cited, did not extend to the conclusion of agreements with third countries.'[45] The Council opposed this teleological interpretation, contending that 'Article [91] relates only to measures *internal* to the [Union], and cannot be interpreted as authorizing the conclusion of international agreements'. The power to enter into agreements with third countries 'cannot be assumed in the absence of an express provision in the Treaty'.[46]

In its judgment, the European Court famously sided with the Commission's extensive stance:

> To determine in a particular case the [Union's] authority to enter into international agreements, regard must be had to the whole scheme of the Treaty no less than to its substantive provisions. *Such authority arises not only from an express conferment by the Treaty—as is the case with [Article 207] for tariff and trade agreements and with [Article 217] for association agreements—but may equally flow from other provisions of the Treaty and from measures adopted, within the framework of those provisions, by the [Union] institutions ...*

---

[42] *Commission v Council (ERTA)*, Case 22/70 [1971] ECR 263.

[43] On this point, see Section 4(a).   [44] *ERTA* (n. 42), para. 6.   [45] Ibid., para. 7.

[46] Ibid., paras 9–10 (emphasis added).

According to [Article 90], the objectives of the Treaty in matters of transport are to be pursued within the framework of a common policy. With this in view, [Article 91 (1)] directs the Council to lay down common rules and, in addition, 'any other appropriate provisions'. By the terms of subparagraph (a) of the same provision, those common rules are applicable 'to international transport to or from the territory of a Member State or passing across the territory of one or more Member States'. This provision is equally concerned with transport from or to third countries, as regards that part of the journey which takes place on [Union] territory. It thus assumes that the powers of the [Union] extend to relationships arising from international law, and hence involve the need in the sphere in question for agreements with the third countries concerned.[47]

The passage spoke the language of teleological interpretation: in the light of the general scheme of the Treaty, the Union's power to adopt 'any other appropriate provision' to give effect to the Union's transport policy objectives was interpreted to include the legal power to conclude international agreements.[48]

This was subsequently confirmed in *Opinion 1/76*, where the Court declared that 'whenever [European] law has created for the institutions of the [Union] powers within its internal system for the purpose of attaining a specific objective, the [Union] has authority to enter into the international commitments necessary for the attainment of that objective even in the absence of an express provision in that connexion'.[49] From the very fact that the Union enjoyed an internal power, the Court implied an external power to conclude international treaties for all matters falling within the scope of the Union's internal competence. The reasoning of the Court was based on the idea of a parallel treaty-making power running alongside the Union's internal legislative power. The European Court here confirmed a doctrine according to which 'treaty power is coextensive with its internal domestic powers', and which thus 'cuts across all areas of its internal domestic competence'.[50]

---

[47] Ibid., paras 15–16 and 23–7.

[48] In the words of the *ERTA* Court: 'With regard to the implementation of the Treaty the system of internal [Union] measures may not therefore be separated from that of external relations' (ibid., para. 19).

[49] *Opinion 1/76 (Laying-up Fund)* [1977] ECR 741, para. 3.

[50] E. Stein, 'External Relations of the European Community: Structure and Process' in *Collected Courses of the Academy of European Law* (Martinus Nijhoff, 1990), Vol. I-1, 115 at 146.

(b) Article 216: Codifying *ERTA*?

The Lisbon Treaty has tried to codify the implied powers doctrine in Article 216 TFEU. The provision states:

> The Union may conclude an agreement with one or more third countries or international organizations where the Treaties so provide or where the conclusion of an agreement is necessary in order to achieve, within the framework of the Union's policies, one of the objectives referred to in the Treaties, or is provided for in a legally binding Union act or is likely to affect common rules or alter their scope.[51]

While recognizing the express treaty-making competences of the Union elsewhere conferred by the EU Treaties, the provision grants the Union a residual competence to conclude international agreements in three situations.

The first alternative mentioned in Article 216 confers a treaty power to the Union 'where the conclusion of an agreement is necessary in order to achieve, within the framework of the Union's policies, one of the objectives referred to in the Treaties'. This formulation is—strikingly—similar to the one found in the Union's general competence in Article 352. Textually, this competence is wider than the judicial doctrine of parallel external powers. For past doctrine insisted that an implied external competence derived from an internal *competence*—and thus did not confer a treaty power to pursue any internal *objective*.[52] Yet the Court has clarified that we are only in the presence of sloppy drafting and that Article 216 TFEU simply codifies the doctrine of parallel powers from *ERTA*.[53]

Article 216 mentions two additional situations. The Union will also be entitled to conclude international agreements, where this 'is provided for in a legally binding act or is likely to affect common rules or alter their scope'. Both alternatives make the existence of an external competence dependent on the existence of secondary Union law. Two objections may be launched against this view. Theoretically, it is difficult to accept that the Union can expand its competences without Treaty amendment through the simple adoption of internal Union acts. Practically, it is also hard to see how either alternative will ever go beyond the first alternative.

---

[51] Art. 216(1) TFEU.

[52] The classic doctrine of implied external powers, as defined in *Opinion 1/76*, thus stated that external powers flowed 'by implication from the provisions of the Treaty creating the internal *power*' (*Opinion 1/76* (*Laying-up Fund*) [1977] ECR 741, para. 4 (emphasis added)).

[53] *Opinion 1/13* (*Hague Convention*), EU:C:2014:2303, para. 67.

4. Categories of Union Competences

Different types of competences constitutionally pitch the *relative degree of power* of two public authorities within a material policy field. The respective differences are of a relational kind: exclusive competences 'exclude' the Member States from acting within the same policy area, while non-exclusive competences permit the Union and the Member States to coexist. Importantly, in order to provide a clear picture of the vertical division of powers, each policy area should ideally correspond to one competence category.

What then are the competence categories developed in the European legal order? The distinction between exclusive and non-exclusive competences emerged early on.[54] The Treaties today distinguish between various categories of Union competence in Article 2 TFEU. The provision reads as follows:

1. When the Treaties confer on the Union exclusive competence in a specific area, only the Union may legislate and adopt legally binding acts, the Member States being able to do so themselves only if so empowered by the Union or for the implementation of Union acts.
2. When the Treaties confer on the Union a competence shared with the Member States in a specific area, the Union and the Member States may legislate and adopt legally binding acts in that area. The Member States shall exercise their competence to the extent that the Union has not exercised its competence. The Member States shall again exercise their competence to the extent that the Union has decided to cease exercising its competence.
3. The Member States shall coordinate their economic and employment policies within arrangements as determined by this Treaty, which the Union shall have competence to provide.
4. The Union shall have competence, in accordance with the provisions of the Treaty on European Union, to define and implement a common foreign and security policy, including the progressive framing of a common defence policy.
5. In certain areas and under the conditions laid down in the Treaties, the Union shall have competence to carry out actions to support, coordinate or supplement the actions of the Member States, without thereby superseding their competence in these areas. Legally binding acts of the Union adopted on the basis of the provisions of the Treaties relating to these areas shall not entail harmonization of Member States' laws or regulations.

---

[54] See R. Schütze, 'Dual Federalism Constitutionalised: The Emergence of Exclusive Competences in the EC Legal Order' (2007) 32 *European Law Review* 3.

| Exclusive | Shared | Coordinating | Complementary |

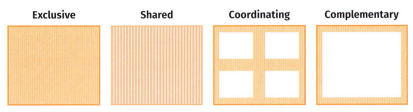

Figure 3.2 Competence categories

Outside the Common Foreign and Security Policy,[55] the Treaties thus expressly recognize four general competence categories: exclusive competences, shared competences, coordinating competences, and complementary competences. And Articles 3 to 6 TFEU correlate the various Union policies to a particular competence category. Figure 3.2 offers a schematic representation of the four ways in which the power between the Union (shaded orange) and the Member State (white) are divided within the four competence types.

(a) Exclusive Competences: Article 3

Exclusive powers are constitutionally guaranteed monopolies. Only the Union is entitled to act autonomously. Exclusive competences are thus double-edged provisions. Their positive side entitles the Union to act, while their negative side 'excludes' the Member States from acting within its scope. For the European legal order, exclusive competences are defined as areas in which 'only the Union may legislate and adopt legally binding acts', while the Member States will only be enabled to act 'if so empowered by the Union or for the implementation of Union acts'.[56]

What are the policy areas of constitutional exclusivity? In the past, the Court has accepted a number of competences to qualify under this type. The first exclusive competence was discovered in the context of the Common Commercial Policy (CCP). In *Opinion 1/75*,[57] the Court found that the existence of a merely shared competence within the field would 'compromise[ ] the effective defence of the common interests of the [Union]'.[58]

A second area of exclusive competence was soon discovered in relation to the conservation of biological resources of the sea. In *Commission v United*

---

[55]   For an analysis of this *sui generis* category, see R. Schütze, *European Union Law* (Cambridge University Press, 2018), ch. 8, section 2(a).

[56]   Art. 2(1) TFEU.

[57]   *Opinion 1/75* (*Draft Understanding on a Local Cost Standard*) [1975] ECR 1355.

[58]   Ibid., para. 13.

Kingdom,[59] the Court found that Member States would 'no longer [be] entitled to exercise any power of their own in the matter of conservation measures in the waters under their jurisdiction.'[60]

Article 3(1) TFEU now expressly mentions five policy areas: (a) the customs union; (b) the establishment of the competition rules necessary for the functioning of the internal market; (c) monetary policy for the Member States whose currency is the euro; (d) the conservation of marine biological resources under the common fisheries policy; and (e) the common commercial policy. In the light of the judicial status quo, this enumeration poses some definitional problems.[61]

Much greater constitutional confusion is, however, created by Article 3(2) TFEU which states:

> The Union shall also have exclusive competence for the conclusion of an international agreement when its conclusion is provided for in a legislative act of the Union or is necessary to enable the Union to exercise its internal competence, or in so far as its conclusion may affect common rules or alter their scope.

In addition to the constitutionally fixed exclusive competences—mentioned in Article 3(1)—the Union legal order thus acknowledges the possibility of a *dynamic* growth of its exclusive competences in the external sphere. According to Article 3(2), the Union may subsequently obtain exclusive treaty-making power, where one of three situations is fulfilled. These three situations are said to codify three famous judicial doctrines. These doctrines were developed in the jurisprudence of the European Court prior to the Lisbon Treaty.[62]

According to the first situation, the Union will obtain a subsequently exclusive treaty-making power when the conclusion of an international agreement 'is provided for in a legislative act'. This formulation corresponds to the so-called 'WTO Doctrine'. In *Opinion 1/94* on the compatibility of the WTO Agreement with the EU Treaties,[63] the Court had indeed stated: '[w]henever the [Union] has concluded in its internal legislative acts provisions relating to the treatment of nationals of non-member countries or expressly conferred on the institutions powers to negotiate with non-member countries, it acquires exclusive external competence in the spheres covered by those

---

[59] *Commission v United Kingdom*, Case 804/79 [1981] ECR 1045.
[60] Ibid., para. 18.   [61] See Schütze, 'Dual Federalism Constitutionalised' (n. 54).
[62] On the three judicial doctrines, see Schütze, 'Parallel External Powers' (n. 41).
[63] *Opinion 1/94 (WTO Agreement)* [1994] ECR I-5267.

acts.'[64] Article 3(2) codifies this judicial doctrine. However, the codification is more restrictive, as it excludes the first alternative ('provisions relating to the treatment of nationals of non-member countries') from its scope.

The second situation mentioned in Article 3(2) grants the Union an exclusive treaty power, where this 'is necessary to enable the Union to exercise its internal competence'. This formulation appears to codify the '*Opinion 1/76* doctrine',[65] albeit in a much *less* restrictive form. In its jurisprudence, the Court had confined this second line of subsequent exclusivity to situations 'where the conclusion of an international agreement is necessary in order to achieve Treaty objectives *which cannot be attained by the adoption of autonomous rules*',[66] and where the achievement of an internal objective is 'inextricably linked' with the external sphere.[67] None of these restrictions can be found in Article 3(2). And in its unqualified openness, the second situation comes close to the wording of the Union's 'residual' competence: Article 352 TFEU. Moreover, the almost identical wording of Article 3(2) and Article 216 TFEU suggests that 'implied shared competence would disappear'; yet, this would be 'a wholly undesirable departure from the case law'.[68]

Finally, the third situation in Article 3(2) appears to refer to the Court's so-called '*ERTA* doctrine'. Under the *ERTA* doctrine,[69] the Member States are deprived of their treaty-making power to the extent that their exercise affects internal European law. Each time the Union 'adopts provisions laying down common rules, whatever form these may take, the Member States no longer have the right, acting individually or even collectively, to undertake obligations with third countries *which affect those rules*'.[70] The principle behind *ERTA* exclusivity is to prevent an international agreement concluded by the Member States from undermining 'the uniform and consistent application of the [Union] rules and the proper functioning of the system which they establish'.[71] Has Article 3(2) properly codified this third judicial line of subsequently exclusive powers? The third alternative in Article 3(2)—strangely—breaks the link between a *Member State* agreement and internal European law, and replaces it with an analysis of the effect of a *Union* agreement on European

---

[64] Ibid., para. 95.

[65] *Opinion 1/76* (*Laying-Up Fund*) [1977] ECR 741. On the evolution of the '*Opinion 1/76* doctrine', see Schütze, 'Parallel External Powers' (n. 41), 258 et seq.

[66] *Opinion 2/92* (*Third Revised Decision of the OECD on National Treatment*) [1995] ECR I-521, Part V, para. 4 (emphasis added).

[67] *Commission v Germany* (*Open Skies*), Case C-476/98 [2002] ECR I-9855, para. 87.

[68] M. Cremona, 'A Constitutional Basis for Effective External Action? An Assessment of the Provisions on EU External Action in the Constitutional Treaty', EUI Working Paper 2006/30, 10.

[69] *Commission v Council* (*ERTA*) (n. 42).   [70] Ibid., para. 18 (emphasis added).

[71] *Opinion 1/03* (*Lugano Convention*) [2006] ECR I-1145, para. 133.

rules. But this is simply an 'editorial mistake', and the Court has clarified that the 'old' *ERTA* case law fully applies here.[72]

(b) Shared Competences: Article 4

Shared competences are the 'ordinary' competences of the European Union. Unless the Treaties expressly provide otherwise, a Union competence will be shared.[73] Within a shared competence, 'the Union and the Member States may legislate';[74] yet according to the formulation in Article 2(2) TFEU, both appear to be prohibited from acting at the same time:

> The Member States shall exercise their competence to the extent that the Union has not exercised its competence.

This formulation invokes the geometrical image of a divided field: the Member States may only legislate in that part which the European Union has not (yet) entered. Within one field, *either* the European Union *or* the Member States can exercise their shared competence.[75]

When viewed against the constitutional status quo ante, this is a mystifying conception of shared competences. For in the past 60 years, shared competences have generally allowed the Union and the Member States to act in the same field at the same time. The (exceptional) exception to that rule concerned situations where the Union fully pre-empted the Member States.[76] The formulation in Article 2(2) TFEU is—sadly—based on that exception. It appears to demand 'automatic [field] pre-emption of Member State action where the Union has exercised its power'.[77] Will the technique of European

---

[72] *Commission v Council*, Case C-114/12, EU:C:2014:2151, esp. para. 66.

[73] Art. 4 TFEU states that Union competences will be shared 'where the Treaties confer on it a competence which does not relate to the areas referred to in Articles 3 and 6', i.e. areas of exclusive or complementary EU competence.

[74] Art. 2(2) TFEU.

[75] The Union may, however, decide to 'cease exercising its competence'. This reopening of legislative space arises 'when the relevant EU institutions decide to repeal a legislative act, in particular better to ensure constant respect for the principles of subsidiarity and proportionality'. See Declaration (No. 18) 'In Relation to the Delimitation of Competences'.

[76] On the various pre-emption types, see Schütze, *European Union Law* (n. 55), ch. 4, section 3.

[77] P. Craig, 'Competence: Clarity, Conferral, Containment and Consideration' (2004) 29 *European Law Review* 323, 334. The Treaties, however, clarify that such field pre-emption would 'only' be in relation to the legislative act (see Protocol (No. 25) 'On the Exercise of Shared Competence': 'With reference to Article 2 of the Treaty on the Functioning of the European Union on shared competence, when the Union has taken action in a certain area, the scope of this exercise of competence only covers those elements governed by the Union act in question and therefore does not cover the whole [competence] area').

minimum harmonization—allowing for higher national standards adopted in addition to the Union standard—thus be in danger? This seems doubtful, since the EU Treaties expressly identify minimum harmonization competences as shared competences.[78]

This pre-emption problem is not the only textual problem. For Article 4 TFEU recognizes a special type of shared competence in paragraphs 3 and 4. Both paragraphs separate the policy areas of research, technological development, and space, as well as development cooperation and humanitarian aid from the 'normal' shared competences. What is so special about these areas? According to paragraphs 3 and 4, the 'exercise of that competence shall not result in Member States being prevented from exercising theirs'. But since that qualification also undermines the essence of what constitutes a 'shared' competence, set out in Article 2(2) TFEU, these policy areas should never have been placed there. This special type of shared competence has been described as parallel competence.

(c) Coordinating Competences: Article 5

Coordinating competences are defined in the third paragraph of Article 2; and Article 5 places 'economic policy', 'employment policy', and 'social policy' within this category. The inspiration for this third competence category was the absence of a political consensus among the Member States drafting the 2004 Constitutional Treaty that transformed into the Lisbon Treaty. Whereas one group wished to place economic and employment coordination within the category of shared competences, an opposing view advocated their classification as complementary competence. The Presidium of the Convention thus came to feel that 'the specific nature of the coordination of Member States' economic and employment policies merits a separate provision'.[79]

The constitutional character of coordinating competences remains largely undefined. From Articles 2 and 5 TFEU, we may solely deduce that the European Union has a competence to provide 'arrangements' for the Member States to exercise their competences in a coordinated manner. The Union's

---

[78] See Art. 4(2)(e) TFEU on the shared 'environment' competence.

[79] Presidium CONV 724/03 (Annex 2), 68. Arguably, the addition of a new competence type was unnecessary in the light of Art. 2(6) TFEU. That provision states: 'The scope of and arrangements for exercising the Union's competences shall be determined by the provisions of the Treaties relating to each area.'

coordination effort may include the adoption of 'guidelines' and 'initiatives to ensure coordination'. It has been argued that the political genesis for this competence category should place it, on the normative spectrum, between shared and complementary competences.[80] If this systematic interpretation is accepted, coordinating competences would have to be normatively stronger than complementary competences.

(d) Complementary Competences: Article 6

The term 'complementary competence' is not used in Article 2(5) TFEU. However, it appears to be the best way generically to refer to 'actions to support, coordinate or supplement the actions of the Member States'.[81] Article 6 lists seven areas: the protection and improvement of human health; industry; culture; tourism; education, vocational training, youth and sport; civil protection; and administrative cooperation. Is this an exhaustive list? This should be the case in the light of the residual character of shared competences.

A good example of a complementary competence is the Union competence to protect human health, which is formulated as follows:

> Union action, which shall *complement* national policies, shall be directed towards improving public health, preventing physical and mental illness and diseases, and obviating sources of danger to physical and mental health. . . The Union shall encourage cooperation between the Member States in the areas referred to in this Article and, if necessary, lend support to their action. *It shall in particular encourage cooperation between the Member States to improve the complementarity of their health services in cross-border areas.*[82]

The contours of this competence type are largely unexplored by jurisprudence. However, after the Lisbon reform, it appears to be a defining characteristic of complementary competences that they do '*not entail harmonization* of Member States' laws or regulations'.[83]

But what exactly is the prohibition of 'harmonization' supposed to mean? Two views can be put forward. According to the first, the exclusion of harmonization means that Union legislation must not modify *existing* or *future* national legislation. From this strict reading, the exclusion of harmonization

---

[80] See in this sense, Craig, 'Competence' (n. 77), 338.
[81] Art. 2(5) TFEU.   [82] Art. 168(1) and (2) TFEU (emphasis added).
[83] Art. 2(5) TFEU, second indent (emphasis added).

would consequently deny any preemptive effect to European legislation.[84] A second and less restrictive view argues that the Union's legislative powers are only trimmed so as to prevent the *de jure* harmonization of national legislation.[85] *Both* views appear problematic. National legislators are—still— quicker in passing legislation than the Union legislator; and if a Member State thus wished to prevent Union action, it could be tempted to swiftly adopt a national law in the same area.

Conclusion

The Union is not a sovereign State that enjoys 'inherent' competences. Its competences are 'enumerated' competences that are 'conferred' by the European Treaties. The majority of the Union's competences are spread across Part III of the TFEU. In each of its policy areas, the Union will typically be given a specific competence. Its competences are here thematically limited; yet, as we saw earlier, the Union legislator has made wide use of its powers by interpreting them teleologically.

In the past, the Union has also extensively used its general competences. Articles 114 and 352 TFEU grant the Union two competences that horizontally cut across (almost) all substantive policy areas. In their most dramatic form, they have even allowed the Union to develop policies that were not expressly mentioned in the Treaties. Within the external relations field, the Union has developed a doctrine of implied parallel external powers. This is codified in Article 216 TFEU—a provision that now comes close to Article 352 TFEU.

Importantly, however, not all competences of the Union provide it with the same power. The Union legal order recognizes various competence categories. The Treaties distinguish between exclusive, shared, coordinating, and complementary competences. Each competence category constitutionally distributes power between the Union and the Member States. Within its exclusive competences, the Union is exclusively competent to legislate; whereas it shares this power with the Member States under its non-exclusive powers.

---

[84] See A. Bardenhewer-Rating and F. Niggermeier, 'Artikel 152', para. 20, in H. von der Groeben and J. Schwarze (eds), *Kommentar zum Vertrag über die EU* (Nomos, 2003).

[85] For Lenaerts 'incentive measures can be adopted in the form of Regulations, Directives, Decisions or atypical legal acts and are thus normal legislative acts of the [Union].' '[T]he fact that a [European] incentive measure may have the indirect effect of harmonizing ... does not necessarily mean that it conflicts with the prohibition on harmonization' (K. Lenaerts, 'Subsidiarity and Community Competence in the Field of Education' (1994–5) 1 *Columbia Journal of European Law* 1 at 13 and 15).

4

Fundamental Rights

Introduction

The protection of human rights is a central task of many modern constitutions.[1] Fundamental rights are here designed to set protective limits to governmental power(s). This protective task is principally transferred onto the judiciary and involves the judicial review of governmental actions.[2] The protection of human rights may be limited to judicial review of the executive.[3] But in its expansive form, it extends to the review of parliamentary legislation.[4]

---

[1] On human rights as constitutional rights, see A. Sajó, *Limiting Government* (Central European University Press, 1999), ch. 8.

[2] See M. Cappelletti, *Judicial Review in the Contemporary World* (Bobbs-Merrill, 1971).

[3] For the classic doctrine of parliamentary sovereignty in the United Kingdom, see A. V. Dicey, *Introduction to the Study of the Law of the Constitution* (Liberty Fund, 1982).

[4] The classic example here is the United States, where the US Supreme Court can invalidate congressional legislation.

The European Union follows this expansive constitutional tradition.[5] It considers itself to be 'founded on the values of respect for human dignity, freedom, democracy, equality, the rule of law and respect for human rights'.[6] Human rights are thus given a 'foundational' status and constitutionally limit the exercise of all Union competences—including its legislative competences.

What are the sources of human rights in the Union legal order? While there was no 'Bill of Rights' in the original Treaties, three sources of European fundamental rights were subsequently developed. The European Court first began distilling general principles protecting fundamental rights from the constitutional traditions of the Member States. This *unwritten* bill of rights was inspired and informed by a second bill of rights: the European Convention on Human Rights. This *external* bill of rights was subsequently—and thirdly—matched by a *written* bill of rights specifically for the European Union: the EU Charter of Fundamental Rights. These three sources of European human rights are now expressly referred to—in reverse order—in Article 6 TEU:

1. The Union recognises the rights, freedoms and principles set out in the Charter of Fundamental Rights of the European Union of 7 December 2000, as adapted at Strasbourg, on 12 December 2007, which shall have the same legal value as the Treaties ...
2. The Union shall accede to the European Convention for the Protection of Human Rights and Fundamental Freedoms. Such accession shall not affect the Union's competences as defined in the Treaties.
3. Fundamental rights, as guaranteed by the European Convention for the Protection of Human Rights and Fundamental Freedoms and as they result from the constitutional traditions common to the Member States, shall constitute general principles of the Union's law.

What is the nature and effect of each source of fundamental rights? And to what extent will they limit the exercise of Union competences? This chapter investigates the three bills of rights of the Union. Section 1 starts with the discovery of an 'unwritten' bill of rights in the form of general principles of European law. Section 2 then moves on to discuss possible structural limits

---

[5]   On this point, see *Parti Écologiste 'Les Verts' v European Parliament*, Case 294/83 [1986] ECR 1339, para. 23: 'a [Union] based on the rule of law, inasmuch as neither its Member States nor its institutions can avoid a review of the question whether the measures adopted by them are in conformity with the basic constitutional charter, the Treaty.' For an extensive discussion of judicial review in the Union legal order, see Chapter 8, Section 3.

[6]   Art. 2(1) TEU.

to European human rights in the form of international obligations flowing from the United Nations Charter. Section 3 analyses the Union's 'written' bill of rights in the form of its Charter of Fundamental Rights. Finally, Section 4 explores the European Convention on Human Rights as an external bill of rights for the European Union.

1. The Birth of European Fundamental Rights

Originally, the European Treaties contained no express reference to human rights.[7] And the birth of EU fundamental rights did not happen overnight. The Court had indeed been invited—as long ago as 1958—to review the constitutionality of a European act in the light of fundamental rights. In *Stork*,[8] the applicant had challenged a European decision on the ground that the Commission had infringed *German* fundamental rights. In the absence of a European bill of rights, this claim drew on the so-called 'mortgage theory'. According to this theory, the powers conferred on the European Union by each of the Member States were tied to a human rights 'mortgage'. *National* fundamental rights binding the Member States would also bind the *European* Union, since the Member States could not have created an organization with more powers than themselves.[9] When they thus transferred powers to the Union, the very transfer was subject to the respective 'constitutional tradition' of each Member State. This argument was however—correctly—rejected by the Court.[10] The task of the European institutions was to apply European laws 'without regard for their validity under national law'.[11] National fundamental rights could be *no direct* source of European human rights.

---

[7] For speculations on the historical reasons for this absence, see P. Pescatore, 'The Context and Significance of Fundamental Rights in the Law of the European Communities' (1981) 2 *Human Rights Journal* 295.

[8] *Stork v High Authority of the European Coal and Steel Community*, Case 1/58 [1958] ECR (English Special Edition) 17.

[9] In Latin, the legal proverb is clear: *Nemo dat quod non habet.*

[10] For a criticism of the 'mortgage theory', see H. G. Schermers, 'The European Communities Bound by Fundamental Rights' (1980) 27 *Common Market Law Review* 249 at 251.

[11] *Stork v High Authority*, Case 1/58 (n. 8), 26: 'Under Article 8 of the [ECSC] Treaty the [Commission] is only required to apply Community law. It is not competent to apply the national law of the Member States. Similarly, under Article 31 the Court is only required to ensure that in the interpretation and application of the Treaty, and of rules laid down for implementation thereof, the law is observed. It is not normally required to rule on provisions of national law. Consequently, the [Commission] is not empowered to examine a ground of complaint which maintains that, when it adopted its decision, it infringed principles of German constitutional law (in particular Articles 2 and 12 of the Basic Law).'

This position of the European Union towards national fundamental rights has never changed. However, the Court's view has significantly evolved with regard to the existence of implied *EU* fundamental rights. Having originally found that European law did 'not contain any general principle, *express or otherwise*, guaranteeing the maintenance of vested rights',[12] the Court subsequently discovered 'fundamental human rights enshrined in the general principles of [European] law'.[13]

This new position was spelled out in *Internationale Handelsgesellschaft*.[14] The Court here—again—rejected the applicability of national fundamental rights to European law. Yet the judgment now also confirmed the existence of an 'analogous guarantee' in European Union law. To quote the renowned passage in full:

> [T]he law stemming from the Treaty, an independent source of law, cannot because of its very nature be overridden by rules of national law, however framed, without being deprived of its character as [Union] law and without the legal basis of the [Union] itself being called in question. Therefore the validity of a [Union] measure or its effect within a Member State cannot be affected by allegations that it runs counter to either fundamental rights as formulated by the constitution of that State or the principles of a national constitutional structure. However, an examination should be made as to whether or not any analogous guarantee inherent in [Union] law has been disregarded. *In fact, respect for fundamental rights forms an integral part of the general principles of law protected by the Court of Justice. The protection of such rights, whilst inspired by the constitutional traditions common to the Member States, must be ensured within the framework of the structure and objectives of the [Union].*[15]

From this moment, fundamental rights were seen as an integral part of the general principles of European law. But where did these fundamental rights come from? The famous answer was that the Union's (unwritten) bill of rights would be '*inspired* by the constitutional traditions *common* to the Member States'.[16] While thus not a direct source, national constitutional rights constituted an *indirect* source of the Union's fundamental rights.

---

[12]   *Geitling Ruhrkohlen-Verkaufsgesellschaft mbH, Mausegatt Ruhrkohlen-Verkaufsgesellschaft mbH and I. Nold KG v High Authority of the European Coal and Steel Community*, Joined Cases 36, 37, 38 and 40/59 [1959] ECR (English Special Edition) 423 at 439 (emphasis added).

[13]   *Stauder v City of Ulm*, Case 29/69 [1969] ECR 419, para. 7.

[14]   *Internationale Handelsgesellschaft mbH v Einfuhr- und Vorratsstelle für Getreide und Futtermittel*, Case 11/70 [1979] ECR 1125.

[15]   Ibid., paras 3–4 (emphasis added).

[16]   Ibid. (emphasis added).

What, however, was the exact nature of this indirect relationship between national rights and European rights? And how would the former influence the latter? A constitutional clarification was offered in *Nold*.[17] Drawing on its previous jurisprudence, the Court held:

> [F]undamental rights form an integral part of the general principles of law, the observance of which it ensures. In safeguarding these rights, the Court is bound to draw inspiration from constitutional traditions common to the Member States, and it cannot therefore uphold measures which are incompatible with fundamental rights recognized and protected by the constitutions of those States. Similarly, international treaties for the protection of human rights on which the Member States have collaborated or of which they are signatories, can supply *guidelines* which should be followed within the framework of [European] law.[18]

In searching for fundamental rights inside the general principles of European law, the Court would thus draw 'inspiration' from the common constitutional traditions of the Member States. One—ingenious—way of identifying a common 'agreement' between the various national constitutional traditions was to use international *agreements* of the Member States. And one such international agreement in place then was the European Convention on Human Rights. Having been ratified by all Member States and dealing specially with human rights,[19] the Convention would soon assume a 'particular significance' in identifying fundamental rights for the European Union.[20] And yet none of this conclusively characterized the legal relationship between European human rights, national human rights, and the European Convention on Human Rights.

---

[17] *Nold v Commission*, Case 4/73 [1974] ECR 491.

[18] Ibid., para. 13 (emphasis added).

[19] When the E(E)C Treaty entered into force on 1 January 1958, five of its Member States were already parties to the European Convention for the Protection of Human Rights and Fundamental Freedoms, signed in Rome on 4 November 1950. Ever since France joined the Convention system in 1974, all Member States have also been members of the European Convention legal order. For an early reference to the Convention in the jurisprudence of the Court, see *Rutili v Ministre de l'intérieur*, Case 36/75 [1975] ECR 1219, para. 32.

[20] See *Höchst v Commission*, Joined Cases 46/87 and 227/88 [1989] ECR 2859, para. 13: 'The Court has consistently held that fundamental rights are an integral part of the general principles of law the observance of which the Court ensures, in accordance with constitutional traditions common to the Member States, and the international treaties on which the Member States have collaborated or of which they are signatories. The European Convention for the Protection of Human Rights and Fundamental Freedoms of 4 November 1950 (hereinafter referred to as "the European Convention on Human Rights") is of particular significance in that regard.'

Let us therefore look at the question of a Union human rights standard first, before analysing the constitutional doctrines on limits to EU human rights.

(a) The European Standard: An 'Autonomous' Standard

Human rights express the fundamental values of a society. Each society may wish to protect distinct values and give them a distinct level of protection.[21] Not all societies may thus choose to protect a constitutional 'right to work',[22] while most liberal societies will protect 'liberty'; yet, the level at which liberty is protected might vary.[23]

Which fundamental rights exist in the European Union, and what is their level of protection? From the very beginning, the Court of Justice did not feel completely free to invent an unwritten bill of rights. Instead, and in the words of the famous *Nold* passage, the Court was '*bound to* draw inspiration from constitutional traditions *common* to the Member States'.[24] But how binding would that inspiration be? Could the Court discover human rights that not all Member States recognize as a national human right? And would the Court consider itself under the obligation to use a particular standard for a human right, where a right's 'scope and the criteria for applying it vary'?[25]

The relationship between the Union standard and the various national standards is not an easy one. Would the obligation to draw inspiration from the constitutional traditions *common* to the Member States not imply a common *minimum* standard? Serious practical problems follow from this view. For if the European Union consistently adopted the lowest common human rights denominator to assess the legality of its acts, this would inevitably lead to charges that the European Court refuses to take human rights seriously. Should the Union thus favour the *maximum* standard among the Member States,[26] as 'the most liberal

---

[21] 'Constitutions are not mere copies of a universalist ideal, they also reflect the idiosyncratic choices and preferences of the constituents and are the highest legal expression of the country's value system.' See B. de Witte, 'Community Law and National Constitutional Values' (1991/2) 2 *Legal Issues of Economic Integration* 1 at 7.

[22] Art. 4 of the Italian Constitution states: 'The Republic recognises the right of all citizens to work and promotes those conditions which render this right effective.'

[23] To illustrate this point with a famous joke: 'In Germany everything is forbidden, unless something is specifically allowed, whereas in Britain everything which is not specifically forbidden, is allowed.' (The joke goes on to claim that: 'In France everything is allowed, even if it is forbidden; and in Italy everything is allowed, especially when it is forbidden.')

[24] *Nold* (n. 17), para. 13 (emphasis added).

[25] *AM & S Europe Ltd v Commission*, Case 155/79 [1982] ECR 1575, para. 19.

[26] In favour of a maximalist approach, see L. Besselink, 'Entrapped by the Maximum Standard: On Fundamental Rights, Pluralism and Subsidiarity in the European Union' (1998) 35 *Common Market Law Review* 629.

interpretation must prevail'?[27] This time, there are serious theoretical problems with this view. For the maximalist approach assumes that courts always balance private rights against public interests. But this is not necessarily the case;[28] and, in any event, the maximum standard is subject to a communitarian critique that insists that the public interest should also be taken seriously.[29] The Court has consequently rejected both approaches.[30]

What about the European Convention on Human Rights as a—common— Union standard? What, indeed, is the status of the Convention in the Union legal order? The relationship between the Union and the European Convention has remained ambivalent (see Figure 4.1). The Court of Justice has not found the European Convention to be formally binding on the Union; and it has also never considered itself materially bound by the interpretation given to the Convention by the European Court of Human Rights. This interpretative freedom has created the possibility of a distinct *Union* standard; yet it

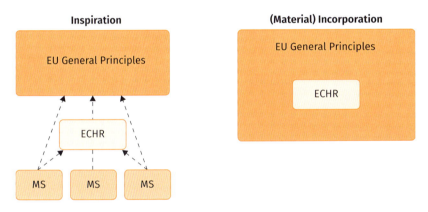

Figure 4.1 Inspiration theory versus incorporation theory

---

[27] This 'Dworkinian' language comes from *Stauder* (n. 13), para. 4.

[28] The Court of Justice was faced with such a right–right conflict in *Society for the Protection of Unborn Children Ireland Ltd v Stephen Grogan and others*, Case C-159/90 [1991] ECR I-4685, but (in)famously refused to decide the case for lack of jurisdiction.

[29] J. Weiler, 'Fundamental Rights and Fundamental Boundaries: On Standards and Values in the Protection of Human Rights' in N. Neuwahl and A. Rosas (eds), *The European Union and Human Rights* (Brill, 1995), 51 at 61: 'If the ECJ were to adopt a maximalist approach this would simply mean that for the [Union] in each and every area the balance would be most restrictive on the public and general interest. A maximalist approach to human rights would result in a minimalist approach to [Union] government.'

[30] For the early (implicit) rejection of the minimalist approach, see *Hauer v Land Rheinland-Pfalz*, Case 44/79 [1979] ECR 3727, para. 32—suggesting that a fundamental right only needs to be protected in '*several* Member States' (emphasis added).

equally entails the danger of diverging interpretations of the European Convention in Strasbourg and Luxembourg.[31]

What is the situation today, and has the 2007 Lisbon Treaty changed this ambivalent relationship? Today, there are indeed strong textual reasons for claiming that the European Convention is *materially* binding on the Union. For according to the (new) Article 6(3) TEU, fundamental rights as guaranteed by the Convention '*shall constitute general principles of the Union's law*'.[32] Will this formulation not mean that all Convention rights are *incorporated* as general principles of Union law? If so, the Convention standard would henceforth provide a direct standard for the Union. But if this route were chosen, the Convention standard would—presumably—only provide a *minimum* standard for the Union's general principles.

In conclusion, the Union standard for the protection of fundamental rights is an *autonomous* standard. While drawing inspiration from the constitutional traditions common to the Member States and the European Convention on Human Rights, the Court of Justice has—so far—not considered itself directly bound by a particular national or international standard. The Court has therefore remained free to distil and protect what it sees as the shared values among the majority of people(s) within the Union and has thereby assisted—dialectically—in the establishment of a shared identity for the people(s) of Europe.[33]

(b) Limitations, and 'Limitations on Limitations'

Within the European constitutional tradition, some rights are absolute rights. They cannot—under any circumstances—be legitimately limited.[34] However, most fundamental rights are *relative* rights that may be limited in accordance with a public interest. Private property may thus be taxed and individual freedom be restricted—*if* such actions are justified by the common good.

---

[31] For an excellent analysis of this point, see R. Lawson, 'Confusion and Conflict? Diverging Interpretations of the Europe Convention on Human Rights in Strasbourg and Luxembourg' in R. Lawson and M. de Blois (eds), *The Dynamics of the Protection of the Rights in Europe* (Martinus Nijhoff, 1994), Vol. III, 219 and esp. 234–50.

[32] Art. 6(3) TEU (emphasis added).

[33] T. Tridimas, 'Judicial Federalism and the European Court of Justice' in J. Fedtke and B. S. Markesinis (eds), *Patterns of Federalism and Regionalism: Lessons for the UK* (Hart, 2006), 149 at 150—referring to the contribution of the judicial process 'to the emergence of a European *demos*'.

[34] The European Court of Justice followed this tradition and recognized the existence of absolute rights in *Schmidberger v Austria*, Case C-112/00 [2003] ECR I-5659, para. 80: 'the right to life or the prohibition of torture and inhuman or degrading treatment or punishment, which admit of no restriction'.

Has the European legal order recognized such limits to human rights? From the very beginning, the Court has indeed clarified that human rights are 'far from constituting unfettered prerogatives',[35] and that they may thus be subject 'to limitations laid down in accordance with the public interest'.[36] Nonetheless, liberal societies would cease to be liberal if they permitted unlimited limitations to human rights in pursuit of the public interest. Many legal orders consequently recognize limitations on public interest limitations. These 'limitations on limitations' to fundamental rights can be relative or absolute in nature.

According to the principle of proportionality, each restriction of a fundamental right must always be 'proportionate' in relation to the public interest pursued.[37] The principle of proportionality is thus a relative principle. It balances interests: the *greater* the public interest protected, the *greater* the right restrictions permitted. And in order to limit this relativist logic, a second principle may come into play. For according to the 'essential core' doctrine,[38] any limitation of human rights—even proportionate ones—must never undermine the very essence of a fundamental right. This sets an absolute limit to all governmental actions by identifying an 'untouchable' core within a fundamental right. The relationship between a fundamental right and (proportionate) public interest limitations and an (untouchable) essential core of that right can be seen in Figure 4.2.

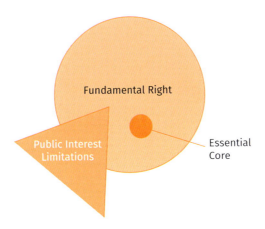

Figure 4.2 Right limitations: relative and absolute

[35] *Nold v Commission*, Case 4/73 (n. 17), para. 14.

[36] Ibid.

[37] *Hauer*, Case 44/79 (n. 30), para. 23. On the proportionality principle in the Union legal order, see Chapter 8, Section 3(b)(ii).

[38] For the German constitutional order, see Art. 19(2) German Constitution: 'The essence of a basic right must never be violated.'

Yet while the principle of proportionality is almost omnipresent in the jurisprudence of the Court,[39] the existence of an 'essential core' doctrine was for a long time unclear. True, the Court had used formulations that came—very—close to the doctrine, but its relationship to the proportionality principle has long remained ambivalent.

The Court did, however, finally confirm the existence of an 'essential core' doctrine in *Zambrano*.[40] Two Colombian parents had challenged the rejection of their Belgian residency permits on the ground that their children had been born in Belgium and thereby assumed Belgian and—thus—European citizenship.[41] And since minor children would inevitably have to follow their parents, the question arose whether the latter's deportation would violate their children's fundamental status as Union citizens. The Court indeed held that the Belgian measures violated the Treaties, as they would 'have the effect of depriving citizens of the Union of the genuine enjoyment of the *substance of the rights* conferred by virtue of their status as citizens of the Union'.[42] The recognition of such an untouchable 'substance' of a fundamental right here functioned like an essential core doctrine; and the Court has subsequently embraced the essential core doctrine as an absolute limit to all public policy limitations to EU fundamental rights.[43]

2. United Nations Law: External Limits to European Human Rights?

The European legal order is a constitutional order based on the rule of law.[44] This implies that an individual, where legitimately concerned,[45] must be able to challenge the legality of a European act on the basis that his

---

[39] See T. Tridimas, *The General Principles of EU Law* (Oxford University Press, 2007), chs 3–5.

[40] *Zambrano v Office national de l'emploi*, Case C-34/09 [2001] ECR I-1177. Admittedly, there are many questions that this—excessively—short case raises (see 'Editorial: Seven Questions for Seven Paragraphs' (2011) 36 *European Law Review* 161).

[41] According to Art. 20(1) TFEU: 'Citizenship of the Union is hereby established. Every person holding the nationality of a Member State shall be a citizen of the Union. Citizenship of the Union shall be additional to and not replace national citizenship.'

[42] *Zambrano* (n. 40), para. 42 (emphasis added); and see also para. 44: 'In those circumstances, those citizens of the Union would, as a result, be unable to exercise the substance of the rights conferred on them by virtue of their status as citizens of the Union.'

[43] For a discussion of this point, see K. Lenaerts, 'Limits on Limitations: The Essence of Fundamental Rights in the EU' (2019) 20 *German Law Journal* 779.

[44] See *Parti Écologiste*, Case 294/83 (n. 5).

[45] On the judicial standing of private parties in the Union legal order, see Chapter 8, Section 3(c).

or her human rights have been violated. Should there be exceptions to this constitutional rule? This question is controversially debated in comparative constitutionalism; and it has, in the context of the European Union, received much attention in a special form: will EU fundamental rights be limited by *international* obligations flowing from the United Nations Charter?

The classic answer to this question was offered by *Bosphorus*.[46] The case dealt with European legislation implementing the United Nations embargo against the Federal Republic of Yugoslavia. Protesting that its fundamental right to property was violated, the plaintiff challenged the European law. The Court had no qualms in judicially reviewing the European legislation at issue—even if a lower review standard was applied.[47] The constitutional message behind the classic approach was thus clear: where the Member States decided to fulfil their international obligations under the United Nations *qua* European law, they would have to comply with the constitutional principles of the Union legal order and, in particular, European human rights.

This classic approach was challenged by the General Court in 2005 by *Kadi*.[48] The applicant was a suspected Taliban terrorist, whose financial assets had been frozen as a result of European legislation that reproduced United Nations Security Council Resolutions. Kadi claimed that his fundamental rights of due process and property had been violated. The Union organs intervened in the proceedings and argued—to the surprise of many—that 'the Charter of the United Nations prevail[s] over every other obligation of international, [European] or domestic law' with the effect that European human rights should be inoperable.[49]

To the even greater surprise—if not shock—of European constitutional scholars,[50] the General Court accepted this argument. How did the Court come to this conclusion? It had recourse to a version of the 'succession doctrine', according to which the Union may be bound by the international

---

[46] *Bosphorus Hava Yollari Turizm ve Ticaret AS v Minister for Transport, Energy and Communications and others*, Case C-84/95 [1996] ECR I-3953.

[47] For a critique of the standard of review, see I. Canor, '"Can Two Walk Together, Except They Be Agreed?" The Relationship between International Law and European Law: The Incorporation of United Nations Sanctions against Yugoslavia into European Community Law through the Perspective of the European Court of Justice' (1998) 35 *Common Market Law Review* 137 at 162.

[48] *Kadi v Council and Commission*, Case T-315/01 [2005] ECR II-3649.

[49] Ibid., paras 156 and 177.

[50] P. Eeckhout, *Does Europe's Constitution Stop at the Water's Edge? Law and Policy in the EU's External Relations* (Europa Law Publishing, 2005); as well as R. Schütze, 'On "Middle Ground": The European Community and Public International Law', EUI Working Paper 2007/13.

obligations of its Member States.[51] While this conclusion was in itself highly controversial, the dangerous part of the judgment related to the consequences of that conclusion. For the General Court recognized 'structural limits, imposed by general international law' on the judicial review powers of the European Court.[52] In the words of the Court:

> Any review of the internal lawfulness of the contested regulation, especially having regard to the provisions or general principles of [European] law relating to the protection of fundamental rights, would therefore imply that the Court is to consider, indirectly, the lawfulness of those [United Nations] resolutions. In that hypothetical situation, in fact, the origin of the illegality alleged by the applicant would have to be sought, not in the adoption of the contested regulation but in the resolutions of the Security Council which imposed the sanctions. In particular, if the Court were to annul the contested regulation, as the applicant claims it should, although that regulation seems to be imposed by international law, on the ground that that act infringes his fundamental rights which are protected by the [Union] legal order, such annulment would indirectly mean that the resolutions of the Security Council concerned themselves infringe those fundamental rights.[53]

The General Court thus declined jurisdiction to judicially review European legislation *because it would entail an indirect review of the United Nations resolutions.* The justification for this self-abdication was that United Nations law was binding on all Union institutions, including the European Courts.

From a constitutional perspective, this reasoning was prisoner to a number of serious mistakes.[54] And in its appeal judgment,[55] the Court of Justice remedied these constitutional blunders and safely returned to the classic *Bosphorus* approach. The Court held:

> [T]he obligations imposed by an international agreement cannot have the effect of prejudicing the constitutional principles of the [European Treaties], which include the principle that all [Union] acts must respect fundamental rights, that respect constituting a condition of their lawfulness which it is for the Court to review in the framework of the complete system of legal remedies established by the Treat[ies].[56]

---

[51] On the doctrine, see Chapter 2, Section 4(d).

[52] *Kadi*, Case T-315/01 (n. 48), para. 212.

[53] Ibid., paras 215–16 (references omitted).

[54] On this point, see R. Schütze, 'On "Middle Ground": The European Union and Public International Law' (n. 50), 19 et seq.

[55] *Kadi and Al Barakaat International Foundation v Council and Commission*, Case C-402/05P [2008] ECR I-6351.   [56] Ibid., para. 285.

The United Nations Charter, while having special importance within the European legal order,[57] would—in this respect—not be different from other international agreements. Like 'ordinary' international agreements, the United Nations Charter might—if materially binding—have primacy over European legislation but '[t]hat primacy at the level of [European] law would not, however, extend to primary law, in particular to the general principles of which fundamental rights form part'.[58] European human rights would thus *not* find an external structural limit in the international obligations stemming from the United Nations.[59] The Union was firmly based on the rule of law, and this meant that all European legislation—regardless of its 'domestic' or international origin—would be limited by the respect for fundamental human rights.[60]

3. The Charter of Fundamental Rights

The desire for a *written* bill of rights for the European Union first expressed itself, by the end of the 1970s, in arguments favouring accession to the European Convention on Human Rights.[61] Yet an alternative strategy became prominent in the late twentieth century: the Union's *own* written bill of rights. The initiative for a 'Charter of Fundamental Rights' came from the European Council,[62] and the idea behind an internal Union codification was to strengthen the protection of fundamental rights in Europe 'by making those rights more visible in a Charter'.[63] The Charter was proclaimed in 2000, but it was *not* yet legally binding. Its status was similar to the European Convention on Human Rights: it provided valuable *inspiration* but imposed no formal obligation on the European institutions.[64] This ambivalent status was immediately perceived as a constitutional problem. But it took almost a

---

[57] Ibid., para. 294 ('special importance').

[58] Ibid., para. 308.   [59] Ibid., para. 327.

[60] The Court in fact identified a breach of the right of defence, especially the right to be heard (ibid., para. 353), as well as an unjustified violation of the right to property (ibid., para. 370).

[61] Commission, Memorandum on the Accession of the European Communities to the European Convention for the Protection of Human Rights and Fundamental Freedoms, [1979] Bulletin of the European Communities—Supplement 2/79, esp. 11 et seq.

[62] On the drafting process, see G. de Búrca, 'The Drafting of the European Union Charter of Fundamental Rights' (2001) 26 *European Law Review* 126.

[63] Charter, Preamble 4.

[64] See *Parliament v Council*, Case C-540/03 [2006] ECR I-5769, para. 38: 'the Charter is not a legally binding instrument'.

decade before the Lisbon Treaty recognized the Charter as having 'the same legal value as the Treaties' in 2009.

The Charter 'reaffirms' the rights that result 'in particular' from the constitutional traditions common to the Member States, the European Convention on Human Rights, and the general principles of European law.[65] This formulation suggested two things. First, the Charter aims to *codify* existing fundamental rights and was thus not intended to create 'new' ones. And, second, it codified European rights from *various* sources—and thus not solely the general principles found in the European Treaties. To help identify the sources behind individual Charter articles, the Member States decided to give the Charter its own commentary. These 'Explanations' are not strictly legally binding, but they must be given 'due regard' in the interpretation of the Charter.[66]

The structure of the Charter is shown in Table 4.1. The Charter divides the Union's fundamental rights into six classes. The classic liberal rights are covered by Titles I to III as well as Title VI. The controversial Title IV codifies the rights of workers; yet, provision is here also made for the protection of the family and the right to health care.[67] Title V deals with 'citizens' rights'; that is, rights that a polity provides exclusively to its members. This includes the right to vote and to stand as a candidate in elections.[68]

The general principles on the interpretation and application of the Charter are finally set out in Title VII. These horizontal provisions establish four fundamental principles. First, the Charter is addressed to the Union and will only exceptionally apply to the Member States.[69] Second, not all provisions within the Charter are 'rights'; that is: directly effective entitlements for individuals.[70] Third, the rights within the Charter can, within limits, be restricted by Union legislation.[71] Fourth, the Charter tries to establish harmonious relations with the European Treaties and the European Convention, as well as with the constitutional traditions common to the Member States.[72] In the context of the present section, only principles two and three warrant special attention.

[65] Charter, Preamble 5.
[66] Art. 6(1) TEU and Art. 52(7) Charter: 'The explanations drawn up as a way of providing guidance in the interpretation of this Charter shall be given due regard by the courts of the Union and of the Member States.' These 'Explanations' are published in [2007] OJ C303/17.
[67] See, respectively, Arts 33 and 35 Charter.
[68] Art. 39 Charter.
[69] Art. 51 Charter. On the application of the Charter to the Member States, see R. Schütze, 'European Fundamental Rights and the Member States: From "Selective" to "Total" Incorporation?' (2011/12) 14 *Cambridge Yearbook of European Legal Studies* 337.
[70] Arts 51(1) and 52(5) Charter.
[71] Art. 52(1) Charter.
[72] Art. 52(2)–(4) as well as (6) of the Charter. But see also Art. 53 on the 'Level of Protection'.

Table 4.1 Structure of the Charter of Fundamental Rights

EU Charter of Fundamental Rights
Preamble
Title I—Dignity
Title II—Freedoms
Title III—Equality
Title IV—Solidarity
Title V—Citizens' Rights
Title VI—Justice
Title VII—General Provisions
Article 51—Field of Application
Article 52—Scope and Interpretation of Rights and Principles
Article 53—Level of Protection
Article 54—Prohibition of Abuse of Rights
Protocol No. 30 on Poland and the United Kingdom
Explanations

(a) (Hard) Rights and (Soft) Principles

It is important to note that the Charter makes a distinction between (hard) 'rights' and (soft) 'principles'. The distinction between rights and principles seems to contradict the jurisprudence of the Court with regard to fundamental *rights* as general *principles* in the context of the European Treaties. Yet what the Charter here means is that only those provisions that have direct effect will be 'rights' in that they can be invoked before a court. And not all provisions within the Charter are rights in this strict sense. The Charter expressly recognizes the separate existence of such 'principles' in Title VII.[73]

What are these principles in the Charter, and what is their effect? The 'Explanations' offer a number of illustrations, for example, Article 37 of the Charter dealing with 'Environmental Protection'. The provision reads: 'A high level of environmental protection and the improvement of the quality of the environment *must be integrated into the policies of the Union* and ensured in accordance with the principle of sustainable development.'[74] This wording

---

[73] Arts 51(1) and 52(5) Charter. For a good discussion of these provisions, and the case law here, see J. Krommendijk, 'Principled Silence or Mere Silence on Principles? The Role of the EU Charter's Principles in the Case Law of the European Court of Justice' (2015) 11 *European Constitutional Law Review* 321.

[74] Emphasis added.

contrasts strikingly with that of a classic right provision. For it constitutes less a *limit* to governmental action than an *aim* for governmental action. Principles indeed come close to orienting values, which 'do not however give rise to direct claims for positive action by the Union institutions'.[75] They are not subjective rights, but *objective guidelines*. In the words of the Charter:

> The provisions of this Charter which contain principles may be implemented by legislative and executive acts taken by institutions . . . They shall be judicially cognisable only in the interpretation of such acts and in the ruling on their legality.[76]

The difference between rights and principles is thus between a hard and a soft judicial claim. An individual will not have an (individual) right to a high level of environmental protection. In line with the classic task of legal principles,[77] the courts must, however, generally draw 'inspiration' from Union principles when interpreting European law.

But how is one to distinguish between 'rights' and 'principles'? Sadly, the Charter offers no catalogue of principles. Nor are its principles neatly grouped into a section within each substantive title. And even the wording of a particular article will not conclusively reveal whether it contains a right or a principle. But, most confusingly, even a single article 'may contain both elements of a right and of a principle'.[78] How is this possible? The best way to make sense of this is to see rights and principles not as mutually exclusive concepts, but as distinct but overlapping legal constructs. 'Rights' are situational crystallizations of principles, and therefore derive from principles. A good illustration may be offered by Figure 4.3 and Article 33 of the Charter on the status of the family and its relation to professional life.

(b) Limitations, and 'Limitations on Limitations'

Every legal order protecting fundamental rights recognizes that some rights can be limited to safeguard the public interest. For written bills of rights, these limitations are often recognized for each constitutional right. While the Charter follows this technique for some articles,[79] it also contains a provision

---

[75] 'Explanations' (n. 66), 35.   [76] Art. 52(5) Charter.

[77] See R. Dworkin, *Taking Rights Seriously* (Duckworth, 1996).   [78] 'Explanations' (n. 66), 35.

[79] Art. 17 (Right to Property) Charter states in para. 1: 'No one may be deprived of his or her possessions, except in the public interest and in the cases and under the conditions provided for by law, subject to fair compensation being paid in good time for their loss. The use of property may be regulated by law in so far as is necessary for the general interest.'

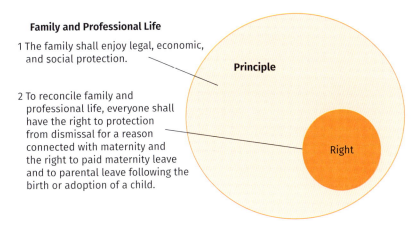

Family and Professional Life

1 The family shall enjoy legal, economic, and social protection.

2 To reconcile family and professional life, everyone shall have the right to protection from dismissal for a reason connected with maternity and the right to paid maternity leave and to parental leave following the birth or adoption of a child.

Principle

Right

Figure 4.3 Principles and rights within the Charter

that defines legitimate limitations to all fundamental rights. These 'limitations on limitations' are set out in Article 52 of the Charter. The provision states:

> Any limitation on the exercise of the rights and freedoms recognised by this Charter must be *provided for by law* and *respect the essence of those rights and free-doms*. Subject to the principle of *proportionality*, limitations may be made only if they are necessary and genuinely meet objectives of general interest recognised by the Union or the need to protect the rights and freedoms of others.[80]

The provision subjects all limitations to EU Charter rights to three constitutional principles.

First, any limitation of a fundamental right must be provided for 'by law'. This requirement seems to prohibit, out of hand, human rights violations that are the result of individual acts based on the Union's autonomous executive powers.[81] However, the problem is still this: will a limitation of someone's fundamental rights require the (democratic) legitimacy behind formal Union legislation? Put differently, must every 'law' limiting a fundamental right be adopted under a 'legislative procedure'?[82] This view would significantly affect the balance between fundamental rights and the pursuit of the common good of the Union. For if Article 52 outlaws all limitations of fundamental rights

---

[80] Art. 52(1) Charter (emphasis added).

[81] See *Knauf Gips v Commission*, Case C-407/08P [2010] ECR I-6371.

[82] In favour of this view, see D. Triantafyllou, 'The European Charter of Fundamental Rights and the "Rule of Law": Restricting Fundamental Rights by Reference' (2002) 39 *Common Market Law Review* 53–64 at 61: 'Accordingly, references to "law" made by the Charter should ideally require a co-deciding participation of the European Parliament[.]'

that are the result of *delegated* executive acts, much of the governmental machinery of the Union would come to a halt. In order to prevent such a petrification of the executive branch, the Court has favoured a material concept of 'law'.[83]

However, Article 52(1) of the Charter mentions, of course, two additional limitations on right limitations. Most importantly, Article 52 has now confirmed the independent existence of an absolute limit to Union interferences with fundamental rights by insisting that each limitation must always 'respect the essence' of the right in question. The codification of the 'essential core' doctrine is to be welcomed; and its independence from the principle of proportionality has been consistently confirmed.[84] Finally, and according to the principle of proportionality, each restriction of fundamental rights must, of course, always be necessary in the light of the general interest of the Union or the rights of others. This imposes a general constitutional obligation on the Union institutions to balance the various rights and interests at stake.

4. The 'External' Bill of Rights: The European Convention on Human Rights

The discovery of an unwritten bill of rights and the creation of a written bill of rights for the Union had been 'internal' achievements. They did 'not result in any form of external supervision being exercised over the Union's institutions'.[85] And by preferring *its* internal human rights over any external international standard, the Court has even been accused of a 'chauvinist' and 'parochial' attitude.[86]

This bleak picture *is* distorted—at the very least, when it comes to one international human rights treaty that has always provided an external standard

---

[83] Such a material reading of the phrase 'provided for by law' was confirmed in *Schecke & Eifert v Land Hessen*, Joined Cases C-92 and 93/09 [2010] ECR I-11063.

[84] *Digital Rights Ireland Ltd v Minister for Communications, Marine and Natural Resources et al.*, Joined Cases C-293 and 594/12 [2014] ECR I-238. The Court here clearly distinguished between a violation of the essential core doctrine (ibid., paras 39–40) and a breach of the principle of proportionality (ibid., paras 45–69). And see most definitely also *Schrems*, Case C-362/14, EU:C:2015:650, paras 94–5.

[85] I. de Jesús Butler and O. de Schutter, 'Binding the EU to International Human Rights Law' (2008) 27 *Yearbook of European Law* 277 at 278. This statement is correct only if limited to *direct* external supervision.

[86] G. de Búrca, 'The European Court of Justice and the International Legal Order After *Kadi*' (2010) 51 *Harvard International Law Journal* 1 at 4.

to the European Union: the European Convention on Human Rights. From the very beginning, the Court of Justice took the Convention very seriously,[87] sometimes even too seriously.[88] The Union has for a long time indeed acted *as if* it was bound by the European Convention; and even the Convention system has developed some form of external review of Union acts. Nonetheless, there *are* still many complexities and shortcomings with the European Convention as long as the Union is not formally bound by this external bill of rights. This fourth section will consequently look at the external standard imposed by the Convention prior to and after an eventual accession by the Union.

(a) Before Accession: Indirect Review of Union Law

The Union is (still) *not* a formal party to the European Convention. Could the Member States thus escape their international obligations under the Convention by transferring decision-making powers to the European Union? In order to avoid a normative vacuum, the European Convention system has developed a form of *indirect* judicial review of Union acts.

   This indirect review is based on the doctrine of (limited) Member State responsibility for acts of its Union. This complex construction draws on the idea of a human rights mortgage: the Convention Member States cannot transfer powers to the European Union without being bound—at least to some extent—by the European Convention to which they are formal parties. In *M & Co. v Germany*,[89] the European Commission of Human Rights thus found that whereas 'the Convention does not prohibit a Member State from transferring powers to international organisations', '*a transfer of powers does not necessarily exclude a State's responsibility under the Convention with regard to the exercise of the transferred powers*'.[90] This would not, however, mean that the State was to be held responsible for all actions of the Union: 'it would be contrary to the very idea of transferring powers to an international organisation to hold the Member States responsible for examining [possible violations] in each individual case.'[91]

   What, then, were the conditions for this indirect review of Union acts? Consistent with its chosen emphasis on *State* responsibility, the Convention system does not concentrate on a concrete Union act, but on the State's

---

[87] See S. Douglas-Scott, 'A Tale of Two Courts: Luxembourg, Strasbourg and the Growing European Human Rights Acquis' (2006) 43 *Common Market Law Review* 629.

[88] See *Spain v United Kingdom*, Case C-145/04 [2006] ECR I-7917.

[89] *M & Co. v Federal Republic of Germany* (1990) 64 DR 138.

[90] Ibid., 145 (emphasis added).   [91] Ibid., 146.

decision to transfer powers to the Union. This transfer of powers is deemed 'not incompatible with the Convention provided that within that organisation fundamental rights will receive an *equivalent protection*'.[92]

This was confirmed in *Bosphorus*.[93] Where the Union protected human rights in an 'equivalent' manner to that of the Convention, the European Court of Human Rights would operate a 'presumption' that the States had not violated the Convention by transferring powers to the European Union. This presumption translates into a lower review standard for acts adopted by the European Union, since the presumption of equivalent protection could only be rebutted where the actual treatment of human rights within the Union was 'manifestly deficient'.[94] This lower review standard represented a compromise between two extremes: no control, as the Union was not a member, and full control even in situations in which the Member States acted as mere agents of the Union. This compromise is 'the price for Strasbourg achieving a level of control over the EU, while respecting its autonomy as a separate legal order'.[95]

(b) Union Accession: Preconditions and Consequences

The EU Commission, long ago, suggested that accession to the Convention should be pursued. But under the original Treaties, the European Union lacked the express power to conclude human rights treaties. The Commission thus originally proposed using the Union's general competence: Article 352 TFEU; yet—famously—the Court rejected this strategy. In *Opinion 2/94*, the Court held that since accession by the Union would have '*fundamental institutional implications*', only a subsequent Treaty amendment could provide the Union with the power of accession.[96]

This competence has today been granted. According to Article 6(2) TEU, the European Union 'shall accede to the European Convention for the Protection of Human Rights and Fundamental Freedoms'. The 'shall' formulation indicates that the Union is even constitutionally obliged to become a member of this international organization. Union accession to the European

---

[92]   Ibid., 145 (emphasis added).

[93]   *Bosphorus Hava v Minister*, Case 84/95 (n. 46).

[94]   Ibid., paras 156–7. See also J. Callewaert, 'The European Convention on Human Rights and European Union Law: A Long Way to Harmony' [2009] *European Human Rights Law Review* 768 at 773: 'through the *Bosphorus*-presumption and its tolerance as regards "non-manifest" deficiencies, the protection of fundamental rights under [European] law is policed with less strictness than under the Convention'.

[95]   Douglas-Scott, 'A Tale of Two Courts' (n. 87), 639.

[96]   On this point, see Chapter 3, Section 2(b).

Convention must, however, pay due regard to the 'specific characteristics of the Union and Union law'.[97]

These 'specific characteristics' have recently been given a controversial interpretation in *Opinion 2/13* (*Accession to the ECHR II*). Indeed, no Opinion has generated more—negative—commentary in recent years![98] What was the main problem for the Court? The Court recalled that the Union is not a State; and that its legal order was a 'new kind of legal order' that was neither international nor national in nature.[99] The special characteristics of the Union were especially manifest in the horizontal relations between the Member States, where they found particular expression in the principles of mutual trust and mutual recognition.[100] The principle of mutual recognition here demands that Member States must generally accept the decisions of other Member States *as if they had adopted these decisions themselves*; and according to the Court, this logic must never be undermined by accession to the European Convention:

> In so far as the ECHR would, in requiring the EU and the Member States to be considered Contracting Parties not only in their relations with Contracting Parties which are not Member States of the EU but also in their relations with each other, including where such relations are governed by EU law, require a Member State to check that another Member State has observed fundamental rights, even though EU law imposes an obligation of mutual trust between those Member States, *accession is liable to upset the underlying balance of the EU and undermine the autonomy of EU law.*[101]

But assuming that this constitutional precondition can be fulfilled, through which procedure would the Union have to accede to the European Convention? On the Union side, accession will principally depend on the Member States of the Union:

> The Council shall . . . act unanimously for the agreement on accession of the Union to the European Convention for the Protection of Human Rights and Fundamental Freedoms; the decision concluding this agreement shall enter into

---

[97] Protocol No. 8 relating to Art. 6(2) of the Treaty on European Union on the Accession of the Union to the ECHR.

[98] See P. Gragl, 'The Reasonableness of Jealousy: *Opinion 2/13* and EU Accession to the ECHR' (2015) 15 *European Yearbook on Human Rights* 27.

[99] Protocol No. 8 (n. 97), paras 156–8.

[100] For a discussion of the principle of mutual recognition, see Chapters 9 and 11.

[101] Protocol No. 8 (n. 97), para. 194 (emphasis added).

force after it has been approved by the Member states in accordance with their respective constitutional requirements.[102]

The Council will thus have to agree unanimously, having previously obtained the consent of the European Parliament,[103] and unlike ordinary international agreements of the Union, the Union accession agreement will only come into force once each and every Member State has also ratified it. The Member States will therefore be able to block Union accession twice: once in the Council and once outside it. And while they technically are under a constitutional obligation to consent to accession as members of the Council, this is not the case for the second consent. For the duty to accede to the Convention expressed in Article 6(2) TEU will only bind the Union—and its institutions—but not the Member States.

Assuming that the Union eventually accedes to the Convention, will the presumption that the Union—in principle—complies with the European Convention on Human Rights disappear with accession? It seems compelling that the *Bosphorus* presumption will indeed cease once the Union accedes to the Convention. For '[b]y acceding to the Convention, the European Union will have agreed to have its legal system measured by the human rights standards of the ECHR', and will 'therefore no longer deserve special treatment'.[104] The replacement of an *indirect* review by a *direct* review should also—at least in theory—lead to the replacement of a *limited* review by a *full* review. Yet the life of law is not always logical, and the Strasbourg Court may well decide to cherish past experiences by applying a lower review standard to the (acceded) European Union. We must wait and see whether or not logic will trump experience.

Conclusion

Fundamental rights constitute a vital constitutional limit to all legislative and executive actions of the Union. They are principally enforced by the judiciary in the form of judicial review.

The Union has, unfortunately, not reserved one place for human rights, but has instead developed three bills of rights. Its unwritten bill of rights results

---

[102] Art. 218(8) TFEU, second indent.
[103] Art. 218(6)(a)(ii) TFEU.
[104] T. Lock, 'EU Accession to the ECHR: Implications for Judicial Review in Strasbourg' (2010) 35 *European Law Review* 777 at 798.

from the general principles of Union law. The Court here indirectly developed EU fundamental rights from the constitutional traditions of the Member States. The Charter of Fundamental Rights adds a written bill of rights for the Union. The relationship between this written bill and the unwritten bill of rights within the EU Treaties remains, however, ambivalent. The same is true for the relationship between the two internal bills of EU rights and the European Convention on Human Rights. The latter has always provided an external bill of rights—yet the exact status of the European Convention in the Union legal order and its influence on the substance of EU fundamental rights remains to be settled. There is thus much potential confusion as to which source of fundamental rights governs a case.

What is, however, certain is that most EU fundamental rights are not absolute rights. They can be limited if the public interest so demands. Yet these public interest limitations are themselves limited by the principle of proportionality and the idea that the essential core of a fundamental right can never be touched.

Part II

European Law: Enforcement

This Part concentrates on the 'enforcement' of Union law in the courts. We shall see that European law establishes rights and obligations that directly affect individuals. The direct effect of European law in the national legal orders will be discussed in Chapter 5. Where a European norm is directly effective, it will also be 'supreme' over national law. The 'primacy' of European law is the subject of Chapter 6. How will individuals enforce their 'supreme' European rights? Chapters 7 and 8 look at the dual enforcement machinery within the Union legal order. Individuals will typically enforce their European rights in national courts. The Union legal order has here required national courts to provide effective remedies for the enforcement of European rights; and in order to assist these courts in their interpretation and application of European law, the Union envisages a preliminary reference procedure. Having discussed the indirect enforcement of European law through the national courts in Chapter 7, the direct enforcement of European law in the European Courts will be explored in Chapter 8.

Direct Effect

Introduction

Classic international law holds that each State can itself determine the relationship between its 'domestic' law and 'international' law. Two—constitutional—theories thereby exist: monism and dualism. Monist States make international law part of their domestic legal order. International law will here directly apply *as if* it were domestic law.[1] By contrast, dualist States consider international law separate from domestic law. International law is viewed as the law *between* States; national law is the law *within* a State. While international treaties are thus binding—externally—'on' States, they cannot be binding 'in' States. International law here needs to be 'transposed' or 'incorporated' into domestic law and may, at most, have *indirect* effects through the medium of national law. For an illustration of the two theories see Figure 5.1.

---

[1] Art. VI, cl. 2 of the United States Constitution (emphasis added): '[A]ll Treaties made, or which shall be made, under the Authority of the United States, shall be the supreme Law of the Land; and the *Judges in every State shall be bound thereby, any Thing in the Constitution or Laws of any State to the Contrary notwithstanding*.'

Figure 5.1 Monism and dualism

Did the European Union leave the choice between monism and dualism to its Member States? Section 1 examines this question in greater detail, and we shall see there that the Union insists on a monistic relationship between European and national law. This, in particular, means that the Union will itself determine the effect of its law in the national legal orders. The remainder of this chapter then explores the doctrine of direct effect for European law. Section 2 starts out with the direct effect of the European Treaties. The European Treaties are, however, mainly framework treaties; that is: they primarily envisage the adoption of European *secondary* law and especially EU legislation. This secondary law may take various forms. These forms are set out in Article 288 TFEU. The provision defines the Union's legal instruments, and states:

[1] To exercise the Union's competences, the institutions shall adopt regulations, directives, decisions, recommendations and opinions.
[2] A regulation shall have general application. It shall be binding in its entirety and directly applicable in all Member States.
[3] A directive shall be binding, as to the result to be achieved, upon each Member State to which it is addressed, but shall leave to the national authorities the choice of form and methods.
[4] A decision shall be binding in its entirety. A decision which specifies those to whom it is addressed shall be binding only on them.
[5] Recommendations and opinions shall have no binding force.

The provision acknowledges three binding legal instruments—regulations, directives, and decisions—and two non-binding instruments. Why was there a need for three types of binding instruments? The answer seems to lie in their specific—direct or indirect—effects in the national legal orders. While regulations and decisions were considered to be Union acts that would contain directly effective legal norms, directives appeared to lack this capacity. Much of the constitutional discussion on the direct effect of European secondary law has consequently concentrated on the direct effect of directives. Section 3 will look at them specifically in much detail. Finally, Section 4 analyses the doctrine of indirect effect within the Union legal order.

1. Direct Applicability and Direct Effect

Would the Union legal order permit a dualist approach towards European law on the part of the Member States? The European Treaties gave some signals in favour of this permissive approach.[2] However, the Treaties also contain strong signals against the 'ordinary' international reading of European law. For not only was the Union entitled to adopt legal acts that were to be 'directly applicable *in* all Member States'.[3] From the very beginning, the Treaties also established a constitutional mechanism that envisaged the direct application of European law by the national courts.[4]

But regardless of whether a monist view had or had not been intended by the founding Member States, the European Court discarded any dualist leanings in one of the most important cases of European law: *Van Gend en Loos*.[5] The Court here expressly cut the umbilical cord with classic international law by insisting that the European legal order was a 'new legal order'. In the famous words of the Court:

> The objective of the E[U] Treaty, which is to establish a common market, the functioning of which is of direct concern to interested parties in the [Union], implies that this Treaty is *more than an agreement which merely creates mutual obligations between the contracting States*. This view is confirmed by the preamble to the Treaty which refers not only to the governments but to peoples. It is also confirmed more specifically by the establishment of institutions endowed with sovereign rights, the exercise of which affects Member States and also their citizens. Furthermore, it must be noted that the nations of the States brought together in the [Union] are called upon to cooperate in the functioning of this [Union] through the intermediary of the European Parliament and the Economic and Social Committee.
>
> In addition the task assigned to the Court of Justice under Article [267], the object of which is to secure uniform interpretation of the Treaty by national courts and tribunals, confirms that the States have acknowledged that [European] law has an authority which can be invoked by their nationals before those courts and tribunals. The conclusion to be drawn from this is that the [Union] constitutes a

---

[2] E.g. there existed an 'international' enforcement machinery in the form of infringement actions before the Court of Justice. On this point, see Chapter 8, Section 1.

[3] Art. 288(2) TFEU.

[4] Art. 267 TFEU. On the provision, see Chapter 7, Sections 3 and 4.

[5] *Van Gend en Loos v Netherlands Inland Revenue Administration*, Case 26/62 [1963] ECR (Special English Edition) 1.

new legal order of international law for the benefit of which the States have limited their sovereign rights, albeit within limited fields, and the subjects of which comprise not only Member States but also their nationals. *Independently of the legislation of Member States*, [European] law therefore not only imposes obligations on individuals but is also intended to confer upon them rights which become part of their legal heritage.[6]

All judicial arguments here marshalled to justify a monistic reading of European law are debatable.[7] But with a stroke of the pen, the Court confirmed the independence of the European legal order from classic international law. Unlike ordinary international law, the European Treaties were more than agreements creating mutual obligations between States. European law was to be enforced in national courts—despite the parallel existence of an international enforcement machinery.[8] Individuals were subjects of European law, and individual rights and obligations could consequently derive *directly* from European law.

Importantly, *all* European law is directly applicable law, and the European Union could therefore *itself* determine the effect and nature of European law within the national legal orders. The direct applicability of European law indeed allowed the Union *centrally* to develop two foundational doctrines of the European legal order: the doctrine of direct effect and the doctrine of supremacy or primacy. The present chapter analyses the doctrine of direct effect; Chapter 6 deals with the doctrine of primacy.

---

⁶ Ibid., 12 (emphasis added).

⁷ For a critical overview, see T. Arnull, *The European Union and its Court of Justice* (Oxford University Press, 2006), 168 et seq.

⁸ *Van Gend en Loos,* Case 26/62 (n. 5), 13: 'In addition the argument based on Articles [258] and [259] of the [TFEU] put forward by the three Governments which have submitted observations to the Court in their statements of [the] case is misconceived. The fact that these Articles of the Treaty enable the Commission and the Member States to bring before the Court a State which has not fulfilled its obligations does not mean that individuals cannot plead these obligations, should the occasion arise, before a national court, any more than the fact that the Treaty places at the disposal of the Commission ways of ensuring that obligations imposed upon those subject to the Treaty are observed, precludes the possibility, in actions between individuals before a national court, of pleading infringements of these obligations. A restriction of the guarantees against an infringement of [ex-] Article 12 [EEC] by Member States to the procedures under Articles [258 and 259] would remove all direct legal protection of the individual rights of their nationals. There is the risk that recourse to the procedure under these Articles would be ineffective if it were to occur after the implementation of a national decision taken contrary to the provisions of the Treaty. The vigilance of individuals concerned to protect their rights amounts to an effective supervision in addition to the supervision entrusted by Articles [258 and 259] to the diligence of the Commission and of the Member States.'

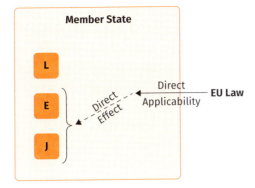

Figure 5.2 Direct applicability and direct effect

What is the doctrine of direct effect? Direct effect means that a norm is directly *enforceable*; that is: it needs no further implementation by the legislature but can be directly applied by the executive or the courts. Not all legal norms have this quality. For example, where a European norm requires Member States to establish a public fund to guarantee unpaid wages for insolvent private companies, yet leaves a wide margin of discretion to the Member States on how to achieve that end, this norm is not intended to have direct effects in a specific situation.[9] While it binds the national *legislator*, the norm is not self-*executing*. It is thus vital to understand that the Court's decision in favour of a monistic relationship between the European and the national legal orders did not mean that all European law would be directly effective. For the concept of direct applicability is wider than the concept of direct effect. Whereas the former refers to the *internal* effect of a European norm within national legal orders, the latter refers to the *enforceable* effect of such a norm in a specific case. Direct effect thus relates to the executive and judicial branches—and not the legislative branch (Figure 5.2).

2. Direct Effect of Primary Law

The European Treaties are framework treaties. They establish the objectives of the European Union, and confer upon it the powers to achieve these objectives. Many of the European policies in Part III of the TFEU thus simply set out the competences and procedures for future Union legislation. The Treaties,

---

[9] This example is of course taken from *Francovich*—a very famous case discussed in Chapter 7, Section 2.

as primary European law, here only offer the constitutional bones. But could this constitutional 'skeleton' itself have direct effect? Would there be Treaty provisions that were sufficiently precise to be enforceable in national courts?

The European Court affirmatively answered this question in *Van Gend en Loos*.[10] The case concerned a central objective of the European Union: the internal market. According to that central plank of the Treaties, the Union was to create a customs union between the Member States. Within a customs union, goods can move freely without any tariffs or other pecuniary charges being levied when crossing borders. The Treaties had chosen to establish the customs union gradually; and to this effect ex-Article 12 EEC contained a standstill obligation: 'Member States shall refrain from introducing between themselves any new customs duties on imports or exports or any charges having equivalent effect, and from increasing those which they already apply in their trade with each other.'[11] The Netherlands appeared to have violated this provision; and believing this to be the case, Van Gend en Loos—a Dutch import company—brought proceedings in a Dutch court against the National Inland Revenue. The Dutch court had doubts about the admissibility and the substance of the case and referred a number of preliminary questions to the European Court of Justice.

Could a private party enforce an international treaty in a national court? And, if so, was this a question of national or European law? In the course of the proceedings before the European Court, the Dutch government heavily disputed that an individual could enforce an international treaty against its own government in a national court. Any alleged infringements had to be submitted to the European Court by the Commission or a Member State under the 'international' infringement procedures set out in Articles 258 and 259 TFEU.[12] The Belgian government, having intervened in the case, equally claimed that the question of what effects an international treaty had within the national legal order 'falls exclusively within the jurisdiction of the Netherlands court'.[13] Conversely, the Commission countered that 'the effects of the provisions of the Treaty on the national law of Member States cannot be determined by the actual national law of each of them but by the Treaty itself'.[14] And since ex-Article 12 EEC was 'clear and complete', it was 'a rule of

---

[10] *Van Gend en Loos*, Case 26/62 (n. 5).

[11] The provision has been repealed. Strictly speaking, it is therefore not correct to identify Art. 30 TEU as the successor provision, for article is based on ex-Arts 13 and 16 EEC. The normative content of ex-Art. 12 EEC solely concerned the introduction of *new* customs duties; and therefore did not cover the abolition of existing tariff restrictions.

[12] *Van Gend en Loos*, Case 26/62 (n. 5), 6. On enforcement actions by the Commission, see Chapter 8, Section 1.

[13] *Van Gend en Loos*, Case 26/62 (n. 5), 6.   [14] Ibid.

law capable of being effectively applied by the national court'.[15] The fact that the European provision was addressed to the States did 'not of itself take away from individuals who have an interest in it the right to require it to be applied in the national courts'.[16]

Two views thus competed before the European Court. According to the 'dualist' view, legal rights of private parties could 'not derive from the [Treaties] or the legal measures taken by the institutions, but [solely] from legal measures enacted by Member States'.[17] According to the 'monist' view, by contrast, European law was capable of directly creating individual rights. The Court famously favoured the second view. It followed from the 'spirit' of the Treaties that European law was no 'ordinary' international law. It would thus of itself be directly applicable in the national legal orders.

But when would a provision have direct effect, and thus entitle private parties to seek its application by a national court? Having briefly presented the general scheme of the Treaty in relation to customs duties,[18] the Court concentrated on the wording of ex-Article 12 EEC and found as follows:

> The wording of [ex-]Article 12 [EEC] contains a *clear and unconditional prohibition* which is not a positive but a *negative obligation*. This obligation, moreover, is not qualified by any reservation on the part of the States, *which would make its implementation conditional upon a positive legislative measure enacted under national law*. The very nature of this prohibition makes it ideally adapted to produce direct effects in the legal relationship between Member States and their subjects. The implementation of [ex-]Article 12 [EEC] does not require any legislative intervention on the part of the States. The fact that under this Article it is the Member States who are made the subject of the negative obligation does not imply that their nationals cannot benefit from this obligation.[19]

While somewhat repetitive, the test for direct effect is here clearly presented: wherever the Treaties contain a 'prohibition' that is 'clear' and 'unconditional', it will have direct effect. Being an unconditional prohibition thereby required two things. First, the European provision had to be an *automatic* prohibition; that is: it should not depend on subsequent positive legislation by

[15] Ibid., 7.   [16] Ibid.
[17] This was the view of the German government (ibid., 8).
[18] The Court considered ex-Art. 12 EEC as an 'essential provision' in the general scheme of the Treaty as it relates to customs duties (ibid., 12).
[19] Ibid., 13 (emphasis added).

the European Union. And, second, the prohibition should ideally be *absolute*; that is: 'not qualified by any reservation on the part of the States'.

This was a—very—strict test. But ex-Article 12 EEC was indeed 'ideally adapted' to satisfy this triple test. It was a clear prohibition and unconditional in the double sense. However, if the Court had insisted on a strict application of all three criteria, very few provisions within the Treaties would have had direct effect. Yet the Court subsequently loosened the test considerably.

(a) Direct Effect: From Strict to Lenient Test

The direct effect test set out in *Van Gend* was informed by three criteria. First, a provision had to be clear. Second, it had to be unconditional in the sense of being an automatic prohibition. And, third, this prohibition would need to be absolute; that is: not allow for reservations. In its subsequent jurisprudence, the Court expanded the concept of direct effect on all three fronts.

First, how clear would a prohibition have to be to be directly effective? Within the Treaties' title on the free movement of goods, we find the follow-ing famous prohibition: 'Quantitative restrictions on imports and all meas-ures having equivalent effect shall be prohibited between Member States.'[20] Was this a clear prohibition? While the notion of 'quantitative restrictions' might have been—relatively—clear, what about 'measures having equivalent effect'? The Commission had realized the open-ended nature of the concept and offered some early semantic help.[21] And yet, despite all the uncertainty involved, the Court found that the provision had direct effect.[22]

What about the second part of the direct effect test? When was a prohibition automatic? Would this ever be the case where the Treaties expressly acknowl-edged the need for positive legislative action by the Union to achieve a Union objective? For example, the Treaty chapter on the right of establishment con-tains not just a prohibition addressed to the Member States;[23] the subsequent

---

[20]   Art. 34 TFEU.

[21]   Directive 70/50/EEC on the abolition of measures which have an effect equivalent to quan-titative restrictions on imports and are not covered by other provisions adopted in pursuance of the EEC Treaty, [1970] OJ (English Special Edition) 17.

[22]   *Iannelli & Volpi SpA v Ditta Paolo Meroni*, Case 74/76 [1977] ECR 557, para. 13: 'The prohi-bition of quantitative restrictions and measures having equivalent effect laid down in Article [34] of the [TFEU] is mandatory and explicit and its implementation does not require any subsequent intervention of the Member States or [Union] institutions. The prohibition therefore has direct effect and creates individual rights which national courts must protect[.]'

[23]   Art. 49(1) TFEU states: 'Within the framework of the provisions set out below, restrictions on the freedom of establishment of nationals of a Member State in the territory of another Mem-ber State shall be prohibited.'

article states: 'In order to attain freedom of establishment as regards a particular activity, the European Parliament and the Council, acting in accordance with the ordinary legislative procedure and after consulting the Economic and Social Committee, shall act by means of directives.' Would this not mean that the freedom of establishment was *conditional* on legislative action? In *Reyners*,[24] the Court rejected this argument. Despite the fact that the general scheme within the chapter on freedom of establishment contained a set of provisions that sought to achieve free movement through subsequent Union legislation,[25] the Court declared the European right of establishment to be directly effective.

Finally, what about the third requirement? Could relative prohibitions, even if clear, ever be directly effective? The prohibition on quantitative restrictions on imports, discussed earlier, is subject to a number of legitimate exceptions according to which it 'shall not preclude [national] prohibitions or restrictions on imports, exports or goods in transit justified on grounds of public morality, public policy or public security'.[26] Was this, then, a prohibition that was 'not qualified by any reservation on the part of the States'? The Court found that this was indeed the case. For although these derogations would 'attach particular importance to the interests of Member States, it must be observed that they deal with exceptional cases which are clearly defined and which do not lend themselves to any wide interpretation'.[27] And since the application of these exceptions was 'subject to judicial control', a Member State's right to invoke them did not prevent the general prohibition 'from conferring on individuals rights which are enforceable by them and which the national courts must protect'.[28]

What, then, is the test for the direct effect of Treaty provisions in the light of these—relaxing—developments? Today, the simple test is this: a provision has direct effect when it is capable of being applied by a national court. Importantly, direct effect does *not* depend on a European norm granting a subjective right; but on the contrary, the subjective right is a result of a directly effective norm.[29] Direct effect simply means that a norm can be 'invoked' in

---

[24] *Reyners v Belgian State*, Case 2/74 [1974] ECR 631. For an excellent discussion of this question, see P. Craig, 'Once Upon a Time in the West: Direct Effect and the Federalization of EEC Law' (1992) 12 *Oxford Journal of Legal Studies* 453 at 463–70.

[25] *Reyners*, Case 2/74 (n. 24), para. 32.

[26] Art. 36 TFEU.

[27] *Salgoil v Italian Ministry of Foreign Trade*, Case 13/68 [1968] ECR 453 at 463.

[28] *Van Duyn v Home Office*, Case 41/74 [1974] ECR 1337, para. 7.

[29] M. Ruffert, 'Rights and Remedies in European Community Law: A Comparative View' (1997) 34 *Common Market Law Review* 307 at 315.

and applied by a court. And this is the case, when the Court of Justice says it is! Today, almost all Treaty *prohibitions* have direct effect—even the most general ones. Indeed, in *Mangold*,[30] the Court held that an—unwritten and vague—*general* principle of European law could have direct effect.

Should we embrace this development? We should, for the direct effect of a legal rule 'must be considered as being the normal condition of any rule of law'. The very questioning of the direct effect of European law was an 'infant disease' of the young European legal order.[31]

(b) Vertical and Horizontal Direct Effect

Where a Treaty provision is directly effective, an individual can invoke European law in a national court (or before the national administration). This will normally be as against the State. This situation is called 'vertical' direct effect, since the State is normatively 'above' its subjects. But what about a situation between two private parties? The legal effect of a norm between private parties is called 'horizontal' effect; and while there has never been any doubt that Treaty provisions can be invoked in a vertical situation, there has been some discussion on their horizontal direct effects.

Should it make a difference whether European law is invoked in proceedings against the Inland Revenue, as in *Van Gend*, or in a civil dispute between two private parties? Should the Treaties be allowed to impose obligations on individuals? The Court in *Van Gend* had accepted this theoretical possibility.[32] And indeed, the horizontal direct effect of Treaty provisions has never been in doubt for the Court.[33]

A good illustration of the horizontal direct effect of Treaty provisions can be found in *Familiapress v Bauer*.[34] The case concerned the interpretation of Article 34 TFEU prohibiting unjustified restriction on the free movement of goods. It arose in a *civil* dispute before the Vienna Commercial Court between Familiapress and a German competitor, Bauer. The latter was

---

[30]   *Mangold v Helm*, Case C-144/04 [2005] ECR I-9981. The case will be discussed later in the chapter.

[31]   P. Pescatore, 'The Doctrine of "Direct Effect": An Infant Disease of Community Law' (1983) 8 *European Law Review* 155.

[32]   *Van Gend en Loos*, Case 26/62 (n. 5), 12: '[European] law therefore not only imposes obligations on individuals[.]'

[33]   The direct effect of Art. 34 TFEU was announced in a 'horizontal' case between two private parties; see *Iannelli & Volpi v Meroni*, Case 74/76 (n. 22).

[34]   *Vereinigte Familiapress Zeitungsverlags- und vertriebs GmbH v Bauer Verlag*, Case C-368/95 [1997] ECR I-3689.

accused of violating the Austrian Law on Unfair Competition by publishing prize crossword puzzles—a sales technique that was deemed unfair under Austrian law. Bauer defended itself in the national court by invoking Article 34 TFEU—claiming that the directly effective European right to free movement prevailed over the Austrian law. And the Court of Justice indeed found that a national law that constituted an unjustified restriction of trade would have to be disapplied in the—civil—proceedings. The European Treaty provision thus had horizontal direct effect.

3. Direct Effect of Secondary Law: Directives

When the European Union was born, the Treaties envisaged two instruments that were designed to contain norms that were directly effective: regulations and decisions. And with regard to both of them, the constitutional principles discussed in Section 2 for primary Union law here apply analogously.[35]

By contrast, a third instrument—the directive—appeared to lack this capacity. For according to Article 288(3) TFEU, a directive is defined as follows:

> A directive shall be binding, as to the result to be achieved, upon each Member State to which it is addressed, but shall leave to the national authorities the choice of form and methods.

This formulation suggested that directives were internationally binding *on* States—not *within* States. And on the basis of such a 'dualist' reading, directives would have no validity in the national legal orders. They seemed *not* to be directly applicable, and would thus need to be 'incorporated' or 'implemented' through national legislation. This dualist view was underlined by the fact that Member States were only bound as to the result to be achieved—as obligations of result are common in classic international law.[36]

But could this indirect Union law nonetheless have direct effects? In a courageous line of jurisprudence, the Court confirmed that directives could—under certain circumstances—have direct effect and thus entitle individuals to have

[35] For 'regulations', see *Azienda Agricola Monte Arcosa Srl*, Case C-403/98 [2001] ECR I-103. And, importantly, while this chapter does not look at EU international agreements, the constitutional principles discussed here also apply, *mutatis mutandis*, to them (see R. Schütze, *European Union Law* (Cambridge University Press, 2018), ch. 3, section 4).

[36] For this view, see L.-J. Constantinesco, *Das Recht der Europäischen Gemeinschaften* (Nomos, 1977), 614.

their European rights applied in national courts. However, the Court subjected this finding to two limitations: one temporal, one normative. Direct effect would only arise *after* a Member State had failed properly to 'implement' the Directive, and then only in relation to the State authorities themselves. The second limitation is known as the 'no-horizontal-direct-effect rule'. And while this constitutional rule has been consistently confirmed, it has itself been limited.

(a) Direct Effect of Directives: Conditions and Limits

That directives could directly give rise to rights that individuals could claim in national courts was accepted in *Van Duyn v Home Office*.[37]

The case concerned a Dutch secretary, whose entry into the United Kingdom had been denied on the ground that she was a member of the Church of Scientology. Britain had tried to justify this limitation on the free movement of persons by reference to an express derogation that allowed such restrictions on grounds of public policy and public security.[38] However, in an effort to harmonize national derogations from free movement, the Union had adopted a directive according to which '[m]easures taken on grounds of public policy or of public security shall be based exclusively on the personal conduct of the individual concerned'.[39] This outlawed national measures that limited free movement for generic reasons, such as membership of a disliked organization. Unfortunately, the United Kingdom had not 'implemented' the Directive into national law. Could Van Duyn nonetheless directly invoke the Directive against the British authorities? The Court of Justice found that this was possible by emphasizing the distinction between direct applicability and direct effect:

> [B]y virtue of the provisions of Article [288] regulations are directly applicable and, consequently, may by their very nature have direct effects, it does not follow from this that other categories of acts mentioned in that Article can never have similar effects. It would be incompatible with the binding effect attributed to a directive by Article [288] to exclude, in principle, the possibility that the obligation which it imposes may be invoked by those concerned. In particular, where the [Union] authorities have, by directive, imposed on Member States the obligation to pursue a particular course of conduct, the useful effect of such an act

---

[37] *Van Duyn*, Case 41/74 (n. 28).   [38] Art. 45(1) and (3) TFEU.

[39] Art. 3(1) Directive 64/221 on the coordination of special measures concerning the movement and residence of foreign nationals which are justified on grounds of public policy, public security or public health, [1963–4] OJ (English Special Edition) 117.

would be weakened if the individuals were prevented from relying on it before their national courts and if the latter were prevented from taking it into consideration as an element of [European] law. Article [267], which empowers national courts to refer to the Court questions concerning the validity and interpretation of all acts of the [Union] institutions, without distinction, implies furthermore that these acts may be invoked by individuals in the national courts.[40]

The Court—rightly—emphasized the distinction between direct applicability and direct effect, yet—wrongly—defined the relationship between these two concepts in order to justify its conclusion. To brush aside the textual argument that regulations are directly applicable while directives are not, it wrongly alluded to the idea that direct effect without direct application was possible.[41] And the direct effect of directives was justified by three different and distinct arguments. First, to exclude direct effect would be incompatible with the 'binding effect' of directives. Second, their 'useful effect' would be weakened if individuals could not invoke them in national courts. Third, since the preliminary reference procedure did not exclude directives, the latter must be capable of being invoked in national courts.

What was the constitutional value of these arguments? Argument one is a sleight of hand: the fact that a directive is not binding in *national law* is not 'incompatible' with its binding effect under *international law*. The second argument is strong, but not of a legal nature: to enhance the useful effect of a rule by making it more binding is a political argument. Finally, the third argument only begs the question: while it is true that the preliminary reference procedure generically refers to all 'acts of the institutions', it could be argued that only those acts that are directly effective can be referred. The decision in *Van Duyn* was right, but sadly without reason.

The lack of a convincing *legal* argument to justify the direct effect of directives soon prompted the Court to propose a fourth argument. 'A Member State which has not adopted the implementing measures required by the Directive in the prescribed periods may not rely, as against individuals, on

---

[40] *Van Duyn*, Case 41/74 (n. 28), para. 12.

[41] In the words of J. Steiner: 'How can a law be enforceable by individuals within a Member State if it is not regarded as incorporated in that State?' (J. Steiner, 'Direct Applicability in EEC Law—A Chameleon Concept' (1982) 98 *Law Quarterly Review* 229–48 at 234). The direct effect of a directive presupposes its direct application. And, indeed, ever since *Van Gend en Loos*, all directives must be regarded as directly applicable (see S. Prechal, *Directives in EC Law* (Oxford University Press, 2005), 92 and 229).

its own failure to perform the obligations which the directive entails.'[42] This fourth reason has become known as the 'estoppel argument'. A Member State that fails to implement its European obligations is 'estopped' from invoking that failure as a defence, and individuals are consequently and collaterally entitled to rely on the directive as against the State. Unlike the three original arguments, this fourth argument is *State*-centric. It locates the rationale for the direct effect of directives not in the nature of the instrument itself, but in the behaviour of the State.

This (behavioural) rationale would result in two important limitations on the direct effect of directives. Even if provisions within a directive were 'unconditional and sufficiently precise' 'those provisions may [only] be *relied upon by an individual against the State* where that State fails to implement the Directive in national law *by the end of the period prescribed or where it fails to implement the directive correctly*'.[43] This direct effect test for directives differed from that for ordinary Union law, as it added a temporal and a normative limitation. *Temporally,* the direct effect of directives could only arise after the failure of the State to implement the directive had occurred. Thus, before the end of the implementation period granted to Member States, no direct effect can take place. And even once this temporal condition has been satisfied, the direct effect would operate only as against the State. This *normative* limitation on the direct effect of directives has become famous as the 'no-horizontal-direct-effect rule'.

(b) The No-Horizontal-Direct-Effect Rule

The Court's jurisprudence of the 1970s had extended the direct effect of Union law to directives. An individual could claim his or her European rights against a State that had failed to implement a directive into national law. This situation was one of 'vertical' direct effect. Could an individual equally invoke a directive against another private party? This 'horizontal' direct effect existed for direct Union law; yet should it be extended to directives? The Court's famous answer is a resolute 'no': directives could not have horizontal direct effects.

The 'no-horizontal-direct-effect rule' was first expressed in *Marshall*.[44] The Court based its negative conclusion on a textual argument:

---

[42] *Ratti*, Case 148/78 [1979] ECR 1629, para. 22.
[43] *Kolpinghuis Nijmegen BV*, Case 80/86 [1987] ECR 3969, para. 7 (emphasis added).
[44] *Marshall v Southampton and South-West Hampshire Area Health Authority*, Case 152/84 [1986] ECR 723.

[A]ccording to Article [288 TFEU] the binding nature of a directive, which constitutes the basis for the possibility of relying on the directive before a national court,
exists only in relation to 'each Member State to which it is addressed'. It follows that a
directive may not of itself impose obligations on an individual and that a provision
of a directive may not be relied upon as such against such a person.[45]

The absence of horizontal direct effect was subsequently confirmed in *Dori*.[46]
A private company had approached Ms Dori for an English language cor-
respondence course. The contract had been concluded in Milan's busy central
railway station. A few days later, she changed her mind and tried to cancel
the contract. A right of cancellation had been provided for by the European directive on consumer contracts concluded outside business premises,[47]
but Italy had not implemented the Directive into national law. Could a private party nonetheless directly rely on the unimplemented directive against
another private party? The Court was firm:

[A]s is clear from the judgment in *Marshall* ... the case-law on the possibility of
relying on directives against State entities is based on the fact that under Article
[288] a directive is binding only in relation to 'each Member State to which it is
addressed'. That case-law seeks to prevent 'the State from taking advantage of its
own failure to comply with [European] law' ... The effect of extending that case-
law to the sphere of relations between individuals would be to recognize a power
in the [Union] to enact obligations for individuals with immediate effect, whereas
it has competence to do so only where it is empowered to adopt regulations. It
follows that, in the absence of measures transposing the directive within the
prescribed time-limit, consumers cannot derive from the directive itself a right
of cancellation as against traders with whom they have concluded a contract or
enforce such a right in a national court.[48]

This denial of any direct effect of directives in *horizontal* situations was
grounded in three arguments.[49] First, a textual argument: a directive is binding in relation to each Member State to which it is addressed. But had the

---

[45] Ibid., para. 48.

[46] *Faccini Dori v Recreb*, Case C-91/92 [1994] ECR I-3325.

[47] Directive 85/577 concerning protection of the consumer in respect of contracts negotiated
away from business premises, [1985] OJ L372/31.

[48] *Dori* (n. 46), paras 22–5.

[49] The Court silently dropped the 'useful effect argument' as it would have worked towards the
opposite conclusion.

Court not used this very same argument to establish the direct effect of directives in the first place? Second, the estoppel argument: the direct effect for directives exists to prevent a State from taking advantage of its own failure to comply with European law. And since individuals were not responsible for the non-implementation of a directive, direct effect should not be extended to them. Third, a systematic argument: if horizontal direct effect was given to directives, the distinction between directives and regulations would disappear. This was a weak argument, for a directive's distinct character could be preserved in different ways.[50] In order to bolster its reasoning, the Court added a fourth argument in subsequent jurisprudence: legal certainty.[51] Since directives were not published, they must not impose obligations on those to whom they are not addressed. This argument has lost some of its force,[52] but continues to be very influential today.

All these arguments may be criticized.[53] But the Court of Justice has stuck to its conclusion: directives cannot *directly* impose obligations on individuals. They lack horizontal direct effect. This constitutional rule of European law has nonetheless been qualified by an important limitation to the rule: the wide ambit of vertical direct effect.

(c) Limitation to the Rule: The Wide Definition of State (Actions)

One way to minimize the no-horizontal-direct-effect rule is to maximize the vertical direct effect of directives. The Court has done this by giving extremely extensive definitions to what constitutes the 'State', and what constitute 'public actions'.

What public authorities count as the 'State'? A minimal definition restricts the concept to a State's central organs. Because they failed to implement the Directive, the estoppel argument suggested them to be vertically bound by the Directive. Yet the Court has never accepted this restriction, and has endorsed a maximal definition of the State. It thus held that directly effective

---

[50] On this point, see R. Schütze, 'The Morphology of Legislative Power in the European Community: Legal Instruments and Federal Division of Powers' (2006) 25 *Yearbook of European Law* 91.

[51] See *The Queen on the Application of Delena Wells v Secretary of State for Transport, Local Government and the Regions*, Case C-201/02 [2004] ECR 723, para. 56: 'the principle of legal certainty prevents directives from creating obligations for individuals'.

[52] The publication of directives is now, in principle, required by Art. 297 TFEU.

[53] For an excellent overview of the principal arguments, see P. Craig, 'The Legal Effect of Directives: Policy, Rules and Exceptions' (2009) 34 *European Law Review* 349.

obligations 'are binding upon *all authorities of the Member States*'; and this included 'all organs of the administration, including decentralised authorities, such as municipalities',[54] even 'constitutionally independent' authorities.[55]

The best formulation of this maximalist approach was given in *Foster*.[56] Was the 'British Gas Corporation'—a statutory corporation for developing and maintaining gas supply—part of the British 'State'? The Court held this to be the case. Vertical direct effect would apply to any body 'whatever its legal form, which has been made responsible, pursuant to a measure adopted by the State, *for providing a public service under the control of the State and has for that purpose special powers* beyond those which result from the normal rules applicable in relations between individuals'.[57] This wide definition of the State consequently covers *private* bodies endowed with *public* functions.

This functional definition of the State, however, in turn suggested that only 'public acts'; that is: acts adopted in pursuit of a public function, would be covered. Yet there are situations where the State acts horizontally like a private person: it might conclude private contracts and employ private personnel. Would these 'private actions' be covered by the doctrine of vertical direct effect?

In *Marshall*, the plaintiff argued that the UK had not properly implemented the Equal Treatment Directive. But could an *employee* of the South-West Hampshire Area Health Authority invoke the direct effect of a directive against this State authority in this horizontal situation? The British government argued that direct effect would only apply:

> against a Member State *qua* public authority and not against a Member State *qua* employer ... As an employer a State is no different from a private employer ... [I]t would not therefore be proper to put persons employed by the State in a better position than those who are employed by a private employer.[58]

This was an excellent argument, but the Court would have none of it. According to the Court, an individual could rely on a directive as against the State

---

[54] *Costanzo SpA v Comune di Milano*, Case 103/88 [1989] ECR 1839, para. 31 (emphasis added).

[55] *Johnston v Chief Constable of the Royal Ulster Constabulary*, Case 222/84 [1986] ECR 1651, para. 49.

[56] *Foster and others v British Gas*, Case C-188/89 [1990] ECR I-3313.

[57] Ibid., para. 20 (emphasis added). For a more recent confirmation of that test, see *Farrell*, Case C-413/15, EU:C:2017:745.

[58] *Marshall*, Case 152/84 (n. 44), para. 43.

'regardless of the capacity in which the latter is acting, whether employer or public authority'.[59]

Vertical direct effect would thus not only apply to *private* parties exercising public functions, but also to public authorities engaged in *private* activities.[60] This double extension of the doctrine of vertical direct effect can be criticized for treating similar situations dissimilarly. For it creates a discriminatory limitation to the no-horizontal-direct-effect rule. However, the Court has recently confirmed that both extensions are an integral result of the *Foster* doctrine.[61]

4. Indirect Effects through National and European Law

Norms can have direct and indirect effects. A European provision lacking direct effect may still have certain indirect effects in the national legal orders. The lack of direct effect simply means that the norm cannot itself—that is *directly*—be invoked. However, European law might still have indirect effects in the national legal orders. For the European Court has created a general duty on national courts (and administrations) to interpret national law as far as possible in the light of all European law. This doctrine of consistent interpretation applies to all sources of European law.[62] However, the doctrine has been mainly developed in the context of directives, and many of the cases will thus refer to this particular Union instrument here.

(a) Consistent Interpretation of National Law

The doctrine of consistent interpretation was given an elaborate definition in *Von Colson*:

---

[59] Ibid., para. 49.   [60] Ibid., para. 51.

[61] *Farrell*, Case C-413/15 (n. 57), where the Court was asked whether the traditional *Foster* definition consisted of two cumulative or two alternative criteria; and the Court expressly clarified that the latter was the case (ibid., esp. para. 33).

[62] In the—brilliant—summary of Advocate General Tizzano in *Mangold*, Case C-144/04 (n. 30), para. 117: 'It must first be recalled that the duty of consistent interpretation is one of the "structural" effects of [European] law which, together with the more "invasive" device of direct effect, enables national law to be brought into line with the substance and aims of [European] law. Because it is structural in nature, the duty applies with respect to all sources of [European] law, whether constituted by primary or secondary legislation, and whether embodied in acts whose legal effects are binding or not. Even in the case of recommendations, the Court has held, "national courts *are bound* to take [them] into consideration in order to decide disputes submitted to them"'.

[T]he Member States' obligation arising from a Directive to achieve the result envisaged by the Directive and their duty under Article [4(3) TEU] to take all appropriate measures, whether general or particular, to ensure the fulfilment of that obligation, is binding on all the authorities of Member States including, for matters within their jurisdiction, the courts. It follows that, in applying the national law, in particular the provisions of a national law specifically introduced in order to implement [a Directive], national courts are required to interpret their national law in the light of the wording and the purpose of the directive in order to achieve the result referred to in the third paragraph of Article [288].[63]

The duty of consistent interpretation is a duty to give effect to a directive by indirect means. Where a national legislator has failed to implement a directive, the task will be (partly) transferred to the national judiciary. National courts are here under an obligation to 'implement' the directive judicially through a 'European' interpretation of national law. Importantly, however, the duty of consistent interpretation only starts applying *after* the implementation period of the directive has passed.[64]

The duty of consistent interpretation thereby applies regardless of 'whether the [national] provisions in question *were adopted before or after the directive*'.[65] The duty to interpret national law as far as possible in the light of European law also extends to all national law—irrespective of whether the national law was intended to implement the directive. However, where domestic law had been specifically enacted to implement the directive, the national courts must even operate under the particularly strong presumption 'that the Member State, following its exercise of the discretion afforded to it under that provision, had the intention of fulfilling entirely the obligations arising from the directive'.[66]

The duty of consistent interpretation may thus lead to the *indirect* implementation of a directive. For it can *indirectly* impose new obligations—both

---

[63] *Von Colson and Elisabeth Kamann v Land Nordrhein-Westfalen*, Case 14/83 [1984] ECR 1891, para. 26. Because this paragraph was so important in defining the duty of consistent interpretation, it is sometimes referred to as the '*Von Colson* principle'.

[64] National courts are not required to interpret their national law in the light of Union law *before* (!) the expiry of the implementation deadline, see *Adeneler and others v Ellinikos Organismos Galaktos (ELOG)*, Case C-212/04 [2006] ECR I-6057.

[65] *Marleasing v La Comercial Internacional de Alimentatión*, Case C-106/89 [1990] ECR I-4135, para. 8 (emphasis added).

[66] *Bernhard Pfeiffer et al. v Deutsches Rotes Kreuz, Kreisverband Walshut eV*, Joined Cases C-397–403/01 [2004] ECR I-8835, para. 112.

vertically and horizontally. An illustration of this horizontal *indirect* effect of directives can be seen in *Webb*.[67] The case concerned a claim by Mrs Webb against her employer. The latter had hired the plaintiff to replace a pregnant co-worker during her maternity leave. Two weeks after she had started work, Mrs Webb discovered that she was pregnant herself, and was dismissed for that reason. She brought proceedings before the Industrial Tribunal, pleading sex discrimination. The Industrial Tribunal rejected this on the ground that the reason for her dismissal had not been her sex but her inability to fulfil the primary task for which she had been recruited. The case went on appeal to the (then) British House of Lords, which confirmed the interpretation of national law but nonetheless harboured doubts about Britain's European obligations under the Equal Treatment Directive. On a preliminary reference, the European Court indeed found that there was sex discrimination under the Directive and that the fact that Mrs Webb had been employed to replace another employee was irrelevant.[68] On receipt of the preliminary ruling, the House of Lords was thus required to change its previous interpretation of national law. Mrs Webb *won* a right, while her employer *lost* the right to dismiss her.

The doctrine of indirect effect here changed the horizontal relations between two private parties; and the duty of consistent interpretation has consequently been said to amount to 'de facto (horizontal) direct effect of the directive'.[69] This de facto horizontal effect is, however, an *indirect* effect. For it operates through the medium of national law.

Are there limits to the indirect effect of directives through the doctrine of consistent interpretation? The duty is very demanding: national courts are required to interpret their national law '*as far as possible, in the light of the wording and the purpose of the directive*'.[70] But what will 'as far as possible' mean? Should national courts be required to behave as if they were the national legislature? This might seriously undermine the (relatively) passive place reserved for judiciaries in many national constitutional orders. And the European legal order has therefore only asked a national court to adjust its interpretation of national law 'in so far as it is given discretion to do so *under national law*'.[71] The European Court thus accepts that there exist established national judicial methodologies and has permitted national courts to

---

[67] *Webb v EMO Air Cargo*, Case C-32/93, [1994] ECR I-3567.
[68] Ibid., paras 26–8.
[69] See Prechal, *Directives in EC Law* (n. 41), 211.
[70] *Marleasing*, Case C-106/89 (n. 65), para. 8 (emphasis added).
[71] *Von Colson*, Case 14/83 (n. 63), para. 28 (emphasis added).

limit themselves to 'the application of interpretative methods recognised by national law'.[72] National courts are not obliged to 'invent' or 'import' novel interpretative methods.[73] However, within the discretion given to the judiciary under national law, the European doctrine of consistent interpretation requires the referring court 'to do whatever lies within its jurisdiction, having regard to the whole body of rules of national law'.[74]

But there are also European limits to the duty of consistent interpretation. The Court has clarified that the duty 'is limited by the general principles of law which form part of [European] law and in particular the principles of legal certainty and non-retroactivity'.[75] This has been taken to imply that the indirect effect of directives cannot aggravate the criminal liability of a private party, as criminal law is subject to particularly strict rules of interpretation.[76] But more importantly, the Court recognizes that the clear and unambiguous wording of a national provision constitutes an absolute limit to its interpretation.[77] National courts are thus not required to interpret national law *contra legem*.[78] The duty of consistent interpretation would find a boundary in the clear wording of a provision. In giving indirect effect to Union law, national courts are therefore not required to stretch the medium of national law beyond breaking point. They are only required to *interpret* the text—and not to *amend* it! The latter continues to be the task of the national legislatures—and not the national judiciaries.

The indirect horizontal effect of European law is consequently *limited* through the medium of national law. The duty of consistent interpretation is therefore a milder incursion on the legislative powers of the Member States than the doctrine of horizontal *direct* effect. This result has, however, been put into question by a second development with regard to the doctrine of indirect effect.

---

[72] *Pfeiffer*, Joined Cases C-397–403/01 (n. 66), para. 116.

[73] See M. Klammert, 'Judicial Implementation of Directives and Anticipatory Indirect Effect: Connecting the Dots' (2006) 43 *Common Market Law Review* 1251 at 1259. For the opposite view, see Prechal, *Directives in EC Law* (n. 41), 213.

[74] *Pfeiffer*, Joined Cases C-397–403/01 (n. 66), para. 118.

[75] *Kolpinghuis*, Case 80/86 (n. 43), para. 13.

[76] *Arcaro*, Case C-168/95 [1996] ECR I-4705.

[77] *Kücükdeveci v Swedex*, Case C-555/07 [2010] ECR I-365, para. 49.

[78] *Adeneler v Ellinikos*, Case C-212/04 (n. 64), para. 110: 'It is true that the obligation on a national court to refer to the content of a directive when interpreting and applying the relevant rules of domestic law is limited by general principles of law, particularly those of legal certainty and non-retroactivity, and that obligation cannot serve as the basis for an interpretation of national law *contra legem*.'

(b) Indirect Effects Through EU Primary Law

The European Court has established a—second—avenue to promote the indirect effect of directives. Instead of mediating them through *national* law, it indirectly translates their content into European law. How so? The way the Court has achieved this has been to capitalize on the general principles of European law, and in particular: EU fundamental rights. For the latter may—as primary Union law—have horizontal direct effect.[79]

This new avenue was opened in *Mangold*.[80] The case concerned the German law on Part-Time Working and Fixed-Term Contracts. It permitted fixed-term employment contracts if the worker had reached the age of 52. However, the German law seemed to violate an EU directive: Directive 2000/78 establishing a general framework for equal treatment in employment and occupation adopted to combat discrimination in the workplace. For according to the Directive, Member States could only establish differences in the workplace on grounds of age if they were objectively and reasonably justified by a legitimate aim. In the present case, a German law firm had hired Mr Mangold, then aged 56, on a fixed-term employment contract; and Mangold claimed that the German law violated Directive 2000/78, as a disproportionate discrimination on grounds of age.

The argument was not only problematic because it was raised in *civil* proceedings between two *private* parties, which seemed to exclude the horizontal *direct* effect of Article 6(1) of the Directive. More importantly, since the implementation period of the Directive had not yet expired, even the horizontal *indirect* effect of the Directive could not be achieved through a 'Union-consistent' interpretation of *national* law. Yet having found that the national law indeed violated the *substance* of the Directive,[81] the Court was out to create a new way to review the legality of the German law. Instead of using the Directive as such—directly or indirectly—it found a fundamental EU human right that stood *behind* the Directive. That right was the principle of non-discrimination on the ground of age; and it was *that* general principle that would bind the Member States when implementing European law. From there, the Court reasoned as follows:

> [O]bservance of the general principle of equal treatment, in particular in respect of age, cannot as such be conditional upon the expiry of the period allowed the Member States for the transposition of a directive intended to lay down a general

---

[79]   On the normative quality of primary Union law, see Section 2 earlier.
[80]   *Mangold v Helm*, Case C-144/04 [2005] ECR I-9981.
[81]   Ibid., para. 65.

framework for combating discrimination on the grounds of age ... In those circumstances it is the responsibility of the national court, hearing a dispute involving the principle of non-discrimination in respect of age, to provide, in a case
within its jurisdiction, the legal protection which individuals derive from the
rules of [European] law and to ensure that those rules are fully effective, setting
aside any provision of national law which may conflict with that law. Having
regard to all the foregoing, the reply to be given to the [national court] must be
that [European] law and, more particularly, *Article 6(1) of Directive 2000/78, must
be interpreted as precluding a provision of domestic law such as that at issue in
the main proceedings which authorises, without restriction, unless there is a close
connection with an earlier contract of employment of indefinite duration concluded
with the same employer, the conclusion of fixed-term contracts of employment once
the worker has reached the age of 52.*[82]

This judgment has been—very—controversial. The regular use of EU primary
law as the medium for secondary law is dangerous 'since the subsidiary applicability of the principles not only gives rise to a lack of legal certainty but
also distorts the nature of the system of sources, converting typical [Union]
acts into merely decorative rules which may be easily replaced by the general
principles'.[83] Put succinctly, if a *special* directive is adopted to make a *general*
principle sufficiently precise, how can the latter have direct effect while the
former has not? Yet to the chagrin of some,[84] the *Mangold* ruling was confirmed *and* consolidated.[85] The indirect effect of directives via the medium
of EU primary law has thus become a second route to create the indirect
horizontal effect of directives (Figure 5.3).

Conclusion

For a norm to be a *legal* norm it must be enforceable.[86] The very questioning
of the direct effect of European law was thus an 'infant disease' of a young
legal order.[87] 'But now that [European] law has reached maturity, direct effect

---

[82] Ibid., paras 76–8 (emphasis added).

[83] Advocate General Ruiz-Jarabo Colomer in *Michaeler et al. v Amt für sozialen Arbeitsschutz
Bozen,* Joined Cases C-55 and 56/07 [2008] ECR I-3135, para. 21.

[84] For the Danish Constitutional Court's opposition here, see Chapter 6, Section 4(a).

[85] *Kücükdeveci v Swedex,* Case C-555/07 [2010] ECR I-365.

[86] On the difference between (merely) 'moral' and (enforceable) 'legal' norms, see H. L. A. Hart,
The Concept of Law (Clarendon Press, 1997).

[87] Pescatore, 'The Doctrine of "Direct Effect"' (n. 31).

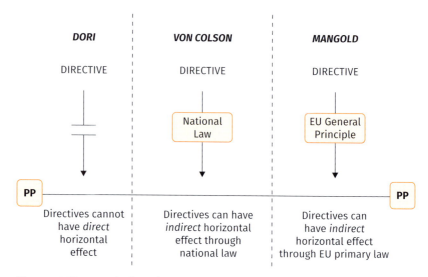

Figure 5.3 Horizontal effect of directives between private parties (PP)

should be taken for granted, as a normal incident of an advanced constitutional order.'[88]

The evolution of the doctrine of direct effect, discussed in this chapter, mirrors this maturation. Today's test for the direct effect of European law is an extremely lenient test. A provision has direct effect, where it is 'unconditional' and thus 'sufficiently clear and precise'—three conditions that probe whether a norm can be enforced in court. All sources of European law have been considered capable of producing law with direct effects; and this direct effect normally applies vertically as well as horizontally.

The exception to this rule is the 'directive'. For directives, the Union legal order prefers their indirect effects. The directive thus represents a form of 'background' or 'indirect' European law.[89] Yet, as we saw earlier, an unimplemented or wrongly implemented directive can come to the fore after its implementation period has passed and also have direct effects. These direct effects will, however, only be vertical direct effects. For the Court has insisted on the 'no-horizontal-direct-effect' rule for EU directives.

[88] A. Dashwood, 'From *Van Duyn* to *Mangold* via *Marshall*: Reducing Direct Effect to Absurdity' [2006/7] 9 *Cambridge Yearbook of European Legal Studies* 81.

[89] *Gibraltar v Council*, Case C-298/89 [1993] ECR I-3605, para. 16 (emphasis added): 'normally a form of *indirect regulatory or legislative measure*'.

6

(Legal) Primacy

Introduction

Since European law is directly applicable in the Member States, it must be recognized alongside national law by national authorities. And since European law may have direct effect, it might come into conflict with national law in a specific situation.

Where two legislative wills come into conflict, courts need to know *how* these conflicts are to be resolved. The resolution of legislative conflicts here requires a hierarchy of norms. Modern federal States typically resolve conflicts between federal and State legislation in favour of the former: federal law is supreme over State law.[1] This *centralized* solution has become so engrained in our constitutional mentalities that we tend to forget that the *decentralized* solution is also possible: local law may reign supreme over central law.[2] Each

---

[1] Art. VI(2) of the US Constitution, e.g., states: 'This Constitution, and the Laws of the United States which shall be made in pursuance thereof; and all treaties made, or which shall be made, under the Authority of the United States, *shall be the supreme Law of the Land*.'

[2] For a long time, the 'subsidiarity solution' structured federal relationships during the Middle Ages. Its constitutional spirit is best preserved in the old legal proverb: 'Town law breaks county law, county law breaks common law.' In the event of a legislative conflict, primacy was thus given to the rule of the *smaller* political entity.

federal order must thus determine which law prevails. The simplest primacy format is one that is absolute: all law from one legal order is superior to all law from the other. Absolute primacy may however be given to the legal system of the smaller *or* the bigger political community. Between these two extremes lies a range of possible nuances.

When the Union was born, the European Treaties did not expressly mention the primacy (or 'supremacy') of European law.[3] Did this mean that primacy was a matter to be determined by each national legal order; or was there a *Union* doctrine of primacy? We shall see in this chapter that there are *two* perspectives on the primacy question. According to the *European* perspective, all Union law prevails over all national law. This 'absolute' view is not, however, shared by the Member States. According to the *national* perspective, the primacy of European law is relative. National challenges to the absolute primacy of European law are thereby traditionally expressed in two contexts. First, some Member States—in particular their supreme courts—have fought a battle over human rights within the Union legal order. They claim that European law cannot violate *national* fundamental rights. The most famous battle over the primacy of European law in this context was the conflict between the European Court of Justice and the German Constitutional Court.[4] A similar contestation occurred in a second context: *ultra vires* control. In denying the Union an unlimited competence to determine the scope of its own competences,[5] Member States here insisted that they have the last word with regard to the competence limits of the Union.

This chapter analyses the primacy doctrine within the Union legal order in four steps. We shall start with the European doctrine of absolute primacy

---

[3] The (failed) Constitutional Treaty *would* have added an express provision (Art. I-6): 'The Constitution and law adopted by the institutions of the Union in exercising competences conferred on it shall have primacy over the law of the Member States.' However, the provision was not taken over by the Lisbon Treaty. Yet the Lisbon Treaty has added Declaration 17 which states: 'The Conference recalls that, in accordance with well settled case law of the Court of Justice of the European Union, the Treaties and the law adopted by the Union on the basis of the Treaties have primacy over the law of Member States, under the conditions laid down by the said case law.'

[4] The following chapter concentrates on the jurisprudence of the German Constitutional Court. The latter has long been the most pressing and—perhaps—prestigious national court in the Union legal order. For the reaction of the French supreme courts, see R. Mehdi, 'French Supreme Courts and European Union Law: Between Historical Compromise and Accepted Loyalty' (2011) 48 *Common Market Law Review* 439. For the views of the Central European constitutional courts, see W. Sadurski, '"*Solange*, Chapter 3": Constitutional Courts in Central Europe—Democracy—European Union' (2008) 14 *European Law Journal* 1.

[5] On the—strange—(German) notion of *Kompetenz-Kompetenz*, see R. Schütze, *European Union Law* (Cambridge University Press, 2018), ch. 2, section 2(a).

in Section 1, before looking at the effect of the principle on national law in Section 2. The subsequent sections, by contrast, analyse the national perspective on the primacy principle in the form of two challenges to the primacy of European law. Section 3 explores the national claim asserting the relative primacy of European law in the context of fundamental human rights. Section 4 extends this analysis to the contested question of who is the ultimate arbiter of the scope of the Union's competences.

1. The European Perspective: Absolute Primacy

The strong dualist traditions within some Member States in 1958 posed a serious legal threat to the unity of the Union legal order.[6] Within dualist States, the status of European law is seen as depending on the national act 'transposing' the European Treaties. Where this was a parliamentary act, any subsequent parliamentary acts could—expressly or impliedly—repeal the national transposition law. This follows from the classic doctrine of parliamentary sovereignty: an 'old' parliament cannot bind a 'new' one. Any 'newer' parliamentary act will thus theoretically prevail over the 'older' European Union (transposition) act. But the primacy of European law could even be threatened in monist States, where a national constitution could—theoretically—stand above European law.

 Would the European legal order insist that its law was to prevail over national law, including national constitutional law? The Court of Justice did just that in a series of foundational cases.

(a) Primacy over Internal Laws of the Member States

Frightened by the decentralized solution to the primacy issue, the Court centralized the question of primacy quickly and turned it into a foundational principle of European law. In *Costa v ENEL*,[7] the European judiciary was asked whether Italian legislation adopted *after* 1958 could prevail over the original Treaties. The litigation involved an unsettled energy bill owed by Costa to the Italian National Electricity Board. The latter had been created by the 1962 Electricity Nationalization Act, which was challenged by the plaintiff as a violation of the 1957 EEC Treaty. The Italian dualist tradition responded that the EU Treaties—like ordinary international law—had been transposed

---

 [6] C. Sasse, 'The Common Market: Between International and Municipal Law' (1965–6) 75 *Yale Law Journal* 696–753.
 [7] *Costa v ENEL*, Case 6/64 [1964] ECR 585.

by national legislation that could—following international law logic—be derogated from by subsequent national legislation.

Could the Member States thus unilaterally determine the status of European law in their national legal order? The Court famously rejected this reading and distanced itself from the international law thesis:

> By contrast with ordinary international treaties, the E[U] Treaty has created its own legal system which, on the entry into force of the Treaty, became an integral part of the legal systems of the Member States and which their courts are bound to apply ... The integration into the laws of each Member State of provisions which derive from the [Union], and more generally the terms and the spirit of the Treaty, make it impossible for the States, as a corollary, to accord precedence to a unilateral and subsequent measure over a legal system accepted by them on a basis of reciprocity. Such a measure cannot therefore be inconsistent with that legal system. The *executive force* of [European] law cannot vary from one State to another in deference to subsequent domestic laws, without jeopardizing the attainment of the objectives of the Treaty ... It follows from all these observations that the law stemming from the Treaty, an independent source of law, could not, because of its special and original nature, be overridden by domestic legal provisions, however framed, without being deprived of its character as [European] law and without the legal basis of the [Union] itself being called into question.[8]

European law ought to be supreme over national law, since its *executive force* must not vary from one State to another. And, since the primacy of Union law could not be derived from classic international law,[9] the Court had to declare the Union legal order autonomous from ordinary international law.

---

[8]   Ibid., 593–4.

[9]   Some legal scholars refer to the 'supremacy' of international law vis-à-vis national law (see F. Morgenstern, 'Judicial Practice and the Supremacy of International Law' (1950) 27 *British Yearbook of International Law* 42). However, the concept of supremacy is here used in an imprecise way. Legal supremacy stands for the priority of one norm over another. For this, two norms must conflict and, therefore, form part of the same legal order. However, classic international law is based on the sovereignty of States and that implies a dualist relation with national law. The dualist veil protected national laws from being overridden by norms adopted by such 'supranational' authorities as the Catholic Church or the Holy Roman Empire. When a State opens up to international law, this 'monistic' stance is a *national* choice. International law as such has never imposed monism on a State. Reference to the international law doctrine of *pacta sunt servanda* will hardly help here. The fact that a State cannot invoke its internal law to justify a breach of international obligations is not supremacy. Behind the doctrine of *pacta sunt servanda* stands the concept of legal responsibility: a State cannot—without legal responsibility—escape its international obligations. The duality of internal and international law is thereby maintained: the former cannot affect the latter (as the latter cannot affect the former).

How supreme was European law? The fact that the European *Treaties* were to prevail over national *legislation* did not automatically imply that *all* secondary law would prevail over *all* national law. Would the Court accept a 'nuanced' solution for certain national norms, such as national constitutional law? The European Court never accepted the relative nature of the primacy doctrine. This was clarified in *Internationale Handelsgesellschaft*.[10] A German administrative court had doubts that European legislation could violate fundamental rights as granted by the German Constitution and raised this very question with the European Court of Justice. Were the fundamental principles of national constitutions, including human rights, beyond the scope of European primacy? The Court disagreed:

> Recourse to the legal rules or concepts of national law in order to judge the validity of measures adopted by the institutions of the [Union] would have an adverse effect on the uniformity and efficiency of [Union] law. The validity of such measures can only be judged in the light of [Union] law.[11]

The validity of Union laws could *not* thus be affected—even by the most fundamental norms within the Member States. The Court's vision of the primacy of European law over national law was an absolute one: 'The whole of [European] law prevails over the whole of national law.'[12]

(b) Primacy over International Treaties of the Member States

While the European doctrine of primacy had quickly emerged with regard to national legislation,[13] its extension to international agreements of the Member States was much slower. From the very beginning, the Treaties here

---

[10] *Internationale Handelsgesellschaft mbH v Einfuhr- und Vorratsstelle für Getreide und Futtermittel*, Case 11/70 [1970] ECR 1125.

[11] Ibid., para. 3.

[12] R. Kovar, 'The Relationship between Community Law and National Law' in EC Commission (ed.), *Thirty Years of Community Law* (EC Commission, 1981), 109 at 112–13.

[13] On the establishment of the *social* acceptance of the doctrine, see K. Alter, *Establishing the Supremacy of European Law: The Making of an International Rule of Law in Europe* (Oxford University Press, 2001).

recognized an express exception to the primacy of European law. According to Article 351 TFEU:

> The rights and obligations arising from agreements concluded before 1 January 1958 or, for acceding States, before the date of their accession, between one or more Member States on the one hand, and one or more third countries on the other, shall not be affected by the provisions of the Treaties.[14]

Article 351 here codifies the 'primacy' of *prior* international agreements of the Member States over conflicting European law. In the event of a conflict between the two, it was European law that could be disapplied *within the national legal orders*. Indeed, Article 351 'would not achieve its purpose if it did not imply a duty on the part of the institutions of the [Union] not to impede the performance of the obligations of Member States which stem from a prior agreement'.[15] This was a severe incursion into the integrity of the European legal order, and as such had to be interpreted restrictively.[16]

But would there be internal or external limits to the primacy of prior international treaties of the Member States? The Court has clarified that there existed internal limits to the provision. Article 351(1) would only allow Member States to implement their *obligations* towards *third* states.[17] Thus, Member States could not rely on Article 351 to enforce their rights; nor could they rely on the provision to fulfil their international obligations between themselves.

These internal limitations are complemented by external limitations. The Court clarified their existence in *Kadi*.[18] While admitting that Article 351 would justify derogations from primary Union law, the Court also insisted

---

[14]   Paragraph 1. The provision continues (para. 2): 'To the extent that such agreements are not compatible with the Treaties, the Member State or States concerned shall take all appropriate steps to eliminate the incompatibilities established. Member States shall, where necessary, assist each other to this end and shall, where appropriate, adopt a common attitude.'

[15]   *Attorney General v Burgoa*, Case 812/79 [1980] ECR 2787, para. 9. This was confirmed in *Criminal Proceedings against Jean-Claude Levy*, Case C-158/91 [1993] ECR I-4287.

[16]   *The Queen v Secretary of State for Home Department, ex p. Evans Medical Ltd and Macfarlan Smith Ltd*, Case C-324/93 [1995] ECR I-563, para. 32.

[17]   *Commission v Italy*, Case 10/61 [1962] ECR 1, 10–11: '[T]he terms "rights and obligations" in Article [351] refer, as regards the "rights", to the rights of third countries and, as regards the "obligations", to the obligations of Member States and that, by virtue of the principles of international law, by assuming a new obligation which is incompatible with rights held under a prior treaty, a State ipso facto gives up the exercise of these rights to the extent necessary for the performance of its new obligation.'

[18]   *Kadi and Al Barakaat International Foundation v Council and Commission*, Case C-402/05P [2008] ECR I-6351. The facts of the case were discussed in Chapter 4, Section 2.

that the provision 'cannot, however, be understood to authorize any derogation from the principles of liberty, democracy and respect for human rights
and fundamental freedoms enshrined in Article [2] [T]EU as a foundation
of the Union'.[19] In the opinion of the Court, 'Article [351 TFEU] may in no
circumstances permit any challenge to the principles that form part of the
very foundations of the [Union] legal order'.[20] The Union's constitutional core
constituted a limit to the primacy of prior international treaties concluded by
the Member States.

Should the—limited—application of Article 351 TFEU be extended, by
analogy, to post-1958 international agreements concluded by the Member
States? The main constitutional thrust behind the argument is that it protects
the effective exercise of the treaty-making powers of the Member States. For
'otherwise the Member States could not conclude any international treaty
without running the risk of a subsequent conflict with [European] law'.[21]
This idea has been criticized: there would be no reason why the 'normal'
constitutional principles characterizing the relationship between European
law and unilateral national acts should not also apply to subsequently
concluded international agreements.[22] A middle position has proposed
limiting the analogous application of Article 351 to situations where the
conflict between post-accession international treaties of Member States and
subsequently adopted European legislation was 'objectively unforeseeable'
and could not therefore be expected.[23]

None of the proposals to extend Article 351 by analogy have been mirrored in the jurisprudence of the European Court of Justice.[24] The Court
has unconditionally upheld the primacy of European law over international
agreements concluded by the Member States after 1958 (or their date of
accession).

In the light of the potential international responsibility of the Member
States, is this a fair constitutional solution? Should it make a difference
whether a national rule is adopted by means of a unilateral measure or

---

[19] Ibid., para. 303.   [20] Ibid., para. 304.

[21] E. Pache and J. Bielitz, 'Das Verhältnis der EG zu den völkerrechtlichen Verträgen ihrer
Mitgliedstaaten' (2006) 41 *Europarecht* 316 at 327 (author's translation).

[22] E. Bülow, 'Die Anwendung des Gemeinschaftsrechts im Verhältnis zu Drittländern' in A.
Clauder (ed.), *Einführung in die Rechtsfragen der europäischen Integration* (Europa-Union Verlag,
1972), 52 at 54.

[23] E.-U. Petersmann, 'Artikel 234' in H. von der Groeben, J. Thiesing, and C.-D. Ehlermann
(eds), *Kommentar zum EWG-Vertrag* (Nomos, 1991), 5725 at 5731 (para. 6).

[24] See *Commission v Belgium* & *Luxembourg*, Joined Cases C-176 and 177/97 [1998] ECR
I-3557.

by means of an international agreement with a third State? Constitutional solutions still need to be found to solve the Member States' dilemma of choosing between the Scylla of liability under the European Treaties and the Charybdis of international responsibility for breach of contract. Should the Union legal order, therefore, be given an *ex ante* authorization mechanism for Member States' international agreements? Or, should the Union share financial responsibility for breach of contract with the Member State concerned? These are difficult constitutional questions. They await future constitutional answers.

2. Primacy's 'Executive' Nature: Disapplication, not Invalidation

What are the legal consequences of the primacy of European law over conflicting national law? Must a national court 'hold such provisions inapplicable to the extent to which they are incompatible with [European] law', or must it 'declare them void'?[25] This question concerns the constitutional effect of the primacy doctrine in the Member States.

The classic answer to the question is found in *Simmenthal II*.[26] The issue raised in the national proceedings was this: 'What consequences flow from the direct applicability of a provision of [Union] law in the event of incompatibility with a subsequent legislative provision of a Member State?'[27] Within the Italian legal order, national legislation could be *repealed* solely by Parliament or the Constitutional Court. Would lower national courts thus have to wait until this happened and, in the meantime, apply national laws that violated Union laws?

Unsurprisingly, the European Court rejected such a reading. Appealing to the 'very foundations of the [Union]', national courts were under a direct obligation to give immediate effect to European law. The primacy of European law meant that 'rules of [European] law must be fully and uniformly applied in all the Member States from the date of their entry into force and for so long as they continue in force'.[28] But did this mean that the national court had to *repeal* the national law? According to one view, primacy indeed

---

[25] This very question was raised in *Firma Gebrüder Luck v Hauptzollamt Köln-Rheinau*, Case 34/67 [1968] ECR 245.

[26] *Amministrazione delle Finanze dello Stato v Simmenthal SpA*, Case 106/77 [1978] ECR 629.

[27] Ibid., para. 13.   [28] Ibid., para. 14.

meant that national courts must declare conflicting national laws void. European law would 'break' national law.[29] Yet the Court preferred a milder—second—view:

> [I]n accordance with the *principle of precedence* of [European] law, the relationship between provisions of the Treaty and directly applicable measures of the institutions on the one hand and the national law of the Member States on the other is such that those provisions and measures not only by their entry into force render *automatically inapplicable* any conflicting provision of current national law but—in so far as they are an integral part of, and take precedence in, the legal order applicable in the territory of each of the Member States—also preclude the valid adoption of new legislative measures to the extent to which they would be incompatible with [European] provisions.[30]

Where national measures conflicted with European law, the primacy of European law would thus not render them void, but only 'inapplicable'. Not 'invalidation' but 'disapplication' was required of national courts, where European laws came into conflict with pre-existing national laws. Yet, in the above passage, the effect of the primacy doctrine appeared stronger in relation to *future* national legislation. Here, the Court said that the primacy of European law would 'preclude the *valid adoption* of new legislative measures to the extent to which they would be incompatible with [European] provisions'.[31] Was this to imply that national legislators were not even *competent* to adopt national laws that would run counter to *existing* European law? Were these national laws void *ab initio*?[32]

In *Ministero delle Finanze v IN.CO.GE.'90*,[33] the Commission picked up this second prong of the *Simmenthal* ruling and argued that 'a Member State has *no power whatever to [subsequently] adopt* a fiscal provision that is incompatible with [European] law, with the result that such a provision . . . must be treated

---

[29] This is the very title of a German monograph by E. Grabitz, *Gemeinschaftsrecht bricht nationales Recht* (L. Appel, 1966). This position was shared by Hallstein: '[T]he supremacy of [European] law means essentially two things: its rules take precedence irrespective of the level of the two orders at which the conflict occurs, and further, [European] law *not only invalidates previous national law but also limits subsequent national legislation*' (W. Hallstein quoted in Sasse, 'The Common Market' (n. 6), 696–753 at 717 (emphasis added)).

[30] *Simmenthal*, Case 106/77 (n. 26), para. 17 (emphasis added).

[31] Ibid., para. 17 (emphasis added).

[32] A. Barav, 'Les Effets du Droit Communautaire Directement Applicable' (1978) 14 *Cahiers de Droit Européen* 265 at 275–6. See also Grabitz, *Gemeinschaftsrecht*, and Hallstein, quoted in Sasse (n. 29).

[33] *Ministero delle Finanze v IN.CO.GE.'90 Srl and others*, Joined Cases C-10–22/97 [1998] ECR I-6307.

as *non-existent*.[34] But the European Court of Justice disagreed with this inter-pretation. Pointing out that *Simmenthal* 'did not draw any distinction between pre-existing and subsequently adopted national law',[35] it held that the incom-patibility of subsequently adopted rules of national law with European law did not have the effect of rendering these rules non-existent.[36] National courts were thus only under an obligation to disapply a conflicting provision of national law—be it prior *or* subsequent to the Union law.

What will this tell us about the nature of the EU primacy doctrine? It tells us that the primacy doctrine is about the 'executive force' of European law. The Union legal order, while integrated with the national legal orders, is not a 'uni-tary' legal order. European law leaves the 'validity' of national norms untouched; and will not negate the underlying legislative competence of the Member States. The primacy principle is thus not addressed to the State legislatures, but to the national executive and judicial branches. (And while in some situations the national *legislator* will be required to amend or repeal national provisions that give rise to legal uncertainty,[37] this additional obligation is not a direct result of the primacy doctrine but derives from Article 4(3) TEU.)[38] The executive force of European law thus generally leaves the normative validity of national law intact. National courts are not obliged to 'break' national law. They must only not apply it when in conflict with European law in a specific case.

This milder primacy doctrine has a number of advantages. First, some national legal orders may not grant their (lower) courts the power to invalidate parliamentary laws. The question of who can invalidate national laws is thus left to the national legal order.[39] Second, comprehensive national laws must only

---

[34] Ibid., para. 18 (emphasis added).

[35] Arguably, the *Simmenthal* Court had indeed not envisaged two different consequences for the primacy principle. While para. 17 (see text earlier and n. 30) appears to make a distinction depending on whether national legislation existed or not, the operative part of the judgment referred to both variants. It stated that a national court should refuse of its own motion to 'apply any conflicting provision of national legislation' (*Simmenthal*, dictum).

[36] *IN.CO.GE.'90*, Cases C-10–22/97 (n. 33), paras 20–1.

[37] *Commission v France*, Case 167/73 [1974] ECR 359. The Court now appears generally to assume that the presence of a national provision that conflicts with European law will *ipso facto* 'give ... rise to an ambiguous state of affairs in so far as it leaves persons concerned in a state of uncertainty as to the possibilities available to them relying on [European] law'; see *Commission v Italy*, Case 104/86 [1988] ECR 1799, para. 12.

[38] See e.g. ibid., para. 13.

[39] *Filipiak v Dyrektor Izby Skarbowej w Poznaniu*, Case C-314/08 [2009] ECR I-11049, para. 82: 'Pursuant to the principle of the primacy of [European] law, a conflict between a provision of nation-al law and a directly applicable provision of the Treaty is to be resolved by a national court applying [European] law, if necessary by refusing to apply the conflicting national provision, and not by a declaration that the national provision is invalid, the powers of authorities, courts and tribunals in that regard being a matter to be determined by each Member State.'

be disapplied to the extent to which they conflict with European law.[40] They will remain operable in purely internal situations. Third, once the Union act is repealed, national legislation may become fully operational again.[41]

3. National Challenges I: Fundamental Rights

The European Union is not a federal State in which the sovereignty question is resolved. The European Union is a federal union of States;[42] and each federal union is characterized by a political dualism. Each citizen is indeed a member of *two* political bodies which will compete for loyalty and, sometimes, the 'national' view on a political question may not correspond with the 'European' view on the matter.

What happens when the political views of a Member State clash with that of the federal Union? Controversies over the primacy of federal law are as old as the (modern) idea of federalism.[43] And while the previous sections analysed the European answer to the primacy doctrine, this absolute vision is—unsurprisingly—not shared by all the Member States. There indeed exists a competing national view—or better, national views—on the primacy issue. The extreme version of such a national view could be found in the British European Union Act 2011. The latter unambiguously stated:

> Directly applicable or directly effective EU law (that is, the rights, powers, liabilities, obligations, restrictions, remedies and procedures referred to in section 2(1) of the European Communities Act 1972) falls to be recognised and available in law in the United Kingdom only by virtue of that Act or where it is required to be recognised and available in law by virtue of any other Act.[44]

A milder national perspective, on the other hand, accepts the primacy of European law over national *legislation*; yet the primacy of European law is still relative, since it is granted and limited by national *constitutional* law.

---

[40] B. de Witte, 'Direct Effect, Supremacy and the Nature of the Legal Order' in P. Craig and G. de Búrca (eds), *The Evolution of EU Law* (Oxford University Press, 1999), 177 at 190.

[41] Ibid.

[42] For an extensive discussion of this classification, see R. Schütze, *European Union Law* (n. 5), ch. 2.

[43] R. Schütze, 'Federalism as Constitutional Pluralism: Letter from America' in J. Kommarek and M. Avbelj (eds), *Constitutional Pluralism in the European Union and Beyond* (Hart, 2012), ch. 8.

[44] European Union Act 2011, s. 18.

A first national challenge to the absolute primacy of European law crystallized around *Internationale Handelsgesellschaft*.[45] For, ironically, after the European Court of Justice had given its absolute view on the primacy of European law, the case moved back to the German Constitutional Court and the German court here defined its perspective on the question.[46] Could national constitutional law, especially national fundamental rights, affect the application of European law in the domestic legal order? Famously, the German Constitutional Court rejected the European Court's absolute vision and replaced it with its counter-theory of the *relative* primacy of European law. The reasoning of the German court was as follows: while the German Constitution expressly allowed for the transfer of sovereign powers to the European Union in its Article 24,[47] such a transfer was itself limited by the 'constitutional identity' of the German State. Fundamental constitutional structures were thus beyond the primacy of European law:

> The part of the Constitution dealing with fundamental rights is an *inalienable essential feature of the valid Constitution of the Federal Republic of Germany and one which forms part of the constitutional structure of the Constitution.* Article 24 of the Constitution does not without reservation allow it to be subjected to qualifications. In this, the present state of integration of the [Union] is of crucial importance. The [Union] still lacks ... in particular a codified catalogue of fundamental rights, the substance of which is reliably and unambiguously fixed for the future in the same way as the substance of the Constitution ...
>
> *So long as* this legal certainty, which is not guaranteed merely by the decisions of the European Court of Justice, favourable though these have been to fundamental rights, is not achieved in the course of the further integration of the [Union], the reservation derived from Article 24 of the Constitution applies ... *Provisionally, therefore, in the hypothetical case of a conflict between [European] law and a part of national constitutional law or, more precisely, of the guarantees of fundamental rights in the Constitution, there arises the question of which system of law takes precedence, that is, ousts the other. In this conflict of norms, the guarantee of fundamental rights in the Constitution prevails so long as the competent organs of the [Union] have not removed the conflict of norms in accordance with the Treaty mechanism.*[48]

---

[45]   *Internationale Handelsgesellschaft*, Case 11/70 (n. 10).

[46]   BVerfGE 37, 271 (*Solange I* (*Re Internationale Handelsgesellschaft*)). For an English translation, see [1974] 2 CMLR 540.

[47]   Art. 24(1) of the German Constitution states: 'The Federation may by a law transfer sovereign powers to international organizations.' A new article was subsequently inserted into the German Constitution expressly dealing with the European Union (see Art. 23 German Constitution).

[48]   *Solange I* [1974] 2 CMLR 540 at 550–1 (paras 23–4, emphasis added).

'So long' as the European legal order had not developed an adequate standard of fundamental rights, the German Constitutional Court would 'disapply' European law that conflicted with the fundamental rights guaranteed in the German legal order. There were thus *national* limits to the primacy of European law. However, these national limits were also *relative*, because they depended on the evolution and nature of European law. This was the very essence of the 'so long' formula. For once the Union legal order had developed equivalent human rights guarantees, the German Constitutional Court would no longer challenge the primacy of European law.

The Union legal order did, indeed, subsequently develop extensive human rights bill(s),[49] and the dispute over the primacy doctrine was significantly softened in the aftermath of a second famous European case with a national coda. In *Wünsche Handelsgesellschaft*,[50] the German Constitutional Court not only recognized the creation of 'substantially similar' fundamental right guarantees, it drew a remarkably self-effacing conclusion from this:

> In view of those developments it must be held that, *so long* as the European [Union], and in particular in the case law of the European Court, generally ensures an effective protection of fundamental rights as against the sovereign powers of the [Union] which is to be regarded as substantially similar to the protection of fundamental rights required unconditionally by the Constitution, and in so far as they generally safeguard the essential content of fundamental rights, the Federal Constitutional Court will no longer exercise its jurisdiction to decide on the applicability of secondary [Union] legislation cited as the legal basis for any acts of German courts or authorities within the sovereign jurisdiction of the Federal Republic of Germany, and it will no longer review such legislation by the standard of the fundamental rights contained in the Constitution[.][51]

This judgment became known as '*So-Long II*', for the German Constitutional Court had again recourse to this famous formulation in determining its relationship with European law. But importantly, this time, the 'so long' condition was inverted. The German Court promised not to question the primacy of European law 'so long' as the latter guaranteed substantially similar fundamental rights to those recognized by the German Constitution. This was not an absolute promise to respect the absolute primacy of European law, but

---

[49] On this point, see Chapter 4.
[50] BVerfGE 73, 339 (*Solange II* (*Re Wünsche Handelsgesellschaft*)). For an English translation, see [1987] 3 CMLR 225.
[51] Ibid., 265 (para. 48) (emphasis added).

a result of the Court's own relative primacy doctrine having been fulfilled. *So-Long II* thus only refined the national perspective on the limited primacy of European law in '*So-Long I*'.

4. National Challenges II: Competence Limits

With the constitutional conflict over fundamental rights (temporarily) settled, a second concern emerged: the ever-growing competences of the European Union. Who was to control and limit the scope of European law? Was it enough to have the *European* legislator centrally controlled by the *European* Court of Justice? Or should the national constitutional courts be entitled to a decentralized *ultra vires* review?

The European view on this is crystal clear: national courts cannot disapply—let alone invalidate—European law.[52] Yet, unsurprisingly, this absolute view has not been shared by all Member States. And it was again the German Constitutional Court that set the tone and provided the vocabulary of the academic debate. The *ultra vires* question was at the heart of its (in)famous *Maastricht* Decision to which we must now turn.

(a) Competence Limits I: From '*Maastricht*' to '*Mangold*'

The German Court set out its *ultra vires* doctrine in *Maastricht*.[53] Starting from the premise that the European Treaties must adhere to the principle of conferred powers, the Court found that the Union ought not to be able to extend its own competences. While the EU Treaties allowed for teleological interpretation especially of its general competences, there existed a clear dividing line 'between a legal development within the terms of the Treaties and a making of legal rules which breaks through its boundaries and is not covered by valid Treaty law'.[54] This led to the following conclusion:

> Thus, if European institutions or agencies were to treat or develop the Union Treaty in a way that was no longer covered by the Treaty in the form that is the basis for the Act of Accession, the resultant legislative instruments would

---

[52] *Foto-Frost v Hauptzollamt Lübeck-Ost*, Case 314/85 [1987] ECR 4199.
[53] BVerfGE 89, 155 (*Maastricht* Decision). For an English translation, see [1994] 1 CMLR 57.
[54] Ibid., 105 (para. 98).

not be legally binding within the sphere of German sovereignty. The German state organs would be prevented for constitutional reasons from applying them in Germany. Accordingly the Federal Constitutional Court will review legal instruments of European institutions and agencies to see whether they remain within the limits of the sovereign rights conferred on them or transgress them ...

Whereas a dynamic extension of the existing Treaties has so far been supported on the basis of an open-handed treatment of Article [352] of the [TFEU] as a 'competence to round-off the Treaty' as a whole, and on the basis of considerations relating to the 'implied powers' of the [Union], and of Treaty interpretation as allowing maximum exploitation of [Union] powers ('effet utile'), in future it will have to be noted as regards interpretation of enabling provisions by [Union] institutions and agencies that the Union Treaty as a matter of principle distinguishes between the exercise of a sovereign power conferred for limited purposes and the amending of the Treaty, so that its interpretation may not have effects that are equivalent to an extension of the Treaty. Such an interpretation of enabling rules would not produce any binding effects for Germany.[55]

The German Constitutional Court thus threatened to disapply European law that it considered to have been adopted *ultra vires*.

This national review power was subsequently confirmed; yet, the doctrine was also limited and refined in *Honeywell*.[56] The case resulted from a constitutional complaint that targeted the European Court's ruling in *Mangold*.[57] The plaintiff argued that the European Court's 'discovery' of a European principle that prohibited discrimination on the ground of age was *ultra vires* as it read something into the Treaties that was not there. In its decision, the German Constitutional Court confirmed its relative primacy doctrine. It claimed the power to disapply European law that it considered not to be covered by the principle of conferral. The principle of primacy was thus not unlimited.[58] However, reminiscent of

[55] Ibid., 105 (para. 99).
[56] 2 BvR 2661/06 (*Re Honeywell*). For an English translation, see [2011] 1 CMLR 1067. For a discussion of the case, see M. Paydandeh, 'Constitutional Review of EU Law after *Honeywell*: Contextualizing the Relationship between the German Constitutional Court and the EU Court of Justice' (2011) 48 *Common Market Law Review* 9.
[57] For a discussion of *Mangold*, see Chapter 5, Section 4(b).
[58] *Honeywell* [2011] 1 CMLR 1067 at 1084: 'Unlike the primacy of application of federal law, as provided for by Article 31 of the Basic Law for the German legal system, the primacy of application of Union law cannot be comprehensive.' (It is ironic that this is said by the German Federal(!) Constitutional Court.)

its judicial deference in *So-Long II*, the Court accepted a presumption that the Union would generally act within the scope of its competences:

> If each Member State claimed to be able to decide through their own courts on the validity of legal acts by the Union, the primacy of application could be circumvented in practice, and the uniform application of Union law would be placed at risk. If however, on the other hand, the Member States were completely to forgo ultra vires review, disposal of the treaty basis would be transferred to the Union bodies alone, even if their understanding of the law led in the practical outcome to an amendment of a Treaty or an expansion of competences. That in the borderline cases of possible transgression of competences on the part of the Union bodies—which is infrequent, as should be expected according to the institutional and procedural precautions of Union law—the [national] constitutional and the Union law perspective do not completely harmonise, is due to the circumstance that the Member States of the European Union also remain the masters of the Treaties . . .
>
> Ultra vires review by the Federal Constitutional Court can moreover *only be considered if it is manifest* that acts of the European bodies and institutions have taken place outside the transferred competences. A breach of the principle of conferral is only manifest if the European bodies and institutions have transgressed the boundaries of their competences *in a manner specifically violating the principle of conferral*, the breach of competences is in other words sufficiently qualified. This means that the act of the authority of the European Union *must be manifestly in violation of competences* and that the impugned act is highly significant in the structure of competences between the Member States and the Union with regard to the principle of conferral and to the binding nature of the statute under the rule of law.[59]

This limits the national review of European law to 'specific' and 'manifest' violations of the principle of conferral. There is thus a presumption that the Union institutions would generally act *intra vires*; and only for clear and exceptional violations would the German Constitutional Court challenge the primacy of European law.

But even if the German court's behaviour was again 'all bark and no bite',[60] another supreme court appears to have recently taken a bite and openly refused to apply European Union law. Rebelling against *Mangold* too, the

---

[59] Ibid., 1085–6 (paras 42 and 46 (emphasis added)).

[60] C. U. Schmid, 'All Bark and No Bite: Notes on the Federal Constitutional Court's "Banana Decision"' (2001) 7 *European Law Journal* 95.

Danish Supreme Court has boldly stated that the idea of a directly effective unwritten general principle of European law was not acceptable. In *Dansk Industri (Ajos)*,[61] it thus held:

> Following the EU Court of Justice's judgments in *Mangold*, C-144/04, EU:C:2005:709, *Kücükdeveci*, C-555/07, EU:C:2010:21, and the present case, we find that the principle prohibiting discrimination on grounds of age is a general principle of EU law which, according to the EU Court of Justice, is to be found in various international instruments and in the constitutional traditions common to the Member States. The EU Court of Justice does not refer to provisions in those treaties covered by the Law on accession as a basis for the principle.
>
> Even though the principle is inferred from legal sources outside the EU Treaties, it is obvious that the three aforementioned judgments must be construed as involving an unwritten principle which applies at treaty level. *There is nothing in those judgments, however, to indicate that there is a specific treaty provision providing the basis for the principle. A situation such as this, in which a principle at treaty level under EU law is to have direct effect (thereby creating obligations) and be allowed to take precedence over conflicting Danish law in a dispute between individuals, without the principle having any basis in a specific treaty provision, is not foreseen in the Law on accession .... It follows from the foregoing that, under the Law on accession, principles developed or established on the basis of Article 6(3) TEU have not been made directly applicable in Denmark.*[62]

The Danish Supreme Court thus found that unwritten general principles of EU law could not have direct effect within Denmark, because the Danish Accession Law simply did not cover the European Court's *Mangold* jurisprudence. The judgment is a novelty and has been criticized as a 'mutual disempowerment' and a 'breakdown of mutual trust' between the European Court of Justice and the Danish Supreme Court.[63]

---

[61] *Dansk Industri, acting on behalf of Ajos v Estate of A*, Case 15/14. For an unofficial English translation, see the book's companion website.

[62] Ibid., pp. 45 and 47 (emphasis added).

[63] For an extensive discussion of the *Ajos* ruling, see M. Madsen, H. Olsen, and U. Šadl, 'Competing Supremacies and Clashing Institutional Rationalities: the Danish Supreme Court's Decision in the *Ajos* Case and the National Limits of Judicial Cooperation' (2017) 23 *European Law Journal* 140.

(b) Competence Limits II: National Constitutional Identities

The *Solange* jurisprudence as well as the *ultra virus* jurisprudence had both set *relative* limits to European integration: *so long as* the Union acknowledged fundamental rights and respected the competence limits *as set by the EU Treaties*, European law could be given primacy over conflicting national law.

This integration-friendly position, however, received an absolute 'national' limit in a third famous judgment by the German Constitutional Court: the *Lisbon Decision*.[64] In this decision, the court now asserted that even in a situation where the German Parliament had agreed to a further transfer of competences to the Union, that (democratic) choice was limited by the 'constitutional identity' of the German State.

What was this constitutional identity and why could it not be limited? This was the answer given by the Constitutional Court:

> From the perspective of the principle of democracy, the violation of the constitutional identity codified in art.79.3 of the Basic Law is at the same time an encroachment upon the constituent power of the people. *In this respect, the constituent power has not granted the representatives and bodies of the people a mandate to dispose of the identity of the constitution.* ... The safeguarding of sovereignty, demanded by the principle of democracy in the valid constitutional system prescribed by the Basic Law in a manner that is open to integration and to international law, does not mean that a pre-determined number or certain types of sovereign rights should remain in the hands of the state .... *European unification on the basis of a treaty union of sovereign states may, however, not be achieved in such a way that not sufficient space is left to the Member States for the political formation of the economic, cultural and social living conditions.* ... Particularly sensitive for the ability of a constitutional state to democratically shape itself are decisions on substantive and formal criminal law (1), on the disposition of the monopoly on the use of force by the police within the state and by the military towards the exterior (2), fundamental fiscal decisions on public revenue and public expenditure, the latter being particularly motivated, inter alia, by social policy considerations (3), decisions on the shaping of living

---

[64]   BVerfGE 123, 267 (*Lisbon Decision*). For an English translation, see [2010] 3 CMLR 276. For an excellent analysis of the decision, see D. Thym, 'In the Name of Sovereign Statehood: A Critical Introduction to the Lisbon Judgment of the German Constitutional Court' (2009) 46 *Common Market Law Review* 1795.

conditions in a social state (4) and decisions of particular cultural importance, for example on family law, the school and education system and on dealing with religious communities (5).[65]

Invoking the idea of (national) democracy, the German Constitutional Court here set absolute limits to European integration—at least European integration within the scope of the German Constitution. In order to remain a 'sovereign' State—what an anachronistic idea in our global times!—national competences must guarantee that 'sufficient space' is left for the national legislature. And in order to guarantee that guarantee, the German court would engage in an 'identify review' that could, in the future, result in 'Union law being declared inapplicable in Germany'.[66]

Conclusion

The doctrine of direct effect demands that a national court *applies* European law. And the doctrine of primacy demands that a national court *disapplies* national law that conflicts with European law.

For the European legal order, the absolute primacy of European law means that all Union law prevails over all national law. The absolute nature of the primacy doctrine is, however, contested by the Member States. While they generally acknowledge the primacy of European law, they have insisted on national constitutional limits. Is this relative nature of primacy a 'novelty' or an 'aberration'?[67] This view is introverted and unhistorical when compared with the constitutional experiences of the United States.[68] Indeed, the normative ambivalence surrounding the primacy principle in the European Union is part and parcel of Europe's *federal* nature.[69]

---

[65] *Lisbon Decision* (n. 64), 332–41 (emphasis added). Article 79(3) of the German Constitution is the so-called 'Eternity Clause' and states: 'Amendments to this Basic Law affecting the division of the Federation into Länder, their participation in the legislative process, or the principles laid down in Articles 1 and 20 shall be inadmissible.'

[66] Ibid., 338.

[67] See N. Walker, 'The Idea of Constitutional Pluralism' (2002) 65 *Modern Law Review* 317 at 338. This—'Eurocentric'—view shockingly ignores the American experience, in which the Union and the States were seen to have 'constitutional' claims and in which the 'Union' was—traditionally—not (!) conceived in statist terms.

[68] Schütze, 'Federalism as Constitutional Pluralism' (n. 43).

[69] On this point, see R. Schütze, *European Union Law* (n. 5), ch. 2.

National Actions

Introduction

National courts are the principal judicial enforcers of European law. 'Ever since *Van Gend en Loos* the Court has maintained that it is the task of the national courts to protect the rights of individuals under [Union] law and to give full effect to [Union] law provisions.'[1] Indeed, whenever European law is directly effective, national courts must apply it; and wherever a Union norm comes into conflict with national law, each national court must disapply the latter. The Union legal order thereby insists that nothing within the national judicial system must prevent national courts from exercising their functions as 'guardians' of the European judicial order.[2] In *Simmenthal*,[3] the Court thus

---

[1] S. Prechal, 'National Courts in EU Judicial Structures' (2006) 25 *Yearbook of European Law* 429.

[2] *Opinion 1/09 (Draft Agreement on the Creation of European and Community Patent Court)* [2011] ECR I-1137, para. 66.

[3] *Amministrazione delle Finanze dello Stato v Simmenthal*, Case 106/77 [1978] ECR 629.

held that each national court must be able to disapply national law—even where the national judicial system traditionally reserved that power to a central constitutional court:

> [E]very national court must, in a case within its jurisdiction, apply [Union] law in its entirety and protect rights which the latter confers on individuals and must accordingly set aside any provision of national law which may conflict with it, whether prior or subsequent to the [Union] rule. Accordingly any provision of a national legal system and any legislative, administrative or judicial practice which might impair the effectiveness of [European] law by withholding from the national court having jurisdiction to apply such law the power to do everything necessary at the moment of its application to set aside national legislative provisions which might prevent [Union] rules from having full force and effect are incompatible with those requirements which are the very essence of [Union] law.[4]

Functionally, the direct effect (and supremacy) of European law thus transforms every single national court into a 'European' court. This decentralized system differs from the judicial system in the United States in which the application of federal law is principally left to 'federal' courts. *Federal* courts here apply *federal* law, while *State* courts apply *State* law. The European system, by contrast, is based on a philosophy of cooperative federalism: *all* national courts are entitled and obliged to apply European law to disputes before them. In opting for the decentralized judicial enforcement via State courts, the EU judicial system thereby comes close to German judicial federalism; yet, unlike the latter, State courts are *not* hierarchically subordinated. Indeed, there is no compulsory appeal procedure from the national to the European Courts; and the relationship between national courts and the European Court is thus based on their *voluntary* cooperation. National courts are consequently only functionally—but not institutionally—Union courts. The three distinct models of judicial federalism can be seen in Figure 7.1.

Has the Union therefore had to take State courts as it finds them? The Union has indeed traditionally recognized the 'procedural autonomy' of the judicial authorities of the Member States:

> Where national authorities are responsible for implementing [European law] it must be recognised that in principle this implementation takes place with due respect for the forms and procedures of national law.[5]

---

[4] Ibid., paras 21–2.
[5] *Norddeutsches Vieh- und Fleischkontor GmbH v Hauptzollamt Hamburg-St. Annen*, Case 39/70 [1971] ECR 49, para. 4.

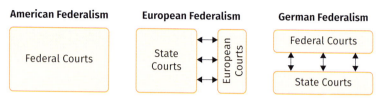

Figure 7.1 Judicial federalism in comparative perspective

This formulation has become known as the principle of 'national procedural autonomy'.[6] It essentially means that in the judicial enforcement of European law, the Union 'piggybacks' on the national judicial systems.[7] Yet the danger of such 'piggybacking' is that there may be situations in which there is a *European right* but no *national remedy* to enforce that right. But rights without remedies are 'pie in the sky': a metaphysical meal. Each right should have its remedy;[8] and for that reason, the autonomy of national enforcement procedures was never absolute. The Union has indeed imposed a number of obligations on national courts. The core duty governing the decentralized enforcement of European law by national courts is thereby rooted in Article 4(3) TEU: the duty of 'sincere cooperation'.[9] It is today complemented by Article 19(1), which states: 'Member States shall provide remedies sufficient to ensure effective legal protection in the fields covered by Union law.'

What does this mean; and to what extent does it limit the procedural autonomy of the Member States? This chapter explores this very question. We shall start with two specific constitutional principles that the Court has derived from the general duty of sincere cooperation: the principle of equivalence and the principle of effectiveness. Both principles have led to a significant *judicial* harmonization of national procedural laws, and this chapter analyses their evolution in Section 1. Section 2 then turns to a

---

[6] For a criticism of the notion, see C. N. Kakouris, 'Do the Member States Possess Judicial Procedural "Autonomy"?' (1997) 34 *Common Market Law Review* 1389.

[7] K. Lenaerts et al., *EU Procedural Law* (Oxford University Press, 2014), 107.

[8] Remedies might be said to fall into two broad categories. *Ex ante* remedies are to prevent the violation of a right (interim relief, injunctions), while *ex post* remedies are used to 'remedy' a violation that has already occurred (damages liability). On the many meanings of 'remedy', see P. Birks, 'Rights, Wrongs, and Remedies' (2000) 20 *Oxford Journal of Legal Studies* 1 at 9 et seq.

[9] Art. 4(3) TEU states: 'Pursuant to the principle of sincere cooperation, the Union and the Member States shall, in full mutual respect, assist each other in carrying out tasks which flow from the Treaties. The Member States shall take any appropriate measure, general or particular, to ensure fulfilment of the obligations arising out of the Treaties or resulting from the acts of the institutions of the Union. The Member States shall facilitate the achievement of the Union's tasks and refrain from any measure which could jeopardise the attainment of the Union's objectives.'

second—and much more intrusive—incursion into the procedural autonomy of the Member States: the State liability principle. If the principles of equivalence and effectiveness ultimately rely on the existence of *national* remedies for the enforcement of European law, this principle establishes a *European* remedy. An individual could here, under certain conditions, claim compensatory damages resulting from a breach of European law.

Finally, we shall explore the procedural bridge that exists between national courts and the European Court of Justice. For in the absence of an 'institutional' connection between the European Court and the national courts, how has the Union legal order guaranteed a degree of uniformity in the decentralized judicial enforcement of European law? From the very beginning, the Treaties contained a mechanism for the interpretative assistance of national courts: the preliminary reference procedure. The general and specific aspects of that procedure will be discussed in Sections 3 and 4. Suffice it to say here that the European Court is only *indirectly* involved in the judgment delivered by the national court. It cannot 'decide' the case, as the principal action continues to be a 'national action'.

1. National Remedies: Equivalence and Effectiveness

The general duty governing the decentralized enforcement of European law by national courts is Article 4(3) TEU. This duty of 'sincere cooperation' has traditionally imposed two limitations on the procedural autonomy of the Member States: the principle of equivalence and the principle of effectiveness. The classic expression of both limitations can be found in *Rewe*:

> [I]n the absence of [European] rules on this subject, it is for the domestic legal system of each Member State to designate the courts having jurisdiction and to determine the procedural conditions governing actions at law intended to ensure the protection of the rights which citizens have from the direct effect of [European] law, it being understood that such conditions cannot be less favourable than those relating to similar actions of a domestic nature ... In the absence of such measures of harmonization the right conferred by [European] law must [thus] be exercised before the national courts in accordance with the conditions laid down by national rules. The position would be different only if the [national rules] made it impossible in practice to exercise the rights which the national courts are obliged to protect.[10]

---

[10] *Rewe*, Case 33/76 [1976] ECR 1989, para. 5. For the modern version, see *Peterbroeck, Van Campenhout & Cie v Belgian State*, Case C-312/93 [1995] ECR I-4599.

The procedural autonomy of the Member States is thus *relative*. First, national procedural rules cannot make the enforcement of European rights less favourable than the enforcement of similar national rights. This prohibition of procedural discrimination is the principle of equivalence. Second, national procedural rules—even if not discriminatory—ought not to make the enforcement of European rights 'impossible in practice'. This would become known as the principle of effectiveness. Both principles have led to a *judicial* harmonization of national procedural laws, and this first section analyses their evolution.

(a) The Equivalence Principle

The idea behind the principle of equivalence is straightforward: national procedures and remedies for the enforcement of European rights 'cannot be less favourable than those relating to similar actions of a domestic nature'.[11] When applying European law, national courts must act *as if* they were applying national law. National procedures and remedies must not discriminate between national and European rights. The principle of equivalence will consequently not affect the substance of national remedies. It only requires the formal extension of those remedies to 'similar' or 'equivalent' actions under European law.

But what are 'equivalent' or 'similar' actions? The devil always lies in the detail, and much case law on the equivalence principle has concentrated on this devilish question. In *Edis*,[12] a company had been required to pay a registration charge. Believing the charge to be contrary to European law, the plaintiff applied for a refund from the State that was rejected by the Italian courts on the ground that the limitation period for such refunds had expired. However, Italian law recognized various limitation periods—depending on whether the refund was due to be paid by public or private parties. The limitation period for public authorities was shorter than that for private parties. And this posed the following question: Was the national court entitled to simply extend the national *public* refund procedure to charges in breach of European law; or was it required to apply the more generous *private* refund procedure? The Court answered as follows:

---

[11]   *Rewe*, Case 33/76 (n. 10), para. 5.
[12]   *Edilizia Industriale Siderurgica Srl (Edis) v Ministero delle Finanze*, Case C-231/96 [1998] ECR I-4951.

> Observance of the principle of equivalence implies, for its part, that the procedural rule at issue applies without distinction to actions alleging infringements of [Union] law and to those alleging infringements of national law, with respect to the same kind of charges or dues. *That principle cannot, however, be interpreted as obliging a Member State to extend its most favourable rules governing recovery under national law to all actions for repayment of charges or dues levied in breach of [European] law.* Thus, [European] law does not preclude the legislation of a Member State from laying down, alongside a limitation period applicable under the ordinary law to actions between private individuals for the recovery of sums paid but not due, special detailed rules, which are less favourable, governing claims and legal proceedings to challenge the imposition of charges and other levies. The position would be different only if those detailed rules applied solely to actions based on [European] law for the repayment of such charges or levies.[13]

In the present case, the 'equivalent' action was thus to be based on the national remedies that existed for refunds from *public* bodies. The existence of a more favourable limitation period for refunds from private parties was irrelevant, since the equivalence principle only required treating like actions alike. And the 'like' action in this case was the refund procedure applicable to a public body. The national procedural rules thus did not violate the principle of equivalence.

However, matters might not be so straightforward.[14] For the equivalence principle requires national courts to evaluate 'whether the actions concerned are similar as regards their purpose, cause of action and essential characteristics'.[15] And this teleological comparability test might require them to look beyond the specific procedural regime for a national right.

(b) The Effectiveness Principle

The power of the effectiveness principle to interfere with the principle of national procedural autonomy was—from the start—much greater. However, the Court's jurisprudence on the principle is disastrously unclear. The best way to analyse the case law is to identify general historical periods and a

---

[13] Ibid., paras 36–7 (emphasis added).
[14] *Levez v Jennings (Harlow Pools) Ltd*, Case C-326/96 [1998] ECR I-7835.
[15] *Preston et al. v Wolverhampton Healthcare NHS Trust and Others*, Case C-78/98 [2000] ECR I-3201, para. 57.

variety of specific thematic lines.[16] The academic literature on the effectiveness principle thereby typically distinguishes between three periods of evolution. A first period of *restraint* is replaced by a period of *intervention*, which in turn gives way to a period of *balance*.[17]

Each of these periods corresponds to a particular effectiveness standard. The European Court began to develop the principle from a minimal standard. National remedies would solely be found ineffective where they 'made it *impossible* in practice to exercise the rights which the national courts are obliged to protect'.[18] With time, the Court, however, increasingly moved to a maximum standard insisting on the 'full effectiveness' of European law.[19] This maximum standard was eventually replaced by a medium standard in a third period. The three standards and their (inverse) relationship to the principle of national procedural autonomy can be seen in Figure 7.2.

Let us now quickly look at each historical period in turn. In a first period, the European Court showed much restraint and respect towards the procedural autonomy of the Member States. The Court indeed pursued a policy of judicial minimalism.[20] The standard for an 'effective remedy' was low and simply required that the national procedures did not make the enforcement of European rights (virtually) impossible. This minimalist approach is exemplified by *Rewe*.[21]

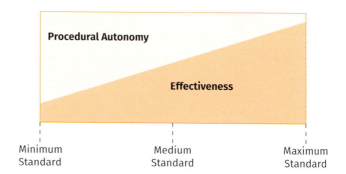

Procedural Autonomy

Effectiveness

| Minimum | Medium | Maximum |
| Standard | Standard | Standard |

Figure 7.2 Standards of effectiveness

---

[16]   For illustrations of this—brilliant and necessary—approach, see M. Dougan, *National Remedies before the Court of Justice: Issues of Harmonisation and Differentiation* (Hart, 2004), chs 5 and 6.

[17]   A. Arnull, *The European Union and its Court of Justice* (Oxford University Press, 2006), 268; as well as Dougan, *National Remedies* (n. 16), 227.

[18]   *Rewe*, Case 33/76 (n. 10), para. 5 (emphasis added).

[19]   *The Queen v Secretary of State for Transport, ex parte Factortame Ltd and others*, Case C-213/89 [1990] ECR I-2433, para. 21.

[20]   A. Ward, *Judicial Review and the Rights of Private Parties in EC Law* (Oxford University Press, 2007), 87.

[21]   *Rewe*, Case 33/76 (n. 10).

In subsequent jurisprudence, the Court however developed a more demanding standard of 'effectiveness'. In *Von Colson*,[22] two female job applicants for a warden position in an all-male prison had been rejected. The State prison had indisputably discriminated against them on the ground that they were women. Their European right to equal treatment had thus been violated, and the question arose how this violation could be remedied under national law. The remedy under German law restricted the claim for damages to the plaintiffs' travel expenses. Was this an effective remedy for the enforcement of their European rights? The Court now clarified that the effectiveness principle required that the national remedy 'be such as to guarantee real and effective judicial protection'.[23] The remedy would need to have 'a real deterrent effect on the employer', and in the context of a compensation claim this meant that the latter 'must in any event be *adequate* in relation to the damage sustained'.[24]

The most famous intervention into the procedural autonomy of a Member State in this second period is, however, to be found in an English case: *Factortame*.[25] The case concerned a violation of the Union's internal market law through a British nationality requirement imposed on fishing vessels. The case went to the (then) House of Lords, and the Lords found that the substantive conditions for granting interim relief were in place, but held 'that the grant of such relief was precluded by the old common-law rule that an interim injunction may not be granted against the Crown, that is to say against the government, in conjunction with the presumption that an Act of Parliament is in conformity with [European] law until such time as a decision on its compatibility with that law has been given'.[26] Unsure whether this common law rule itself violated the effectiveness principle under European law, the House of Lords referred the case to Luxembourg. And the European Court answered as follows:

[A]ny provision of a national legal system and any legislative, administrative or judicial practice which might impair the effectiveness of [European] law by withholding from the national court having jurisdiction to apply such law the power to do everything necessary at the moment of its application to set aside national legislative provisions which might prevent, even temporarily, [European] rules from having full force and effect are incompatible with those requirements, which

---

[22] *Von Colson and Elisabeth Kamann v Land Nordrhein-Westfalen*, Case 14/83 [1984] ECR 1891.

[23] Ibid., para. 23.   [24] Ibid. (emphasis added).

[25] *The Queen v Secretary of State for Transport, ex parte Factortame Ltd and others*, Case C-213/89 (n. 19).

[26] Ibid., para. 13.

are the very essence of [European] law. It must be added that the *full effectiveness* of [European] law would be just as much impaired if a rule of national law could prevent a court seized of a dispute governed by [European] law from granting interim relief in order to ensure the full effectiveness of the judgment to be given on the existence of the rights claimed under [European] law. It follows that a court which in those circumstances would grant interim relief, if it were not for a rule of national law, is obliged to set aside that rule.[27]

While short of creating a new remedy, this came very close to demanding a maximum standard of effectiveness. Yet the Court soon withdrew from this highly interventionist stance and thereby entered into a third period in the evolution of the effectiveness principle. In this third period, the Court tried—and still tries—to find a balance between the minimum and the maximum standard of effectiveness.[28]

The retreat from the second period of high intervention can be seen in *Steenhorst-Neerings*,[29] where the Court developed a distinction between national procedural rules whose effect was to totally *preclude* individuals from enforcing European rights and those national rules that merely *restrict* their remedies.[30] In *Preston*,[31] the Court had to deal with the British Equal Pay Act whose section 2(4) barred any claim that was not brought within a period of six months following cessation of employment. And instead of concentrating on the 'full effectiveness' or 'adequacy' of the national remedy, the Court stated that '[s]uch a limitation period does not render impossible *or excessively difficult* the exercise of rights conferred by the [European] legal order and is not therefore liable to strike at the very essence of those rights'.[32] The Court here had recourse to a—stronger—alternative to the (minimal) impossibility standard: national procedures that would make the exercise of European rights 'excessively difficult' would equally fall foul of the principle

---

[27]   Ibid., paras 20–1 (emphasis added).

[28]   F. G. Jacobs, 'Enforcing Community Rights and Obligations in National Courts: Striking the Balance' in A. Biondi and J. Lonbay (eds), *Remedies for Breach of EC Law* (Wiley, 1996).

[29]   *Steenhorst-Neerings v Bestuur van de Bedrijfsvereniging voor Detailhandel, Ambachten en Huisvrouwen*, Case C-338/91 [1993] ECR I-5475.

[30]   On the distinction, see Ward, *Judicial Review* (n. 20), 131. The distinction was elaborated in *Johnson v Chief Adjudication Officer*, Case C-31/90 [1991] ECR I-3723.

[31]   *Preston v Wolverhampton*, Case C-78/98 (n. 15).

[32]   Ibid., para. 34 (emphasis added).

of effectiveness. This medium standard lies in between the minimum and the maximum standard.[33]

2. State Liability: The *Francovich* Doctrine

Even if the Court had pushed for a degree of uniformity in the decentralized enforcement of European law via the principles of equivalence and effectiveness, it would still be *national* remedies whose scope or substance was extended. But what would happen if no national remedy existed? Would the non-existence of a national remedy not be an absolute barrier to the enforcement of European law? For a long time, the Court appeared to insist that the European Treaties were 'not intended to create new remedies in the national courts to ensure the observance of [Union] law other than those already laid down by national law'.[34]

In what was perceived as a dramatic turn of events, the European Court renounced this position and proclaimed the existence of a *European* remedy for breaches of European law in *Francovich*.[35] The Court here held that in certain situations the State was liable to compensate losses caused by its violation of European law. This section will look at the birth of the State liability doctrine first, before analysing its conditions.

(a) The Birth of the *Francovich* Doctrine

For a clairvoyant observer there was 'little doubt that one future day the European Court will be asked to say, straightforwardly, whether [European] law requires a remedy in damages to be made available in the national courts'.[36] This day came on 8 January 1990. On this day, the Court received a series of preliminary questions in *Francovich and others v Italy*.[37]

---

[33] When would this medium standard of effectiveness be violated? Instead of providing hard-and-fast rules, the Court has come to prefer a contextual test spelled out for the first time in *Peterbroeck*, Case C-312/93 (n. 10). In order to discover whether a national procedural rule makes the enforcement of European rights 'excessively difficult', the Court analyses each case 'by reference to the role of that provision in the procedure, its progress and its special features, viewed as a whole, before the various national instances' (ibid., para. 14).

[34] *Rewe Handelsgesellschaft et al. v Hauptzollamt Kiel* (*Butter-Cruises*), Case 158/80 [1981] ECR 1805.

[35] *Francovich and Bonifaci et al. v Italy*, Joined Cases C-6 and 9/90 [1991] ECR I-5357.

[36] A. Barav, 'Damages in the Domestic Courts for Breach of Community Law by National Public Authorities' in H. G. Schermers et al. (eds), *Non-Contractual Liability of the European Communities* (Nijhoff, 1988), 149 at 165.

[37] *Francovich and Bonifaci*, Joined Cases C-6 and 9/90 (n. 35).

The facts of the case are memorably sad.[38] Italy had flagrantly flouted its obligations under the Treaty by failing to implement a European directive designed to protect employees in the event of their employer's insolvency.[39] The Directive had required Member States to pass national legislation guaranteeing the payment of outstanding wages. Francovich had been employed by an Italian company, but had hardly received any wages. He brought proceedings against his employer; yet the employer had become insolvent, and for that reason Francovich brought a separate action against the Italian State to recover his losses. In the course of these second proceedings, the national court asked the European Court whether the State itself would be obliged to cover the losses of employees. The European Court found that the Directive had left the Member States a 'broad discretion with regard to the organization, operation and financing of the guarantee institutions', and it therefore lacked direct effect.[40] It followed that 'the persons concerned cannot enforce those rights against the State before the national courts where no implementing measures are adopted within the prescribed period'.[41]

But this was not the end of the story! The Court—unhappy with the negative result flowing from the lack of direct effect—continued:

> [T]he principle where by a State must be liable for loss and damage caused to individuals as a result of breaches of [European] law for which the State can be held responsible is inherent in the system of the Treaty. A further basis for the obligation of Member States to make good such loss and damage is to be found in Article [4(3)] of the Treaty [on European Union], under which the Member States are required to take all appropriate measures, whether general or particular, to ensure fulfilment of their obligations under [European] law. Among these is the obligation to nullify the unlawful consequences of a breach of [European] law. It follows from all the foregoing that it is a principle of [European] law that the Member States are obliged to make good loss and damage caused to individuals by breaches of [European] law for which they can be held responsible.[42]

---

[38] Opinion of Advocate General Mischo (ibid., para. 1): 'Rarely has the Court been called upon to decide a case in which the adverse consequences for the individuals concerned of failure to implement a directive were as shocking as in the case now before us.'

[39] The Court had already expressly condemned this failure in *Commission v Italian Republic,* Case 22/87 [1989] ECR 143.

[40] *Francovich and Bonifaci,* Joined Cases C-6 and 9/90 (n. 35), para. 25.

[41] Ibid., para. 27.   [42] Ibid., paras 33–7.

The European Court here took a qualitative leap in the context of remedies. Up to this point, it could still be argued that the principle of national procedural autonomy precluded the creation of European remedies as the principles of equivalence and effectiveness solely required the extension of *national* remedies to violations of European law. With *Francovich*, the Court clarified that the right to reparation for such violations was 'a right founded directly on [European] law'.[43] The action for State liability was thus a *European* remedy that had to be made available in the national courts.

How did the Court justify this 'revolutionary' result? It had recourse to the usual constitutional suspects: the very nature of the European Treaties and the general duty under Article 4(3) TEU. A more sophisticated justification was added by a later judgment. In *Brasserie du Pêcheur*,[44] the Court found:

> Since the Treaty contains no provision expressly and specifically governing the consequences of breaches of [European] law by Member States, it is for the Court, in pursuance of the task conferred on it by Article [19] of the [EU] Treaty of ensuring that in the interpretation and application of the Treaty the law is observed, to rule on such a question in accordance with generally accepted methods of interpretation, in particular by reference to the fundamental principles of the [Union] legal system and, where necessary, general principles common to the legal systems of the Member States. Indeed, it is to the general principles common to the laws of the Member States that the second paragraph of Article [340] of the [TFEU] refers as the basis of the non-contractual liability of the [Union] for damage caused by its institutions or by its servants in the performance of their duties. The principle of the non-contractual liability of the [Union] expressly laid down in Article [340] of the [TFEU] is simply an expression of the general principle familiar to the legal systems of the Member States that an unlawful act or omission gives rise to an obligation to make good the damage caused. That provision also reflects the obligation on public authorities to make good damage caused in the performance of their duties.[45]

The principle of State liability was thus rooted in the constitutional traditions common to the Member States and was equally recognized in the principle of *Union* liability for breaches of European law.[46] There was consequently a

---

[43] Ibid., para. 41.

[44] *Brasserie du Pêcheur SA v Bundesrepublik Deutschland* and *The Queen v Secretary of State for Transport, ex parte Factortame Ltd and others*, Joined Cases C-46 and 48/93 [1996] ECR I-1029.

[45] Ibid., paras 27–9.

[46] On this point, see Chapter 8, Section 4.

parallel between *State* liability and *Union* liability for tortious acts of public authorities. And this parallelism would have a decisive effect on the conditions for State liability for breaches of European law.

(b) The Three Conditions for State Liability

Having created the liability principle for State actions, the *Francovich* Court had nonetheless made the principle dependent on the fulfilment of three conditions:

> The first of those conditions is that the result prescribed by the directive should entail the grant of rights to individuals. The second condition is that it should be possible to identify the content of those rights on the basis of the provisions of the directive. Finally, the third condition is the existence of a causal link between the breach of the State's obligation and the loss and damage suffered by the injured parties. Those conditions are sufficient to give rise to a right on the part of individuals to obtain reparation, a right founded directly on [European] law.[47]

The original liability test was thus as follows: the Union law must have been intended to grant individual rights, and these rights would—even if they lacked direct effect—have to be identifiable.[48] If this was the case, and if European law was breached by a Member State not guaranteeing these rights, any loss that was caused by that breach could be claimed by the individual.[49] On its face, this test appeared to be complete and was therefore one of *strict* liability: any breach of an identifiable Union right would give rise to State liability. But the Court subsequently clarified that this was *not* the case. The *Francovich* test was to be confined to the specific context of a flagrant non-implementation of a European directive.

Drawing on its jurisprudence on *Union* liability, the Court indeed introduced a more restrictive principle of State liability in *Brasserie du Pêcheur*.[50]

---

[47] *Francovich and Bonifaci*, Joined Cases C-6 and 9/90 (n. 35) paras 40–1.

[48] For an analysis of this criterion, see Dougan, *National Remedies* (n. 16), 238 et seq. For a case in which the European Court found that a directive did not grant rights, see *Paul et al. v Germany*, Case C-222/02 [2004] ECR I-9425.

[49] For an analysis of this criterion, see particularly *Brinkmann Tabakfabriken GmbH v Skatteministeriet*, Case C-319/96 [1998] ECR I-5255.

[50] *Brasserie du Pêcheur*, Joined Cases C-46 and 48/93 (n. 44), para. 42: 'The protection of the rights which individuals derive from [European] law cannot vary depending on whether a national authority or a [Union] authority is responsible for the damage.' On the constitutional principles governing Union liability, see Chapter 8, Section 4.

The Court here clarified that State liability was to be confined to 'sufficiently serious' breaches. To cover up the fact that it had implicitly added a 'fourth' condition to its *Francovich* test, the Court replaced the new condition with the second criterion of its 'old' test. The new liability test could thus continue to insist on three—necessary and sufficient—conditions, but now read as follows:

> [European] law confers a right to reparation where three conditions are met: the rule of law infringed must be intended to confer rights on individuals; the breach must be sufficiently serious; and there must be a direct causal link between the breach of the obligation resting on the State and the damage sustained by the injured parties.[51]

The Court justified its limitation of State liability to 'sufficiently serious' breaches by reference to the wide discretion that Member States might enjoy, especially when exercising legislative powers. The 'limited liability' of the legislature is indeed a common constitutional tradition of the Member States and equally applies to the Union legislature. Where legislative functions are concerned, Member States 'must not be hindered by the prospect of actions for damages'.[52] The special democratic legitimacy attached to parliamentary legislation thus provided an argument against public liability for breaches of private rights, 'unless the institution concerned has manifestly and gravely disregarded the limits on the exercise of its powers'.[53] And in analysing whether a breach was sufficiently serious in the sense of a 'manifest … and grave … disregard', the Court would balance a number of diverse factors,[54] such as the degree of discretion enjoyed by the Member States as well as the clarity of the Union norm breached.

Unfortunately, there are very few hard-and-fast rules to determine when a breach is sufficiently serious. Indeed, the second criterion of the *Brasserie* test has been subject to much uncertainty. Would the manifest and grave

---

[51] Ibid., para. 51.   [52] Ibid., para. 45.

[53] Ibid. See also *The Queen v H.M. Treasury, ex parte British Telecommunications*, Case C-392/93 [1996] ECR I-10631, para. 42.

[54] *Brasserie du Pêcheur*, Joined Cases C-46 and 48/93 (n. 44), para. 56: 'The factors which the competent court may take into consideration include the clarity and precision of the rule breached, the measure of discretion left by that rule to the national or [Union] authorities, whether the infringement and the damage caused was intentional or involuntary, whether any error of law was excusable or inexcusable, the fact that the position taken by a [Union] institution may have contributed towards the omission, and the adoption or retention of national measures or practices contrary to [European] law.'

disregard test only apply to the legislative function? The Court appears to have answered this question in *Hedley Lomas*,[55] when dealing with the failure of the national *executive* to correctly apply European law. The Court found:

> [W]here, at the time when it committed the infringement, the Member State in question was not called upon to make any legislative choices and had only considerably reduced, or even no, discretion, the mere infringement of [European] law may be sufficient to establish the existence of a sufficiently serious breach[.][56]

This confirmed the potential liability of the (national) executive branch and clarified that the less discretion enjoyed by the latter, the more likely would be the liability of a State.[57] The Court here seemed to acknowledge two alternatives within the second *Brasserie* condition—depending on whether the State violated European law via its legislative or executive branch. The existence of these two alternatives would find expression in *Larsy*,[58] where the Court found:

> [A] breach of [European] law is sufficiently serious where a Member State, in the exercise of its legislative powers, has manifestly and gravely disregarded the limits on its powers and, secondly, that where, at the time when it committed the infringement, the Member State in question had only considerably reduced, or even no, discretion, the mere infringement of [European] law may be sufficient to establish the existence of a sufficiently serious breach.[59]

For an executive failure, the threshold for establishing State liability is thus much lower than the liability threshold for legislative actions. While the incorrect *application* of a clear European norm by the national executive will incur automatic liability, the incorrect implementation of a directive by the national legislature may not.[60] Nonetheless, the European Court strictly distinguishes the *incorrect* implementation of a directive from its *non*-implementation. The use of a stricter liability regime for legislative *non*-action makes much sense, for

---

[55] *The Queen v Ministry of Agriculture, Fisheries and Food, ex parte Hedley Lomas*, Case C-5/94 [1996] ECR I-2553.

[56] Ibid., para. 28.

[57] *Haim v Kassenzahnärztliche Vereinigung Nordrhein*, Case C-424/97 [2000] ECR I-5123, para. 38.

[58] *Larsy v Institut national d'assurances sociales pour travailleurs indépendants*, Case C-118/00 [2001] ECR I-5063.

[59] Ibid., para. 38.

[60] *Denkavit et al. v Bundesamt für Finanzen*, Cases C-283 and 291–2/94 [1996] ECR I-4845.

the failure of the State cannot be excused by reference to the exercise of legislative discretion. The Court has consequently held that the non-implementation of a directive could per se constitute a sufficiently serious breach.[61]

What about the third branch of government: the judiciary? Common sense typically identifies the 'State' with its legislative and executive branches. Yet there exists, of course, a third power within the State: the national judiciary. The benign neglect of the 'least dangerous branch' stems from two reductionist perceptions. First, the judiciary is reduced to a passive organ that merely represents the 'mouth of the law'. Second, its independence from the legislature and executive is mistaken as an independence from the State. Both perceptions are of course misleading: for in resolving disputes between private parties and in controlling the other State branches, the judiciary exercises *State* functions. And like the national executive, the national judiciary may breach European law by misapplying it in the national legal order. This misapplication could constitute a violation that triggers State liability under EU law; and the European Court of Justice has indeed held that a sufficiently serious breach of EU law by a national court can give rise to *Francovich* liability.[62]

3. Preliminary Rulings I: General Aspects

From the beginning, the Treaties contained a mechanism for the interpretative assistance of national courts. Where national courts encounter problems relating to the interpretation of European law, they can refer 'preliminary questions' to the European Court. The questions are 'preliminary', since they *precede* the application of European law by the national court. Thus, importantly, the European Court will not 'decide' the case. It is only *indirectly* involved in the judgment delivered by the national court; and for that reason preliminary rulings are called 'indirect actions'. The preliminary rulings procedure constitutes the cornerstone of the Union's judicial federalism.

---

[61] *Dillenkofer v Germany*, Case C-178/94 [1996] ECR I-4845, para. 29: '[F]ailure to take any measure to transpose a directive in order to achieve the result it prescribes within the period laid down for that purpose constitutes per se a serious breach of [European] law and consequently gives rise to a right of reparation for individuals suffering injury if the result prescribed by the directive entails the grant to individuals of rights whose content is identifiable and a causal link exists between the breach of the State's obligation and the loss and damage suffered.'

[62] Case C-224/01, *Köbler v Austria* [2003] ECR I-10239. For a detailed discussion of the case, see M. Breuer, 'State Liability for Judicial Wrongs and Community Law' (2004) 29 *European Law Review* 243.

This federalism is *cooperative* in nature: the European Court and the national courts collaborate in the adjudication of a single case.

The procedure for preliminary rulings is set out in Article 267 TFEU, which reads:

[1] The Court of Justice of the European Union shall have jurisdiction to give preliminary rulings concerning:
   (a) the interpretation of the Treaties;
   (b) the validity and interpretation of acts of the institutions, bodies, offices or agencies of the Union.
[2] Where such a question is raised before any court or tribunal of a Member State, that court or tribunal may, if it considers that a decision on the question is necessary to enable it to give judgment, request the Court to give a ruling thereon.
[3] Where any such question is raised in a case pending before a court or tribunal of a Member State against whose decisions there is no judicial remedy under national law, that court or tribunal shall bring the matter before the Court.[63]

The provision establishes a constitutional nexus between the European and the national courts. This section looks at the general aspects of preliminary rulings. We start by analysing the jurisdiction of the European Court under the procedure, and then move to the nature and effect of preliminary rulings in the Union legal order.

(a) The Jurisdiction of the European Court

The European Court's jurisdiction, set out in paragraph 1 of Article 267, covers all Union law—including international agreements of the Union.[64] It is, however, limited to *European* law. 'The Court is not entitled, within the framework of Article [267 TFEU], to interpret rules pertaining to national law.'[65] Nor can it theoretically give a ruling on the compatibility of national rules with Union law.

The Court's competence with regard to European law extends to questions on the 'validity and interpretation' of that law. Preliminary references may

---

[63] The (omitted) fourth paragraph states: 'If such a question is raised in a case pending before a court or tribunal of a Member State with regard to a person in custody, the Court of Justice of the European Union shall act with the minimum of delay.'

[64] *Haegemann*, Case 181/73 [1974] ECR 449.

[65] *Hoekstra (née Unger)*, Case 75/63 [1964] ECR 177, para. 3.

thus be made in relation to *two* judicial functions. They can concern the *validity* of European law; and in exercising its judicial review function, the European Court will be confined to providing a ruling on the validity of Union acts below the Treaties. National courts can, however, equally ask about the *interpretation* of European law. This includes all types of European law—ranging from the deepest constitutional foundations to the loftiest soft law.

The *application* of European law is—theoretically—not within the power of the Court. Article 267 'gives the Court no jurisdiction to apply the Treat[ies] to a specific case'.[66] However, the distinction between 'interpretation' and 'application' is sometimes hard to make. The Court has tried to explain it as follows:

> When it gives an interpretation of the Treat[ies] in a specific action pending before a national court, the Court limits itself to deducing the meaning of the [European] rules from the wording and spirit of the Treat[ies], it being left to the national court to apply in the particular case the rules which are thus interpreted.[67]

Theoretically, this should mean that the Court of Justice cannot decide whether or not a national law, in fact, violates Union law. And yet, the Court has often made this very assessment.[68]

A famous illustration of the blurred line between 'interpretation' and 'application' is provided by the 'Sunday trading cases'.[69] Would the national prohibition on trading on Sundays conflict with the Union's internal market provisions? Preliminary references had been made by a number of English courts to obtain an interpretation on the EU Treaties' free movement of goods provisions. The Court found that national rules governing opening hours could be justified on public interest grounds, but asked the referring national courts 'to ascertain whether the effects of such national rules exceed what is necessary to achieve the aim in view'.[70] Yet the decentralized application of this proportionality test led to judicial chaos in the United Kingdom. Simply

---

[66] *Costa v ENEL*, Case 6/64 [1964] ECR 585 at 592.

[67] *Da Costa et al. v Netherlands Inland Revenue Administration*, Joined Cases 28–30/62 [1963] ECR 31 at 38.

[68] For an excellent analysis of this category of cases, see T. Tridimas, 'Constitutional Review of Member State Action: The Virtues and Vices of an Incomplete Jurisdiction' (2011) 9 *International Journal of Constitutional Law* 737.

[69] See M. Jarvis, 'The *Sunday Trading* Episode: In Defence of the Euro-Defence' (1995) 44 *International and Comparative Law Quarterly* 451.

[70] *Torfaen Borough Council*, Case C-145/88 [1989] ECR I-3851, para. 15.

put, different national courts decided differently. The European Court thus ultimately took matters into its own hands and centrally applied the proportionality test.[71] And in holding that the British Sunday trading rules were not disproportionate interferences with the internal market, the Court crossed the line between 'interpretation' and 'application' of the Treaties.

(b) The Legal Nature of Preliminary Rulings

What is the nature of preliminary rulings from the European Court? Preliminary references are *not* appeals. They are—principally—discretionary acts of a national court asking for interpretative help from the European Court. The decision to refer to the European Court of Justice thus lies entirely with the national court—not the parties to the dispute.[72] But once the European Court has given a preliminary ruling, this ruling will be binding. But *whom* will it bind—the parties to the national dispute or the national court(s)?

Preliminary rulings cannot bind the parties in the national dispute, since the European Court will not 'decide' their case. It is therefore misleading to even speak of a binding effect *inter partes* in the context of preliminary rulings.[73] The Court's rulings are addressed to the national court requesting the reference; and the Court has clarified that 'that ruling is binding on the national court as to the interpretation of the [Union] provisions and acts in question'.[74] Yet, will the binding effect of a preliminary ruling extend beyond the referring national court? In other words, is a preliminary ruling equivalent to a 'decision' addressed to a single court; or will the European Court's interpretation be generally binding on all national courts?

The Court has long clarified that a preliminary ruling is *not* a 'decision'; indeed, it is not even seen as an (external) act of a Union institution.[75] What then is the nature of preliminary rulings? The question has been hotly debated in the academic literature. And we may contrast two views competing with

---

[71]   *Stoke-on-Trent City Council v B&Q*, Case C-169/91 [1992] ECR I-6635.

[72]   *Kempter v Hauptzollamt Hamburg-Jonas*, Case C-2/06 [2008] ECR I-411, para. 41: 'the system established by Article [267 TFEU] with a view to ensuring that [European] law is interpreted uniformly in the Member States instituted direct cooperation between the Court of Justice and the national courts by means of a procedure which is completely independent of any initiative by the parties'.

[73]   *Contra* A. Toth, 'The Authority of Judgments of the European Court of Justice: Binding Force and Legal Effects' (1984) 4 *Yearbook of European Law* 1.

[74]   *Benedetti v Munari*, Case 52/76 [1977] ECR 163, para. 26.

[75]   *Wünsche Handelsgesellschaft v Germany*, Case 69/85 (Order) [1986] ECR 947, para. 16.

each other. According to the common law view, preliminary rulings are legal precedents that generally bind all national courts. Judgments of the European Court are binding *erga omnes*.[76]

The problem with this—masterful yet mistaken—theory is that the European Court subscribes to a second constitutional view: the civil law tradition. Accordingly, its judgments do not create 'new' legal rules but only clarify 'old' ones. In the words of the Court:

> The interpretation which, in the exercise of the jurisdiction conferred upon it by Article [267 TFEU], the Court of Justice gives to a rule of [European] law clarifies and defines where necessary the meaning and scope of that rule as it must be or ought to have been understood and applied from the time of its coming into force[.][77]

The Court of Justice thus adopts the—(in)famous—'declaration theory'. Judgments only declare pre-existing positive law and thus reach back in time to when the positive law was adopted.

In the light of the 'civilian' philosophy of the European Court, its judgments are *not* generally binding.[78] There is no vertical or multilateral effect of judicial decisions, as 'judgments of the European Courts are *not sources* but *authoritative evidences* of [European] law': '[A]n interpretation given by the Court becomes an integral part of the provision interpreted and cannot fail to affect the legal position of all those who may derive rights and obligations from that provision.'[79]

Are there constitutional problems with the Union's civil law philosophy? There are, indeed, temporal problems. For the 'declaratory' effect of preliminary rulings generally generates 'retroactive' effects.[80] In *Kühne & Heitz*,[81]

---

[76] See A. Trabucchi, 'L'Effet "erga omnes" des Décision Préjudicielles rendus par la Cour de Justice des Communautés Européennes' (1974) 10 *Revue Trimestrielle de Droit Européen* 56.

[77] *Amministrazione delle Finanze dello Stato v Denkavit*, Case 61/79 [1980] ECR 1205, para. 16; and more recently *Kühne & Heitz v Productschap voor Pluimvee en Eieren*, Case C-453/00 [2004] ECR I-837, para. 21.

[78] In this sense, see Toth, 'The Authority of Judgments' (n. 73), 60: 'in the cases under discussion the Court itself has never meant to attribute, as is sometimes suggested, a general binding force to interpretative preliminary rulings'.

[79] Ibid., 70 and 74 (emphasis added).

[80] On this point, see G. Bebr, 'Preliminary Rulings of the Court of Justice: Their Authority and Temporal Effect' (1981) 18 *Common Market Law Review* 475, esp. 491: 'The retroactive effect of a preliminary interpretative ruling is, according to the Court, the general rule.'

[81] *Kühne & Heitz*, Case C-453/00 (n. 77).

the Court thus held that a (new) interpretation of European law must be applied 'even to legal relationships which arose or were formed before the Court gave its ruling on the question on interpretation'.[82] The Court has nonetheless recognized that its civil law philosophy must—occasionally— be tempered by the principles of legal certainty and financial equity.[83] It has therefore—exceptionally—limited the temporal effects of its preliminary rulings to an effect *ex nunc*; that is: an effect from the time of the ruling. However, the Court has equally clarified that legal certainty will not prevent the retroactive application of a (new) interpretation, where the judgment of a national court of final instance 'was, in the light of a decision given by the Court subsequent to it, based on a misinterpretation of [European] law which was adopted without a question being referred to the Court for a preliminary ruling under the third paragraph of Article [267]'.[84]

4. Preliminary Rulings II: Special Aspects

Article 267(2) defines the competence of national courts to ask preliminary questions. The provision allows 'any court or tribunal of a Member State' to ask a European law question that 'is necessary to enable it to give judgment'. But while any national courts 'may' refer a question to the European Court under paragraph 2, Article 267(3) imposes an obligation on certain courts. Article 267(3) defines these as courts 'against whose decisions there is no judicial remedy under national law'.

Let us look at each of these special aspects of the preliminary reference procedure in turn.

(a) 'Who': National Courts and Tribunals

The formulation 'court or tribunal' in Article 267 directly refers to *judicial* authorities. This removes *administrative* authorities, which have indeed been systematically excluded from the scope of the judicial cooperation procedure.[85]

---

[82]   Ibid., para. 22.

[83]   For the former rationale, see *Kempter*, Case C-2/06 (n. 72); for the latter rationale, see *Defrenne v Sabena*, Case 43/75 [1976] ECR 455.

[84]   *Kempter*, Case C-2/06 (n. 72), para. 39. For a critical analysis of this case, see A. Ward, 'Do unto Others as you would have them do unto you: "Willy Kempter" and the Duty to Raise EC Law in National Litigation' (2008) 33 *European Law Review* 739.

[85]   See *Corbiau*, Case C-24/92 [1993] ECR I-1277.

But what exactly is a 'court or tribunal' that can refer questions to the Court of Justice? The Treaties provide no positive definition. Would the concept therefore fall within the competence of the Member States? Unsurprisingly, the European Court has not accepted this idea and has provided a European definition of the phrase. Its definition is extremely wide. In *Dorsch Consult*,[86] the Court thus held:

> In order to determine whether a body making a reference is a court or tribunal for the purposes of Article [267] of the Treaty, which is a question governed by [Union] law alone, the Court takes account of a number of factors, such as whether the body is established by law, whether it is permanent, whether its jurisdiction is compulsory, whether its procedure is inter partes, whether it applies rules of law and whether it is independent.[87]

The last criterion is often controlling. Therefore, an authority that is not independent from the State's executive branch is not a court or tribunal in the meaning of European law.[88]

The still enormous breadth of this European definition is illustrated in *Broekmeulen*.[89] The plaintiff had obtained a medical degree from Belgium and tried to register as a 'General Practitioner' in the Netherlands. The registration was refused on the ground that Dutch professional qualifications were not satisfied. The plaintiff appealed before the Appeals Committee for General Medicine—a professional body set up under private law. This Appeals Committee was not a court or tribunal under Dutch law. Would it nonetheless be a 'court or tribunal' under Article 267(2); and, as such, be entitled to make a preliminary reference? The European Court found as follows:

> In order to deal with the question of the applicability in the present case of Article [267 TFEU], it should be noted that it is incumbent upon Member States to take the necessary steps to ensure that within their territory the provisions adopted by the [Union] institutions are implemented in their entirety. If, under the legal

---

[86] *Dorsch Consult Ingenieurgesellschaft v Bundesbaugesellschaft Berlin*, Case C-54/96 [1997] ECR I-4961.

[87] Ibid., para. 23.

[88] *Syfait et al. v GlaxoSmithKline*, Case C-53/03 [2005] ECR I-4609. On the general question whether national competition authorities should be considered 'courts or tribunals' in the sense of Art. 267 TFEU, see A. Komninos, 'Article 234 EC and National Competition Authorities in the Era of Decentralisation' (2004) 29 *European Law Review* 106.

[89] *Broekmeulen v Huisarts Registratie Commissie*, Case 246/80 [1981] ECR 2311.

system of a Member State, the task of implementing such provisions is assigned to a professional body acting under a degree of governmental supervision, and if that body, in conjunction with the public authorities concerned, creates appeal procedures which may affect the exercise of rights granted by [European] law, it is imperative, in order to ensure the proper functioning of [Union] law, that the Court should have an opportunity of ruling on issues of interpretation and validity arising out of such proceedings. As a result of all the foregoing considerations and in the absence, in practice, of any right of appeal to the ordinary courts, the Appeals Committee, which operates with the consent of the public authorities and with their cooperation, and which, after an adversarial procedure, delivers decisions which are recognized as final, must, in a matter involving the application of [European] law, be considered as a court or tribunal of a Member State within the meaning of Article [267 TFEU].[90]

Can a higher national court limit the power of a lower national court to refer preliminary questions? The European legal order has given short shrift to the attempt to break the cooperative nexus between the European Court and *each level of the national judiciary*. In Rheinmühlen,[91] the Court thus held that 'a rule of national law whereby a court is bound on points of law by the rulings of a superior court cannot deprive the inferior courts of their power to refer to the Court questions of interpretation of [Union] law involving such rulings'.[92] For if inferior courts could not refer to the Court of Justice, 'the jurisdiction of the latter to give preliminary rulings and the application of [European] law *at all levels of the judicial systems* of the Member States would be compromised'.[93]

Any national court or tribunal, at any level of the national judicial hierarchy, and at any stage of its judicial procedure, is thus entitled to refer a preliminary question to the European Court of Justice. National rules allowing for an appeal against the decision of a national court to refer a preliminary question to the European Court will thus violate 'the autonomous jurisdiction which Article [267 TFEU] confers on the referring court'.[94] For the German judicial hierarchy, the judicial federalism constructed by the European Court thus looks as Figure 7.3.

---

[90] Ibid., paras 16–17.

[91] *Rheinmühlen-Düsseldorf*, Case 166/73 [1974] ECR 33.

[92] Ibid., para. 4.

[93] Ibid. (emphasis added). For confirmation, see *Elchinov v Natsionalna zdravnoosiguritel-nakasa*, Case C-173/09 [2010] ECR I-8889, para. 27.

[94] *Cartesio*, Case C-210/06 [2008] ECR I-9641 para. 95.

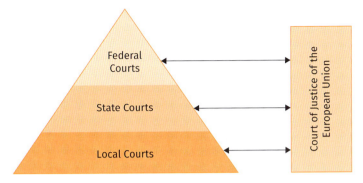

Figure 7.3 Preliminary rulings under Article 267

(b) 'What': Necessary Questions

National courts are entitled to request a preliminary ruling, where—within a pending case—there is a 'question' on which they consider it 'necessary' for judgment to be given. In the past, the European Court has been eager to encourage national courts to ask preliminary questions. For these questions offered the Court formidable opportunities to say what the European constitution 'is'. Thus, even where questions were 'imperfectly formulated', the Court was willing to extract the 'right' ones.[95] Moreover, the Court will generally not 'criticize the grounds and purpose of the request for interpretation'.[96] In the words of a seminal judgment on the issue:

> As regards the division of jurisdiction between national courts and the Court of Justice under Article [267] of the [TFEU] the national court, which is alone in having a direct knowledge of the facts of the case and of the arguments put forward by the parties, and which will have to give judgment in the case, is in the best position to appreciate, with full knowledge of the matter before it, the relevance of the questions of law raised by the dispute before it and the necessity for a preliminary ruling so as to enable it to give judgment.[97]

Nonetheless, in—very—exceptional circumstances the Court may reject a request for a preliminary ruling. This happened in *Foglia v Novello (No. 1)*,[98] where the Court insisted that questions referred to it must be raised

---

[95]   *Costa v ENEL*, Case 6/64 (n. 66) 593: '[T]he Court has the power to extract from a question imperfectly formulated by the national court those questions which alone pertain to the interpretation of the Treaty.'
[96]   Ibid.   [97]   *Pigs Marketing Board v Raymond Redmond*, Case 83/78 [1978] ECR 2347, para. 25.
[98]   *Foglia v Novello*, Case 104/79 [1980] ECR 745.

in a 'genuine' dispute.[99] Where the parties to the national dispute agreed, in advance, on the desirable outcome, the Court will decline jurisdiction. In a sequel to this case, the Court justified this jurisdictional limitation as follows:

> [T]he duty assigned to the Court by Article [267] is not that of delivering advisory opinions on general or hypothetical questions but of assisting in the administration of justice in the Member States. It accordingly does not have jurisdiction to reply to questions of interpretation which are submitted to it within the framework of procedural devices arranged by the parties in order to induce the Court to give its views on certain problems of [European] law which do not correspond to an objective requirement inherent in the resolution of a dispute.[100]

The Court of Justice has consequently imposed *some* jurisdictional control on requests for preliminary rulings. To prevent an abuse of the Article 267 procedure, the Court will 'check, as all courts must, whether it has jurisdiction'.[101] Yet, the Court has been eager to emphasize that it wishes 'not in any way [to] trespass upon the prerogatives of the national courts'.[102] The Court here pledged to 'place as much reliance as possible upon the assessment by the national court of the extent to which the questions submitted are essential'.[103] The Court therefore declines jurisdiction 'only if it is manifest that the interpretation of [European] law or the examination of the validity of a rule of [European] law sought by that court bears no relation to the true facts or the subject-matter of the main proceedings'.[104] There is thus a 'presumption of relevance' that the EU law questions asked will be relevant for the national case at hand.

(c) The Obligation to Refer and '*Acte Clair*'

While any national court or tribunal 'may' refer a question to the European Court under paragraph 2, Article 267(3) imposes an obligation:

> Where any such question is raised in a case pending before a court or tribunal of a Member State against whose decisions there is no judicial remedy under national law, that court or tribunal shall bring the matter before the Court.

---

[99]   G. Bebr, 'The Existence of a Genuine Dispute: an Indispensable Precondition for the Jurisdiction of the Court under Article 177 EEC?' (1980) 17 *Common Market Law Review* 525.

[100]   *Foglia v Novello (No. 2)*, Case 244/80 [1981] ECR 3045, para. 18.

[101]   Ibid., para. 19.   [102]   Ibid., para. 18.   [103]   Ibid., para. 19.

[104]   *Imperial Chemical Industries (ICI) v Kenneth Hall Colmer (Her Majesty's Inspector of Taxes)*, Case C-264/96 [1998] ECR I-4695, para. 15.

What is the scope of this obligation? Two theoretical options exist. Under an 'institutional' theory, the formulation refers to the highest judicial *institution* in the country. This would restrict the obligation to refer preliminary questions to a single court in a Member State—in the Netherlands, the Supreme Court. By contrast, a 'procedural' reading links the definition of the court of last instance to the judicial *procedure* in the particular case. This broadens the obligation to refer to every national court whose decision cannot be appealed in the particular case.

The Court of Justice has—from the very beginning—favoured the second reading.[105] The key concept in Article 267(3) is thus the 'appeal*ability*' of a judicial decision. What counts is the *ability* of the parties to appeal to a higher court. (The fact that the merits of the appeal are subject to a prior declaration of admissibility by a superior court may not therefore deprive the parties of that ability.[106]) Where an appeal is *procedurally* possible, the obligation under Article 267(3) will *not* apply.

Apart from the question as to what are courts 'against whose decisions there is no judicial remedy under national law', the wording of Article 267(3) appears relatively clear. Yet, this picture is—misleadingly—deceptive. For the European Court has judicially 'amended' the provision in two very significant ways.

The first 'amendment' relates to references on the validity of European law. For despite the restrictive wording of paragraph 3, the European Court has here insisted that *all* national courts—even courts that are not courts of last resort—are under an obligation to refer *when they are in doubt about the validity of a Union act*.[107] This *expansion* of the scope of Article 267(3) follows from the structure of the Union's judicial federalism, which grants the exclusive power to invalidate European law to the Court of Justice.[108]

---

[105] The procedural theory received support in *Costa v ENEL*, Case 6/64 (n. 66), where the ECJ treated an Italian court of *first* instance as a court against whose decision there was no judicial remedy.

[106] *Lyckeskog*, Case C-99/00 [2002] ECR I-4839, paras 16–17: 'Decisions of a national appellate court which can be challenged by the parties before a supreme court are not decisions of a court or tribunal of a Member State against whose decisions there is no judicial remedy under national law within the meaning of Article [267 TFEU]. The fact that examination of the merits of such appeals is subject to a prior declaration of admissibility by the Supreme Court does not have the effect of depriving the parties of a judicial remedy.'

[107] See *The Queen on the Application of International Air Transport Association et al. v Department for Transport*, Case C-344/04 [2006] ECR I-403, para. 30.

[108] Within the Union legal order, the power to annul a Union act is an *exclusive* competence of the European Court: *Foto-Frost v Hauptzollamt Lübeck-Ost*, Case 314/85 [1987] ECR 4199. On this power, see: Chapter 8, Section 3.

By contrast, a second 'amendment' has limited the obligation to refer preliminary questions. This *limitation* follows from constitutional common sense. For to ask a question implies uncertainty as to the answer. And where the answer is 'clear', there may be no need to raise a question. Yet, on its textual face, Article 267(3) treats national courts 'as perpetual children': they are forbidden from interpreting European law—even if the answers are crystal clear.[109] And in order to counter this, the Union legal order has imported a French legal doctrine under the name of *acte clair*. The doctrine simply means that where it is *clear* how to *act*, a national court need not ask a preliminary question.

The doctrine of *acte clair* began its European career in *Da Costa*.[110] In this case, the Court held:

> [T]he authority of an interpretation under Article [267] already given by the Court may deprive the obligation of its purpose and thus empty it of its substance ... Such is the case especially when the question raised is *materially identical* with a question which has already been the subject of a preliminary ruling in a similar case.[111]

The Court subsequently clarified that this covered a second situation. Where the European Court had already given a negative answer to a question relating to the *validity* of a Union act, another national court need not raise the same question again.[112]

But general guidelines on the constitutional scope of the *acte clair* doctrine were only offered in *CILFIT*.[113] The Court here generally widened the doctrine to all situations 'where previous decisions of the Court have already dealt with the *point of law* in question, irrespective of the nature of the proceedings which led to those decisions, even though the questions at issue are not strictly identical'.[114] Yet national courts will only be released from their obligation to refer questions under Article 267(3) TFEU where the correct application of European law is 'so obvious as to leave no scope for any reasonable doubt as to the matter in which the question raised is to be resolved'.[115] This is an extremely high threshold, which the Court linked to the fulfilment

---

[109] J. C. Cohen, 'The European Preliminary Reference and U.S. Supreme Court Review of State Court Judgments: A Study in Comparative Judicial Federalism' (1996) 44 *American Journal of Comparative Law* 421 at 438.

[110] *Da Costa et al. v Netherlands Inland Revenue Administration*, Joined Cases 28–30/62 [1963] ECR 31.

[111] Ibid., 38 (emphasis added).

[112] *International Chemical Corporation*, Case 66/80 [1981] ECR 1191, paras 12–13.

[113] *CILFIT and others v Ministry of Health*, Case 283/81 [1982] ECR 3415.

[114] Ibid., para. 14 (emphasis added).   [115] Ibid., para. 16.

of a number of very (!) restrictive conditions.[116] These *CILFIT* conditions are 'designed to prevent national courts from abusing the doctrine in order to evade their obligation to seek a preliminary ruling where they are disinclined to adhere to the Court's case-law'.[117]

Conclusion

Functionally, national courts are Union courts; yet the decentralized application of European law by national courts means that the procedural regime for the enforcement of European law is principally left to the Member States.

This rule of 'national procedural autonomy' is, however, qualified. The two constitutional principles judicially developed by the Court here are the equivalence and the effectiveness principles. The former requests national courts to extend existing national remedies to similar European actions. The latter demands that these national remedies must not make the enforcement of European law 'excessively difficult'. There is a third important qualification: the liability principle. The *Francovich* doctrine obliges national courts to provide for damages actions that compensate for losses resulting from (sufficiently serious) breaches of European law by a Member State.

In order to guarantee a degree of uniformity in the interpretation of European law, the EU Treaties finally provide for a 'preliminary reference procedure'. This is not an appeal procedure, but allows national courts to ask—if they want to—questions relating to the interpretation of European law. This voluntary cooperative arrangement is replaced by a constitutional obligation for national courts of last resort. In this way, a question of European law should always—at least once—be referred to the European Court of Justice.

---

[116] Ibid., paras 16–20. For a very long time, not much was known about the *CILFIT* conditions. In a recent judgment, the Court has helpfully added some clarity as to when the obligation under Art. 267(3) would be breached. In *Ferreira da Silva e Brito and others*, Case C-160/14, EU:C:2015:565, the Court clarified that the existence of contradictory decisions of lower national courts was 'not a conclusive factor capable of triggering the obligation set out in the third paragraph of Article 267 TFEU' because a higher court may hold a distinct interpretation that it believes to be beyond reasonable doubt (ibid., paras 41–2). While disagreement *within one national legal* order is thus not a conclusive trigger, the Court of Justice nevertheless held that wherever there exists 'a great deal of uncertainty on the part of *many national courts and tribunals*', '[t]hat uncertainty shows not only that there are difficulties of interpretation, but also that there is a risk of divergences in judicial decisions within the European Union' (ibid., para. 43). And, importantly, this was a question that the European Court itself felt very happy to—centrally—decide.

[117] K. Lenaerts et al., *EU Procedural Law* (n. 7), 100.

European Actions

Introduction

The European Treaties establish a dual enforcement mechanism for European Union law. Apart from decentralized enforcement by national courts, the Union legal order also envisages centralized enforcement of European law in the European Courts. The judicial competences of the European Courts are enumerated in the section of the Treaty on the Functioning of the European Union dealing with the Court of Justice of the European Union (Table 8.1).

Four classes of judicial actions will be discussed in this chapter. The first class is typically labelled an 'enforcement action' in the strict sense of the term. This action is set out in Articles 258 and 259 TFEU and concerns the failure of a Member State to act in accordance with European law (Section 1).

Table 8.1 Judicial competences and procedures

Judicial Competences and Procedures (Arts 258–81 TFEU)	
Article 258	Enforcement Action brought by the Commission
Article 259	Enforcement Action brought by another Member State
Article 260	Action for a Failure to Comply with a Court judgment
Article 261	Jurisdiction for Penalties in Regulations
Article 262	(Potential) Jurisdiction for Disputes relating to European intellectual property rights
Article 263	Action for Judicial Review
Article 265	(Enforcement) Action for the Union's Failure to Act
Article 267	Preliminary Rulings
Article 268	Jurisdiction in Damages Actions under Article 340
Article 269	Jurisdiction for Article 7 TEU
Article 270	Jurisdiction in Staff Cases
Article 271	Jurisdiction for Cases involving the European Investment Bank and the European Central Bank
Article 272	Jurisdiction granted by Arbitration Clauses
Article 273	Jurisdiction granted by special agreement between the Member States
Article 274	Jurisdiction of national courts involving the Union
Article 275	Non-Jurisdiction for the Union's Common Foreign and Security Policy
Article 276	Jurisdictional Limits within the Area of Freedom, Security and Justice
Article 277	Collateral (Judicial) Review for acts of general application

The three remaining actions 'enforce' the European Treaties against the Union itself. These actions can be brought for a failure to act (Section 2), for judicial review (Section 3), and for damages (Section 4).

1. Enforcement Actions against Member States

Where a Member State breaches European law, the central way to 'enforce' the EU Treaties is to bring that State before the European Court. As can be seen in Figure 8.1, this does not happen too often—even if it happens more often to some Member States!

The Union legal order thereby envisages two potential applicants for such enforcement or infringement proceedings (both names are often used

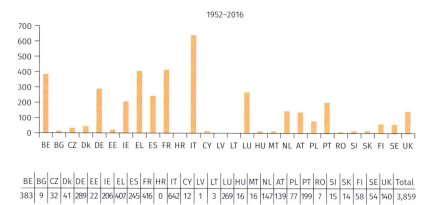

Figure 8.1 Infringement proceedings against Member States

BE	BG	CZ	Dk	DE	EE	IE	EL	ES	FR	HR	IT	CY	LV	LT	LU	HU	MT	NL	AT	PL	PT	RO	SI	SK	FI	SE	UK	Total
383	9	32	41	289	22	206	407	245	416	0	642	12	1	3	269	16	16	147	139	77	199	7	15	14	58	54	140	3,859

interchangeably) against a failing Member State: the Commission and another Member State. The procedure governing the former scenario is set out in Article 258; and the—almost—identical procedure governing the second scenario is set out in Article 259. Both procedures are inspired by international law logic. For not only are individuals excluded from enforcing their rights under that procedure, the European Court also cannot repeal national laws that violate European law. Its judgment will simply 'declare' that a violation of European law has taken place. However, as we shall see later, this declaration may now be backed up by financial sanctions.

(a) Procedural Conditions under Article 258

Enforcement actions against a Member State are 'the *ultima ratio* enabling the [Union] interests enshrined in the Treat[ies] to prevail over the inertia and resistance of Member States'.[1] They are typically brought by the Commission.[2] For it is the Commission, acting in the general interest of the Union, that is charged with ensuring that the Member States give effect to European law.[3]

---

[1] *Italy v High Authority*, Case 20/59 [1960] ECR 325 at 339.

[2] The following section therefore concentrates on proceedings brought by the Commission. Member States very rarely bring actions against another Member State; but see *Spain v United Kingdom*, Case C-145/04 [2006] ECR I-7917.

[3] See *Commission v Germany*, Case C-431/92 [1995] ECR I-2189. On the Commission's powers in this context, see Chapter 1, Section 3(c).

The procedural regime for enforcement actions brought by the Commission is set out in Article 258 TFEU, which states:

> If the Commission considers that a Member State has failed to fulfil an obligation under the Treaties, it shall deliver a reasoned opinion on the matter after giving the State concerned the opportunity to submit its observations. If the State concerned does not comply with the opinion within the period laid down by the Commission, the latter may bring the matter before the Court of Justice of the European Union.

The provision clarifies that before the Commission can bring the matter to the Court, it must pass through an *administrative* stage. The purpose of this pre-litigation stage is 'to give the Member State concerned an opportunity, on the one hand, to comply with its obligations under [European] law and, on the other, to avail itself of its right to defend itself against the complaints made by the Commission'.[4] This administrative stage expressly requires a 'reasoned opinion', and before that—even if not expressly mentioned in Article 258—a 'letter of formal notice'. In the 'letter of formal notice' the Commission will notify the State that it believes it to violate European law, and ask it to submit its observations. Where the Commission is not convinced by the explanations offered by a Member State, it will then issue a 'reasoned opinion'; and after that second administrative stage,[5] it will go to court.

What violations of European law may be litigated under the infringement procedure? Apart from two general exceptions,[6] the Commission can raise any violation of European law, including breaches of the Union's international agreements.[7] However, the breach must be committed by the 'State'. This includes its legislature, its executive, and—in theory—its judiciary. The Member State might also be responsible for violations of Union law by territorially autonomous regions.[8] And even the behaviour of its nationals may—exceptionally—be attributed to the Member State.[9]

Are there any defences that a State can raise to justify its breach of European law? Early on, the Court clarified that breaches of European law by one Member State cannot justify breaches by another. In *Commission v*

---

[4] *Commission v Belgium*, Case 293/85 [1988] ECR 305, para. 13.

[5] The Court has insisted that the Member State must—again—be given a reasonable period to correct its behaviour; see *Commission v Belgium*, Case 293/85 (n. 4).

[6] See Arts 275 and 276 TFEU.

[7] *Commission v Germany (IDA)*, Case C-61/94 [1996] ECR I-3989.

[8] See *Commission v Germany*, Case C-383/00 [2002] ECR I-4219.

[9] *Commission v Ireland (Buy Irish)*, Case 249/81 [1982] ECR 4005.

Luxembourg and Belgium,[10] the defendants had argued that 'since international law allows a party, injured by the failure of another party to perform its obligations, to withhold performance of its own, the Commission has lost the right to plead infringement of the Treaty'.[11] The Court did not accept this 'international law' reading of the European Treaties. The latter were 'not limited to creating reciprocal obligations between the different natural and legal persons to whom it is applicable, but establish … a new legal order, which governs the powers, rights and obligations of the said persons, as well as the necessary procedures for taking cognizance of and penalizing any breach of it'.[12] The binding effect of European law was thus comparable to the effect of 'institutional' law.[13] The Court has also denied the availability of 'internal' constitutional problems,[14] or budgetary restraints, as justifications.[15] However, one of the arguments that the Court has accepted in the past is the idea of force majeure in an emergency situation.[16]

(b) Judicial Enforcement Through Financial Sanctions

The European Court is not entitled to void national laws that violate European law. It can only *declare* national laws or practices incompatible with European law.[17] Where the Court has found that a Member State has failed to fulfil an obligation under the Treaties, 'the State shall be required to take the necessary measures to comply with the judgment of the Court'.[18] Inspired by international law logic, the European legal order here builds on the normative distinctiveness of European and national law. It remains within the exclusive competence of the Member States to remove national laws or practices that are incompatible with European law.

Nonetheless, the Union legal order may 'punish' violations by imposing financial sanctions on a recalcitrant State. The sanction regime for breaches by

---

[10] *Commission v Luxembourg and Belgium*, Joined Cases 90–91/63 [1964] ECR 625.

[11] Ibid., 631.   [12] Ibid.

[13] P. Pescatore, *The Law of Integration: Emergence of a New Phenomenon in International Relations Based on the Experience of the European Communities* (Sijthoff, 1974), 67 and 69.

[14] See *Commission v Ireland*, Case C-39/88 [1990] ECR I-4271, para. 11: 'a Member State may not plead internal circumstances in order to justify a failure to comply with obligations and time-limits resulting from [European] law'.

[15] See *Commission v Italy*, Case 30/72 [1973] ECR 161.

[16] For an excellent discussion of the case law, see L. Prete and B. Smulders, 'The Coming of Age of Infringement Proceedings' (2010) 47 *Common Market Law Review* 9 at 44.

[17] *France v Commission*, Joined Cases 15 and 16/76 [1979] ECR 32.

[18] Art. 260(1) TFEU.

a Member State is set out in Article 260(2) and (3) TFEU. Importantly, financial sanctions will not automatically follow from every breach of European law. According to Article 260(2), the Commission may only apply for a 'lump sum or penalty payment',[19] where a Member State has failed to comply with a *judgment of the Court*. And even in this limited situation, the Commission must bring a second (!) case before the Court.[20] There is only one exception to the requirement of a second judgment. This 'exceptional' treatment corresponds to a not too exceptional situation: the failure of a Member State properly to transpose a 'directive'.[21] Where a Member State fails to fulfil its obligation 'to notify measures transposing a directive adopted under a legislative procedure',[22] the Commission can apply for a financial sanction in the first enforcement action. The payment must take effect on the date set by the Court in its judgment, and is thus directed at the specific breach of European law.

2. Actions Against the Union: Failure to Act

Enforcement actions primarily target a Member State's failure to act (properly). However, infringement proceedings can also be brought against Union institutions. Actions for failure to act are thereby governed by Article 265 TFEU, which states:

> Should the European Parliament, the European Council, the Council, the Commission or the European Central Bank, in infringement of the Treaties, fail to act, the Member States and the other institutions of the Union may bring an action before the Court of Justice of the European Union to have the infringement established. This Article shall apply, under the same conditions, to bodies, offices and agencies of the Union which fail to act.
>
> The action shall be admissible only if the institution, body, office or agency concerned has first been called upon to act. If, within two months of being so

---

[19] The Court has held that Art. 265 TFEU allows it to impose a 'lump sum' *and* a 'penalty payment' at the same time (see *Commission v France* (*French Fisheries II*), Case C-304/02 [2005] ECR I-6262).

[20] The Court has softened this procedural requirement somewhat by specifically punishing 'general and persistent infringements'; see *Commission v Ireland* (*Irish Waste*), Case C-494/01 [2005] ECR I-3331. For an extensive discussion of this type of infringement, see P. Wennerås, 'A New Dawn for Commission Enforcement under Articles 226 and 228 EC: General and Persistent (GAP) Infringements, Lump Sums and Penalty Payments' (2006) 43 *Common Market Law Review* 31 at 33–50.

[21] On the legal instrument 'Directive', see Chapter 5, Section 3.

[22] Art. 260(3) TFEU.

called upon, the institution, body, office or agency concerned has not defined its position, the action may be brought within a further period of two months.

Any natural or legal person may, under the conditions laid down in the preceding paragraphs, complain to the Court that an institution, body, office or agency of the Union has failed to address to that person any act other than a recommendation or an opinion.

An action for failure to act can thus be brought against any Union institution or body—with the exception of the Court of Auditors and the European Court. It can be brought by another Union institution or body, a Member State, and even a private party.[23]

What are the procedural stages of this action? As with infringement actions against a Member State, the procedure is divided into an administrative and a judicial stage. The judicial stage will only commence once the relevant institution has been 'called upon to act', and has not 'defined its position' within two months.[24]

What types of 'inactions' can be challenged? In its early jurisprudence, the Court appeared to interpret the scope of Article 265 in parallel with the scope of Article 263 (to be discussed later).[25] This suggested that only those inactions with (external) legal effects might be challenged. However, the wording of the provision points the other way—at least for non-private applicants. And this wider reading was confirmed in *Parliament v Council (Comitology)*,[26] where the Court found that '[t]here is no necessary link between the action for annulment and the action for failure to act'.[27] Actions for failure to act can thus also be brought in relation to 'preparatory acts'.[28] The material scope of Article 265 is, in this respect, wider than that of Article 263.

However, in one important respect the scope of Article 265 is much narrower than that of Article 263. For the European Court has added an 'unwritten' limitation that cannot be found in the text of Article 265.

---

[23]   However, with regard to private parties, the Court appears to read a 'direct and individual concern' criterion into Art. 265 TFEU; see *T. Port GmbH & Co. v Bundesanstalt für Landwirtschaft und Ernährung*, Case C-68/95 [1996] ECR I-6065.

[24]   On what may count as a 'defined' position, see *Parliament v Council*, Case 377/87 [1988] ECR 4017, and *Pesquer as Echebastar v Commission*, Case C-25/91 [1993] ECR I-1719.

[25]   *Chevallery v Commission*, Case 15/70 [1970] ECR 975, para. 6: '[T]he concept of a measure capable of giving rise to an action is identical in Articles [263] and [265], as both provisions merely prescribe one and the same method of recourse.'

[26]   *Parliament v Council*, Case 302/87 [1988] ECR 5615.

[27]   Ibid., para. 1.   [28]   *Parliament v Council*, Case 377/87 (n. 24).

It insists that a finding of a failure to act requires the existence of an *obligation to act*. Where an institution has 'the right, but not the duty' to act, no failure to act can be established.[29] This is, for example, the case with regard to the Commission's competence to bring enforcement actions under Article 258. Under this article 'the Commission is not bound to commence the proceedings provided for in that provision but in this regard has a discretion which excludes the right for individuals to require that institution to adopt a specific position'.[30] The existence of institutional discretion thus excludes an obligation to act.

In *Parliament v Council* (*Common Transport Policy*),[31] the Court offered further commentary on what the existence of an obligation to act requires. Parliament had brought proceedings against the Council claiming that it had failed to lay down a framework for the common transport policy. The Council responded by arguing that a failure to act under Article 265 'was designed for cases where the institution in question has a legal obligation to adopt a *specific* measure and that *it is an inappropriate instrument for resolving cases involving the introduction of a whole system of measures* within the framework of a complex legislative process'.[32] The Court joined the Council and rejected the idea that enforcement proceedings could be brought for failure to fulfil the *general* obligation to develop a Union policy. The failure to act would have to be 'sufficiently defined'; and this would only be the case where the missing Union act could be 'identified individually'.[33]

What are the consequences of an established failure to act on the part of the Union? According to Article 266, the institution 'whose failure to act has been declared contrary to the Treaties shall be required to take the necessary measures to comply with the judgment of the Court of Justice of the European Union'. And in the absence of an express time limit for such compliance, the Court acknowledges that the institution 'has a reasonable period for that purpose'.[34]

---

[29] *Star Fruit Co. v Commission*, Case 247/87 [1989] ECR 291, esp. para. 12.

[30] Ibid., para. 11.

[31] *Parliament v Council*, Case 13/83 [1985] ECR 1513.

[32] Ibid., para. 29 (emphasis added).

[33] Ibid., para. 37. The Court thus held in para. 53 that 'the absence of a common policy which the Treaty requires to be brought into being does not in itself necessarily constitute a failure to act sufficiently specific in nature to form the subject of an action under Article [265]'.

[34] Ibid., para. 69.

3. Annulment Actions: Judicial Review

The action for judicial review in the European Union legal order is set out in Article 263 TFEU. The provision reads:

[1] The Court of Justice of the European Union shall review the legality of legislative acts, of acts of the Council, of the Commission and of the European Central Bank, other than recommendations and opinions, and of acts of the European Parliament and of the European Council intended to produce legal effects vis-à-vis third parties. It shall also review the legality of acts of bodies, offices or agencies of the Union intended to produce legal effects vis-à-vis third parties.

[2] It shall for this purpose have jurisdiction in actions brought by a Member State, the European Parliament, the Council or the Commission on grounds of lack of competence, infringement of an essential procedural requirement, infringement of the Treaties or of any rule of law relating to their application, or misuse of powers.

[3] The Court shall have jurisdiction under the same conditions in actions brought by the Court of Auditors, by the European Central Bank and by the Committee of the Regions for the purpose of protecting their prerogatives.

[4] Any natural or legal person may, under the conditions laid down in the first and second paragraphs, institute proceedings against an act addressed to that person or which is of direct and individual concern to them, and against a regulatory act which is of direct concern to them and does not entail implementing measures ...

[6] The proceedings provided for in this Article shall be instituted within two months of the publication of the measure, or of its notification to the plaintiff, or, in the absence thereof, of the day on which it came to the knowledge of the latter, as the case may be.[35]

Where an action for judicial review is well founded, the Court of Justice 'shall declare the acts concerned to be void'.[36] The Union will henceforth 'be required to take the necessary measures to comply with the judgment of the

---

[35] The omitted para. 5 lays down special rules for Union agencies and bodies. It states: 'Acts setting up bodies, offices and agencies of the Union may lay down specific conditions and arrangements concerning actions brought by natural or legal persons against acts of these bodies, offices or agencies intended to produce legal effects in relation to them.' The following section will not deal with this special aspect of judicial review.

[36] Art. 264(1) TFEU. However, according to Art. 264(2) TFEU, the Court can—exceptionally— 'if it considers this necessary, state which of the effects of the act which it has declared void shall be considered as definitive'.

Court of Justice of the European Union';[37] and may even be subject to pay compensation for damage caused by the illegal act.[38]

What are the procedural requirements for a judicial review action? Article 263 follows a complex structure; and the easiest way to understand its logic is to break it down into four constituent components starting with four 'w's. Paragraph 1 concerns the question *whether* the Court has the power to review particular types of Union acts. Paragraph 2 tells us *why* there can be judicial review; that is: on what grounds one can challenge the legality of a Union act. Paragraphs 2–4 concern the question of *who* can ask for judicial review and thereby distinguish between three classes of applicants. Finally, paragraph 6 tells us *when* an application for review must be made; namely, within two months.

(a) 'Whether': The Existence of a 'Reviewable' Act

Paragraph 1 determines whether there can be judicial review. This question has two dimensions. The first dimension relates to *whose* acts may be challenged; the second dimension clarifies *which* acts might be reviewed.

Whose acts can be challenged in judicial review proceedings? According to Article 263(1), the Court is entitled to review 'legislative acts'; that is: acts whose joint authors are the European Parliament and the Council both following the ordinary or a special legislative procedure. It can also review executive acts of all Union institutions and bodies, except for the Court of Auditors. By contrast, the Court cannot judicially review acts of the Member States. And this exclusion covers unilateral national acts, as well as international agreements of the Member States. (The European Treaties thus cannot—despite their being the foundation of European law—be reviewed by the Court.) So even if national acts or international agreements of the Member States fall within the scope of EU law, they cannot be attributed to the Union institutions, and as such are beyond the review powers of the European Court.

Which acts of the Union institutions can be reviewed? Instead of a positive definition, Article 263(1) only negatively tells us which acts cannot be reviewed. Accordingly, there will be no judicial review for 'recommendations' or 'opinions'. The reason for this exclusion is that both instruments 'have no binding force',[39] and there is thus no need to challenge their *legality*. The provision equally excludes judicial review for acts of the European

---

[37] Art. 266 TFEU.

[38] Arts 268 and 340 TFEU. On this point, see Section 4.

[39] Art. 288(5) TFEU.

Parliament, the European Council, and of other Union bodies not 'intended to produce legal effects vis-à-vis third parties'. The rationale behind this limitation is to exclude acts that are 'internal' to an institution. And despite being textually limited to *some* Union institutions, the requirement of an 'external' effect has been extended to all Union acts.

The Court has thus clarified that purely preparatory acts of the Commission or the Council cannot be challenged because 'an act is open to review only if it is a measure definitely laying down the position of the Commission or the Council'.[40] In a legislative or executive procedure involving several stages, all preparatory acts are consequently considered 'internal' acts; and as such cannot be reviewed.

But apart from these—minor—limitations, the Court has embraced a wide teleological definition of which acts may be reviewed. The nature of the act would thereby be irrelevant. In *ERTA*,[41] the Court thus found:

> Since the only matters excluded from the scope of the action for annulment open to the Member States and the institutions are 'recommendations or opinions'—which by the final paragraph of Article [288 TFEU] are declared to have no binding force—Article [263 TFEU] treats as acts open to review by the Court all measures adopted by the institutions which are intended to have legal force. The objective of this review is to ensure, as required by Article [19 TEU], observance of the law in the interpretation and application of the Treaty. It would be inconsistent with this objective to interpret the conditions under which the action is admissible so restrictively as to limit the availability of this procedure merely to the categories of measures referred to by Article [288 TFEU]. *An action for annulment must therefore be available in the case of all measures adopted by the institutions, whatever their nature or form, which are intended to have legal effects.*[42]

The Court's wide review jurisdiction is, however, externally limited by Articles 275 and 276 TFEU.[43]

---

[40] *International Business Machines (IBM) v Commission*, Case 60/81 [1981] ECR 2639, para. 10.
[41] *Commission v Council (ERTA)*, Case 22/70 [1971] ECR 263.
[42] Ibid., paras 39–42 (emphasis added).
[43] The Treaties acknowledge two general limitations on the jurisdiction of the European Court: Arts 275 and 276 TFEU. The former declares that the European Court 'shall not have jurisdiction with respect to the provisions relating to the common foreign and security policy nor with respect to acts adopted on the basis of those provisions' (Art. 275(1) TFEU). And Art. 276 TFEU decrees that the European Court 'shall have no jurisdiction to review the validity or proportionality of operations carried out by the police or other law-enforcement services of a Member State or the exercise of the responsibilities incumbent upon Member States with regard to the maintenance of law and order and the safeguarding of internal security'.

(b) 'Why': Legitimate Grounds for Review

Not every reason is a sufficient reason to request judicial review. While the existence of judicial review is an essential element of all political orders subject to the 'rule of law', the extent of judicial review will differ depending on whether a procedural or a substantive version is chosen.

The British or French legal orders have historically followed a *procedural* definition of the rule of law. Accordingly, courts are (chiefly) entitled to review whether in the adoption of an act the respective legislative or executive procedures have been followed. The 'merit' or substance of a legislative act is here beyond the review powers of the courts. By contrast, the American or German constitutional orders have traditionally followed a substantive definition of the rule of law. Courts are here obliged to review the content of a legislative act and, in particular, whether it violates fundamental human rights as guaranteed in the Constitution.

For the European legal order, Article 263(2) TFEU limits judicial review to four legitimate grounds: 'lack of competence', 'infringement of an essential procedural requirement', 'infringement of the Treaties or any rule of law relating to their application', and 'misuse of powers'. Do these reasons indicate whether the Union subscribes to a formal or substantive rule of law?

Let us look at this general question first, before analysing the principle of proportionality as a specific ground of review in a second step.

(i) 'Formal' and 'Substantive' Grounds

The Union legal order recognizes three 'formal' grounds of review.

First, a European act can be challenged on the ground that the Union lacked the competence to adopt it. The *ultra vires* review of European law thereby extends to all secondary and tertiary Union law. The review of the former originates in the principle of conferral.[44] Since the Union may only exercise those powers conferred on it by the Treaties, any action beyond these powers is *ultra vires* and thus voidable.

Second, a Union act can be challenged if it infringes an essential procedural requirement. According to this second ground of review, not all procedural irregularities may invalidate a Union act, only those that are 'essential'. When are 'essential' procedural requirements breached? The constitutional rules developed under this jurisdictional head are the result of an extensive 'legal basis litigation'.[45]

---

[44] On the principle of conferral, see Chapter 3, Introduction.

[45] On the phenomenon of 'legal basis litigation' in the Union legal order, see H. Cullen and A. Worth, 'Diplomacy by Other Means: the Use of Legal Basis Litigation as a Political Strategy by the European Parliament and Member States' (1999) 36 *Common Market Law Review* 1243.

An essential procedural step is breached when the Union adopts an act under a procedure that leaves out an institution that was entitled to be involved.[46] Alternatively, the Union may have adopted an act on the basis of a wrong voting arrangement *within* one institution. Thus, where the Council voted by unanimity instead of a qualified majority, an essential procedural requirement is breached.[47] By contrast, no essential procedural requirement is infringed when the Union acts under a 'wrong' competence, which nonetheless envisages an identical legislative procedure.[48]

The third formal ground of review is 'misuse of powers', which has remained relatively obscure.[49] The subjective rationale behind it is the prohibition on pursuing a different objective from the one underpinning a legal competence.[50]

Finally, a Union act can be challenged on the ground that it represents an 'infringement of the Treaties or any other rule of law relating to their application'. This constitutes a 'residual' ground of review. The European Court has used it as a constitutional passepartout to import a range of general principles into the Union legal order.[51] These general principles include, most importantly, the principle of proportionality. And with the introduction of such principles, the rule of law has received a *substantive* dimension in the European Union. The most important expression of this substantive rule of law idea is the ability of the European Courts to review Union acts against EU fundamental rights. They impose substantive limits on all governmental powers of the Union; and in the light of their importance, they have already been dealt with in Chapter 4.

(ii) Proportionality: A Substantive Ground

The constitutional function of the proportionality principle is to protect liberal values.[52] It constitutes one of the 'oldest' general principles of the Union

---

[46] See *Commission v Council* (*ERTA*), Case 22/70 (n. 41), as well as *Parliament v Council* (*Chernobyl*), Case C-70/88 [1990] ECR I-2041.

[47] See *United Kingdom v Council*, Case 68/86 [1988] ECR 855, as well as *Commission v Council*, Case C-300/89 [1991] ECR I-2867.

[48] *Commission v Council*, Case 165/87 [1988] ECR 5545, para. 19: 'only a purely formal defect which cannot make the measure void'.

[49] For a more extensive discussion of this ground of review, see H. Schermers and D. Waelbroeck, *Judicial Protection in the European Union* (Kluwer, 2001), 402 et seq.

[50] See *Gutmann v Commission*, Joined Cases 18 and 35/65 [1965] ECR 103.

[51] On the general principles in the Union legal order, see T. Tridimas, *General Principles* (Oxford University Press, 2007).

[52] On the origins of the proportionality principle, see J. Schwarze, *European Administrative Law* (Sweet & Maxwell, 2006), 678–9.

legal order. Beginning its career as an unwritten principle, the proportionality principle is now codified in Article 5(4) TEU:

> Under the principle of proportionality, the content and form of Union action shall not exceed what is necessary to achieve the objectives of the Treaties.[53]

The proportionality principle has been characterized as 'the most far-reaching ground for review', and 'the most potent weapon in the arsenal of the public law judge'.[54]

But how will the Court assess the proportionality of a Union act? The Court has developed a proportionality test. In its most elaborate form, the test follows a tripartite structure.[55] It analyses the *suitability*, *necessity*, and *proportionality* (in the strict sense) of a Union act. However, the Court does not always distinguish between the second and third prongs. Within its suitability review, the Court will check whether the European measure was suitable to achieve a given objective. This might be extremely straightforward.[56] The necessity test is, on the other hand, more demanding. The Union will have to show that the act adopted represents the *least restrictive means* of achieving a given objective. Finally, even the *least* restrictive means of achieving a public policy objective might disproportionately interfere with individual rights. Proportionality in a strict sense thus weighs whether the burden imposed on an individual is excessive or not.

While this tripartite test may—in theory—be hard to satisfy, the Court has granted the Union a wide margin of appreciation wherever it enjoys a sphere of discretion. The legality of a discretionary Union act will only be affected 'if the measure is manifestly inappropriate'.[57] This relaxed standard of review

---

[53] The provision continues: 'The institutions of the Union shall apply the principle of proportionality as laid down in the Protocol on the application of the principles of subsidiarity and proportionality.'

[54] Tridimas, *General Principles* (n. 51), 140.

[55] See *The Queen v Minister of Agriculture, Fisheries and Food and Secretary of State for Health, ex parte Fedesa and others*, Case C-331/88 [1990] ECR I-4023, para. 13: '[T]he principle of proportionality is one of the general principles of [Union] law. By virtue of that principle, the lawfulness of the prohibition of an economic activity is subject to the condition that the prohibitory measures are appropriate and necessary in order to achieve the objectives legitimately pursued by the legislation in question; when there is a choice between several appropriate measures recourse must be had to the least onerous, and the disadvantages caused must not be disproportionate to the aims pursued.'

[56] For a—rare—example where the test was not satisfied, see *Crispoltoni v Fattoria autonoma tabacchi di Città di Castello*, Case C-368/89 [1991] ECR I-3695, esp. para. 20.

[57] *Fedesa*, Case C-331/88 (n. 55), para. 14. See also *Germany v Council (Bananas)*, Case C-122/95 [1998] ECR I-973, para. 79.

has meant that the European Court rarely finds a Union measure to be disproportionately interfering with, say, fundamental rights.

We find a good illustration of a disproportionate Union act in *Kadi*.[58] In its fight against international terrorism, the Union had adopted a regulation freezing the assets of people suspected to be associated with Al-Qaeda. The applicant alleged, inter alia, that the Union act disproportionately restricted his right to property. The Court held that the right to property was not absolute and 'the exercise of the right to property may be restricted, provided that those restrictions in fact correspond to objectives of public interest pursued by the [Union] and do not constitute, in relation to the aim pursued, a disproportionate and intolerable interference, impairing the very substance of the right so guaranteed'.[59] And this required that 'a fair balance has been struck between the demands of the public interest and the interest of the individuals concerned'.[60] This fair balance had not been struck for the applicant; and the Union act would, so far as it concerned the applicant,[61] have to be annulled.

(c) 'Who': Legal Standing before the European Courts

The Treaties distinguish between three types of applicants in three distinct paragraphs of Article 263 TFEU.

Paragraph 2 mentions the applicants that can always bring an action for judicial review. These 'privileged' applicants are: the Member States, the European Parliament,[62] the Council, and the Commission. The reason for their privileged status is that they are *ex officio* deemed to be affected by the adoption of every Union act.

---

[58] *Kadi and Al Barakaat International Foundation v Council and Commission*, Case C-402P [2008] ECR I-6351.

[59] Ibid., para. 355.   [60] Ibid., para. 360.

[61] Ibid., para. 372. However, the Court found that the Union act as such could, in principle, be justified (ibid., para. 366).

[62] Under the original Rome Treaty, the European Parliament was not a privileged applicant. The reason for this lay in its mere 'consultative' role in the adoption of Union law. With the rise of parliamentary involvement after the Single European Act, this position became constitutionally problematic. How could Parliament cooperate or even co-decide in the legislative process, yet not be able to challenge an act that infringed its procedural prerogatives? To close this constitutional gap, the Court judicially 'amended' ex-Art. 173 EEC by giving the Parliament the status of a 'semi-privileged' applicant (see *Parliament v Council* (*Chernobyl*), Case 70/88 (n. 46)). This status was codified in the Maastricht Treaty; and the Nice Treaty finally recognized Parliament's status as a fully privileged applicant under ex-Art. 230(2) EC.

Paragraph 3 lists applicants that are 'semi-privileged'. These are the Court of Auditors, the European Central Bank, and the Committee of the Regions. They are only partly privileged, as they may solely bring review proceedings 'for the purpose of protecting their prerogatives'.[63]

Paragraph 4—finally—addresses the standing of natural or legal persons. These applicants are 'non-privileged' applicants, as they must demonstrate that the Union act affects them specifically. This fourth paragraph has been highly contested in the past 60 or so years. And in order to make sense of the Court's jurisprudence, we must start with a historical analysis of its 'Rome formulation', before moving to the current 'Lisbon formulation' of that paragraph.

(i) The Rome Formulation and its Judicial Interpretation

The Rome Treaty granted individual applicants the right to apply for judicial review in ex-Article 230 EC. Paragraph 4 of that provision stated:

> Any natural or legal person may … institute proceedings against a *decision* addressed to that person or against a *decision* which, although in the form of a regulation or *decision* addressed to another person, is of *direct and individual concern* to the former.[64]

This 'Rome' formulation must be understood against the background of two constitutional choices. First, the drafters of the Rome Treaty had wished to confine the standing of private parties to challenges of individual 'decisions'; that is: EU administrative acts. The Rome Treaty thereby distinguished between three types of decisions: decisions addressed to the applicant, decisions addressed to another person, and decisions 'in the form of a regulation'. This third decision was a decision 'in substance', which had been put into the wrong legal form.[65] Judicial review was here desirable to avert an abuse of powers.

---

[63] For a definition of this phrase in the context of Parliament's struggle to protect its prerogatives before the Nice Treaty, see *Parliament v Council*, Case C-316/91 [1994] ECR I-625, as well as *Parliament v Council*, Case C-187/93 [1994] ECR I-2857.

[64] Ex-Art. 230(4) EC (emphasis added).

[65] On the various instruments in the European legal order, see Chapter 5, Introduction. On the material distinction between 'decisions' and 'regulations', see *Confederation nationale des producteurs de fruits et légumes and others v Council*, Joined Cases 16–17/62 [1962] ECR 471, where the Court found that the Treaty 'makes a clear distinction between the concept of a "decision" and that of a "regulation"' (ibid., 478). Regulations were originally considered the sole 'generally applicable' instrument of the European Union, and their general character distinguished them from individual decisions.

Second, not every challenge of a decision by private parties was permitted. Only those decisions that were of 'direct and individual concern' to a private party could be challenged. And while this concern was presumed for decisions addressed to the applicant, it had to be proven for all other decisions. Private applicants were thus 'non-privileged' applicants in a dual sense. Not only could they *not* challenge all legal acts, they were—with the exception of decisions addressed to them—not presumed to have a legitimate interest in challenging the act.

Both constitutional choices severely restricted the standing of private parties and were heavily disputed. In the Union legal order prior to Lisbon, they were subject to extensive judicial and academic commentary.[66]

In a first line of jurisprudence, the Court succeeded significantly in 're-writing' ex-Article 230(4) EC by deserting the text's insistence on an (administrative) 'decision'. While it had originally paid homage to that text in denying private party review of generally applicable acts,[67] the Court famously abandoned its classic test and clarified that the legal nature of a Union act was irrelevant. In *Codorniu*,[68] the Court thus found:

> Although it is true that according to the criteria in the [fourth] paragraph of [ex-] Article [230] of the [EC] Treaty the contested provision is, by nature and by virtue of its sphere of application, of a legislative nature in that it applies to the traders concerned in general, that does not prevent it from being of individual concern to some of them.[69]

This judicial 'amendment' cut the Gordian knot between the 'administrative' nature of an act and ex-Article 230(4) EC. Private parties could henceforth challenge single provisions within *any* legal act—even generally applicable

---

[66] For the academic controversy (in chronological order), see A. Barav, 'Direct and Individual Concern: an Almost Insurmountable Barrier to the Admissibility of Individual Appeal to the EEC Court' (1974) 11 *Common Market Law Review* 191; H. Rasmussen, 'Why is Article 173 Interpreted Against Private Plaintiffs?' (1980) 5 *European Law Review* 112; A. Arnull, 'Private Applicants and the Action for Annulment since *Codorniu*' (2001) 38 *Common Market Law* 8; and A. Ward, *Judicial Review and the Rights of Private Parties in EU Law* (Oxford University Press, 2007).

[67] The Court's classic test concentrated on whether—from a material point of view—the challenged act was a 'real' regulation. The 'test' is spelled out in *Calpak v Commission*, Case 790/79 [1980] ECR 1949, paras 8–9: 'By virtue of the second paragraph of Article [288] of the [TFEU] the criterion for distinguishing between a regulation and a decision is whether the measure at issue is of general application or not.'

[68] *Codorniu v Council*, Case C-309/89 [1994] ECR I-1853.

[69] Ibid., para. 19.

acts like regulations or directives—as long as they could demonstrate 'direct and individual concern'.

This brings us to the second famous battleground under ex-Article 230(4) EC. What was the meaning of the 'direct and individual concern' formula? The criterion of direct concern was taken to mean that the contested measure *as such* would have to *directly* affect the position of the applicant. This would not be the case where the contested measure allowed for any form of discretionary implementation. Where an additional—and intervening—act was envisaged, there would be no 'direct' link between the measure and the applicant.[70] (In this case, the Union legal order would require the applicant to challenge the implementing measure—and not the 'parent' act.)

Sadly, the criterion of 'individual concern' was less straightforward. It was given an authoritative interpretation in *the* seminal case on the standing of private parties under ex-Article 230(4) EC: the *Plaumann* case. Plaumann, an importer of clementines, had challenged a Commission decision refusing to lower European customs duties on that fruit. But since the decision was not addressed to him—it was addressed to his Member State: Germany—he had to demonstrate that the decision was of 'individual concern' to him. The European Court defined the criterion as follows:

> Persons other than those to whom a decision is addressed may only claim to be individually concerned if that decision affects them by reason of certain attributes which are peculiar to them or by reason of circumstances in which they are differentiated from all other persons and by virtue of these factors distinguishes them individually just as in the case of the person addressed.[71]

This formulation became famous as the '*Plaumann* test'. If private applicants wish to challenge an act not addressed to them, it is not sufficient to rely on the adverse—absolute—effects that the act has on them. Instead, they must show that—relative to everybody else—the effects of the act are 'peculiar to

---

[70] See *Les Verts*, Case 294/83 [1986] ECR 1339, para. 31: 'The contested measures are of direct concern to the applicant association. They constitute a complete set of rules which are sufficient in themselves and which require no implementing provisions.' In *Regione Siciliana v Commission*, Case C-417/04P [2006] ECR I-3881, the Court however clarified that 'direct concern' was not about whether or not there—formally—needed to be additional implementing measures. It was only interested in whether the act directly determined—in a substantive sense—the situation of the applicant. Directives could thus be of direct concern—even if they always formally require implementation by the Member States.

[71] *Plaumann v Commission*, Case 25/62 [1963] ECR 95 at 107.

them'. This *relational* standard insists that they must be 'differentiated from all other persons'. The applicants must be *singled* out as if they were specifically addressed. In the present case, the Court denied this *individual* concern, as Plaumann was seen to be only *generally* concerned 'as an importer of clementines, that is to say, by reason of a commercial activity which may at any time be practised by any person'.[72] The *Plaumann* test is therefore *very* strict: whenever a private party is a member of an 'open group' of persons—anybody could decide to become an importer of clementines tomorrow—legal standing under ex-Article 230(4) EC is denied.[73] A person must belong to a 'closed group' so as to be entitled to challenge a Union act (see Figure 8.2).

Unsurprisingly, this restrictive reading of private party standing was heavily criticized as an illiberal limitation of an individual's fundamental right to judicial review. And the Court would partly soften its stance in specific areas of European law.[74] However, it generally refused to introduce a more liberal approach to the standing of private applicants. In *Unión de Pequeños*

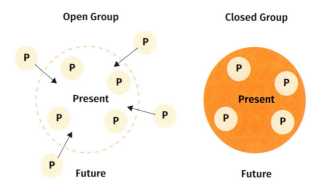

Figure 8.2 The *Plaumann* test

[72] Ibid.

[73] Even assuming that Plaumann was the only clementine importer in Germany at the time of the decision, the category of 'clementine importers' was open: future German importers could wish to get involved in the clementine trade.

[74] This had happened, e.g., in the area of European competition law; see *Metro-SB-Großmärkte v Commission*, Case 26/76 [1977] ECR 1875.

Agricultores (UPA),[75] the Court indeed expressly rejected the invitation to overrule its own jurisprudence on the following—disingenuous[76]—ground:

> While it is, admittedly, possible to envisage a system of judicial review of the legality of [Union] measures of general application different from that established by the founding Treaty and never amended as to its principles, it is for the Member States, if necessary, in accordance with Article 48 TEU, to reform the system currently in force.[77]

Has this—requested—constitutional amendment of the EU Treaties taken place? Let us look at the Lisbon formulation dealing with the standing of private parties today.

(ii) The Lisbon Formulation and its Interpretative Problems

The Lisbon Treaty has substantially amended the Rome formulation. The standing of private parties is now enshrined in Article 263(4) TFEU. The provision states:

> Any natural or legal person may . . . institute proceedings against an *act* addressed to that person or which is of *direct and individual concern* to them, and against a *regulatory act* which is of direct concern to them and does not entail implementing measures.[78]

The new formulation of paragraph 4 textually recognizes the decoupling of private party standing from the nature of the Union act challenged. In codifying *Codorniu*, an individual can thus potentially challenge any Union 'act' with legal effects. However, depending on the nature of the act, Article 263(4) TFEU still distinguishes three scenarios.

First, decisions addressed to the applicant can automatically be challenged.

Second, with regard to 'regulatory acts'—whatever they are—a private party must prove 'direct concern'. S/he also needs to prove that the act does

---

[75] *Unión de Pequeños Agricultores (UPA) v Council*, Case C-50/00 [2002] ECR I-6677.

[76] The *Plaumann* test is a result of the Court's own interpretation of what 'individual concern' means, and the Court could have therefore—theoretically—'overruled' itself. This has happened in other areas of European law; see *Criminal Proceedings against Keck and Mithouard*, Joined Cases C-267 and 268/91 [1993] ECR I-6097.

[77] *Unión de Pequeños Agricultores (UPA) v Council*, Case C-50/00 (n. 75), para. 45.

[78] Art. 263(4) TFEU (emphasis added).

not require implementing measures.[79] This has introduced an additional formal hurdle that may be hard to overcome. Because it seems that any type of act—even a formal communication—whether by the Union or the Member States may count as an implementing measure.[80]

Third, for all other acts, the applicant must continue to show 'direct *and individual concern*'. The Lisbon amendment thus abandons the requirement of an 'individual concern' only for the second but not the third category of acts; and the dividing line between the second and third categories was thus poised to become *the* post-Lisbon interpretative battlefield within Article 263(4) TFEU. This dividing line is determined by the concept of 'regulatory act'.

What, then, are 'regulatory acts'? The term is not defined in the EU Treaties. Two constitutional options exist. According to a first view, 'regulatory acts' are defined as all 'generally applicable acts'.[81] This reading liberalizes the standing of private applicants significantly, as the second category would cover all legislative as well as executive acts of a general nature. According to a second view, on the other hand, the concept of 'regulatory act' should be defined in contradistinction to 'legislative acts'. Regulatory acts are here understood as non-legislative acts.[82] This view places acts adopted under the—ordinary or special—legislative procedure outside the second category. The judicial review of formal legislation would consequently require 'direct *and* individual concern', and would thus remain largely immune from private party challenges.

How have the European Courts decided? In *Inuit I*,[83] the General Court sided with the second—narrower—view. The case involved a challenge by traders of seal products to a Union regulation banning the marketing of such products

[79] 'Direct concern' should theoretically mean that no implementing act is needed. Why then does Art. 263(4) TFEU repeat this expressly? The answer lies in the prior jurisprudence of the Court (see especially *Regione Siciliana v Commission*, Case C-417/04P (n.70)—discussed earlier. From this perspective, the new Art. 263(4) TFEU, and its insistence on the absence of an implementing act, might signal the wish of the Lisbon Treaty-makers for a return to a more restrictive—formal—position. This result should mean that a regulatory act adopted in the form of a 'directive' should never fall within the second class of acts within Art. 263(4), since they—by definition—always require a formal act of implementation by the Member States. On the format of the 'directive' see, Chapter 5, Section 3.

[80] See *Kyocera v Commission*, Case C-553/14P, EU:C:2015:805, para. 55.

[81] J. Bast, 'Legal Instruments and Judicial Protection' in A. von Bogdandy and J. Bast (eds), *Principles of European Constitutional Law* (Hart, 2009), 345 at 396.

[82] A. Ward, 'The Draft EU Constitution and Private Party Access to Judicial Review of EU Measures' in T. Tridimas and P. Nebbia (eds), *European Union Law for the Twenty-First Century* (Hart, 2005), 201 at 221.

[83] *Inuit v Parliament & Council*, Case T-18/10 [2011] ECR II-5599.

in the internal market. Having been adopted on the basis of Article 114 TFEU, under the ordinary legislative procedure, the question arose to what extent Union legislation could be challenged by interested private parties. After a comprehensive analysis of the various arguments for and against the inclusion of legislative acts into the category of regulatory acts, the General Court found the two classes of acts to be mutually exclusive. In the words of the General Court:

> [I]t must be held that the meaning of 'regulatory act' for the purposes of the fourth paragraph of Article 263 TFEU must be understood as covering all acts of general application *apart from legislative acts.*[84]

The judgment was confirmed on appeal,[85] where the Court of Justice held as follows:

> [T]he purpose of the alteration to the right of natural and legal persons to institute legal proceedings, laid down in the fourth paragraph of [ex-]Article 230 EC, was to enable those persons to bring, under less stringent conditions, actions for annulment of acts of general application other than legislative acts. The General Court was therefore correct to conclude that the concept of 'regulatory act' provided for in the fourth paragraph of Article 263 TFEU does not encompass legislative acts.[86]

For private party challenges to legislative acts (as well as decisions not addressed to the applicant), the Union legal order thus continues to require proof of a 'direct *and individual* concern'. Any reports on the death of *Plaumann* have thus turned out to be greatly exaggerated. For the Court in *Inuit I* expressly identified 'individual concern' under Article 263(4) TFEU with the *Plaumann* test. And rejecting the argument that the Lisbon Treaty-makers had wished to replace the 'old' test with a 'new' less restrictive test, the Court here held:

> In that regard, it can be seen that the second limb of the fourth paragraph of Article 263 TFEU corresponds ... to the second limb of the fourth paragraph of [ex-]Article 230 EC. The wording of that provision has not been altered. Further, there is nothing to suggest that the authors of the Treaty of Lisbon had any intention of altering the scope of the conditions of admissibility already laid

---

[84] Ibid., para. 56 (emphasis added).
[85] *Inuit v Parliament & Council*, Case C-583/11P, EU:C:2013:625.
[86] Ibid., paras 60–1.

> down in the fourth paragraph of [ex-]Article 230 EC ... In those circumstances, it must be held that the content of the condition that the act of which annulment is sought should be of individual concern, as interpreted by the Court in its settled case-law since *Plaumann* v *Commission*, was not altered by the Treaty of Lisbon ... According to that case-law, natural or legal persons satisfy the condition of individual concern only if the contested act affects them by reason of certain attributes which are peculiar to them or by reason of circumstances in which they are differentiated from all other persons, and by virtue of these factors distinguishes them individually just as in the case of the person addressed[.][87]

The Court thus refused to replace the 'old' *Plaumann* test with a 'new' less restrictive test; and yet there are good reasons for this change. The strongest critique of the *Plaumann* test has come from the pen of Advocate General Jacobs. In *Unión de Pequeños Agricultores* (*UPA*),[88] his learned opinion pointed to the test's anomalous logic. It is indeed absurd that 'the greater the number of persons affected the less likely it is that effective judicial review is available'.[89] But what alternative test might then be suitable? 'The only satisfactory solution is therefore to recognise that an applicant is individually concerned by a [Union] measure where the measure has, or is liable to have, a *substantial adverse effect* on his interests.'[90] However, as we saw in the previous subsection, the Court has consistently rejected this reinterpretation on the formal ground that abandoning *Plaumann* would require Treaty amendment. The various tests applying under Article 263(4) can be seen in Figure 8.3.

4. Damages Actions: Union Liability

Where the Union legislature or executive has acted in violation of EU law, can the Court grant damages for losses incurred? The European Treaties do acknowledge an action for damages in Article 268 TFEU;[91] yet, for a

---

[87]   Ibid., paras 70–2.
[88]   *Unión de Pequeños Agricultores*, Case C-50/00 (n. 75).
[89]   Opinion of Advocate General Jacobs, in ibid., para. 59.
[90]   Ibid., para. 102 (emphasis added).
[91]   Art. 268 TFEU: 'The Court of Justice of the European Union shall have jurisdiction in disputes relating to compensation for damage provided for in the second and third paragraphs of Article 340.'

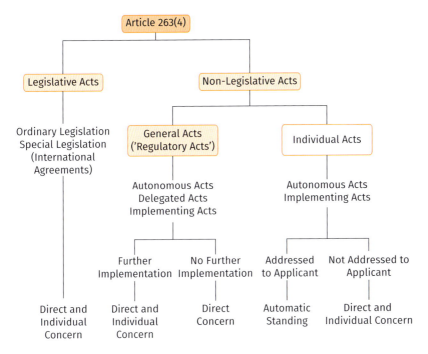

Figure 8.3 Types of acts under Article 263(4)

strange reason the article refers to another provision: Article 340 TFEU. This
provision reads:

> The contractual liability of the Union shall be governed by the law applicable to
> the contract in question.
>
> In the case of non-contractual liability, the Union shall, in accordance with the
> general principles common to the laws of the Member States, make good any dam-
> age caused by its institutions or by its servants in the performance of their duties.[92]

The provision distinguishes between contractual liability in paragraph 1, and
non-contractual liability in paragraph 2. While the former is governed by
national law, the latter is governed by *European* law. Paragraph 2 recognizes
that the Union can do 'wrong' either as an institution or through its servants,[93] and that it will be under an obligation to make good damage incurred.

---

[92] Art. 340(1) and (2) TFEU.

[93] As regards the Union's civil servants, only their 'official acts' will be attributed to the Union.
With regard to their personal liability, Art. 340(4) TFEU states: 'The personal liability of its servants towards the Union shall be governed by the provisions laid down in their Staff Regulations
or in the Conditions of Employment applicable to them.'

What are the European constitutional principles underpinning an action for the non-contractual liability of the Union? Article 340(2) has had a colourful and complex constitutional history. It has not only been transformed from a dependent action into an independent action; its substantial conditions have changed significantly. This final section will briefly analyse the procedural and substantive conditions of Union liability actions.

(a) Procedural Conditions: From Dependent to Independent Action

The action for damages under Article 340(2) started its life as a dependent action; that is, an action that hinged on the prior success of another action. In *Plaumann*—a case discussed in the previous section—a clementine importer had brought an annulment action against a Union decision, while at the same time asking for compensation equivalent to the customs duties that had been paid as a consequence of the challenged European decision. However, as we saw earlier, the action for annulment failed due to the restrictive standing requirements under Article 263(4); and the Court found that this would equally end the liability action for damages:

> In the present case, the contested decision has not been annulled. An administrative measure which has not been annulled cannot of itself constitute a wrongful act on the part of the administration inflicting damage upon those whom it affects. The latter cannot therefore claim damages by reason of that measure. The Court cannot by way of an action for compensation take steps which would nullify the legal effects of a decision which, as stated, has not been annulled.[94]

A liability action thus had to be preceded by a (successful) annulment action. The *Plaumann* Court here insisted on a 'certificate of illegality' before even considering the substantive merits of Union liability. This, however, dramatically changed in *Lütticke*.[95] The case constitutes the 'declaration of independence' for liability actions:

> Article [340] was established by the Treaty as an independent form of action with a particular purpose to fulfil within the system of actions and subject to conditions for its use, conceived with a view to its specific purpose.[96]

---

[94] *Plaumann*, Case 25/62 (n. 71), 108.
[95] *Lütticke v Commission*, Case 4/69 [1971] ECR 325.   [96] Ibid., para. 6.

According to the Court, it would be contrary to 'the independent nature' of this action as well as to 'the efficacy of the general system of forms of action created by the Treaty' to deny admissibility of the damages action on the ground that it might lead to a similar result as an annulment action.[97]

What are the procedural requirements for liability actions? The proceedings may be brought against any Union action or inaction that is claimed to have caused damage. The act (or omission) must normally be an 'official act'; that is: it must be attributable to the Union.[98] Unlike Article 263 TFEU, there are no limitations on the potential applicants: anyone who feels 'wronged' by a Union (in)action can bring proceedings under Article 340(2).[99] And against whom? With the exception of the European Central Bank,[100] the provision only generically identifies the Union as the potential defendant. However, the Court has clarified that 'in the interests of a good administration of justice', the Union 'should be represented before the Court by the institution or institutions against which the matter giving rise to liability is alleged'.[101]

When will the action have to be brought? Unlike the strict two-month limitation period for annulment actions, liability actions can be brought within a five-year period.[102] The procedural requirements for liability actions are thus much more liberal than the procedural regime governing annulment actions.

(b) Substantive Conditions: From *Schöppenstedt* to *Bergaderm*

The constitutional regime governing the substantive conditions for liability actions can be divided into two historical phases. In a first phase, the European Court distinguished between 'administrative' and 'legislative' Union acts. The former were subject to a relatively low liability threshold. The Union would be

---

[97] Ibid. In the present case, the Court dealt with an infringement action for failure to act under Art. 265 TFEU (see Section 2), but the same result applies to annulment actions; see *Schöppenstedt v Council*, Case 5/71 [1971] ECR 975.

[98] The Union must be the author of the act, and this means that the Treaties themselves—as collective acts of the Member States—cannot be the basis of a liability action (see *Compagnie Continentale France v Council*, Case 169/73 [1975] ECR 117, para. 16).

[99] See *CMC Cooperativa muratori e cementisti and others v Commission*, Case 118/83 [1985] ECR 2325.

[100] Art. 340(3) TFEU.

[101] *Werhahn Hansamühle and others v Council*, Joined Cases 63–69/72 [1973] ECR 1229, para. 7.

[102] Art. 46 Statute of the Court.

liable for (almost) any illegal action that had caused damage.[103] By contrast, legislative acts were subject to the so-called '*Schöppenstedt* formula'.[104] This formula stated as follows:

> [W]here *legislative* action involving measures of economic policy is concerned, the [Union] does not incur non-contractual liability for damage suffered by individuals as a consequence of that action, by virtue of the provisions contained in Article [340], second paragraph, of the Treaty, *unless a sufficiently flagrant violation of a superior rule of law for the protection of the individual has occurred.*[105]

This formula made Union liability for legislative acts dependent on the breach of a 'superior rule' of Union law—whatever that meant—which aimed to grant rights to individuals.[106] And the breach of that rule would have to be sufficiently serious.[107]

This test was significantly reformed in *Bergaderm*.[108] The reason for this reform was the Court's wish to align the liability regime for breaches of European law by the Union with the liability regime governing the Member States.[109] Today, European law confers a right to reparation:

> where three conditions are met: the rule of law infringed must be intended to confer rights on individuals; the breach must be sufficiently serious; and there must be a direct causal link between the breach of the obligation resting on the State and the damage sustained by the injured parties.[110]

Two important changes were reflected in the '*Bergaderm* formula'. First, the Court abandoned the distinction between 'administrative' and 'legislative' acts. The new test would apply to all Union acts regardless of their nature.[111] Second, the Court dropped the idea that a 'superior rule' had to be infringed.

---

[103] See *Adams v Commission*, Case 145/83 [1985] ECR 3539, para. 44: '[B]y failing to make all reasonable efforts . . . the Commission has incurred liability towards the applicant in respect of that damage.'

[104] *Schöppenstedt v Council*, Case 5/71 (n. 97).

[105] Ibid., para. 11 (emphasis added).

[106] *Vreugdenhil BV v Commission*, Case C-282/90 [1992] ECR I-1937.

[107] See *Bayerische HNL Vermehrungsbetriebe and others v Council and Commission*, Joined Cases 83 and 94/76 and 4, 15 and 40/77 [1978] ECR 1209.

[108] *Bergaderm et al. v Commission*, Case C-352/98P [2000] ECR I-5291.

[109] Ibid., para. 41. This inspiration was 'mutual'. For, as we saw in Chapter 7, Section 2, the Court used Art. 340(2) TFEU as a rationale for the creation of a liability regime for the Member States.

[110] Ibid., para. 42.   [111] Ibid., para. 46.

Henceforth, it was only necessary to show that the Union had caused damage by breaching a rule intended to confer individual rights, and that the breach was sufficiently serious. And the decisive test for finding that a breach of European law was sufficiently serious was whether the Union 'manifestly and gravely disregarded the limits on its discretion'.[112]

Conclusion

This chapter looked at four judicial actions that can be brought directly before the Court of Justice of the European Union. Three of these actions are relatively straightforward. The Treaties distinguish between infringement actions against the Member States, and proceedings against the Union for a failure to act. Proceedings against the Union can also be brought where the Union is liable for non-contractual damages.

The European Court is also empowered to review the legality of European (secondary) law. The Union legal order has thereby opted for a strong 'rule of law' version. It allows the Court to review the formal and substantive legality of European law. However, in the past, there existed severe procedural limitations on the right of individual applicants to request judicial review proceedings. The Lisbon Treaty has partly liberalized these procedural restrictions for 'regulatory' acts; yet the *Plaumann* test continues to apply to all legislative acts.

---

[112] Ibid., para. 43. However, where there was no discretion, 'the mere infringement of [Union] law may be sufficient to establish the existence of a sufficiently serious breach' (ibid., para. 44).

Part III

European Law: Substance

This Part analyses the substantive heart of European law. When the Union was founded, its central aim was the creation of a 'common' or 'internal' market between the Member States. Such an internal market was to go well beyond a free trade area or a customs union. Its aim was to create an area without internal frontiers to the free movement of goods, persons, services, and capital. To guarantee these four fundamental freedoms, the EU Treaties pursue a dual strategy: negative and positive integration. Negative integration refers to the removal of illegal national barriers to trade, whereas positive integration means Union legislation that 'harmonizes' national laws. Chapters 9 and 10 will explore both strategies in the context of the free movement of goods. Chapter 11 then analyses the free movement of persons—which allows European citizens and companies to work and live within another Member State. Finally, Chapter 12 offers an 'introduction' to EU competition law. The latter is traditionally seen as a functional complement to the internal market.

Internal Market: Goods I

Introduction

How can the Union create a 'single' internal market out of 'diverse' national markets? To create an internal market, the EU Treaties pursue a dual strategy: negative and positive integration.[1] The Union is first charged to 'free' the internal market from unjustified national barriers to trade in goods; and, in order to do so, the Treaties contain a number of constitutional prohibitions 'negating' illegitimate obstacles to intra-Union trade. This strategy of *negative* integration is complemented by a—second—strategy of *positive* integration. The Union is here charged to adopt positive legislation to remove obstacles to intra-Union trade arising from diverse national laws. For that purpose,

---

[1] J. Pinder, 'Positive and Negative Integration: Some Problems of Economic Union in the EEC' (1968) 24 *The World Today* 88.

the Treaties confer a number of legislative competences that allow the Union to 'harmonize' national laws in the internal market. The most general and famous provision here is Article 114, which entitles the Union to adopt harmonization measures that 'have as their object the establishment and functioning of the internal market'.[2] This chapter explores the Union's negative integration tools in the context of the free movement of goods, while the next chapter investigates the Union harmonization competences.

What is the 'negative integration' regime governing goods? In order to create an internal market in goods, the Union insists that illegal barriers to intra-Union trade must be removed. Its constitutional regime is, however, split over two sites in Part III of the TFEU (see Table 9.1). It finds its principal place in Title II governing the free movement of goods, which is complemented by a chapter on 'Tax Provisions' in Title VII. Within these two sites, we find three important prohibitions. Section 1 examines the prohibition on customs duties. These are fiscal duties charged when goods cross national borders. Section 2 moves to the second type of fiscal charge: discriminatory taxes imposed on foreign goods. Section 3 then investigates the legality of

Table 9.1 Treaty provisions on the free movement of goods

Title II: Free Movement of Goods	Title VII: Competition, Taxation, Approximation
Chapter 1: Customs Union	*Chapter 1: Rules on Competition*
Article 30: Prohibition on CD and CEE	
Article 31: Common Customs Tariff	*Chapter 2: Tax Provisions*
Article 32: Commission Duties	Article 110: Prohibition of Discriminatory Taxes
Chapter 2: Customs Cooperation	Article 111: Repayment of Internal Taxes
Chapter 3: Quantitative Restrictions	Article 112: Countervailing Charges
Article 34: Prohibition of QR and MEE on Imports	
Article 35: Prohibition of QR and MEE on Exports	Article 113: Harmonisation of Indirect Taxes
Article 36: Justifications	*Chapter 3: Approximation of Laws*
Article 37: State Monopolies of a Commercial Character	

---

[2] Art. 114 TFEU.

regulatory restrictions to the free movement of goods. Regulatory restrictions are not, unlike fiscal duties, pecuniary charges. They simply 'regulate' access to the national market by—for example—establishing product or labelling requirements. Finally, Section 4 will look at possible justifications for regulatory restrictions to trade in goods.

1. Fiscal Barriers I: Customs Duties

Customs duties are the classic commercial weapon of the protectionist state. They are traditionally employed to 'protect' domestic goods against cheaper imports. Customs duties here operate like a 'countervailing' charge or tax, which is typically demanded at the national border. Yet within a customs union, these pecuniary charges are prohibited.

Within the European Union, they are outlawed by Article 30 TFEU. The provision states:

> Customs duties on imports and exports and charges having equivalent effect shall be prohibited between Member States. The prohibition shall also apply to customs duties of a fiscal nature.

Textually, the prohibition applies to charges on imports and exports; and no exceptions are made.[3] The fact that Article 30 constitutes an absolute prohibition has indeed been confirmed; yet, as we shall see later, the Court has nonetheless allowed for objective justifications that may exceptionally permit charges imposed by Member States.

(a) Article 30: An Absolute Prohibition

What is a customs duty? With no formal definition in the EU Treaties, the Court has defined the concept in a general way. A customs duty is:

> any pecuniary charge, however small and whatever its designation and mode of application, which is imposed on goods by reason of the fact that they cross a frontier[.][4]

---

[3] According to Art. 28(2) TFEU, the prohibition even applies 'to products coming from third countries which are in free circulation in Member States'.

[4] *Commission v Italy* (*Statistical Levy*), Case 24/68 [1969] ECR 193, para. 7.

However, the Treaties not only outlaw customs duties in this strict sense. For Article 30 extends its prohibition to 'charges having equivalent effect' (CEE); and in *Commission v Italy*,[5] the Court defined a CEE as:

> any charge which, by altering the price of an article exported, has the same restrictive effect on the free circulation of that article as a customs duty[.][6]

The purpose of the charge is thereby irrelevant, as Article 30 'ma[de] no distinction based on the purpose of the duties and charges the abolition of which it requires'.[7] All that mattered was the effect of a charge, and even the smallest of effects would matter.[8]

Would Article 30 nonetheless require a *protectionist* effect; that is: an effect that protected domestic goods? Despite a brief flirtation with a protectionist rationale,[9] the Court has chosen a different standard. The mere presence of a *restricting* effect on the free movement of goods will trigger Article 30. This constitutional choice was made in *Statistical Levy*.[10] Italy had imposed a levy on goods leaving (or entering) Italy for the purpose of collecting statistical data. Since the levy applied universally to all goods crossing the national border, it argued that the measure could not constitute a CEE 'since any protection of domestic production or discrimination is eliminated'.[11] The Court disagreed:

> [T]he purpose of the abolition of customs barriers is not merely to eliminate their protective nature, as the Treaty sought on the contrary to give general scope and effect to the rule on the elimination of customs duties and charges having equivalent effect, in order to ensure the free movement of goods. It follows from the system as a whole and from the general and absolute nature of the prohibition of any customs duty applicable to goods moving between Member States that customs duties are prohibited independently of any consideration of the purpose for which they were introduced and the destination of the revenue obtained there from.[12]

---

[5] *Commission v Italy* (*Art Treasures*), Case 7/68 [1968] ECR 423.

[6] Ibid., 429.   [7] Ibid.

[8] *Commission v Italy* (*Statistical Levy*), Case 24/68 (n. 4), para. 14: 'The very low rate of the charge cannot change its character with regard to the principles of the Treaty[.]'

[9] *Commission v Luxembourg and Belgium*, Joined Cases 2 and 3/62 [1962] ECR (English Special Edition) 425 at 432.

[10] *Commission v Italy* (*Statistical Levy*), Case 24/68 (n. 4).

[11] Ibid., para. 12.   [12] Ibid., paras 6–7.

Statistical Levy thus clarified that Article 30 outlawed *all* restrictions—including non-discriminatory restrictions devoid of a protectionist effect.[13] The 'general and absolute nature of the prohibition of any customs duties' was confirmed in subsequent jurisprudence.[14] '[A]ny pecuniary charge—however small—imposed on goods by reason of the fact that they cross a frontier constitutes an obstacle to the movement of such goods.'[15] And such an obstacle remained an obstacle 'even if it is not imposed for the benefit of the State, is not discriminatory or protective in effect or if the product on which the charge is imposed is not in competition with any domestic product'.[16]

This *absolute* restriction rationale underlying Article 30 originally stemmed from the jurisdictional scope of Article 30. For the prohibition appeared to only outlaw national measures that imposed a charge on the frontier-crossing of goods; and these measures are—by definition—distinctly applicable to imports or exports.[17]

This also explains an important conceptual limit to the scope of Article 30. For if it only applies to *frontier* measures it cannot cover measures qualifying as *internal* taxation. The question thus arises as to when a fiscal charge constitutes an 'external' customs duty, and when it constitutes an internal tax. In its past jurisprudence, the Court has tried to answer this question by excluding from the scope of Article 30 'financial charges within a general system of internal taxation *applying systematically to domestic and imported products according to the same criteria* [that] are not to be considered as charges having equivalent effect'.[18] Equally, applicable fiscal charges that apply the 'same criteria' to domestic and imported goods will thus not fall under Article 30.

(b) Objective 'Justifications'

Can a State exceptionally impose customs duties in certain situations? There are no express justifications for fiscal barriers to trade in goods. This absence

---

[13] Ibid., para. 9.

[14] *Sociaal Fonds voor de Diamantarbeiders v S.A. Ch. Brachfeld & Sons and Chougol Diamond Co.*, Case 2/69 [1969] ECR 211, paras 11–14.

[15] Ibid.   [16] Ibid., paras 15–18.

[17] This—convincing—external limit to Art. 30 has, however, partly been overruled by a string of cases in the 1990s dealing with non-discriminatory customs charges *within* Member States (cf. *Lancry SA v Direction Générale des Douanes and others*, Joined Cases C-363 and 407–11/93 [1994] ECR I-3957). For a discussion of this development, see R. Schütze, *European Union Law* (Cambridge University Press, 2018), 508–9.

[18] *Capolongo v Azienda Agricole*, Case 77/72 [1973] ECR 611, para. 12 (emphasis added).

contrasts with the presence of such express justifications for regulatory barriers under Article 36.[19]

Could the latter provision nonetheless apply by analogy to fiscal barriers? In *Commission v Italy*,[20] the defendant tried to justify a charge on the export of goods with artistic or historical value by pointing to Article 36. Yet the Court rejected this reasoning. Exceptions to the free movement of goods had to be interpreted restrictively. With regard to Article 36 this meant that it 'is not possible to apply the exception laid down in the latter provision to measures which fall outside the scope of the prohibitions referred to in the chapter relating to the elimination of quantitative restrictions between Member States'.[21] Article 36 was thus confined to *regulatory* restrictions and could not be extended to *fiscal* charges. And since there were no specific justifications for measures falling into Article 30, the Court concluded that the provision 'does not permit of any exceptions'.[22]

The Court, however, subsequently recognized two *implied* exceptions. The first exception relates to the situation where a fiscal charge constitutes consideration for a service rendered. In *Statistical Levy*,[23] the Italian government had argued that its wish to create statistical data for imports and exports generally benefited individual traders, and that this commercial advantage 'justifies their paying for this public service' as a quid pro quo.[24] The Court indeed accepted the abstract idea;[25] yet it nonetheless found against Italy, since the charge was not consideration for a *specific service* benefiting *individual traders*. The statistical information was only 'beneficial to the economy as a whole', and the advantage was thus 'so general' that the charge could not be regarded 'as the consideration for a *specific* benefit'.[26]

The second (implied) justification from the absolute prohibition of fiscal charges are charges that a Member State levies as compensation for frontier

---

[19] See Table 9.1 earlier. For the text of Art. 36 and its interpretation, see Section 4.

[20] *Commission v Italy* (*Art Treasures*), Case 7/68 (n. 5).

[21] Ibid., 430.

[22] *Commission v Italy* (*Statistical levy*), Case 24/68 (n. 4), para. 10; and see also *Sociaal Fonds voor de Diamantarbeiders v S.A. Ch. Brachfeld*, Case 2/69 (n. 14), paras 19–21.

[23] *Commission v Italy* (*Statistical Levy*), Case 24/68 (n. 4).

[24] Ibid., para. 15.

[25] Ibid., para. 11: 'Although it is not impossible that in certain circumstances a specific service actually rendered may form consideration for a possible proportional payment for the service in question, this may only apply in specific cases which cannot lead to the circumvention of the provisions of [Article 30] of the Treaty.'

[26] Ibid., para. 16 (emphasis added).

checks that are required under European law.[27] The rationale behind this exception is that the Member States here act on behalf of the Union, and in a way that facilitates the free movement of goods.

2. Fiscal Barriers II: Discriminatory Internal Taxation

With regard to fiscal barriers, the prohibition of customs duties and the prohibition of protectionist taxation are two sides of the same coin. In the Union legal order, Article 110 is meant to tackle discriminatory taxation and here complements Article 30 TFEU:

> Article [110] supplements the provision[] on the abolition of customs duties and charges having equivalent effect. Its aim is to ensure free movement of goods between the Member States in normal conditions of competition by the elimination of all forms of protection which may result from the application of internal taxation.[28]

Despite their complementary aims, the jurisdictional scopes of Articles 30 and 110 are, however, fundamentally different. The former catches national measures that impose a charge on goods when crossing an external (national) frontier; whereas Article 110 is to apply where foreign goods are subject—with domestic goods—to internal taxation. Like two sides of the same coin, the two prohibitions within Articles 30 and 110 are thus bound together yet mutually exclusive.[29]

The difference in their jurisdictional scope also implies a fundamental difference with regard to the material test applicable within each prohibition. Article 30 is based, as we saw earlier, on an (absolute) test for distinctly applicable measures. Article 110, on the other hand, is centred on a (relative) discrimination

---

[27] In *Bauhuis v The Netherlands*, Case 46/76 [1977] ECR 5, the Court had been asked to deal with a Union law that required veterinary and public health inspections by the exporting Member State so as to make multiple frontier inspections unnecessary. The health inspections were thus not unilaterally imposed by a Member State but reflected 'the general interest of the [Union]' (ibid., para. 29); and as such, they would not hinder trade in goods (ibid., para. 30). National charges for these 'Union' inspections were thus legal (ibid., para. 31). For a subsequent codification of the *Bauhuis* test, see *Commission v Germany*, Case 18/87 [1988] ECR 5427.

[28] *Bergandi v Directeur général des impôts*, Case 252/86 [1988] ECR 1342, para. 24.

[29] *Compagnie Commerciale de l'Ouest and others v Receveur Principal des Douanes de La Pallice Port*, Case C-78/90 [1992] ECR I-1847, para. 22: 'The provisions on charges having equivalent effect and those on discriminatory internal taxation cannot be applied together. The scope of each of those provisions must therefore be defined.'

test for indistinctly applicable measures; that is: measures that apply both to foreign *and* domestic goods. Article 110 thus states:

> [1]   No Member State shall impose, directly or indirectly, on the products of other Member States any internal taxation of any kind *in excess of* that imposed directly or indirectly on similar domestic products.
>
> [2]   Furthermore, no Member State shall impose on the products of other Member States any internal taxation of such a nature to afford *indirect protection* to other products.

According to the structure of Article 110, the provision thus outlaws two types of national taxes. Paragraph 1 declares illegal all national tax laws that *discriminate* between foreign and domestic goods. Discrimination here means that 'similar' foreign goods are treated dissimilarly. Paragraph 2 then covers a second variant of fiscal protectionism. Strictly speaking, it is not based on a discrimination rationale, since its scope is wider than outlawing the dissimilar treatment of 'similar' goods.[30] Yet by prohibiting the 'indirect protection to other products', the better view regards Article 110(2) as outlawing all general forms of discrimination; and the relationship between the two paragraphs may thus best be described as one of *lex specialis* to *lex generalis*.[31]

Let us look at both protectionist variants in turn.

(a)   Paragraph 1: Discrimination against 'Similar' Foreign Goods

Article 110(1) prohibits foreign goods to be taxed 'in excess of' similar domestic goods. This outlaws internal taxes that discriminate between national and imported products. This might occur through direct or indirect means. Direct discrimination takes place where national tax legislation *legally* disadvantages foreign goods by—for example—imposing a higher tax rate on foreign as opposed to domestic goods.[32] Indirect discrimination occurs

---

[30]   On the two distinct tests for Art. 110(1) and (2) TFEU, see *Fink-Frucht GmbH v Hauptzollamt München-Landsbergerstrasse*, Case 27/67 [1967] ECR 223.

[31]   *Co-Frutta*, Case 193/85 [1987] ECR 2085, para. 19: '[W]here the requirement of similarity prescribed by the first paragraph of Article [110] is not fulfilled, the second paragraph of that article is intended to cover all forms of indirect tax protection in the case of products which, without being similar within the meaning of the first paragraph of Article [110], are nevertheless in competition, even partial, indirect or potential competition, with each other.'

[32]   See *Lütticke GmbH v Hauptzollamt Sarrelouis*, Case 57/65 [1966] ECR 205; as well as *Hansen & Balle v Hauptzollamt de Flensburg*, Case 148/77 [1978] ECR 1787.

where the same national tax formally applies to both foreign and domestic goods, but materially imposes a *heavier* fiscal burden on the former.

The key to the prohibition behind Article 110(1) lies in the concept of 'similarity'. When are domestic and foreign goods *similar*? Early on, the Court clarified that similarity is wider than identity;[33] and that similarity relates to comparability.[34] Comparability thereby means that two goods 'have similar characteristics and meet the same needs from the point of view of consumers'.[35] But are 'whisky' and 'cognac' comparable drinks?[36] Or should it make a difference that the former is seen as an *apéritif*, while the latter constitutes a *digestif*?[37] In its jurisprudence, the Court has endorsed a 'broad interpretation of the concept of similarity',[38] which however takes account of 'objective' differences between two seemingly similar products.

An excellent illustration of this approach is *Humblot*.[39] Monsieur Humblot had acquired a (German) Mercedes car in France. The car possessed 36 CV (fiscal horsepower) and he had to pay a tax imposed by the French Revenue Code, which distinguished between a progressive annual tax for cars up to 16 CV and a single special tax for cars above this rate. The special tax was nearly five times higher than the highest rate of the general progressive tax. And as France did not produce any cars above 16 CV, the question arose whether the special tax was 'in excess of' the national tax on domestic goods. But are small (French) cars comparable to big (German) cars? The French government defended its internal tax regime by arguing that 'the special tax is charged solely on luxury vehicles, which are *not similar*, within the meaning of the first paragraph of Article [110] to cars liable to the differential tax'.[40] The Court disagreed. For while it acknowledged the power of the Member States to 'subject products such as cars to a system of road tax which increases progressively in amount depending on an *objective criterion*, such as the power rating',[41] the French tax system did not do so adequately and thus indirectly discriminated against foreign cars.

---

[33] See *Hansen & Balle v Hauptzollamt de Flensburg*, Case 148/77 (n. 32), para. 19: 'The application of that provision is based not on a strict requirement that the products should be identical but on their "similarity".'

[34] See *Commission v France* (*Whisky v Cognac*), Case 168/78 [1980] ECR 347, para. 5.

[35] *Rewe-Zentrale des Lebensmittel-Großhandels GmbH v Hauptzollamt Landau/Pfalz*, Case 45/75 [1976] ECR 181.

[36] *Commission v France* (*Whisky v Cognac*), Case 168/78 (n. 34).

[37] Ibid., para. 33.

[38] *John Walker v Ministeriet for Skatter og Afgifter*, Case 243/84 [1986] ECR 875, para. 11.

[39] *Humblot v Directeur des Services Fiscaux*, Case 112/84 [1985] ECR 1367.

[40] Ibid., para. 9 (emphasis added).

[41] Ibid., para. 12 (emphasis added).

What 'objective' criteria could be used fiscally to distinguish between seemingly similar products? This question is—misleadingly—called the question of 'objective justification'.[42] What stands behind this misnomer is the idea that while a national tax system must be neutral towards foreign goods, it can discriminate between goods 'on the basis of objective criteria'.[43] Thus: where a Member State discriminates on the basis of a regional policy objective, such a public policy objective will not amount to protectionist discrimination. The discrimination is here 'justified' by 'objective' criteria that distinguish two products.

This logic can be seen in *Commission v France* (*Natural Sweet Wines*).[44] The Commission had brought proceedings against a French tax scheme that exempted naturally sweet wines from the higher consumption duty on liqueur wines. The French government defended this differential treatment by pointing to the fact that 'natural sweet wines are made in regions characterized by low rainfall and relatively poor soil, in which the difficulty of growing other crops means that the local economy depends heavily on their production'.[45] This regional policy objective gave preferential treatment to a 'traditional and customary production' over similar goods resulting from industrial production. This 'objective' criterion did not discriminate against foreign goods.[46]

(b) Paragraph 2: Protection against 'Competing' Foreign Goods

Even when an internal tax does not discriminate against 'similar' domestic goods, it might still fall within the second paragraph of Article 110. Strictly speaking, the rationale behind Article 110(2) is indeed broader than a prohibition on discriminatory taxation. Yet the better way is to see Article 110(2) as an extension of the discrimination rationale in Article 110(1). Its reach is simply wider when outlawing all internal taxes that grant 'indirect protection' to domestic goods. For the provision targets national taxes that *generally disadvantage foreign goods*. The Court has, however, held that such indirect protection can only occur where domestic goods are *in competition* with imported goods.[47] And Article 110(2) consequently requires two elements

---

[42]   The term is used in *Commission v Italy* (*Regenerated Oil*), Case 21/79 [1980] ECR 1, para. 16: 'objectively justified'.

[43]   *John Walker v Ministeriet for Skatter og Afgifter*, Case 243/84 (n. 38), para. 23.

[44]   *Commission v France* (*Natural Sweet Wines*), Case 196/85 [1987] ECR 1597.

[45]   Ibid., para. 9.   [46]   Ibid., para. 10.

[47]   Where this is not the case, Art. 110(2) will indeed not apply; see *De Danske Bilimportorer v Skatteministeriet, Toldog Skattestyrelsen*, Case C-383/01 [2003] ECR I-6065.

to be fulfilled before a national tax is found to hinder the free movement of goods. First, the national law will tax *competing* goods differently; and, second, this differentiation indirectly protects *national* goods and thus indirectly 'discriminates' against foreign goods.

When will two goods be in competition? Within Article 110(2), the Court has generally adopted a flexible approach. This can be seen in *Commission v United Kingdom (Beer & Wine).*[48] The Commission had brought infringement proceedings against Great Britain in the belief that its tax regime for wine granted indirect protection to British beer. The excise tax on wine was indeed significantly higher than that on beer, and as Britain produced very little wine but a lot of beer, the suspicion of indirect protectionism arose. Britain counterclaimed that there was no competitive relationship between beer and wine, and that there could thus be no such protectionist effect. Not only were the two products 'entirely different' with regard to their production and price structure,[49] the goods would hardly ever be substituted by consumers.[50] The Court was not impressed with this line of argument, and espoused its dynamic understanding of product substitution:

> In order to determine the existence of a competitive relationship under the second paragraph of Article [110], it is necessary to consider not only the present state of the market but also the possibilities for development within the context of the free movement of goods at the [Union] level and the further potential for the substitution of products for one another which may be revealed by intensification of trade, so as fully to develop the complementary features of the economies of the Member States in accordance with the objectives laid down by Article [3] of the [EU] Treaty . . . For the purpose of measuring the degree of substitution, it is impossible to restrict oneself to consumer habits in a Member State or in a given region. In fact, those habits, which are essentially variable in time and space, cannot be considered to be a fixed rule; the tax policy of a Member State must not therefore crystallize given consumer habits so as to consolidate an advantage acquired by national industries concerned to comply with them.[51]

---

[48] *Commission v United Kingdom (Beer & Wine, Interim Judgment)*, Case 170/78 [1980] ECR 417.

[49] Ibid., para. 13.

[50] Ibid.: 'As regards consumer habits, the Government of the United Kingdom states that in accordance with long-established tradition in the United Kingdom, beer is a popular drink consumed preferably in public-houses or in connexion with work; domestic consumption and consumption with meals is negligible. In contrast, the consumption of wine is more unusual and special from the point of view of social custom.'

[51] Ibid., paras 6 and 14.

The Court here brilliantly attacked the chicken-and-egg problem within Article 110(2). For two goods might not presently be in competition *because* of the artificial price differences created by internal taxation. The British argument that its tax policy only reflected a social habit in which beer was mass-consumed, while wine was an 'elitist' drink, disregarded the fact that the social habit might itself—at least partly—be the product of its fiscal policy. And once this fiscal policy disappeared, beer and wine *could* be in competition. This *dynamic* understanding of product substitutability acknowledges the ability of fiscal regimes to *dynamically* shape consumer preferences.

Once a foreign product has been found to be in competition with a domestic product, the Court will investigate whether the national tax regime generates a protectionist effect. In the above case, the Court indeed found that the higher tax burden on wine would afford protection to domestic beer production.[52] And in another case involving 'drinks in Luxembourg,'[53] the Court considered a clear protectionist effect to exist where 'an essential part of domestic production' came within the most favourable tax category whereas competing products—'almost all of which [were] imported from other Member States'—were subject to higher taxation.[54]

3. Regulatory Barriers: Quantitative Restrictions

Regulatory barriers are legal obstacles to trade which cannot be overcome by the payment of money.[55] They potentially range from a complete ban on (foreign) products to the partial restriction of a product's use.

What types of legal barriers to the free movement of goods do the EU Treaties prohibit? The Treaty regime for regulatory barriers is set out in Chapter 3 of Title II. The chapter outlaws quantitative restrictions on imports (Art. 34) and exports (Art. 35); yet it also contains a provision according to which restrictions on imports or exports can be justified (Art. 36) by specific public interests.

---

[52] *Commission v United Kingdom* (*Beer & Wine, Final Judgment*), Case 170/78 [1983] ECR 2265, para. 27.

[53] G. Rodrigues Iglesias, 'Drinks in Luxembourg: Alcoholic Beverages and the Case Law of the European Court of Justice' in D. O'Keeffe (ed.), *Judicial Review in European Union Law: Liber Amicorum in Honour of Lord Slynn of Hadley* (Kluwer, 2000), 523.

[54] *Commission v France* (*Whisky v Cognac*), Case 168/78 (n. 34), para. 41.

[55] This general rule was expressed in *Iannelli & Volpi v Meroni*, Case 74/76 [1977] ECR 557, para. 9: '[O]bstacles which are of a fiscal nature or have equivalent effect and are covered by Articles [30 and 110] of the Treaty do not fall within the prohibition in Article [34].'

Two features of this constitutional arrangement strike the attentive eye. First, unlike the legal regime governing customs duties, the Treaties expressly distinguish between *two* prohibitions: one for imports, and one for exports. And, second, the constitutional regime for regulatory barriers expressly allows for public policy exceptions. This section deals with the first feature and analyses the—respective—prohibitions for quantitative restrictions on imports and exports. Section 4 will then examine the express (and implied) justifications for regulatory restrictions on the free movement of goods.

(a) Quantitative Restrictions on Imports: Article 34

The central provision governing regulatory barriers to imports is Article 34 TFEU. It states:

> Quantitative restrictions on imports and all measures having equivalent effect shall be prohibited between Member States.

The core of this prohibition consists of the concept of 'quantitative restrictions'. These are restrictions that limit the *quantity* of imported goods to a fixed amount.[56] Quantitative restrictions are quotas, which—in their most extreme form—amount to a total ban.[57] Import quotas here operate as 'border measures'. For once a quota for a product is exhausted, foreign imports cannot legally enter the domestic market. They are blocked at the national border.

The text of Article 34, however, equally covers—like that of Article 30 on customs duties—a second category of measures, namely 'Measures having an Equivalent Effect to Quantitative Restrictions' (MEEQRs); and it is this category that has been at the centre of judicial and academic attention in the past half-century.

What are these mysterious MEEQRs? We find a first (legislative) definition of these measures in Directive 70/50.[58] The Directive distinguishes between

---

[56] See *Geddo v Ente Nazionale Risi*, Case 2/73 [1973] ECR 865, para. 7: 'The prohibition on quantitative restrictions covers measures which amount to a total or a partial restraint of, according to the circumstances, imports, exports, or goods in transit.'

[57] *R. v Henn and Darby*, Case 34/79 [1979] ECR 3795, para. 12: '[A ban] is the most extreme form of restriction.'

[58] Commission Directive 70/50 on the abolition of measures which have an effect equivalent to quantitative restrictions on imports and are not covered by other provisions adopted in pursuance of the EEC Treaty, [1970] OJ L13/29.

two types of MEEQRs. National measures that are *not* 'applicable equally' to domestic and foreign products and 'which hinder imports which could otherwise take place' are dealt with in its Article 2. They are seen as MEEQRs per se that operate at the 'border', and which must be completely removed. By contrast, 'internal' measures that are 'applicable equally' to foreign and domestic products were generally not considered MEEQRs.[59] For their restrictive effects on the free movement of goods were seen as '*inherent in the disparities* between rules applied by Member States'.[60] And these legislative disparities would need to be removed through the Union's harmonization powers.[61]

Despite the directive's impact on the early case law,[62] the Court eventually developed its own—famous—definition in *Dassonville*.[63] The case involved the legality of Belgian rules that made the sale of Scotch whisky dependent on having a 'certificate of origin' from the British customs authorities. Was this certification requirement an MEEQR? The Court thought so, and gave the following famous definition:

> All trading rules enacted by Member States which are capable of hindering, directly or indirectly, actually or potentially, intra-[Union] trade are to be considered as measures having an effect equivalent to quantitative restrictions.[64]

This formulation became known as the '*Dassonville* formula'. On its surface, the formula did not distinguish between equally and non-equally applicable rules; yet like Directive 70/50, it is best understood as establishing an absolute test for 'border measures'; that is: measures that are distinctly applicable to imports when they cross a national border.[65]

What, then, about 'internal measures', that is: measures that technically apply both to imported and domestic goods? A lasting and well-known answer to this question was given in *Cassis de Dijon*.[66] The case concerned a German marketing rule that fixed the minimum alcohol strength of liqueurs at 25 per cent. This national rule prohibited the sale of Cassis de Dijon as a liqueur in Germany, for the distinguished French drink only had an alcohol

---

[59] Ibid., recital 8.   [60] Ibid. (emphasis added).

[61] On the scope of Art. 114 TFEU, see Chapter 10, Section 1.

[62] See *Commission v Germany*, Case 12/74 [1975] ECR 181.

[63] *Procureur du Roi v Dassonville*, Case 8/74 [1974] ECR 837.

[64] Ibid., para. 5.

[65] For a historical reconstruction of the *Dassonville* judgment, see R. Schütze, 'Re-reading *Dassonville*: Meaning and Understanding in the History of European Law' (2018) 24 *European Law Journal* 376.

[66] *Rewe-Zentral AG v Bundesmonopolverwaltung für Branntwein*, Case 120/78 [1979] ECR 649.

content below 20 per cent. Formally, the national measure applied equally to foreign and domestic goods and was thus an internal measure. Which test would here apply? The Court gave the following answer:

> Obstacles to movement within the [Union] resulting from disparities between national laws relating to the marketing of the products in question must be accepted in so far as those provisions may be recognized as being necessary in order to satisfy mandatory requirements relating in particular to the effectiveness of fiscal supervision, the protection of public health, the fairness of commercial transactions and the defence of the consumer . . .
>
> [T]he requirements relating to the minimum alcohol content of alcoholic beverages do not serve a purpose which is in the general interest and such as to take precedence over the requirements of the free movement of goods, which constitutes one of the fundamental rules of the [Union] . . . There is therefore no valid reason why, provided that they have been lawfully produced and marketed in one of the Member States, alcoholic beverages should not be introduced into any other Member State; the sale of such products may not be subject to a legal prohibition on the marketing of beverages with an alcohol content lower than the limit set by the national rules.[67]

Notably, the Court here implicitly overruled the presumption that trade restrictions flowing from disparities between equally applicable 'internal' requirements will generally not qualify as MEEQRs. *Cassis* indeed inverts this presumption of legality, and transforms it into a presumption of illegality. Thus, *unless* there are mandatory requirements in the general interest, Member States are *not* entitled to impose their domestic product standards on imported goods. This presumption of illegality would become known as the 'principle of mutual recognition'. Member States must—in principle— mutually recognize each other's product standards.

After *Cassis*, it thus seemed that a discrimination test would not apply to Article 34. And in its subsequent jurisprudence, the Court came to cultivate an absolute prohibition for all regulatory restrictions to trade in goods. A striking illustration of this anti-regulatory philosophy is *Torfaen*.[68] The case formed part of the 'Sunday trading cases'.[69] It had been brought by Torfaen Borough Council, which alleged that B&Q had infringed the 1950 (British)

---

[67]   Ibid., paras 8 and 14.
[68]   *Torfaen Borough Council v B&Q*, Case 145/88 [1989] ECR 3851.
[69]   For an analysis of these cases, see C. Barnard, 'Sunday Trading: A Drama in Five Acts' (1994) 57 *Modern Law Review* 449.

Shops Act by trading on Sunday. The defendant counterclaimed that the British restriction on opening times of shops was an MEEQR. The national law reduced the absolute amount of total sales; and since a percentage of these sales were foreign goods, the Sunday trading ban constituted a restriction on imports. The European Court indeed held that the Shops Act would constitute an MEEQR if 'the effects of such national rules exceed what is necessary to achieve the aim in view'.[70]

This judicial signal was fatally effective. For it encouraged commercial traders to challenge virtually all national laws that somehow restricted the marketing of goods on the basis of Article 34. It soon dawned on the Court that its jurisprudence had gone too far. And it therefore announced a judicial retreat in *Keck*.[71] In this case, criminal proceedings had been brought against a supermarket manager who had allowed products to be sold at a loss. This form of sales promotion was prohibited in France, but Keck argued that the prohibition constituted an MEEQR because it restricted intra-Union trade in goods.[72] The Court disagreed and held that certain measures would only fall foul of Article 34 if they were discriminatory:

> National legislation imposing a general prohibition on resale at a loss is not designed to regulate trade in goods between Member States. Such legislation may, admittedly, restrict the volume of sales, and hence the volume of sales of products from other Member States, in so far as it deprives traders of a method of sales promotion. But the question remains whether such a possibility is sufficient to characterize the legislation in question as a measure having equivalent effect to a quantitative restriction on imports ...
>
> It is established by the case-law beginning with 'Cassis de Dijon' that, in the absence of harmonization of legislation, obstacles to free movement of goods which are the consequence of applying, to goods coming from other Member States where they are lawfully manufactured and marketed, rules that lay down requirements to be met by such goods (such as those relating to designation, form, size, weight, composition, presentation, labelling, packaging) constitute measures of equivalent effect prohibited by Article [34]. This is so even if those rules apply without distinction to all products unless their application can be justified by a public-interest objective taking precedence over the free movement of

---

[70] *Torfaen*, Case 145/88 (n. 68), para. 15. The Court expressly referred to Art. 3 of Directive 70/50 (n. 58) as inspiration for this test.

[71] *Criminal Proceedings against Keck and Mithouard*, Joined Cases C-267 and 268/91 [1993] ECR I-6097.

[72] Ibid., para. 3.

goods. *By contrast, contrary to what has previously been decided, the application to products from other Member States of national provisions restricting or prohibiting certain selling arrangements is not such as to hinder directly or indirectly, actually or potentially, trade between Member States within the meaning of the* Dassonville *judgment, so long as those provisions apply to all relevant traders operating within the national territory and so long as they affect in the same manner, in law and in fact, the marketing of domestic products and of those from other Member States.*[73]

The case constitutes a symbolic watershed. Drawing a distinction between 'product requirements' and 'selling arrangements',[74] *Keck* clarified that the latter would only constitute MEEQRs where they *discriminated* against the marketing of foreign goods.[75] Only discriminatory selling arrangements would violate the free movement of goods provisions.[76] Product requirements, by contrast, would still not need to be discriminatory to fall within the scope of Article 34. And in the light of the two distinct constitutional tests, the distinction between product requirements and selling arrangements became *the* classificatory battle in the post-*Keck* jurisprudence.[77]

One must, however, bear in mind that 'product requirements' and 'selling arrangements' are only two specific categories of measures that potentially constitute MEEQRs. Other categories may equally fall foul of Article 34. However, for a very long time it seemed that all MEEQRs would need to be rules that somehow interfered with the commercial chain leading from production and trading to the selling of goods. Rules that limited the *consumer*'s use of goods appeared to be outside the scope of Article 34. But even this implied limitation was challenged in *Italian Trailers*.[78]

The case involved a provision in the Italian Highway Code that prohibited the use of trailers on motorcycles and mopeds. The Commission considered the provision to constitute an MEEQR and brought proceedings against

---

[73] Ibid., paras 12–16 (emphasis added).

[74] The distinction had been—academically—suggested by E. White, 'In Search of the Limits of Article 30 of the EEC Treaty' (1989) 26 *Common Market Law Review* 235.

[75] For an important first evaluation of *Keck*, see S. Weatherill, 'After *Keck*: Some Thoughts on How to Clarify the Clarification' (1996) 33 *Common Market Law Review* 885.

[76] See *Konsumentombudsmannen (KO) v Gourmet*, Case C-405/98 [2001] ECR I-1795, esp. para. 25.

[77] See *Familiapress v Bauer Verlag*, Case C-368/95 [1997] ECR I-3689. On the general classification of advertising restrictions as selling arrangements, see *Hünermund and others v Landes apothekerkammer Baden-Württemberg*, Case C-292/92 [1993] ECR 6787.

[78] *Commission v Italy* (*Italian Trailers*), Case C-110/05 [2009] ECR I-519.

Italy. Italy defended itself by insisting that 'a rule concerning use is covered by Article [34] only if it prohibits all uses of a product or its only use, if the product only has one', whereas 'if there is a discretion as to the possible uses of the product, the situation no longer falls under Article [34]'.[79] In its ruling, the Court picked up this distinction and differentiated between trailers for general use and trailers specifically designed for motorcycles.[80] With regard to the latter, the question was this: Would the *prohibition* on using motor trailers on a public highway constitute an MEEQR? The Court answered this question positively:

> It should be noted in that regard that a prohibition on the use of a product in the territory of a Member State has a considerable influence on the behaviour of consumers, which, in its turn, affects the access of that product to the market of that Member State. Consumers, knowing that they are not permitted to use their motorcycle with a trailer specially designed for it, have practically no interest in buying such a trailer. Thus, Article 56 of the Highway Code prevents a demand from existing in the market at issue for such trailers and therefore hinders their importation. It follows that the prohibition laid down in Article 56 of the High-way Code, to the extent that its effect is to hinder access to the Italian market for trailers which are specially designed for motorcycles and are lawfully produced and marketed in Member States other than the Italian Republic, constitutes a measure having equivalent effect to quantitative restrictions on imports within the meaning of Article [34 TFEU], unless it can be justified objectively.[81]

This extension of the scope of Article 34 to national measures that limit consumer use has been confirmed.[82] The Court there clarified that there was no need to show discrimination. Its sole concern was whether the rules totally or 'greatly' prevented consumers from using products that were lawfully produced in another Member State; and if this was the case, the national measure would negatively influence consumers and thus hinder 'access to the domestic market' of foreign products. And in limiting market access, these rules violated Article 34.[83] Today, there are therefore four distinct lines of case law on Article 34, which can be seen in Figure 9.1. For consumer restrictions, a market-access test determines which national laws are allowed—and which not.

---

[79] Ibid., para. 19.   [80] Ibid., paras 51 et seq.
[81] Ibid., paras 56–8.
[82] *Åklagaren v Mickelsson and Roos*, Case C-142/05 [2009] ECR I-4273.
[83] Ibid., para. 28.

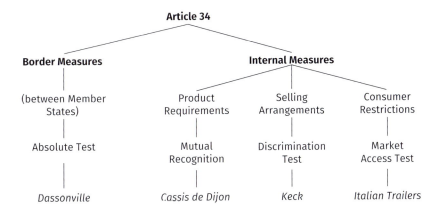

Figure 9.1 Article 34: four main jurisprudential lines

(b) Quantitative Restrictions on Exports: Article 35

The wording in Article 35 mirrors that of Article 34:

> Quantitative restrictions on exports, and all measures having equivalent effect, shall be prohibited between Member States.

Would it not be logical if the constitutional principles governing quantitative restrictions on exports mirrored those on imports? This argument will work for some measures;[84] yet—importantly—not for others. The reason for this asymmetry is the fact that the scope of Article 35 is indirectly limited by the scope of Article 34. For if the *Cassis* principle of mutual recognition is to work, the product standards of the exporting State must be presumed legitimate. With regard to product requirements, the Court has consequently interpreted Article 35 to include only those national laws that specifically discriminate against exports.

This logical extension of *Cassis* was made in *Groenveld*.[85] A wholesaler of horsemeat had challenged the legality of a Dutch law prohibiting the (industrial) production of horsemeat sausages. The law had been adopted in order to protect Dutch meat exports in the light of the fact that the consumption of horsemeat was not allowed in the national markets of some important

---

[84] See *Procureur de la République de Besançon v Les Sieurs Bouhelier and others*, Case 53/76 [1977] ECR 197.

[85] *Groenveld v Produktschap voor Vee en Vlees*, Case 15/79 [1979] ECR 3409.

trading partners. The Court held that the prohibition on the (industrial) production of horsemeat sausages did *not* constitute an MEEQR on exports:

> [Article 35] concerns national measures which have as their specific object or effect the restriction of patterns of exports and thereby the establishment of a difference in treatment between the domestic trade of a Member State and its export trade in such a way as to provide a particular advantage for national production or for the domestic market of the State in question at the expense of the production or of the trade of other Member States. This is not so in the case of a prohibition like that in question which is applied objectively to the production of goods of a certain kind without drawing a distinction depending on whether such goods are intended for the national market or for export.[86]

Equally applicable product requirements would thus *not* constitute MEEQRs on exports. But did this mean that Article 35 would never apply to equally applicable national laws? It took almost 30 years before the Court gave a decisive answer to this question in *Gysbrechts*.[87] The case involved a Belgian law that prohibited distance-selling contracts from requiring the consumer to provide his or her credit card number within seven working days (within which withdrawal from the contract was possible).[88] Was this an MEEQR on exports? The Court found that the national measure indeed 'deprive[d] the traders concerned of an efficient tool with which to guard against the risk of non-payment', and thus restricted trade. But in the light of the equally applicable nature of the measure, did it fulfil the *Groenveld* formula?[89] The Court found that this was indeed the case, since 'its actual effect is none the less greater on goods leaving the market of the exporting Member State than on the marketing of goods in the domestic market of that Member State.'[90] Equally applicable measures may thus constitute MEEQRs on exports, where they indirectly *discriminate*. And the discriminatory selling arrangement in the present case would thus need to be justified.

---

[86] Ibid., para. 7.

[87] *Gysbrechts and Santurel Inter*, Case C-205/07 [2008] ECR I-9947. For an analysis of this case, see M. Szydlo, 'Export Restrictions within the Structure of Free Movement of Goods. Reconsideration of an Old Paradigm' (2010) 47 *Common Market Law Review* 753.

[88] *Gysbrechts*, Case C-205/07 (n. 87), para. 13.

[89] The Court expressly confirmed *Groenveld*, Case 15/79 (n. 85) in *Gysbrechts*, Case C-205/07 (n. 87), para. 40.

[90] Ibid., para. 43. This point was explained in para. 42: 'As is clear from the order for reference, the consequences of such a prohibition are generally more significant in cross-border sales made directly to consumers, in particular, in sales made by means of the internet, by reason, inter alia, of the obstacles to bringing any legal proceedings in another Member State against consumers who default, especially when the sales involve relatively small sums.'

4. Justifying Regulatory Barriers: Article 36 and Mandatory Requirements

From the very beginning, the Treaty acknowledged that some quantitative restrictions or measures having equivalent effect could be justified on public policy grounds. This express acknowledgement reflected the fact that regulatory barriers to trade often pursue a legitimate *regulatory* interest. These legitimate interests are set out in Article 36, which states:

> The provisions of Articles 34 and 35 shall not preclude prohibitions or restrictions on imports, exports or goods in transit justified on grounds of public morality, public policy or public security; the protection of health and life of humans, animals or plants; the protection of national treasures possessing artistic, historic or archaeological value; or the protection of industrial and commercial property. Such prohibitions or restrictions shall not, however, constitute a means of arbitrary discrimination or a disguised restriction on trade between Member States.

The provision expressly exempts national laws that hinder the free movement of goods on six grounds, namely public morality,[91] public policy,[92] public security,[93] public health,[94] national treasures,[95] and the protection of intellectual property.[96] The Court has found this list to be exhaustive: the exceptions listed in Article 36 'cannot be extended to cases other than those specifically laid down'.[97] The Court has further found that since Article 36 'constitutes a derogation from the basic rule that all obstacles to the free movement of goods between Member States shall be eliminated', it 'must be interpreted strictly'.[98] And yet, despite limiting the scope of the Treaty's express derogations, the Court has allowed for implied derogations. These implied justifications for restrictions to the free movement of goods are called 'mandatory requirements'.

---

[91] See *R. v Henn and Darby*, Case 34/79 (n. 57).

[92] See *R. v Thompson, Johnson & Woodiwiss*, Case 7/78 [1978] ECR 2247.

[93] See *Campus Oil and others v Minister for Industry and Energy and others*, Case 72/83 [1984] ECR 2727.

[94] See *Commission v United Kingdom*, Case 40/82 [1982] ECR 2793.

[95] According to P. Oliver et al., *Free Movement of Goods in the European Union* (Hart, 2010), 281 there is no case law on the application of this ground.

[96] See *Van Zuylen frères v Hag AG*, Case 192/73 [1974] ECR 731.

[97] *Commission v Ireland* (*Irish Souvenirs*), Case 113/80 [1981] ECR 1625, para. 7.

[98] *Bauhuis*, Case 46/76 (n. 27), para. 12.

(a) Implied Justifications: Mandatory Requirements

Despite having found the *express* exceptions in Article 36 to be exhaustive, the Court has acknowledged the existence of *implied* justifications. In *Cassis de Dijon*,[99] the Court thus exempted obstacles to the free movement of goods that were 'necessary in order to satisfy *mandatory requirements* relating in particular to the effectiveness of fiscal supervision, the protection of public health, the fairness of commercial transactions and the defence of the consumer'.[100] These additional justifications were originally called 'mandatory requirements'; but the Court increasingly refers to them as 'imperative requirements' or 'overriding reason[s] relating to the public interest'.[101]

The best explanation for the acceptance of implied justifications by the Court is the dramatically expanded scope of Article 34 after *Cassis*—a scope that henceforth also potentially outlawed non-discriminatory obstacles to trade. And, importantly, the Court has indeed clarified that these implied justifications or imperative requirements could solely justify national laws 'which apply without discrimination to both domestic and imported products'.[102]

The nature of a national restriction—whether discriminatory or not—thus determines which justifications are available to a Member State. Discriminatory national measures can only be justified by reference to the express—and exhaustive—list of public interest grounds in Article 36.[103] By contrast, national measures that do not discriminate will benefit from an open-ended list of implied 'mandatory requirements'.[104] This distinction may be criticized; and the Court has sometimes tried to evade it by sharp scholastic means, or by bluntly fudging the issue of the (non-)discriminatory character of a national measure.[105] One of the interesting questions in this context is whether selling arrangements that fall within the scope of Article 34 can ever be justified by

---

[99] *Rewe-Zentral AG v Bundesmonopolverwaltung für Branntwein*, Case 120/78 (n. 66).

[100] Ibid., para. 8 (emphasis added).

[101] *Italian Trailers* (n. 78), paras 59–60.

[102] *Criminal Proceedings against Gilli and Andres*, Case 788/79 [1980] ECR 2071, para. 6.

[103] *Commission v Ireland* (*Irish Souvenirs*), Case 113/80 (n. 97), esp. para. 11.

[104] This list is very long and includes, inter alia: consumer protection (see *Commission v Germany*, Case 178/84 [1987] ECR 1227); the prevention of unfair competition (*Cassis de Dijon*, Case 120/78 (n.66)); the protection of the environment (see *Commission v Denmark*, Case 302/86 [1988] ECR 4607); the improvement of working conditions (see *Oebel*, Case 155/80 [1981] ECR 1993); the diversity of the press (see *Familiapress v Bauer*, Case C-368/95 (n. 77)) and many others.

[105] *Preussen Elektra v Schleswag*, Case C-379/98 [2001] ECR I-2099.

mandatory requirements. Theoretically, this should not be the case if constitutional logic is followed.[106] However, the Court has given reason to believe that a softer rule might apply in practice.[107]

(b) The Proportionality Principle and National Standards

The fact that a national restriction comes under one of the express or implied grounds of justification is only a first step. For even if a legitimate public interest can be found to potentially justify a national measure, restrictions on the free movement of goods will be subject to a proportionality test. The Court has thus insisted that national laws authorized by Article 36 'only comply with the Treaty in so far as they are justified, that is to say, *necessary* for the attainment of the objectives referred to by this provision'.[108] And this proportionality test has been extended to all (implied) imperative requirement justifications.[109]

What will proportionality in this context mean? Proportionality generally means 'that national legislation which restricts or is liable to restrict intra-[Union] trade must be proportionate to the objectives pursued and that those objectives must not be attainable by measures which are less restrictive of such trade'.[110] This least-restrictive-means test constitutes the cornerstone of the proportionality inquiry. But behind this test stands an important question: What standard of protection will it be based on? If the Polish legislature favours a high level of public morality and bans all imports of pornography, should it matter that other Member States do not prefer to stand on such high moral ground? Or, should Germany be allowed to insist on 'beer purity' as the highest standard of consumer protection, while other Member States allow their beer to be brewed with artificial ingredients? The question of proportionality is thus intrinsically linked to the desirable standard of protection. And, unfortunately, this is a question to which the Court has not given consistent answers.[111]

---

[106] We saw earlier that solely discriminatory selling arrangements can constitute MEEQRs, and therefore these national measures could, in theory, solely be justified on the grounds mentioned in Art. 36.

[107] See *Konsumentombudsmannen v De Agostini*, Case C-34/95 [1997] ECR I-3843.

[108] *Simmenthal v Ministero delle Finanze italiano*, Case 35/76 [1976] ECR 1871, para. 10 (emphasis added).

[109] *Rewe-Zentral v Bundesmonopolverwaltung für Branntwein*, Case 120/78 (n. 66).

[110] See *Aher-Waggon GmbH v Germany*, Case C-389/96 [1998] ECR I-4473, para. 20.

[111] On this point, see G. de Búrca, 'The Principle of Proportionality and its Application in EC Law' (1993) 13 *Yearbook of European Law* 105.

We find acceptance of a State's (high) national standard in *Henn and Darby*.[112] The case concerned the importation of pornographic films and magazines from Denmark, which violated the British import ban for such goods. Could this national law be justified on the ground of public morality, or would the 'lower' Danish standard provide an argument that public morality can survive in a society that is more permissive of pornography? The Court chose the higher British standard as its baseline. It held that it was, as a rule, 'for each Member State to determine in accordance with its own scale of values and in the form selected by it the requirements of public morality in its territory'.[113] However, the Court subsequently clarified that 'a Member State may not rely on grounds of public morality in order to prohibit the importation of goods from other Member States when its legislation contains no prohibition on the manufacture or marketing of the same goods on its territory'.[114] Yet this qualification did not 'preclude the authorities of the Member State concerned from applying to those goods, once imported, the same restrictions on marketing which are applied to similar products manufactured and marketed within the country'.[115] Indeed, it did not undermine the legality of a (high) national standard, but only eliminated 'arbitrary discriminations' that led to a 'disguised restriction on trade between Member States'.[116]

In other areas, by contrast, the Court has not deferred to a high national standard. In *Commission v Germany* (*Beer Purity*),[117] the Court thus rejected the claim that a German law confining the designation 'beer' to beverages brewed without artificial additives was a proportionate means to protect consumers.[118] Pointing to its dynamic consumer perception, it found that German consumers could be sufficiently protected by suitable labelling requirements.[119] In the Court's view, a high national standard must thus not 'crystallize given consumer habits so as to consolidate an advantage acquired by national industries concerned to comply with them'.[120]

---

[112] *R. v Henn and Darby*, Case 34/79 (n. 57).

[113] Ibid., para. 15.

[114] *Conegate v HM Customs & Excise*, Case 121/85 [1986] ECR 1007, para. 16. In this respect *Conegate* overruled *Henn and Darby*.

[115] *Conegate v HM Customs & Excise*, Case 121/85 (n. 114), para. 21.

[116] Art. 36 TFEU, second sentence.

[117] *Commission v Germany*, Case 178/84 [1987] ECR 1227.

[118] Ibid., para. 53: '[I]n so far as the German rules on additives in beer entail a general ban on additives, their application to beers imported from other Member States is contrary to the requirements of [Union] law as laid down in the case-law of the Court, since that prohibition is contrary to the principle of proportionality.'

[119] *Commission v Germany*, Case 178/84 (n. 117), para. 35.   [120] Ibid., para. 32.

The Court consequently did not allow Germany to choose its own 'scale of values' and insisted on the European standard of the 'reasonably circumspect consumer'.[121] And it is against this Court-chosen standard that the necessity of a national restriction on the free movement of goods is often judged.

Conclusion

The aim of this chapter has been to explore the degree of negative integration in the context of the free movement of goods. The constitutional regime governing this 'first' fundamental freedom is more complex than that for the other three freedoms. For instead of one single prohibition of illegal trade barriers, the EU Treaties distinguish between fiscal and regulatory barriers; and for fiscal barriers, the Treaties further distinguish between customs charges and internal taxation. For customs charges, the Court has traditionally constructed Article 30 as an absolute prohibition that applies to all charges between Member States. By contrast, the prohibition of discriminatory tax measures under Article 110 is still informed by a discrimination rationale.

For regulatory measures adopted by the Member States, the Court's rationale has changed over time, and Article 34 now seems to comprise a number of tests that apply to different categories of national measures. This differential approach also applies to justifications to regulatory restrictions. Express justifications for regulatory barriers to trade are found in Article 36. These grounds have been enriched by implied justifications called 'imperative requirements'. The latter will however—in theory—only apply to non-discriminatory restrictions; yet the Court seems to have also played with the idea of extending them to discriminatory measures. The central problem with regard to justifying national restrictions is, however, not so much the grounds of justification but the standard against which national restrictions are reviewed.

---

[121] See *Verein gegen Unwesen in Handel und Gewerbe Köln eV v Mars*, Case C-470/93 [1995] ECR I-1923, para. 24.

10

Internal Market: Goods II

Introduction

The gradual integration of the various national markets into a 'common' or 'internal' European market can be achieved by two complementary mechanisms. First, the Treaties may themselves 'negate' certain national barriers to intra-Union trade. For the free movement of goods, this form of negative integration was discussed in the previous chapter. A second constitutional technique is 'positive integration'. The Union here adopts positive legislation to—partly or completely—remove obstacles to trade arising from the differences in national laws. This idea of integration through legislation stands behind Article 26 TFEU. It states:

> The Union shall adopt measures with the aim of establishing or ensuring the functioning of the internal market, in accordance with the relevant provisions of the Treaties.[1]

Legislative competences for positive integration are often placed within the specific policy areas of the Union.[2] However, the Treaties also contain a number of horizontal harmonization competences that generally allow the Union to

---

[1] Art. 26(1) TFEU.

[2] On this point, see Chapter 3, Introduction.

create an 'internal market'. These 'internal market' competences can be found in Chapter 3 of Title VII of the TFEU. They have been the bedrock of the Union's positive integration programme. Articles 114 and 115 here provide the Union with a legislative competence 'for the approximation of the provisions laid down by law, regulation or administrative action in Member States *which have as their object the establishment and functioning of the internal market*'.[3]

These two general internal market competences apply to all four fundamental freedoms.[4] They are complemented by more specific internal market competences. With regard to fiscal measures, Article 113 thus allows the Union to harmonize legislation on 'forms of indirect taxation to the extent that such harmonisation is necessary to ensure the establishment and functioning of the internal market and to avoid distortions of competition'. Article 116 specifically targets distortions of competition, while Article 118 empowers the Union '[i]n the context of the establishment and functioning of the internal market' to 'establish measures for the creation of European intellectual property rights'.[5] An overview of all these competences can be found in Table 10.1.

This chapter explores the constitutional principles and limits governing positive integration in the context of the free movement of goods. Section 1 analyses the scope and nature of the general internal market competence(s): Articles 114 and 115 TFEU. We shall see there that the Union has an—almost—unlimited competence to harmonize national laws that affect the establishment or functioning of the internal market. Section 2 looks at the

Table 10.1 Harmonization competences

Chapter 2: Tax Provisions	Chapter 3: Approximation of Laws
Article 110: Discriminatory Taxation	Article 114: General Competence I
Article 111: Export Repayments	Article 115: General Competence II
Article 112: Export Repayments Approval	Article 116: Specific Competence: Competition
Article 113: Specific Competence: Taxes	Article 117: Commission Consultation
	Article 118: Specific Competence: Intellectual Property

---

[3] Art. 114(1) TFEU (emphasis added).

[4] According to Art. 26(2) TFEU: '[t]he internal market shall comprise an area without internal frontiers in which the free movement of goods, persons, services and capital is ensured in accordance with the provisions of the Treaties.'

[5] Art. 118(1) TFEU.

relationship between Article 114 and other legislative competences within the Union legal order. Section 3 investigates the extent to which Member States can derogate from harmonized Union standards; and, finally, Section 4 is dedicated to a specific area of Union harmonization: tax harmonization.

1. Internal Market Competences: General Issues

Originally, the sole harmonization competences for the internal market were Articles 115 and 116 TFEU. The former entitled the European Union to 'issue directives for the approximation of such provisions laid down by law, regulation or administrative action in Member States as directly affect the establishment or functioning of the common market'. Article 116 was more specific. It allowed the Union to issue directives where the differences between national laws are 'distorting the conditions of competition in the internal market'. The competence was designed as the positive integration platform for the EU's competition policy; yet despite its more specific focus, it quickly declined into oblivion.[6]

Article 115, by contrast, turned out to be legally 'quite simply unlimited'.[7] Yet the competence had an important *political* hurdle: it required unanimity in the Council; and this political safeguard substantially limited the exercise of the Union's internal market competence in its early life.[8] This, however, dramatically changed after the Single European Act. The latter provided Article 115 with a 'brilliant assistant': Article 114.[9] This new constitutional neighbour not only widened the Union's internal market competence;[10]

---

[6] U. Everling, 'Zur Funktion der Rechtsangleichung in der Europäischen Gemeinschaft: vom Abbau der Verzerrungen zur Schaffung des Binnenmarktes' in F. Capotorti et al. (eds), *Du droit international au droit de l'integration: liber amicorum Pierre Pescatore* (Nomos, 1987), 227 at 232.

[7] P. Leleux, 'Le rapprochement des législations dans la communauté economique européenne' (1968) 4 *Cahiers de Droit Européen* 129 at 138.

[8] On this point, see A. Dashwood, 'Hastening Slowly: The Community's Path Towards Harmonization' in H. Wallace, W. Wallace, and C. Webb (eds), *Policy-Making in the European Community* (Wiley & Sons Ltd, 1983), 177.

[9] D. Vignes, 'The Harmonisation of National Legislation and the EEC' (1990) 15 *European Law Review* 358 at 367.

[10] Constitutionally, Art. 114 TFEU no longer contained the—by now obsolete—reference to 'directives' as instruments of harmonization; nor did it mention the 'direct [e]ffect' of national laws on the internal market.

it—importantly—no longer required a unanimous decision of all Member States. Today Article 114 states:

1. Save where otherwise provided in the Treaties, the following provisions shall apply for the achievement of the objectives set out in Article 26. The European Parliament and the Council shall, acting in accordance with the ordinary legislative procedure and after consulting the Economic and Social Committee, adopt the measures for the approximation of the provisions laid down by law, regulation or administrative action in Member States which have as their object the establishment and functioning of the internal market.
2. Paragraph 1 shall not apply to fiscal provisions, to those relating to the free movement of persons nor to those relating to the rights and interests of employed persons.
3. The Commission, in its proposals envisaged in paragraph 1 concerning health, safety, environmental protection and consumer protection, will take as a base a high level of protection, taking account in particular of any new development based on scientific facts. Within their respective powers, the European Parliament and the Council will also seek to achieve this objective.[11]

This gave the Union legislator a general competence, save where otherwise provided,[12] to harmonize national laws that affected the internal market. Positive harmonization could thereby be adopted by a qualified majority of the Member States within the Council.

   This departure from the unanimity requirement within the Council would not, however, extend to all areas within the internal market. Indeed, Article 114(2) expressly states that Article 114(1) would 'not apply to fiscal provisions, to these relating to the free movement of persons nor to those relating to the rights and interests of employed persons'. (These politically 'sensitive' matters would thus continue to fall under Article 115 TFEU or one of the specific legal competences within the relevant Treaty titles.) The fear of 'unqualified' qualified majority voting also led to the inclusion of two further qualifications. First, Article 114(3) obliges the Commission to base its legislative proposals on a 'high level of protection' with regard to these interests. And, second, Article 114(4)–(5) TFEU—quoted later—allowed, for the first time in the Union's history, for differential positive integration.[13]

---

[11]   Art 114(1)–(3) TFEU. For the text of paras 4 and 5, see Section 3.

[12]   On the 'residual' nature of Art. 114, see Section 2.

[13]   For the historical justification of these paragraphs, see Advocate General Tesauro in *France v Commission*, Case C-41/93 [1994] ECR I-1829, para. 4.

Despite these qualifications, Article 114 is, apart from Article 352, the broadest competence of the Union. Indeed, its horizontal and supranational nature have turned Article 114 into 'the' preferred legislative base for the Union's positive integration programme. This section explores the scope of Article 114 by analysing the concept of 'harmonization' and the substantive conditions that need to be satisfied before the Union is entitled to activate its 'internal market' competence.

(a) The Concept of 'Approximation' or 'Harmonization'

The Union's internal market competences are based on the idea of 'approximation' or 'harmonization'. The idea suggests that two or more diverse national laws are brought closer together by means of a European Union act; and, as such, it seems to require the existence of national laws *before* and *after* the Union legislation. Yet is that really the case?

For a long time, European constitutional thought indeed strongly linked the concept of harmonization to the *subsequent* existence of national laws. This was originally the result of the harmonization instrument of the 'directive'.[14] Directives require Member States to adopt national legislation that implements the Union command. A directive thus results in 'harmonized' *national* rules; and it consequently seemed that the *subsequent* existence of national rules was a conceptual characteristic of the notion of harmonization. This, however, changed with Article 114 TFEU, which 'decoupled' the idea of harmonization from the directive. The Union can henceforth adopt any measure under its internal market competence—and this includes 'regulations' as instruments of Union legislation, which did not necessarily require the subsequent existence of national laws.

Could a harmonization of national laws even take place through an (executive) Union *decision*? In *Germany v Council*,[15] this constitutional delicacy was placed on the judicial table. Germany had argued that the power to 'harmonize' did not entitle the Union to adopt decisions (dis)approving certain

---

[14]   According to Art. 288(3) TFEU, '[a] directive shall be binding, as to the result to be achieved, upon each Member State to which it is addressed, but shall leave to the national authorities the choice of form and methods'. On the Union instrument of 'directive', see Chapter 5, Section 3.

[15]   *Germany v Council*, Case C-359/92 [1994] ECR I-3681.

products because no harmonization of national laws had taken place.[16] The Court held otherwise:

> The measures which the Council is empowered to take under that provision are aimed at 'the establishment and functioning of the internal market'. In certain fields, and particularly in that of product safety, the approximation of general laws alone may not be sufficient to ensure the unity of the market. *Consequently, the concept of 'measures for the approximation' of legislation must be interpreted as encompassing the Council's power to lay down measures relating to a specific product or class of products and, if necessary, individual measures concerning those products.*[17]

Despite its reference to harmonization, Article 114 TFEU would thus entitle the Union to adopt specific executive decisions that did not formally harmonize national laws. But could Article 114 also be employed for the establishment of a centralized authorization procedure operated by the Commission, or even the creation of the Union's own executive infrastructure? Subsequent jurisprudence clarified that Article 114 could indeed be used for both purposes. The cause célèbre here is *United Kingdom v Parliament and Council*.[18] It concerned the validity of a Union regulation that tried to ensure the effective functioning of the internal market through a Union authorization procedure for food products.[19] The British government protested: 'The legislative power conferred by Article [114 TFEU] is a power to *harmonise* national laws, *not a power to establish [Union] bodies or to confer tasks on such*

---

[16] Germany's principal claim in this respect is quoted in para. 17: 'The German Government objects to that argument essentially on the ground that the sole aim of Article [114] et seq. of the [TFEU], and of Article [114(1)] in particular, is the approximation of laws and that those articles do not therefore confer power to apply the law to individual cases in the place of the national authorities[.]

[17] *Germany v Council*, Case C-359/92 (n. 15), paras 37–8 (emphasis added).

[18] *United Kingdom v Parliament and Council*, Case C-66/04 [2005] ECR I-10553. In relation to Art. 114 TFEU's use to create a Union body, see *United Kingdom v Parliament and Council (ENISA)*, Case C-217/04 [2006] ECR I-3771, especially para. 44: 'The legislature may deem it necessary to provide for the establishment of a [Union] body responsible for contributing to the implementation of a process of harmonisation in situations where, in order to facilitate the uniform implementation and application of acts based on that provision, the adoption of non-binding supporting and framework measures seems appropriate.'

[19] Regulation 2065/2003 on smoke flavourings used or intended for use in or on foods, [2003] OJ L309/1, Art. 9(1)(b) as well as Art. 11(1).

bodies, or to establish procedures for the approval of lists of authorised products.'[20] Yet in its judgment the Court confirmed this very power.[21] The Union legislator would thus enjoy 'a discretion, depending on the general context and the specific circumstances of the matter to be harmonised, as regards the harmonisation technique'.[22] The Union was thus entitled to create a Union agency and endow it with the power to adopt—binding—executive decisions.

In sum, the Union enjoys an (almost) total freedom with regard to the formal type of harmonization act. This freedom of form is matched by a freedom of substance. For the Court has never identified the concept of harmonization with a 'medium' regulatory standard—located somewhere in between the various national standards. Instead, it grants the Union legislator a wide substantive discretion.[23]

What about the *prior* existence of national laws as a precondition for Article 114 TFEU? This question was the subject of *Spain v Council*.[24] The European legislator here believed the national protection for medicinal patents to be insufficient, and saw this insufficiency as penalizing European pharmaceutical research. It therefore created an additional protection certificate on the basis of Article 114 that could be granted under the same conditions as national patents by each of the Member States.[25] However, two major constitutional hurdles seemed to oppose the legality of this European law. First, could Article 114 TFEU be used to create *new* property rights; or could it only harmonize *existing* rights?[26] Second, since at the time of the adoption of the Union law only *two* Member States had legislation concerning a supplementary certificate, could one speak of a harmonization of national laws at all?

The Court took the first hurdle by force. It simply rejected the claim that the European law created a new right.[27] Concentrating on the second hurdle, the Court then addressed the question whether Article 114 required the

---

[20]   *United Kingdom v Parliament and Council*, Case C-66/04 (n. 18), para. 18 (emphasis added).
[21]   Ibid., para. 64.
[22]   Ibid., para. 45. This was confirmed in *United Kingdom v Parliament and Council* (*ESMA*), Case C-270/12, EU:C:2014:18.
[23]   For an early version of this argument, see T. Vogelaar, 'The Approximation of the Laws of the Member States under the Treaty of Rome' (1975) 12 *Common Market Law Review* 211 at 213.
[24]   *Spain v Council*, Case C-350/92 [1995] ECR I-1985.
[25]   Regulation 1768/92 concerning the creation of a supplementary protection certificate for medicinal products, [1992] OJ L182/1.
[26]   Union legislation that creates 'new' rights will have to be based on Art. 352 TFEU, cf. *Spain v Council* (n. 24), para. 23 (with reference to *Opinion 1/94* [1994] ECR I-5267, para. 59).
[27]   *Spain v Council* (n. 24), para. 27.

pre-existence of diverse national laws before Union harmonization could take place; and, in the eyes of the Court, this was not the case! The Union could also use its internal market competence 'to *prevent the heterogeneous development of national laws* leading to further disparities which would be likely to create obstacles to the free movement of medicinal products within the [Union] and thus directly affect the establishment and the functioning of the internal market'.[28] The Union was thus entitled—even in the absence of diverse national laws on a specific point at a specific time—to use its harmonization power to prevent the *future* adoption of diverse national laws so as to prevent *future* obstacles to trade.[29]

This judicial ruling was confirmed in *Vodafone*;[30] and it seems to have emptied the concept of harmonization of any content. If there are, indeed, conceptual limits to Article 114, they have to be found somewhere else.

(b) The 'Establishment' or 'Functioning' of the Internal Market

The Union's internal market competence is a horizontal competence. It is horizontal because it is not thematically limited to a particular policy area. (The 'internal market' is not a policy area but potentially cuts across all areas of Union law.) Article 114 indeed applies to *any* national measure that somehow affects the establishment or functioning of the internal market.

This horizontal scope thereby refers to two alternatives. The first alternative deals with the 'establishment' of the internal market and concerns obstacles to free movement. The second alternative refers to the 'functioning' of the internal market and addresses distortions of competition resulting from disparities between national laws. Importantly, the combination of these two objectives means that the scope of positive integration under Article 114 TFEU is wider than the scope of negative integration, say, under Article 34 TFEU.[31]

---

[28] Ibid., para. 35 (emphasis added).

[29] On the idea of 'preventive' harmonization in the internal market, see M. Seidel, 'Präventive Rechtsangleichung im Bereich des Gemeinsamen Marktes' (2006) 41 *Europarecht* 26.

[30] *Vodafone and others v Secretary of State for Business, Enterprise and Regulatory Reform*, Case C-58/08 [2010] ECR I-4999.

[31] This means that even where a national law is outside the scope of Art. 34 TFEU— e.g. non-discriminatory selling arrangements after *Keck* (see Chapter 9, Section 3(a)), these selling arrangements could be harmonized under Art. 114 TFEU if they affect the functioning of the internal market. For an overview of the debate on the (only partial) connection between Arts 34 and 114 TFEU, see G. Davies, 'Can Selling Arrangements be Harmonised?' (2005) 30 *European Law Review* 370.

To what extent would Union legislation have to serve the 'establishment' or 'functioning' of the internal market? Until the end of the twentieth century, the jurisprudence of the Court unequivocally confirmed the widest possible reading of the Union's general competence: almost anything, it seemed, could be based on Article 114. Yet this perception significantly changed with *Germany v Parliament and Council (Tobacco Advertising)*.[32] The famous judgment confirmed the existence of constitutional limits for Article 114.

The bone of contention in this case was a Union law that banned the advertising and sponsorship of tobacco products.[33] Germany disliked the idea and claimed that a prohibition or even a ban of a product could never be based on the Union's *internal market* competence. Article 114 could only be used to 'establish' trade and this was not the case where Union legislation limited trade in tobacco products.[34] And while admitting that Article 114 could, in the alternative, still be used to ensure the proper functioning of the internal market, this second alternative within Article 114 should only apply to cases where the distortion of competition was 'considerable'.[35]

To the surprise of many, the Court accepted these arguments and annulled, for the first time in its history, a Union law on the grounds that it went beyond the internal market competence. Emphatically, the Court underlined that Article 114 could not grant the Union a general power to regulate the internal market:

> *To construe that article as meaning that it vests in the [Union] legislature a general power to regulate the internal market would not only be contrary to the express wording of the provisions cited above but would also be incompatible with the principle embodied in Article [5 TEU] that the powers of the [Union] are limited to those specifically conferred on it.* Moreover, a measure adopted on the basis of Article [114] of the Treaty must genuinely have as its object the improvement of the conditions for the establishment and functioning of the internal market. If a mere finding of

---

[32] *Germany v Parliament and Council (Tobacco Advertising)*, Case C-376/98 [2000] ECR I-8419.

[33] Directive 98/43 on the approximation of the laws, regulations and administrative provisions of the Member States relating to the advertising and sponsorship of tobacco products, [1998] OJ L.213/9.

[34] Germany had pointed out that the sole form of advertising allowed under the Directive was advertising at the point of sale, which only accounted for 2 per cent of the tobacco industry's advertising expenditure (*Tobacco Advertising* (n. 32), para. 24).

[35] Ibid., para. 29.

disparities between national rules and of the abstract risk of obstacles to the exercise of fundamental freedoms or of distortions of competition liable to result therefrom were sufficient to justify the choice of Article [114] as a legal basis, judicial review of compliance with the proper legal basis might be rendered nugatory.[36]

What consequences did the Court draw from this statement of principle? The Court split its ruling into an 'establishment' and 'functioning' part and analysed, in turn, the two alternative applications of the Union's harmonization competence.

Regarding the elimination of obstacles to free movement, the Court here qualified its generous ruling in *Spain v Council*.[37] While accepting that 'recourse to Article [114] as a legal basis is possible if the aim is to prevent the emergence of future obstacles to trade resulting from multifarious development of national laws', the Court nonetheless insisted that '*the emergence of such obstacles must be likely* and the measure in question must be designed to prevent them'.[38] Were future obstacles to intra-Union trade in tobacco advertising likely? The Court accepted this for press products; yet 'for numerous types of advertising of tobacco products', the prohibition within the Directive 'cannot be justified by the need to eliminate obstacles to the free movement of advertising media or the freedom to provide services in the field of advertising'.[39] The Union legislature had thus not been entitled to rely on its internal market power on the ground that the measure would eliminate obstacles to free movement.

But recourse to the competence could possibly still be justified by means of the second alternative in Article 114: the elimination of distortions of competition. In previous jurisprudence, the Court had interpreted this condition widely by allowing all harmonizing measures that 'deal with disparities between the laws of the Member States in areas where such disparities are liable to create or maintain distorted conditions of competition'.[40] This suggested that *any* disparities in national laws liable to create *any* distortion of competition could be harmonized.

Yet *Tobacco Advertising* now also corrected this excessive reading for the 'functioning' part of the internal market competence. For the Court here

---

[36] Ibid., paras 83–4 (emphasis added).
[37] *Spain v Council*, Case C-350/92 (n. 24).
[38] *Tobacco Advertising* (n. 32), para. 86 (emphasis added).
[39] Ibid., paras 97 and 99.
[40] Cf. *Commission v Council* (*Titanium dioxide*), Case C-300/89 [1991] ECR I-2867, para. 15.

accepted Germany's invitation: distortions of competition would have to be *appreciable* to entitle the Union to act under Article 114. Constitutionally, the Union legislator was thus not entitled to pass laws under Article 114 'with a view to eliminating the smallest distortions of competition'.[41] And since the national laws at issue had only a 'remote and indirect' effect on competition, disparities between them could not lead to distortions that were appreciable.[42] The Directive was thus not legitimately based on the second alternative of the competence either, and the Court consequently annulled the European directive.

In conclusion, with *Tobacco Advertising*, the Court expressly accepted *some* constitutional limits to the Union's internal market power. First, a simple disparity in national laws would theoretically not be enough to trigger the Union's harmonization competence. The disparity must either give rise to obstacles in trade or lead to appreciable distortions in competition. And while Article 114 could still be used to harmonize *future* disparities in national laws, it had to be 'likely' that this divergent development of national laws would lead to obstacles in trade or appreciable distortions of competition. (The Court has, occasionally, come to verbalize this requirement by extending the constitutional criterion of a 'direct effect'—textually mandated only in Article 115—to Article 114.[43]) Second, the Union measure must *actually contribute* to the elimination of obstacles to trade or distortions of competition,[44] and where this is not the case the Union measure is not a measure of positive integration and will thus be annulled.

These two constitutional limits to the Union's 'internal market' competence have been confirmed *in abstracto* by subsequent jurisprudence; yet, their concrete application has led to renewed accusations that Article 114 grants the Union a general competence for the internal market. A good illustration of this development is *Philip Morris*.[45] The Court here found that the Union labelling

---

[41]   *Tobacco Advertising* (n. 32), para. 107.

[42]   Ibid., para. 109.

[43]   See *R. (on the application of Vodafone Ltd and Others) v Secretary of State for Business, Enterprise and Regulatory Reform*, Case C-58/08 [2010] ECR I-4999, para. 32: 'While a mere finding of disparities between national rules and the abstract risk of infringements of fundamental freedoms or distortion of competition is not sufficient to justify the choice of Article [114 TFEU] as a legal basis, the [Union] legislature may have recourse to it in particular where there are differences between national rules which are such as to obstruct the fundamental freedoms and thus have a direct effect on the functioning of the internal market.'

[44]   *British American Tobacco*, Case C-491/01 [2002] ECR I-11453, para. 60.

[45]   *Philip Morris Brands SARL and Others v Secretary of State for Health*, Case C-547/14, EU:C:2016:325.

requirement demanding that 65 per cent of the surface of tobacco products be covered by health warnings was legitimately based on Article 114.

2. Relationship to 'Sectoral' Legislative Competences

Article 114 TFEU presents itself with an understatement. With false modesty, it states that it only applies 'save where otherwise provided in the Treaties'. This is deeply misleading. For it suggests that the provision is but a residual competence that only applies where no more specific competence is available.[46] The question thus arises when the Union can actually use its general internal market competence under Article 114 and when it must rather use—say—its special environmental competence if it wishes to set environmental standards for industrial machinery.

Had the Court here taken a strict view on the residual nature of Article 114, hardly any matters might have fallen within its scope. Yet the Court has rejected this view and treats Article 114 like a 'normal' legislative competence. This was confirmed in *Titanium Dioxide*.[47] The Court here acknowledged that internal market measures would typically have a dual aim, namely an internal market aim as well as a specific *substantive* policy aim.[48] And in deciding whether or not Article 114 or a specific legal competence applies, the Court would have recourse to the 'centre of gravity' doctrine.[49] The latter makes the choice of competence dependent on whether the Union measure *principally* deals with the internal market or with the more specific substantive interest. And where a Union law's 'weight' falls more heavily on the internal market side, Article 114 will apply.

There are however two qualifications to this picture. First, Article 114 itself expressly excludes three matters from its legislative scope because it states in

---

[46] This is, however, the case for Art. 352 TFEU. For an analysis of this point, see R. Schütze, 'Organized Change towards an "Ever Closer Union": Article 308 EC and the Limits of the Community's Legislative Competence' (2003) 22 *Yearbook of European Law* 79 at 99 et seq.

[47] *Commission v Council* (*Titanium dioxide*), Case C-300/89 (n. 40).

[48] Ibid., para. 11.

[49] Cf. *Commission v Council* (*Waste*), Case C-155/91 [1993] ECR I-939; as well as *Parliament v Council* (*Waste II*), Case C-187/93 [1994] ECR I-2857. For an academic analysis of the phenomenon of legal basis litigation, esp. in relation to Art. 114 TFEU, see R. Barents, 'The Internal Market Unlimited: Some Observations on the Legal Basis of Community Legislation' (1993) 30 *Common Market Law Review* 85; as well as H. Cullen and A. Charlesworth, 'Diplomacy by Other Means: The Use of Legal Basis Litigation as a Political Strategy by the European Parliament and Member States' (1999) 36 *Common Market Law Review* 1243.

paragraph 2 that the general competence 'shall not apply to *fiscal* provisions, to those relating to the *free movement of persons* nor to those relating to the *rights and interests of employed persons*'. These three areas can thus never be harmonized on the basis of Article 114. If Union legislation is here deemed necessary, this will have to be done either under Article 115—requiring unanimity—or one of the special substantive competences dealing with taxation, the free movement of persons, or employment. In the past, the Court has given a broad interpretation to the scope of the excluded policy fields in Article 114(2).[50]

But is the list in Article 114(2) exhaustive? The Court has indeed held this to be the case. The Member States have nonetheless tried to 'shield' some special Union competences from the general internal market competence. How so? In their capacity as Masters of the Treaties, they have increasingly included clauses within specific policy areas that expressly exclude the harmonization of national laws within a specific policy area. For example, under its 'public health' competence in Article 168, the Union is entitled to adopt health measures but only '*excluding any harmonisation* of the laws and regulations of the Member States'.[51]

These clauses limit the ability of the Union legislator to adopt harmonization measures under these special competences, but do they also limit the scope of Article 114? The European Court appears to have expressed a negative view in *Tobacco Advertising*.[52] Germany had here partly challenged the use of Article 114 for the Tobacco Advertising Directive on the ground that the Directive was a 'health measure' and that it should therefore have been based on Article 168; and since the latter excluded any harmonization, the Directive should be annulled.

The Court, however, rejected this argument in full. While admitting that '[t]he national measures *affected* [were] to a large extent inspired by public health policy objectives',[53] the Court clarified that the exclusion of harmonization in Article 168(5) did 'not mean that harmonising measures adopted

---

[50]   For a wide and teleological interpretation of the phrase 'fiscal provisions' in Art. 114(2) TFEU, see *Commission v Council*, Case C-338/01 [2004] ECR I-4829, para. 63: 'With regard to the interpretation of the words "fiscal provisions", there is nothing in the Treaty to indicate how that concept should be construed. It is, however, necessary to point out that, by reason of their general character, those words cover not only all areas of taxation, without drawing any distinction between the types of duties or taxes concerned, but also all aspects of taxation, whether material rules or procedural rules.'

[51]   Art. 168(5) TFEU (emphasis added).

[52]   *Germany v Council* (*Tobacco Advertising*), Case C-376/98 (n. 32).

[53]   Ibid., para. 76 (emphasis added).

on the basis of other provisions of the Treaty cannot have any impact on the protection of human health'.[54] '[T]he [Union] legislature cannot be prevented from relying on [Article 114] on the ground that public health protection is a decisive factor in the choices to be made'.[55]

In conclusion, then, the exclusion of harmonization in a specific (complementary) competence appears thus *not* to operate as a limitation on Article 114 TFEU. Yet the Court has also warned the Union legislator. The latter must not use its internal market power 'to circumvent the express exclusion[s] of harmonisation' that are laid down in the Treaties.[56] Such 'abuses' of legislative power would be sanctioned in the future.

3. 'Opting Up': Derogation Clauses in Article 114

Once the Union has adopted a harmonization measure, all national rules that conflict with the Union measure should—theoretically—have to be disapplied. This follows from the primacy of European law. When Article 114 TFEU was drafted, some Member States, however, feared that the introduction of qualified majority voting in the Council could undermine higher national standards in politically sensitive areas; and they consequently insisted on a constitutional mechanism that allowed them to 'justify' these—derogating—national laws. This was greeted with theoretical outrage;[57] yet the practical consequences of the 'public policy' justifications in Article 114(4)–(5) have been very limited.

 Drafted in parallel with Article 36 TFEU, the fourth and fifth paragraphs of Article 114 state:

4. If, after the adoption of a harmonisation measure by the European Parliament and the Council, by the Council or by the Commission, a Member State deems it necessary to *maintain* national provisions *on grounds of major needs referred to in Article 36, or relating to the protection of the environment or the working environment*, it shall notify the Commission of these provisions as well as the grounds for maintaining them.

5. Moreover, without prejudice to paragraph 4, if, after the adoption of a harmonisation measure by the European Parliament and the Council, by the Council

---

[54] Ibid., para. 78.   [55] Ibid., para. 88.   [56] Ibid., para. 79.

[57] P. Pescatore, 'Some Critical Remarks on the "Single European Act"' (1987) 24 *Common Market Law Review* 9.

> or by the Commission, a Member State deems it necessary to *introduce* national provisions based on *new scientific evidence relating to the protection of the environment or the working environment on grounds of a problem specific to that Member State arising after the adoption of the harmonisation measure*, it shall notify the Commission of the envisaged provisions as well as the grounds for introducing them.[58]

The two paragraphs allow a Member State to 'maintain' or 'introduce' national measures that 'conflict' with the harmonized Union measure. Importantly, conflict here means that a Member State does *not comply with Union legislation adopted under Article 114*. Article 114(4) and (5) TFEU thus do not cover situations where a Member State is entitled—under the harmonization measure—to adopt stricter or higher national norms.[59] They exclusively refer to the situation where a Member State would 'breach' Union legislation by insisting on a standard that is *higher* than the—mandatory and exhaustive—Union standard. Article 114(4) thereby covers the situation where a Member State wishes to 'maintain'—existing—national laws, whereas Article 114(5) refers to the power of Member States to 'introduce'—new—national laws. Both situations are subject to an administrative procedure conducted by the Commission,[60] which can subsequently be reviewed by the European Court.[61]

Article 114(4) entitles a Member State to apply to the Commission for permission to maintain its higher laws '*on grounds of major needs referred to in Article 36, or relating to the protection of the environment or the working environment*'.[62] The list of public interest grounds is limited to the express public interest derogations for the free movement of goods and two—and only two—unwritten mandatory requirements recognized by the Court.[63] By contrast, Article 114(5) does not mention the public policy grounds in Article 36.

---

[58] Emphasis added.

[59] On the various harmonization techniques, see R. Schütze, *European Union Law* (Cambridge University Press, 2018), ch. 14, section 3.

[60] For the elaborate administrative and procedural regime, see Art. 114(6)–(8) TFEU. For an overview of these provisions, see N. de Sadeleer, 'Procedures for Derogation from the Principle of Approximation of Laws under Article 95 EC' (2003) 40 *Common Market Law Review* 889.

[61] Art. 114(9) TFEU provides: 'By way of derogation from the procedure laid down in Articles 258 and 259, the Commission and any Member State may bring the matter directly before the Court of Justice of the European Union if it considers that another Member State is making improper use of the powers provided for in this Article.'

[62] Emphasis added.

[63] On these mandatory requirements, see Chapter 9, Section 4(a).

It insists on new scientific evidence and even demands a problem specific to a Member State. Article 114(5) thus appeared from the very beginning much stricter than Article 114(4).

This view was judicially confirmed in *Denmark v Commission*,[64] where the Court held as follows:

> The difference between the two situations envisaged in Article [114] is that, in the first, the national provisions predate the harmonisation measure. They are thus known to the [Union] legislature, but the legislature cannot or does not seek to be guided by them for the purpose of harmonisation. It is therefore considered acceptable for the Member State to request that its own rules remain in force ...
>
> By contrast, in the second situation, the adoption of new national legislation *is more likely to jeopardise harmonisation*. The [Union] institutions could not, by definition, have taken account of the national text when drawing up the harmonisation measure. In that case, the requirements referred to in Article [36 TFEU] are not taken into account, and only grounds relating to protection of the environment or the working environment are accepted, on condition that the Member State provides new scientific evidence and that the need to introduce new national provisions results from a problem specific to the Member State concerned arising after the adoption of the harmonisation measure.
>
> It follows that neither the wording of Article [114(4) TFEU] nor the broad logic of that article as a whole entails a requirement that the applicant Member State prove that maintaining the national provisions which it notifies to the Commission is justified by a problem specific to that Member State ... Analogous considerations apply to the requirement for new scientific evidence. That condition is imposed under Article [114(5) TFEU] for the introduction of new derogating national provisions, but it is not laid down in Article [114(4) TFEU] for the maintenance of existing derogating national provisions. It is not one of the conditions imposed for maintaining such provisions.[65]

The Court here found that the Commission was entitled, in the exercise of its administrative discretion, to be much stricter in granting derogations under Article 114(5).

This was confirmed in subsequent administrative and judicial practice. In *Upper Austria v Commission*,[66] Austria had applied for a specific derogation under Article 114(5) in relation to the Union directive on genetically

---

[64] *Denmark v Commission*, Case C-3/00 [2003] ECR I-2643.

[65] Ibid., paras 58–62 (emphasis added).

[66] *Land Oberösterreich and Republic of Austria v Commission*, Joined Cases T-366/03 and 235/04 [2005] ECR II-4005.

modified organisms (GMOs). The Austrian measure intended to prohibit the cultivation of seed composed of or containing GMOs as well as the breeding of transgenic animals. The Commission, however, refused to allow the stricter national law on the ground that 'Austria failed to provide new scientific evidence or demonstrate that a specific problem in [that country] arose'.[67] Austria appealed to the General Court against that administrative decision, and this gave the Court an opportunity to explain the criteria in Article 114(5).

The Court unambiguously clarified that the criteria of 'new scientific evidence' and the existence of 'a problem specific to the Member State' were cumulative conditions;[68] and that the burden of proof for both criteria squarely lay with the Member State concerned.[69] Unhappy with this ruling, Austria appealed to the Court of Justice. However, the Court equally confirmed the negative Commission decision; yet additionally alluded that the reference to a 'specific' national problem would not require the existence of a 'unique' problem within one Member State.[70]

4. Tax Harmonization, in Particular: Article 113

From the very beginning, the EU Treaties contained one competence that expressly envisaged the harmonization of national taxation. It can today be found in Article 113 TFEU and states:

> The Council shall, acting unanimously in accordance with a special legislative procedure and after consulting the European Parliament and the Economic and Social Committee, adopt provisions for the *harmonisation of legislation concerning turnover taxes, excise duties and other forms of indirect taxation* to the extent that such harmonisation is necessary to ensure the establishment and the functioning of the internal market and to avoid distortion of competition.[71]

The provision allows the Union, when backed up by the unanimous consent of all national governments in the Council, to harmonize all forms of 'indirect taxation'. Indirect taxes are taxes that are imposed indirectly. (While direct taxes look at the value added by a production *activity*, indirect taxes impose a tax on a product's *price*.) Indirect taxes are consumption or consumer taxes.

---

[67] Ibid., para. 15.   [68] Ibid., para. 54.   [69] Ibid., para. 63.
[70] *Land Oberösterreich and Republic of Austria v Commission*, Joined Cases C-439 and 454/05P [2007] ECR I-7141, paras 65 et seq.
[71] Art. 113 TFEU (emphasis added).

They are collected from the person who is not directly responsible for the economic change that is taxed. The two principal forms of indirect taxation expressly mentioned by Article 113 are turnover (sales) taxes and excise duties. The founding fathers of the Union regarded these two indirect taxes as 'a matter of primary importance',[72] because they posed a particularly serious danger for the establishment and functioning of the internal market.

In the past, the Union has slowly engaged in the harmonization of both forms of indirect taxes. With regard to turnover taxation, it has thereby followed the French tradition and adopted a Union-wide system of 'Value Added Tax' (VAT). This system is codified in Directive 2006/112 'on the common system of value added tax'.[73] VAT is here defined as the application to goods (and services) of 'a general tax on consumption exactly proportional to the price of the goods'.[74] The standard rate for that tax is currently 15 per cent.[75] The rate is, however, a minimum rate that allows Member States to charge a higher VAT rate in their territory.[76]

The wording of Article 113 conceptually excludes the harmonization of *direct* taxes, such as income and corporation tax. It is nonetheless important to recall that the harmonization of direct taxes is *not* beyond the scope of positive integration as such. For while the second paragraph of Article 114 TFEU excludes their harmonization by qualified majority, these taxes may still be harmonized by a unanimous Council on the basis of Article 115 TFEU.

In sum, all tax harmonization is still subject to a 'fiscal veto'. Each Member State holds on to its political 'sovereignty' over taxation. This fiscal veto has made the harmonization of taxation very difficult. EU legislation in this area is piecemeal and thin.[77] The main pressing issue for the future would probably be the harmonization of corporate tax. The latter differs significantly between the Member States, which leads to significant distortions in the functioning of the internal market (see Table 10.2). Yet instead of harmonizing a common—minimum—corporation tax, the Union has here relied on the idea of fiscal

---

[72] European Communities, 'The Value-Added Tax in the European Community' (European Communities, 1970), 3: 'It seems clear from the marked difference between the approach to harmonisation of indirect taxes on the one hand, and of direct taxes on the other, that the authors of the Rome Treaty regarded harmonisation of turnover taxes and excise duties as a matter of primary importance.'

[73] Directive 2006/112 on the common system of value added tax, [2006] OJ L347/1.

[74] Ibid., Art. 1(2).   [75] Ibid., Art. 97.

[76] The highest VAT (standard) rate in a Member State is currently set at 27 per cent in Hungary. Croatia, and Denmark, and Sweden has a VAT (standard) rate of 25 per cent.

[77] A. Hinarejos and R. Schütze (eds), *EU Fiscal Federalism: Past, Present, Future* (Oxford University Press, forthcoming).

Table 10.2 Corporate tax rates—national differences

Lowest Tax Member States		Highest Tax Member States	
Hungary	9%	Malta	35%
Bulgaria	10%	Belgium	34%
Cyprus	12%	France	33%
Ireland	12%	Germany	30%
Latvia	15%	Luxembourg	29%
Lithuania	15%	Greece	25%

competition between the national legal orders. This competition has drained the resources of European States and must be urgently addressed.[78]

Conclusion

This chapter has tried to explore the scope and nature of positive integration within the internal market. While focusing on the free movement of goods, the principles discussed within this chapter apply, *mutatis mutandis*, to all fundamental freedoms within the internal market.

What is the scope of positive integration? Section 1 explored the limits to the Union's internal market competences. We saw there that the Union has not been eager to limit its harmonization competences. It has refused to give a specific content to the technique of 'harmonization', and it has traditionally interpreted the requirement that Union harmonization must serve the establishment or functioning of the internal market extremely widely. An important—symbolic—turning point did, however, occur with *Tobacco Advertising*. The Court here annulled for the first time a Union measure on the ground that it was not covered by the general competence under Article 114. Importantly, and as we saw in Section 2, the Union's general harmonization competence in Article 114 is not limited by specific legislative competences within the EU Treaties. Whenever the centre of gravity of a Union act falls onto the internal market side, legislative harmonization under Article 114 is possible.

Once harmonization has occurred, the Member States are, in principle, obliged to follow the harmonized Union standard; yet the Union legal order has also

---

[78] Ibid.

recognized a limited number of derogations in Article 114(4) and (5). These derogations exceptionally allow a Member State to maintain or introduce a higher (!) national standard—even if this partly undermines the free movement of goods.

Finally, Section 4 looked at the very sensitive issue of tax harmonization. The Union's harmonization powers are here still subject to a 'fiscal veto' by each Member State; and this political safeguard has blocked many—necessary—harmonization efforts within this area.

Internal Market: Persons

Introduction

Apart from goods, the EU Treaties also aim to guarantee the free movement of persons. This constitutional choice for an internal 'market' in persons was originally informed by an economic rationale. For the second fundamental freedom had been created to assist people wishing to *work* in another Member State and was consequently confined to economically active persons.

The Treaties thereby distinguished between two classes of economic migrants, namely, *employed* and *self-employed* persons; and today's Treaty title dealing with persons still addresses 'Workers' and the 'Right of Establishment' in two separate chapters. Each of the two chapters thereby contains a central prohibition that outlaws restrictions to the free movement of persons and which covers both 'import' restrictions as well as 'export' restrictions that persons may face when wishing to move from one State to another.[1] Both chapters also contain a number of harmonization competences for the Union. These competences have been widely exercised in the past; and for this reason, European law on the free movement of persons is a rich mixture of primary and secondary law.

With the 1992 Maastricht Treaty, the two special chapters on persons were complemented by the general rules on EU citizenship; and the introduction of EU citizenship partially cut the economic link that was traditionally required for EU free movement rights. Article 20 TFEU now grants every European citizen the 'right to move and reside freely within the territory of the Member States'.[2] This general movement right is a residual right: it must 'be exercised in accordance with the conditions and limits defined by the Treaties and by the measures adopted thereunder'.[3] And, unsurprisingly, there has therefore been a complex relationship between the two specific sources of free movement rights and the EU citizenship provisions (Table 11.1). Their symbiotic relationship is particularly embodied in the 'Citizenship Directive'.[4]

This chapter explores the complex constitutional arrangements governing the free movement of persons in four sections. Sections 1 and 2 analyse the two special free movement rights for economically active persons, that is: workers and the self-employed. Section 3 investigates the general free movement rights granted to all European citizens. Finally, Section 4 explores the possible justifications for Member State restrictions on the free movement of persons.

---

[1] With regard to workers, see *Scholz v Opera Universitaria di Cagliari and Cinzia Porcedda*, Case C-419/92 [1994] ECR I-505; and with regard to self-employed persons, see *Knoors v Staatssecretaris van Economische Zaken*, Case 115/78 [1979] ECR 399.

[2] Art. 20(2)(a) TFEU, which is elaborated in Art. 21 TFEU. A similar right is enshrined in Art. 45 ECHR.

[3] Art. 20(2) TFEU, last indent.

[4] Directive 2004/38 on the right of citizens of the Union and their family members to move and reside freely within the territory of the Member States, [2004] OJ L158/77.

Table 11.1 Treaty provisions on the free movement of persons

Free Movement of Persons: Three Sources	
Citizenship Rights (Articles 20–5)	
Free Movement of Workers	*Freedom of Establishment*
Article 45: Prohibition on (unjustified) restrictions	Article 49: Prohibition on national restrictions
Article 46: Union Competence: Free movement of workers	Article 50: Union Competence: Freedom of establishment
Article 47: Duty to encourage the exchange of young workers	Article 51: Official Authority Exception for self-employed persons
Article 48: Union Competence: Social security	Article 52: Legitimate justifications for national restrictions
	Article 53: Union Competence: Mutual recognition
	Article 54: Legal persons (companies)
	Article 55: Establishment through participation in a company's capital

Secondary Law (Selection)
Regulation 492/2011 on Freedom of Movement of Workers
Directive 2004/38 on the Rights of Citizens (Citizenship Directive)

1. Free Movement of Workers

The Treaty contains a single provision that governs the principle of and possible restrictions to the free movement of workers. The text of Article 45 TFEU reads as follows:

1. Freedom of movement for workers shall be secured within the Union.
2. Such freedom of movement shall entail the abolition of any discrimination based on nationality between workers of the Member States as regards employment, remuneration and other conditions of work and employment.
3. It shall entail the right, subject to limitations justified on grounds of public policy, public security or public health:
   (a) to accept offers of employment actually made;
   (b) to move freely within the territory of Member States for this purpose;

(c) to stay in a Member State for the purpose of employment in accordance with the provisions governing the employment of nationals of that State laid down by law, regulation or administrative action;

(d) to remain in the territory of a Member State after having been employed in that State, subject to conditions which shall be embodied in regulations to be drawn up by the Commission.

4. The provisions of this Article shall not apply to employment in the public service.

The article has been given direct effect.[5] It thus directly grants Union rights that individuals can enforce in national courts. Yet many of the rights workers enjoy under Article 45 are also codified in Union legislation. The two most important pieces of legislation in this regard are Regulation 492/2011 'on freedom of movement of workers within the Union' (the 'Workers Regulation'),[6] and Directive 2004/38 'on the right of citizens and their family members to move and reside freely within the territory of the Member States' (the 'Citizenship Directive').[7] In combination with Article 45 TFEU, both Union acts have given concrete content to the personal and material scope of the rights granted to workers in the European Union.

What is the personal and material scope of the rights granted by Article 45 and the relevant Union legislation? Who is considered to be a 'worker'? And what types of national restrictions are prohibited? Let us look at both aspects in turn.

(a) Personal Scope: Workers and 'Quasi-Workers'

When is a person a 'worker'? Is part-time work sufficient? And are persons searching for work already 'workers'? These questions concern the personal scope of Article 45, which defines the categories of persons falling within the scope of the provision.[8] The Court of Justice has thereby insisted that

---

[5] On the doctrine of direct effect with regard to Treaty provisions, see Chapter 5, Section 2.

[6] Regulation 492/2011 on freedom of movement for workers within the Union, [2011] OJ L141/1.

[7] Directive 2004/38 on the right of citizens of the Union and their family members to move and reside freely within the territory of the Member States (n. 4).

[8] The section concentrates on the 'worker' as the primary beneficiary of Art. 45 TFEU. However, the provision, and in particular European legislation on the matter, equally entitles additional classes of persons and especially a worker's family.

it alone enjoys the 'hermeneutic monopoly' to determine the scope of the term 'worker'.[9] It held:

> [I]f the definition of this term were a matter within the competence of national law, it would therefore be possible for each Member State to modify the meaning of the concept of 'migrant worker' and to eliminate at will the protection afforded by the Treaty to certain categories of persons.[10]

The concept of 'worker' is thus a European legal concept, as 'the Treaty would be frustrated if the meaning of such a term could be unilaterally fixed and modified by national law'.[11] What, then, is the European scope of the concept of 'worker'? The Court has given it an extremely broad definition in *Lawrie-Blum*:

> The concept must be defined in accordance with objective criteria which distinguish the employment relationship by reference to the rights and duties of the persons concerned. The essential feature of an employment relationship, however, is that *for a certain period of time a person performs services for and under the direction of another person in return for which he receives remuneration.*[12]

This definition contains three criteria. First, a person would have to be 'settled'.[13] Second, the person would have to be under the direction of someone else; and consideration for this subordination was—third—the payment of remuneration.[14]

(i) Employment: A Minimalist Definition

What form of remuneration would be required to trigger the scope of Article 45? In *Levin*,[15] a British national was refused a residence permit in the Netherlands on the ground that she was not engaged in full-time work that provided

---

[9] F. Mancini, 'The Free Movement of Workers in the Case-Law of the European Court of Justice' in D. Curtin and D. O'Keeffe (eds), *Constitutional Adjudication in the European Community and National Law* (Butterworths, 1992), 67.

[10] *Hoekstra (nee Unger) v Bestuur der Bedrijfsvereniging voor Detailhandel en Ambachten*, Case 75/63 [1964] ECR 177, 184.

[11] Ibid.

[12] *Lawrie-Blum v Land Baden-Württemberg*, Case 66/85 [1986] ECR 2121, para. 17 (emphasis added).

[13] This requirement of 'permanency' distinguishes 'workers' under Art. 45 TFEU from 'posted workers' who fall within the scope of the free movement of services. On 'posted workers' as a distinct category, see R. Schütze, *European Union Law* (Cambridge University Press, 2018), ch. 16, section 2(a).

[14] In this sense, see *Trojani v Centre public d'aide sociale de Bruxelles*, Case C-456/02 [2004] ECR I-7573, para. 22: 'the constituent elements of any paid employment relationship, namely subordination and the payment of remuneration'.

[15] *Levin v Staatssecretaris van Justitie*, Case 53/81 [1982] ECR 1035.

her with remuneration 'commensurate with the means of subsistence considered as necessary by the legislation of the Member State'.[16] Would the rights under Article 45 thus depend on receiving a minimum salary within the host Member State? The Court, anxious to avoid a definition of 'worker' that differed depending on the Member State involved, held otherwise:

> Since part-time employment, although it may provide an income lower than what is considered to be the minimum required for subsistence, constitutes for a large number of persons an effective means of improving their living conditions, the effectiveness of [Union] law would be impaired and the achievement of the objectives of the Treaty would be jeopardized if the enjoyment of rights conferred by the principle of freedom of movement for workers were reserved solely to persons engaged in full-time employment and earning, as a result, a wage at least equivalent to the guaranteed minimum wage in the sector under consideration ...
>
> In this regard no distinction may be made between those who wish to make do with their income from such an activity and those who supplement that income with other income, whether the latter is derived from property or from the employment of a member of their family who accompanies them. *It should however be stated that whilst part-time employment is not excluded from the field of application of the rules on freedom of movement for workers, those rules cover only the pursuit of effective and genuine activities, to the exclusion of activities on such a small scale as to be regarded as purely marginal and ancillary.*[17]

The Court here defined a 'worker' as a person remunerated for an 'effective and genuine' activity. Under this minimalist definition, the number of working hours and the level of remuneration is irrelevant, except where the activity is so small that it is 'purely marginal and ancillary'. Subsequent jurisprudence has consolidated this minimalist standard.[18] It thus confirmed that benefits in kind could be considered 'remuneration' as long as the work done was 'capable of being regarded as forming part of the normal labour market'.[19] But what about people who could not support themselves in the host State? The Court here insisted that even where a person needs financial assistance *from the State* to supplement his or her income, this would still be irrelevant

---

[16] Ibid., para. 10.

[17] Ibid., paras 15–17 (emphasis added).

[18] See *Kempf v Staatssecretaris van Justitie*, Case 139/85 [1986] ECR 1741; as well as *Trojani*, Case C-456/02 (n. 14).

[19] Ibid., para. 24.

for the status as a 'worker' as long as he or she was engaged in an effective and genuine activity.[20]

The idea of an 'effective and genuine' working activity is thus the conceptual core of the personal scope of Article 45. It covers full-time, part-time, occasional, and even zero-hour work as long as there is an employment relationship with regard to work that is 'not purely marginal or ancillary'.

(ii) Beyond Employment: Former Workers and Jobseekers

The Court's minimalist definition of 'worker' has given an extremely broad personal scope to Article 45; but it still hinged on the *presence* of a genuine employment relationship. But would Article 45 also cover people searching for *future* employment, or persons who had engaged in *past* employment?

The Court has indeed found these 'quasi-workers' to fall into the personal scope of Article 45. For former employees, this solution is suggested by the provision itself;[21] and the Court has confirmed this in *Lair*.[22] A French national had brought proceedings against a German university for refusing to award her a maintenance grant. This was a social advantage which a worker would have been entitled to claim under Article 45.[23] But could Mrs Lair claim this right *after* having ceased work in the host State? Three Member States intervened in the case and argued that 'a person loses the status of worker, on which the social advantages depend, when, in the host State, [s]he gives up either [her] previous occupational activity or, if unemployed, [her] search for employment in order to pursue full-time studies'.[24] The Court disagreed:

---

[20] *Kempf v Staatssecretaris van Justitie*, Case 139/85 (n. 18), para. 14: 'It follows that the rules on this topic must be interpreted as meaning that a person in effective and genuine part-time employment cannot be excluded from their sphere of application merely because the remuneration he derives from it is below the level of the minimum means of subsistence and he seeks to supplement it by other lawful means of subsistence. In that regard it is irrelevant whether those supplementary means of subsistence are derived from property or from the employment of a member of his family, as was the case in *Levin*, or whether, as in this instance, they are obtained from financial assistance drawn from the public funds of the Member State in which he resides, provided that the effective and genuine nature of his work is established.'

[21] Art. 45(3)(d) TFEU expressly refers to the right 'to remain in the territory of a Member State after having been employed in that State, subject to conditions which shall be embodied in regulations to be drawn up by the Commission'.

[22] *Lair v Universität Hannover*, Case 39/86 [1988] ECR 3161.

[23] Ibid., para. 28. On the material scope of Art. 45 TFEU and the notion of social advantage under Art. 7(2) of Regulation 492/2011, see Section 1(b).   [24] Ibid., para. 29.

> [T]he rights guaranteed to migrant workers do not necessarily depend on the actual or continuing existence of an employment relationship. . . . Persons who have previously pursued in the host Member State an effective and genuine activity as an employed person as defined by the Court but who are no longer employed are nevertheless considered to be workers under certain provisions of [Union] law. . . . It is therefore clear that migrant workers are guaranteed certain rights linked to the status of worker even when they are no longer in an employment relationship.[25]

Non-employed persons may thus continue to enjoy worker rights; yet these rights require 'some continuity' with the previous occupational activity. This qualification is to prevent abuses of the host State's social welfare system.[26]

With regard to retired pensioners, the Court has also held that 'the fact that a person is no longer in an employment relationship does not deny him certain guaranteed rights which are linked to the status of a worker and that a retirement pension, whose grant is dependent on the prior existence of an employment relationship, which has come to an end, falls within that category of rights'.[27] Pensioners, who previously worked in a Member State other than their own, are thus constitutionally entitled to stay. By contrast, pensioners who never worked outside their home State and only moved to another Member State after they retired 'cannot therefore rely on the free movement guaranteed by Article 45 TFEU'.[28]

What about persons seeking future employment? The Court has deliberately expanded the personal scope of Article 45 to jobseekers in *Antonissen*.[29] The case arose from a preliminary question by an English High Court on the compatibility of a British law permitting the deportation of foreigners after six months of unemployment. Was such a temporal limitation on the status of (potential) workers possible? While the Court confirmed that the personal scope of Article 45 included jobseekers, it accepted that the mobility of workers would not be undermined by national measures offering 'a reasonable time' to find work.[30] And in the absence of Union harmonization on the matter, a period of six months was considered reasonable.[31] The Court was

---

[25] Ibid., para. 36.

[26] In *Brown v The Secretary of State for Scotland*, Case 197/86 [1988] ECR 3205, the Court thus imposed strict requirements when a former worker was entitled to educational rights, such as a grant for university studies.

[27] *Kohl and Kohl-Schlesser*, Case C-300/15, EU:C:2016:361, para. 25 (with reference to prior case law).

[28] Ibid., para.26 (with references to previous case law).

[29] *The Queen v Immigration Appeal Tribunal, ex parte Antonissen*, Case C-292/89 [1991] ECR I-745.

[30] Ibid., para. 16.   [31] Ibid., para. 21.

nonetheless eager to add that 'if after the expiry of that period the person concerned provides evidence that he is continuing to seek employment and that he has genuine chances of being engaged', the jobseeker could not be forced to leave the territory of the host Member State.[32]

(b) Material Scope: Discrimination and Beyond

Which rights will workers enjoy on the basis of Article 45 TFEU and Union legislation? Article 45(2) expressly refers to 'the abolition of any discrimination based on nationality between workers of the Member States as regards employment, remuneration and other conditions of work and employment'; and Article 45(3) clarifies that this 'shall entail the right' to accept offers, to move freely, and to stay within the territory of a Member State for that purpose.

  These textual bones were given flesh by two central pieces of Union legislation: the Citizenship Directive (Directive 2004/38) and the Workers Regulation (Regulation 492/2011). With regard to workers, the latter is the more important one as it sets out the specific rights for workers and their families.[33] In addition to outlawing access restrictions to the labour market of the host State,[34] the Regulation also confirms the principle of equal treatment during an employment relationship. The central provision here is Article 7, which states:

1. A worker who is a national of a Member State may not, in the territory of another Member State, be *treated differently from national workers by reason of his nationality* in respect of any conditions of employment and work, in particular as regards remuneration, dismissal, and, should he become unemployed, reinstatement or re-employment.
2. He shall enjoy the *same social and tax advantages* as national workers.[35]

Despite the direct effect of Article 45 TFEU, Article 7 of the Regulation plays a profound role in the EU case law. It provides a negative expression of the equal treatment principle in paragraph 1, and a positive expression of that principle in paragraph 2.

---

[32] Ibid.

[33] These rights are set out in Chapter 1 of the Regulation. Chapter 1 is divided into three sections: Section 1 is on 'Eligibility for Employment' (Arts 1–6). Section 2 deals with 'Employment and Equality of Treatment' (Arts 7–9), while Section 3 concerns 'Workers' Families' (Art. 10).

[34] See Art. 4(1) of the Regulation: 'Provisions laid down by law, regulation or administrative action of the Member States which restrict by number or percentage the employment of foreign nationals in any undertaking, branch of activity or region, or at a national level, shall not apply to nationals of the other Member States.'

[35] Emphasis added.

Was Article 7(1) inspired by a discrimination rationale; and, if so, which one? It is clear that the provision captures direct discrimination, like lower pay for foreign workers. In *Sotgiu*,[36] the Court, however, also clarified that the formulation 'by reason of his nationality' was not confined to direct discrimination only:

> The rules regarding equality of treatment, both in the Treaty and in Article 7 of Regulation [492/2011], forbid not only overt discrimination by reason of nationality but also *all covert forms of discrimination* which, by the application of other criteria of differentiation, lead in fact to the same result.[37]

Article 7(1) of the Regulation thus covers both direct and indirect discrimination. Subsequent jurisprudence thereby crystallized two situations in which national laws would appear to be *indirectly* discriminatory. The first situation concerns national laws that 'although applicable irrespective of nationality' nonetheless 'affect essentially migrant workers or the great majority of those affected are migrant workers'.[38] By contrast, the second situation arises where national laws 'are indistinctly applicable but can more easily be satisfied by national workers than by migrant workers or where there is a risk that they may operate to the particular detriment of migrant workers'.[39] Unless the differential treatment can here be objectively justified, both types of national laws would violate Article 7(1) of the Regulation.

A positive expression of the equal treatment rights for migrant workers is set out in Article 7(2) of the Regulation. Foreign workers are here granted 'the same social and tax advantages as national workers'.[40] The notion of 'advantage' has received a wide teleological meaning. In *Cristini*,[41] the Court found the phrase to refer to 'all social and tax advantages, whether or not attached to the contract of employment';[42] and this included travel reductions in fares for large families offered by the State. This definition was confirmed

---

[36] *Sotgiu v Deutsche Bundespost*, Case 152/73 [1974] ECR 153.

[37] Ibid., para. 11 (emphasis added).

[38] *O'Flynn v Adjudication Officer*, Case C-237/94 [1996] ECR I-2617, para. 18.

[39] Ibid. (with extensive references to the case law).

[40] Originally, the Court had excluded jobseekers from the scope of the provision. In *Centre public d'aide sociale de Courcelles v Lebon*, Case 316/85 [1987] ECR 2811, the Court held (ibid., para. 26): '[T]he right to equal treatment with regard to social and tax advantages applies only to workers. Those who move in search of employment qualify for equal treatment only as regards access to employment in accordance with Article [45] of the [FEU] Treaty and Articles 2 and 5 of Regulation 1612/68.' This judgment was qualified in *Collins v Secretary of State for Work and Pensions*, Case C-138/02 [2004] ECR I-2703.

[41] *Cristini v SNCF*, Case 32/75 [1975] ECR 1085.   [42] Ibid., para. 13.

in *Lair*,[43] where the Court further broadened the concept of social advantage to all advantages which entailed 'the possibility of improving [a worker's] living and working conditions and promoting his social advancement'.[44] This included all advantages that:

> whether or not linked to a contract of employment, are generally granted to national workers primarily because of their status as workers or by virtue of the mere fact of their residence on the national territory and whose extension to workers who are nationals of other Member States therefore seems likely to facilitate the mobility of such workers within the [Union].[45]

However, as under Article 7(1) of the Regulation, Member States are entitled, under Article 7(2) of the Regulation, to justify differential treatment 'if it is based on objective considerations that are independent of the nationality of the persons concerned and proportionate to the legitimate aim of the national provisions'.[46] A residence requirement might thus be legitimate, where a Member State wishes 'to ensure that there is a *genuine link* between an applicant for an allowance in the nature of a social advantage within the meaning of Article 7(2) of Regulation'.[47]

Finally, what about *non*-discriminatory restrictions to the free movement of workers? While much of the case law on workers focuses on discriminatory national laws, the Court accepts that non-discriminatory measures might equally fall within the scope of Article 45 TFEU. The famous confirmation of that possibility is *Bosman*.[48] The case concerned a professional football rule according to which a footballer could not be employed by another club unless the latter paid a transfer or training fee. This was a non-discriminatory rule that applied to nationals and non-nationals alike.[49] Nonetheless, the Court found that:

> [p]rovisions which preclude or deter a national of a Member State from leaving his country of origin in order to exercise his right to freedom of movement therefore constitute an obstacle to that freedom even if they apply without regard to the nationality of the workers concerned. . . . Since they provide that a professional footballer

---

[43] *Lair v Universität Hannover*, Case 39/86 (n. 22).
[44] Ibid., para. 20.   [45] Ibid., para. 21.
[46] *Collins v Secretary of State for Work and Pensions*, Case C-138/02 (n. 40), para. 66.
[47] Ibid., para. 67.
[48] *Union royale belge des sociétés de football association ASBL v Jean-Marc Bosman*, Case C-415/93 [1995] ECR I-4921.   [49] Ibid., para. 98.

may not pursue his activity with a new club established in another Member State unless it has paid his former club a transfer fee agreed upon between the two clubs or determined in accordance with the regulations of the sporting associations, the said rules constitute an obstacle to freedom of movement for workers.[50]

Formulated as a general principle, this suggests that '[n]ational provisions which *preclude or deter a national of a Member State from leaving his country of origin* in order to exercise his right to freedom of movement therefore constitute restrictions on that freedom even if they apply without regard to the nationality of the workers concerned'.[51] Non-discriminatory restrictions are thus covered by Article 45 TFEU.

2. Freedom of Establishment

Freedom of establishment constitutes the second side of the economic coin on the free movement of persons. It guarantees the free movement of *self-employed persons*. To achieve this aim, the relevant Treaty chapter contains a prohibition on illegal national barriers, and grants the Union two legislative competences.[52] This section will concentrate on the prohibition in the form of Article 49,[53] which states:

Within the framework of the provisions set out below, restrictions on the freedom of establishment of nationals of a Member State in the territory of another Member State shall be prohibited. Such prohibition shall also apply to restrictions on the setting-up of agencies, branches or subsidiaries by nationals of any Member State established in the territory of any Member State.

Freedom of establishment shall include the right to take up and pursue activities as self-employed persons and to set up and manage undertakings, in particular companies or firms within the meaning of the second paragraph of Article 54, under the conditions laid down for its own nationals by the law of the country where such establishment is effected, subject to the provisions of the Chapter relating to capital.

---

[50] Ibid., paras 96 and 100.

[51] *Olympique Lyonnais v Bernard and Newcastle UFC*, Case C-325/08 [2010] ECR I-2177, para. 34 (emphasis added).

[52] See Arts 50 and 53 TFEU. This section will not deal with the various legislative instruments in this context. The most important instrument adopted under Art. 53 TFEU is Directive 2005/36 on the recognition of professional qualifications, [2005] OJ L255/22.

[53] The provision was given direct effect in *Reyners v Belgium*, Case 2/74 [1974] ECR 631.

(a) Personal Scope: Self-Employed Persons (and Companies)

The personal scope of Article 49 captures 'self-employed' persons. Like workers, self-employed persons will need to be engaged in a *genuine economic activity*. However, unlike workers, self-employed persons do not work under the direction of an employer and will not receive a 'salary' compensating for their subordination. The personal scopes of Articles 45 and 49 are thus 'mutually exclusive'.[54] The definition of 'worker' thereby negatively determines the personal scope of the freedom of establishment. And importantly, self-employed persons might be natural *or* legal persons. For Article 54 TFEU expressly provides that the freedom of establishment covers companies and firms.[55]

Self-employed persons (and companies) will typically produce goods or perform services. And while there are no delineation problems with regard to goods, the Union legal order had to delimit the personal scope of Article 49 from the perspective of the free movement of services. For this third freedom protects, among other things, persons offering a service in another State.[56]

What, then, is the characteristic feature underlying the personal scope of the freedom of establishment? The Court has identified it as follows:

> The right of establishment, provided for in Articles [49] to [54] of the Treaty, is granted both to legal persons within the meaning of Article [54] and to natural persons who are nationals of a Member State of the [Union]. Subject to the exceptions and conditions laid down, it allows all types of self-employed activity to be taken up and pursued on the territory of any other Member State, undertakings to be formed and operated, and agencies, branches or subsidiaries to be set up ...
>
> The concept of establishment within the meaning of the Treaty is therefore a very broad one, allowing a [Union] national to participate, *on a stable and*

---

[54] *Gebhard v Consiglio dell'Ordine degli Avvocati e Procuratori di Milano*, Case 55/94 [1995] ECR I-4165, para. 20.

[55] Art. 54 TFEU states: 'Companies or firms formed in accordance with the law of a Member State and having their registered office, central administration or principal place of business within the Union shall, for the purposes of this Chapter, be treated in the same way as natural persons who are nationals of Member States. "Companies or firms" means companies or firms constituted under civil or commercial law, including cooperative societies, and other legal persons governed by public or private law, save for those which are non-profit-making.' For a discussion of the free movement of companies, see Schütze, *European Union Law* (n. 13), ch. 15, section 3.

[56] According to Art. 56 TFEU, 'restrictions on freedom to provide services within the Union shall be prohibited in respect of nationals of Member States who are established in a Member State other than that of the person for whom the services are intended'. This 'third' freedom is beyond the scope of this book.

continuous basis, in the economic life of a Member State other than his State of origin and to profit there from, so contributing to economic and social interpenetration within the [Union] in the sphere of activities as self-employed persons. In contrast, where the provider of services moves to another Member State, the provisions of the chapter on services, in particular the third paragraph of Article [57], envisage that he is to pursue his activity there on a temporary basis.[57]

The decisive criterion distinguishing 'established' service providers from 'temporary' service providers is thus the 'stable and continuous basis' on which the former participate in the economy of the host Member State. A 'stable and continuous' presence will trigger the personal scope of the freedom of *establishment*. However, the concept of establishment will not require exclusive presence in the host State (as this would rule out secondary establishment). The applicability of Article 49 is determined by the 'duration', 'regularity, periodicity or continuity' of the services provided,[58] and such a continuous presence will not need to take the form of a 'branch' or 'agency' but may consist of an 'office'.[59] Yet the existence of some infrastructure—like an office—is not conclusive evidence in favour of establishment.[60]

(b) Material Scope: Discrimination and Beyond

Article 49 prohibits 'restrictions on the freedom of establishment'. The prohibition thereby expressly covers primary and secondary establishment. *Primary* establishment occurs where a natural or legal person establishes itself for the first time. The right to establishment is, however, 'not confined to the right to create a single establishment within the [Union]', but includes 'freedom to set up and maintain, subject to observance of the professional rules of conduct, more than one place of work within the [Union]'.[61]

Secondary establishment thus covers 'the setting-up of agencies, branches or subsidiaries by nationals of any Member State [already] established in the

---

[57] *Gebhard*, Case 55/94 (n. 54), paras 23–6 (emphasis added). The third paragraph of Art. 57 TFEU states that '[w]ithout prejudice to the provisions of the Chapter relating to the right of establishment, the person providing a service may, in order to do so, temporarily pursue his activity in the Member State where the service is provided, under the same conditions as are imposed by that State on its own nationals'.

[58] *Gebhard*, Case 55/94 (n. 54), para. 27.

[59] See *Commission v Germany*, Case 205/84 [1986] ECR 3755, para. 21.

[60] *Gebhard*, Case 55/94 (n. 54), para. 27.

[61] *Ordre des avocats au Barreau de Paris v Klopp*, Case 107/83 [1984] ECR 2971, para. 19.

territory of any Member State'.[62] This right of secondary establishment is given to every person or company lawfully established in a Member State of the Union, even if it has no business in the State of primary establishment.[63] This constitutional choice allows a company to freely choose its Member State of incorporation within the Union. However, where a company moves to another Member State, it may lose its legal personality in its original home State.[64] This principle—which partly restricts the right of secondary establishment—follows from the right of each Member State to decide when a company is 'primarily' established.[65]

Which types of restrictions on primary or secondary establishment will Article 49 prohibit? The wording of the provision clearly covers discriminatory measures. This includes *directly* discriminatory national laws, and equally prohibits *indirect* discrimination on the ground of nationality.

A good illustration for direct discrimination is offered in *Reyners*.[66] The plaintiff had been born in Brussels to Dutch parents and had himself retained Dutch nationality. Having been resident in Belgium all his life, he had received his legal education there and had graduated with a Belgian law degree. Yet when applying to become a barrister, his application was denied because a 1919 Belgian law stated that only Belgian nationals could practise the legal profession. Such direct discrimination on the ground of nationality was clearly in breach of Article 49.

A good illustration for indirect discrimination can be found in *Klopp*.[67] The case involved a German barrister registered with the Düsseldorf (Germany) Bar, who had applied for secondary registration at the Paris (France) Bar. His application there was however rejected by the Paris Bar

---

[62] Art. 49 TFEU, first indent.

[63] *Segers v Bestuur van de Bedrijfsvereniging voor Bank- en Verzekeringswezen, Groothandel en Vrije Beroepen*, Case 79/85 [1986] ECR 2375. The *Segers* principle was confirmed in *Centros v Erhvervs-og Selskabsstyrelsen*, Case C-212/97 [1999] ECR I-1459.

[64] *The Queen v HM Treasury and Commissioners of Inland Revenue, ex parte Daily Mail*, Case 81/87 [1988] ECR 5483. This distinguishes legal persons from natural persons, as the latter will not lose their nationality when moving their primary establishment to another Member State.

[65] This is recognized in Art. 54 TFEU, which defers to the laws of the Member States with regard to the formation of companies. National laws typically follow one of two theories. According to the 'incorporation theory', a company is 'established' through the simple act of formal registration. This contrasts with the 'seat theory', which makes formal registration dependent on the company having its managerial and business centre within the State of registration.

[66] *Reyners v Belgium*, Case 2/74 [1974] ECR 631.

[67] *Ordre des avocats au Barreau de Paris v Onno Klopp*, Case 107/83 [1984] ECR 2971.

Council on the ground that he did not satisfy a French law that required barristers to join or establish a set of chambers in one place only. This law was not directly discriminatory, since it also applied to French barristers; yet the Court had no problem in finding indirect discrimination to have taken place:

> It should be emphasized that under the second paragraph of Article [49] free-dom of establishment includes access to and the pursuit of the activities of self-employed persons 'under the conditions laid down for its own nationals by the law of the county where such establishment is effected'. It follows from that provision and its context that in the absence of specific [Union] rules on the matter each Member State is free to regulate the exercise of the legal profession in its territory. Nevertheless that rule does not mean that the legislation of a Member State may require a lawyer to have only one establishment throughout the [Union] territory. Such a restrictive interpretation would mean that a law-yer once established in a particular Member State would be able to enjoy the freedom of the Treaty to establish himself in another Member State only at the price of abandoning the establishment he already had.[68]

Whether the scope of Article 49 also covered non-discriminatory measures remained uncertain for some time. This uncertainty was ultimately removed in *Gebhard*.[69] The case involved a German lawyer who had practised in Italy under the title 'avvocato' without being formally admitted to the Italian Bar. This violated the relevant national rules on the organization of the legal pro-fession. Yet despite their 'non-discriminatory' character, the Court unambig-uously found them to violate Article 49 because they were 'liable to hinder or make less attractive' the freedom of establishment.[70] This market-access for-mula potentially covers all types of regulatory barriers. However, the Court appears to limit its negative ambit to national measures that hinder '[a]ccess to the market' to foreign establishments.[71]

---

[68]   Ibid., paras 17–18.
[69]   *Gebhard*, Case 55/94 (n. 54).
[70]   Ibid., para. 37.
[71]   *Caixa Bank France v Ministère de l'Économie, des Finances et de l'Industrie*, Case C-442/02 [2004] ECR I-8961, para. 14. For an analysis of the case law on persons in the light of the market access test, see E. Spaventa, *Free Movement of Persons in the European Union: Barriers to Move-ment in Their Constitutional Context* (Kluwer, 2007), ch. 5.

3. European Citizenship: A General Right to Move?

With the formal introduction of the provisions on European citizenship,[72] the European Treaties recognize a range of rights that pertain to all 'Europeans' by virtue of being Union citizens.[73] These rights are generally set out in Article 20 TFEU, and are subsequently specified in the following articles. With regard to free movement, Article 21 TFEU states:

1. Every citizen of the Union shall have the right to move and reside freely within the territory of the Member States, subject to the limitations and conditions laid down in the Treaties and by the measures adopted to give them effect.
2. If action by the Union should prove necessary to attain this objective and the Treaties have not provided the necessary powers, the European Parliament and the Council, acting in accordance with the ordinary legislative procedure, may adopt provisions with a view to facilitating the exercise of the rights referred to in paragraph 1.

The central question behind paragraph 1 has been whether the provision grants a directly effective right to all Union citizens to move within the Union that is independent from the free movement of workers and freedom of establishment discussed previously. Would there be a third—general—right to move freely within the Union? Regardless of whether or not there exists such a constitutional right under Article 21(1), Article 21(2) grants the Union a legislative competence, and this competence has been used to adopt the 'Citizenship' Directive.[74] This directive fleshes out the content of the free movement rights for all categories of natural persons within the Union. Importantly, companies are not covered by the citizenship provisions (see Figure 11.1).

---

[72] The citizenship provisions were introduced by the (old) Treaty on European Union concluded in Maastricht. For an early analysis of these provisions, see C. Closa, 'The Concept of Citizenship in the Treaty on European Union' (1992) 29 *Common Market Law Review* 1137.

[73] This European citizenship is 'additional' to national citizenship (see Art. 20(1) TFEU): every citizen of a Member State is thus also a Union citizen.

[74] The Citizenship Directive was adopted on the legal bases of Art. 18 TFEU (non-discrimination), Art. 46 TFEU (workers), Art. 50 TFEU (establishment), and Art. 59 TFEU (services).

Figure 11.1 Relationship between citizenship and special freedoms

(a) Article 21(1): A Direct Source of Movement Rights

Would Article 21(1) TFEU be directly effective, and therefore generally grant movement rights to all European citizens? Having approached the matter in various indirect ways,[75] the Court finally gave a straight answer in *Baumbast*.[76] The case concerned the fight of a German father to stay with his daughters in the United Kingdom while they continued their education at a British school. The fundamental question put before the European Court was this: Would a Union citizen, who no longer enjoyed a right of residence as a migrant worker, nonetheless enjoy an independent right of residence on the basis of Article 21(1) alone?

The United Kingdom government vehemently rejected this view. '[A] right of residence cannot be derived directly from Article [21(1) TFEU]', because '[t]he limitations and conditions referred to in that paragraph show that it is not intended to be a free-standing provision'.[77] The Court famously found otherwise:

[T]he Treaty on European Union does not require that citizens of the Union pursue a professional or trade activity, whether as an employed or self-employed person, in order to enjoy the rights provided in Part Two of the [TFEU], on

---

[75] See *Martínez Sala v Freistaat Bayern*, Case C-85/96 [1998] ECR I-2691; and *Grzelczyk v Centre public d'aide sociale d'Ottignies-Louvain-la-Neuve*, Case C-184/99 [2001] ECR I-6193. In the latter case the Court famously held (ibid., para. 31) that 'Union citizenship is destined to be the fundamental status of nationals of the Member States'.

[76] *Baumbast and R v Secretary of State for the Home Department*, Case C-413/99 [2002] ECR I-7091.

[77] Ibid., para. 78.

citizenship of the Union. Furthermore, there is nothing in the text of that Treaty to permit the conclusion that citizens of the Union who have established themselves in another Member State in order to carry on an activity as an employed person there are deprived, where that activity comes to an end, of the rights which are conferred on them by the [TFEU] by virtue of that citizenship. *As regards, in particular, the right to reside within the territory of the Member States under Article [21(1)] that right is conferred directly on every citizen of the Union by a clear and precise provision of [that] Treaty.*

Purely as a national of a Member State, and consequently a citizen of the Union, Mr Baumbast therefore has the right to rely on Article [21(1)]. Admittedly, that right for citizens of the Union to reside within the territory of another Member State is conferred subject to the limitations and conditions laid down by the [Treaties] and by the measures adopted to give it effect. However, the application of the limitations and conditions acknowledged in Article [21(1)] in respect of the exercise of that right of residence is subject to judicial review. Consequently, any limitations and conditions imposed on that right do not prevent the provisions of Article [21(1)] from conferring on individuals rights which are enforceable by them and which the national courts must protect.[78]

The Court here clarified four things. First, Article 21(1) had direct effect and would thus grant general movement rights that could be invoked against national law. The fact that these rights were subject to limitations and conditions was no barrier to their direct effect. Second, the personal scope of the citizenship provisions did not depend on the economic status of a person. Europeans enjoyed free movement rights as *citizenship* rights; and citizenship was a 'fundamental status' independent of someone's economic position.[79] Third, the citizenship provisions would be residual provisions. They would not apply whenever one of the specialized movement regimes was applicable. Fourth, any limitation on citizenship rights through European legislation would be subject to judicial review. And where these legislative limitations were disproportionate, the Court could strike them down on the basis of Article 21(1).[80]

---

[78] Ibid., paras 83–6 (emphasis added) (with express reference to the reasoning in *Van Duyn v Home Office*, Case 41/74 [1974] ECR 1337).

[79] Ibid., para. 82 (with reference to *Grzelczyk*, Case C-184/99 (n. 75)).

[80] Ibid., paras 91–3.

(b) Citizenship Directive: Rights and Limitations

The directive on the right of citizens to move and reside freely within the Union was adopted to codify in 'a single legislative act' the various secondary sources governing the free movement of persons.[81] It was designed to lay down, in a horizontal manner, 'the conditions governing the *exercise* of the right of free movement and residence within the territory of the Member States by Union citizens' (and their family members).[82]

The Directive thereby contains five substantive chapters. Chapter II concerns the rights of exit and entry (Arts 4–5). Chapter III details the rights of residence (Arts 6–15). Chapter IV lays down rules for the right of permanent residence (Arts 16–21). Chapter V assembles provisions that are common to the right of (temporary) residence and permanent residence (Arts 22–6). Finally, Chapter VI provides detailed rules on legitimate restrictions to the right of entry and residence on grounds of public policy, public security, or public health (Arts 27–33).

What are the most important rights recognized in the Directive? Having spelled out the right to exit and enter a Member State on condition of a valid identity card or passport, the Directive distinguishes three classes of residency rights. According to Article 6, all Union citizens will have the short-term right to reside in the territory of another Member State for a period of up to three months 'as long as they do not become an unreasonable burden on the social assistance system of the host Member State'.[83] A second class of residency rights is established by Article 7, whose first paragraph states:

> All Union citizens shall have the right of residence on the territory of another Member State for a period of longer than three months if they:
>
> (a) are workers or self-employed persons in the host Member State; or
> (b) have sufficient resources for themselves and their family members not to become a burden on the social assistance system of the host Member State during their period of residence and have comprehensive sickness insurance cover in the host Member State; or
> (c) – are enrolled at a private or public establishment, accredited or financed by the host Member State on the basis of its legislation or administrative

---

[81] Directive 2004/38, Preamble 4.

[82] Ibid., Art. 1(a). Art. 3, however, restricts the personal scope to 'Union citizens who move to or reside in a Member State *other than that of which they are a national*' (emphasis added).

[83] Ibid., Art. 14(1).

> practice, for the principal purpose of following a course of study, including vocational training; and
> – have comprehensive sickness insurance cover in the host Member State and assure the relevant national authority, by means of a declaration or by such equivalent means as they may choose, that they have sufficient resources for themselves and their family members not to become a burden on the social assistance system of the host Member State during their period of residence[.]

The provision acknowledges three categories of persons who will benefit from mid-term residency rights. Subparagraph (a) refers to the economically active migrants expressly recognized by the Treaties. This is extended to all persons with 'sufficient resources' and with 'comprehensive sickness insurance' (subpara. b),[84] with students benefiting from a slightly more generous treatment (subpara. c).

Finally, the Directive grants a third right: the 'right of permanent residence' in certain situations. The general rules for this are laid down in Article 16, which confers such a right after lawful presence in the host State 'for a continuous period of five years'.[85] Importantly, this right of long-term residency is *independent of the economic status and the financial means of the person concerned*.

Once a person is legally resident in another Member State, the Directive also expressly grants this person a right to equal treatment in Article 24. The connection between *lawful residence* and *equal treatment* has been firmly established in the jurisprudence of the European Court.[86] In principle, a Member State must thus treat all legally resident Union citizens within its territory— but only those—like its own nationals. This general principle is, however, subject to such 'specific provisions as are expressly provided for in the Treaty and

---

[84] Art. 8(4) of the Directive thereby partly defines 'sufficient resources' by stating: 'Member States may not lay down a fixed amount which they regard as "sufficient resources", but they must take into account the personal situation of the person concerned. In all cases this amount shall not be higher than the threshold below which nationals of the host Member State become eligible for social assistance, or, where this criterion is not applicable, higher than the minimum social security pension paid by the host Member State.'

[85] Art. 17 thereby establishes a more preferable regime for former workers or self-employed persons, and Art. 18 deals with the acquisition of the right of permanent residence by certain family members.

[86] See esp. *Dano and Dano v Jobcenter Leipzig*, Case C-333/13, EU:C:2014:2358.

secondary law'.[87] Controversially, the equality principle has specifically been derogated by Article 24(2) with regard to social assistance and maintenance aid for studies.

4. Justifying Restrictions on (Self-)Employed Persons

Member States are entitled to restrict the free movement of persons but only where these restrictions are justified on the basis of legitimate public interests. For workers, Article 45(3) expressly allows for 'limitations justified *on grounds of public policy, public security or public health*'. For the freedom of establishment, Article 52 permits the 'special treatment for foreign nationals *on grounds of public policy, public security or public health*'. Finally, Article 21(1) subjects the free movement of EU citizens generally 'to the limitations and conditions laid down in the Treaties and by the measures adopted to give them effect'.

Many problems encountered in Chapter 9 in the context of goods will apply, *mutatis mutandis*, to justified restrictions on the free movement of persons.[88] However, unlike the provisions on goods, the Treaties here recognize an additional justification for national restrictions: the public service exception.

(a) Express Justifications and (Implied) Imperative Requirements

The express justifications for restrictions on persons mentioned in the Treaties are substantially identical to those on goods. However, unlike the casuistic approach governing goods, the Citizenship Directive has partly codified the case law.[89] Article 27 of the Directive thereby confirms the power of the Member States to 'restrict the freedom of movement and residence of Union citizens and their family members, irrespective of nationality, on grounds of public policy, public security or public health'.

With regard to the first two public interest grounds, the Directive further clarifies that national restrictions must 'be based exclusively on the personal conduct of the individual concerned',[90] and that this personal conduct 'must represent a genuine, present and sufficiently serious threat affecting one of

---

[87] Directive 2004/38, Art. 24(1).
[88] On justified restrictions to the free movement of goods, see Chapter 9, Section 4.
[89] Directive 2004/38, Chapter VI (Arts 27–33).
[90] Ibid., Art. 27(2), first indent. For an early judicial definition of what constitutes personal conduct, see *Van Duyn v Home Office*, Case 41/74 (n.78).

the fundamental interests of society'.[91] With regard to public health, Article 29 of the Directive subsequently determines that only 'diseases with epidemic potential' and the like will justify measures restricting free movement.[92]

Is the list of public interest justifications exhaustive? The Court has indeed held that discriminatory measures—whether direct or indirect—can solely be justified by reference to the express justifications recognized by the Treaty (or Union secondary law).[93] Yet as soon as the Court had acknowledged that non-discriminatory measures could potentially violate the free movement provisions, it also recognized—just like for the free movement of goods—the existence of additional—implied—justifications. These implied justifications are called 'imperative requirements' or 'overriding requirements' relating to the public interest. And, as with the free movement of goods, the Court here accepts an unlimited and thus extremely wide range of imperative requirements.[94]

The constitutional principles governing these imperative requirements are set out in *Gebhard*,[95] where the Court held:

> [N]ational measures liable to hinder or make less attractive the exercise of fundamental freedoms guaranteed by the Treaty must fulfil four conditions: they must be applied in a non-discriminatory manner; they must be justified by imperative requirements in the general interest; they must be suitable for securing the attainment of the objective which they pursue; and they must not go beyond what is necessary in order to attain it.[96]

Imperative requirements offered by the Member States as potential justifications will thus only apply to *non*-discriminatory measures and will be subject to the principle of proportionality.[97]

---

[91]   Directive 2004/38, Art. 27(2), second indent. For an early judicial definition of what constitutes a 'present' threat, see *Regina v Pierre Bouchereau*, Case 30/77 [1977] ECR 1999.

[92]   Directive 2004/38, Art. 29(1).

[93]   See *Engelmann*, Case C-64/08 [2010] ECR I-8219, para. 34.

[94]   Such imperative requirements include consumer protection (see *Commission v France*, Case 220/83 [1986] ECR 3663), environmental protection (see *De Coster*, Case C-17/00 [2001] ECR I-9445), and many, many more!

[95]   *Gebhard*, Case 55/94 (n. 54).

[96]   Ibid., para. 37.

[97]   On the principle of proportionality in the context of the free movement of goods, see Chapter 9, Section 4(b).

(b) In Particular: the Public Service Exception

Many States still prefer to reserve 'State jobs' for their nationals. And the EU Treaties concede a public service exception for restrictions on the free movement of persons. For workers, we find this special justification in Article 45(4) TFEU, which states that '[t]he provisions of this Article shall not apply to *employment in the public service*'.[98] For the freedom of establishment, this special limitation can be found in Article 51 excluding activities 'connected, even occasionally, with the *exercise of official authority*'.

On the surface, both provisions appear to exclude different things from their respective scopes. For workers, the wording of Article 45 suggests that all employment in a State institution can be excluded, and it therefore seems based on an *institutional* definition. By contrast, the provision on establishment seems to adopt a *functional* definition that focuses on whether public functions are exercised.

Yet despite these textual disparities, the Court has opted for a uniform definition for both derogations. This choice in favour of a single—functional—definition of 'public service' can be seen in *Commission v Belgium*.[99] The Court here held in the context of Article 45(4):

> [D]etermining the sphere of application of Article [45(4)] raises special difficulties since in the various Member States authorities acting under powers conferred by public law have assumed responsibilities of an economic and social nature or are involved in activities which are not identifiable with the functions which are typical of the public service yet which by their nature still come under the sphere of application of the Treaty. In these circumstances the effect of extending the exception contained in Article [45(4)] to posts which, whilst coming under the State or other organizations governed by public law, still do not involve any association with tasks belonging to the public service properly so called, would be to remove a considerable number of posts from the ambit of the principles set out in the Treaty and to create inequalities between Member States according to the different ways in which the state and certain sectors of economic life are organized.[100]

Because the meaning of the concept 'public service' required a 'uniform interpretation',[101] the Court has consequently rejected an institutional (national) definition and favours a functional (European) definition in Article 45(4).

---

[98] Emphasis added.

[99] *Commission v Belgium*, Case 149/79 [1980] ECR 3881.

[100] Ibid., para. 11.   [101] Ibid., para. 12.

This functional classification 'depends on whether or not the posts in question are typical of the specific activities of the public service in so far as the exercise of powers conferred by public law and responsibility for safeguarding the general interest of the State are vested in it'.[102] This definition of public service potentially includes employees of a private company, where the latter performs public functions.[103] The Court has, however, subjected its functional test to 'very strict conditions'.[104] The work must involve 'a *special relationship of allegiance* to the State and reciprocity of rights and duties which form the foundation of the bond of nationality'.[105]

In a separate jurisprudential line, the Court has moreover clarified that the public service exception only permits restrictions on the *access to*—but not *discriminations inside*—a position involving public power. Thus, where foreigners have been admitted to a public service post, they will benefit from the equal treatment principle. In the words of the Court:

> [Article 45(4)] cannot justify discriminatory measures with regard to remuneration or other conditions of employment against workers once they have been admitted to the public service. The very fact that they have been admitted shows indeed that those interests which justify the exceptions to the principle of non-discrimination permitted by Article [45(4)] are not at issue.[106]

The reasoning under Article 45(4) applies, *mutatis mutandis*, to Article 51 and restrictions to professions involving public power.

Conclusion

The free movement of persons is a complex fundamental freedom. It not only comprises the free movement of workers and the freedom of establishment for self-employed persons as well as companies, but the European Treaties also grant a (limited) movement right to all citizens of the Union. These three distinct constitutional sources of free movement rights were discussed in this chapter. Each of the three sources is complemented by

---

[102] Ibid.

[103] *Anker et al. v Germany*, Case C-47/02 [2003] ECR I-10447.

[104] *Lawrie-Blum*, Case 66/85 (n. 12), para. 28.

[105] *Commission v Belgium*, Case 149/79 (n. 99), para. 10 (emphasis added).

[106] *Sotgiu v Deutsche Bundespost*, Case 152/73 (n. 36), para. 4. And see also *Commission v Belgium*, Case 149/79 (n. 99), esp. paras 20–2.

secondary law; and the interplay between negative and positive integration has resulted in a mixture of primary and secondary Union law that makes this area of European law rich in technical nuances.

In order to navigate these technical waters, two elements—one qualitative, one quantitative—should be kept in mind. Despite the introduction of the horizontal provisions on Union citizenship, the Union legal order continues to qualitatively distinguish between categories of person exercising movement rights. Economically active Union 'workers' and 'professionals' will thus generally be entitled to full assimilation into the host State, while non-economically active citizens will not. Within the latter category, the Union has moreover adopted a gradual approach. The number of rights that a migrant Union citizen can claim will depend on the degree of his or her integration into the host society.

Competition Law: Cartels

Introduction

Competitive markets are markets in which economic rivalry is to enhance efficiency. Market 'forces' determine the winners and losers of this rivalry, and competition will—ultimately—force inefficient losers out of the market.

Who, however, forces the winner(s) to act efficiently? By the end of the nineteenth century, this question was first raised in the United States. After a period of intense competition, 'the winning firms were seeking instruments to assure themselves of an easier life';[1] and they started to use—among other

---

[1] G. Amato, *Antitrust and the Bounds of Power: The Dilemma of Liberal Democracy in the History of the Market* (Hart, 1997), 8.

things—the common law 'trust' to coordinate their behaviour within the market. To counter the anti-competitive effects of these trusts, the American legislator adopted the first competition law of the modern world: the Sherman Antitrust Act (1890).[2] The Act attacked two cardinal sins within all competition law: anti-competitive agreements[3] and monopolistic markets.[4]

The US experience has significantly shaped the competition law of the European Union;[5] yet the inclusion of a Treaty chapter on EU competition law was originally rooted not so much in competition concerns as such. It was, instead, the 'general agreement that the elimination of tariff barriers would not achieve its objectives if private agreements of economically powerful firms were permitted to be used to manipulate the flow of trade'.[6] EU competition law was thus—at first—primarily conceived as a complement to the internal market.[7]

This also explains the position of the competition provisions within the EU Treaties. They are found in Chapter 1 of Title VII of the TFEU. The chapter is divided into two sections—one dealing with classic competition law, that is: '[r]ules applying to undertakings'; the other with public interferences in the internal market through '[a]ids granted by States'. Table 12.1 provides an overview of the various competition rules within the EU Treaties.

EU competition law is thereby built on four pillars. The first pillar deals with anti-competitive cartels and can be found in Article 101. The second pillar concerns situations where a dominant undertaking abuses its market power and is covered in Article 102. The third pillar is unfortunately

---

[2] The Act was named after Senator John Sherman, who proposed it.

[3] Sherman Act, Section 1: 'Every contract, combination in the form of trust or otherwise, or conspiracy, in restraint of trade or commerce among the several States, or with foreign nations, is declared to be illegal[.]'

[4] Ibid., Section 2: 'Every person who shall monopolize, or attempt to monopolize, or combine or conspire with any other person or persons, to monopolize any part of the trade or commerce among the several States, or with foreign nations, shall be deemed guilty of a felony[.]'

[5] On the direct influence of American law and its indirect influence via German law, see D. Gerber, *Law and Competition in Twentieth-Century Europe: Protecting Prometheus* (Oxford University Press, 2001).

[6] Ibid., 343.

[7] This link between the internal market and EU competition law continues to be textually anchored in the Treaties. According to Art. 3(3) TEU (emphasis added), '[t]he Union shall establish an internal market. It shall work for the sustainable development of Europe based on balanced economic growth and price stability, [and] a highly *competitive* social market economy, aiming at full employment and social progress.' The meaning of the provision is clarified in Protocol (No. 27) 'On the Internal Market and Competition', according to which 'the internal market as set out in Article 3 of the Treaty on European Union *includes a system ensuring that competition is not distorted*' (emphasis added).

Table 12.1 Competition rules—overview

TFEU—Title VII—Chapter 1			
Section 1:	**Rules Applying to Undertakings**	**Section 2:**	**Aids Granted by States**
Article 101	Anti-competitive Agreements	Article 107	State Aid Prohibition
Article 102	Abuse of a Dominant Position	Article 108	Commission Powers
Article 103	Competition Legislation I	Article 109	Competition Legislation II
Article 104	'Transitional' Provisions		
Article 105	Commission Powers		
Article 106	Public Undertakings (and Public Services)		

invisible: when the Treaties were concluded, they did not mention the control of mergers. This constitutional gap has never been closed by subsequent Treaty amendments; yet it has received a legislative closing in the form of the European Union Merger Regulation (EUMR). The fourth pillar of EU competition law concerns 'public' interferences into free competition, and in particular State aids.

This final chapter on substantive EU law 'introduces' European competition law by exploring only the first pillar: Article 101. This article is in many respects emblematic for the 'European' approach to competition law. We start by considering the 'jurisdictional' aspects of the provision in Sections 1 and 2. The 'substantive' criteria within Article 101, and their relationship to each other, will then be discussed in Sections 3 and 4.

1. Article 101: Jurisdictional Aspects

Article 101 outlaws anti-competitive collusions between undertakings; that is: 'cartels'. Historically, this form of illegal behaviour has been the most dangerous anti-competitive practice. The prohibition on any collusion between undertakings to restrict competition in the internal market is thereby set out in Article 101. It states:

1. The following shall be prohibited as incompatible with the internal market: all agreements between undertakings, decisions by associations of undertakings and concerted practices which may affect trade between Member States

and which have as their object or effect the prevention, restriction or distortion of competition within the internal market . . .

2. Any agreements or decisions prohibited pursuant to this Article shall be automatically void.

3. The provisions of paragraph 1 may, however, be declared inapplicable in the case of:

- any agreement or category of agreements between undertakings,
- any decision or category of decisions by associations of undertakings,
- any concerted practice or category of concerted practices,

which contributes to improving the production or distribution of goods or to promoting technical or economic progress, while allowing consumers a fair share of the resulting benefit, and which does not:

(a) impose on the undertakings concerned restrictions which are not indispensable to the attainment of these objectives;

(b) afford such undertakings the possibility of eliminating competition in respect of a substantial part of the products in question.

Article 101 follows a tripartite structure. Paragraph 1 prohibits collusions between undertakings that are anti-competitive by object or effect if they affect trade between Member States. Paragraph 3 exonerates certain collusions that are justified by their overall pro-competitive effects for the Union economy. In between this dual structure of prohibition and justification—oddly—lies paragraph 2, which determines that illegal collusive practices are automatically void and thus cannot be enforced in court.[8]

This section looks at two jurisdictional aspects of Article 101(1)—and all EU competition law generally; namely, the kinds of undertakings caught as well as the requirement of an 'effect on trade between Member States'.

(a) The Concept of 'Undertaking'

The English word 'undertaking' has traditionally not meant what the EU Treaties want it to mean.[9] The word is a translation from the German and French

---

[8] This is not the sole consequence of a violation of Art. 101 TFEU. The Union has typically used its powers to impose significant fines on undertakings violating the provision. On the enforcement of European competition law generally, see W. Wils, *Principles of European Antitrust Enforcement* (Hart, 2005).

[9] In its saddest form, the word refers to the preparations for a funeral service.

equivalents, and was deliberately chosen to avoid pre-existing meanings in British company law.[10] According to the famous definition in *Höfner & Elser*, the concept of undertaking means this:

> [T]he concept of an undertaking encompasses every entity engaged in an economic activity, regardless of the legal status of the entity and the way in which it is financed[.][11]

This definition ties the notion of undertaking to an *activity*; and this *functional* definition broadens the personal scope of the competition rules to include entities that may—formally—not be regarded as companies. It catches natural persons,[12] and includes 'professionals'—such as barristers.[13] Even the 'State' and its public bodies may sometimes be regarded as an undertaking, when they engage in an economic activity.[14] The advantage of this broad functional definition is its flexibility; its disadvantage, however, is its uncertainty. Indeed, depending on its actions, an entity may or may not be an 'undertaking' within the meaning of EU competition law in particular situations.[15]

What, then, are economic activities? The Court has consistently held that 'any activity consisting in offering goods or services on a given market is an economic activity'.[16]

This comprehensive definition will nevertheless find a limit when public functions are exercised. In *Poucet & Pistre*,[17] the Court thus refused to consider organizations managing a public social security system as 'undertakings', since their activities were 'based on the principle of national solidarity' and

---

[10] R. Lane, *EC Competition Law* (Longman, 2001), 33.

[11] *Höfner and Elser v Macrotron*, Case C-41/90 [1991] ECR I-1979, para. 21.

[12] Cf. *Hydrotherm v Compact*, Case 170/83 [1984] ECR 2999, para. 11.

[13] Cf. *Wouters et al. v Algemene Raad van de Nederlandse Orde van Advocaten*, Case C-309/99 [2002] ECR I-1577, para. 49.

[14] See *Commission v Italy*, Case 118/85 [1987] ECR 2599.

[15] Advocate General Jacobs, *Firma Ambulanz Glöckner v Landkreis Südwestpfalz*, Case C-475/99 [2001] ECR I-8089, para. 72: '[T]he notion of undertaking is a relative concept in the sense that a given entity might be regarded as an undertaking for one part of its activities while the rest falls outside the competition rules.'

[16] *Pavlov and Others v Stichting Pensioenfonds Medische Specialisten*, Case C-180/98 [2000] ECR I-6451, para. 75.

[17] *Poucet & Pistre*, Joined Cases C-159 and 160/91 [1993] ECR I-637.

'entirely non-profit-making'.[18] A private body may thus not count as an undertaking where it is engaged in 'a task in the public interest which forms part of the essential functions of the State'.[19] However, what counts as an essential public function is not always easy to tell. The Court has refused to be bound by a 'historical' or 'traditional' understanding of public services. In *Höfner & Elser*, it consequently found that '[t]he fact that employment procurement activities are normally entrusted to public agencies cannot affect the economic nature of such activities', since '[e]mployment procurement has not always been, and is not necessarily, carried out by public entities'.[20]

In conclusion, then, the Court has so far not found a convincing definition of what counts as an economic activity.[21]

(b) Effect on Trade between Member States

Not all anti-competitive behaviour falls within the jurisdictional scope of EU competition law, and in particular Article 101. Article 101 only catches cartels that may 'affect trade between Member States'.[22]

What is the point behind this jurisdictional limitation around Article 101? The answer lies—partly—in the principle of conferral.[23] The *European* Union should only concern itself with agreements that have a *European* dimension, which is manifested through a (potential) effect on trade *between* Member States. In the words of the European Court:

> The concept of an agreement 'which may affect trade between Member States' is intended to define, in the law governing cartels, the boundary between the areas respectively covered by [European] law and national law. It is only to the extent to

---

[18] Ibid., paras 18–19. This was confirmed in *Albany International BV v Stichting Bedrijfspensioenfonds Textielindustrie*, Case C-67/96 [1999] ECR I-5751. The latter case has been particularly controversial.

[19] *Cali & Figli Srl v Servizi ecologici porto di Genova*, Case C-343/95 [1997] ECR I-1547, esp. paras 22–3.

[20] *Höfner & Elser v Macrotron*, Case C-41/90 (n. 11).

[21] For an academic analysis of the case law, see O. Odudu, 'The Meaning of Undertaking within 81 EC' (2006) 7 *Cambridge Yearbook of European Legal Studies* 211.

[22] The following sections refer to 'agreements', but the analysis applies, *mutatis mutandis*, also to decisions of associations of undertakings, and concerted practices.

[23] On the principal of 'conferral' in the Union legal order, see Chapter 3.

which the agreement may affect trade between Member States that the deterioration in competition caused by the agreement falls under the prohibition of [European] law contained in Article [101]; otherwise it escapes that prohibition.[24]

Agreements must thus have an *interstate* dimension—otherwise they will be outside the sphere of European competition law. But what is this 'European' sphere of competition law? The jurisdictional scope of Article 101 has been—very—expansively interpreted.[25] And the Court has developed a number of constitutional tests as to when interstate trade has been affected. A famous formula was devised in *Société Technique Minière*, where the Court held Article 101 to apply to any agreement that 'may have an influence, direct or indirect, actual or potential, on the *pattern of trade between Member States*'.[26] This 'pattern of trade' test is extremely broad as it captures both quantitative as well as qualitative changes to trade.[27]

The fact that an agreement relates to a single Member State will not necessarily mean that Article 101 is not applicable.[28] What counts are the (potential) *effects* of a national agreement on the European markets.[29] And when measuring the effect of an agreement on trade between Member States, the Court will take into account whether or not the agreement forms part of a broader network of agreements:

The existence of similar contracts is a circumstance which, together with others, is capable of being a factor in the economic and legal context within which the contract must be judged.[30]

---

[24]   *Consten and Grundig v Commission*, Joined Cases 56 and 58/64 [1964] ECR 299 at 341.

[25]   Art. 101 TFEU. For a general analysis of this criterion, see Commission, 'Guidelines on the effect on trade concept contained in Articles [101 and 102] of the Treaty', [2004] OJ C101/81.

[26]   *Société Technique Minière v Maschinenbau Ulm*, Case 56/65 [1965] ECR 235 at 249 (emphasis added).

[27]   On the substantive 'neutrality' of the 'pattern of trade' test, see Commission, 'Guidelines on the effect on trade concept contained in Articles [101 and 102] of the Treaty' (n. 25), paras 34–5: 'The term "pattern of-trade" is neutral. It is not a condition that trade be restricted or reduced. Patterns of trade can also be affected when an agreement or practice causes an increase in trade.'

[28]   See *Belasco and others v Commission*, Case 246/86 [1989] ECR 2117, para. 38: 'Accordingly, although the contested agreement relates only to the marketing of products in a single Member State, it must be held to be capable of influencing intra-[Union] trade.'

[29]   See *Brasserie de Haecht v Wilkin-Janssen (II)*, Case 48/72 [1973] ECR 77, paras 26 et seq.

[30]   *Brasserie de Haecht v Consorts Wilkin-Janssen (I)*, Case 23/67 [1967] ECR 407 at 416.

This 'contextual' view of agreements was developed in *Delimitis*.[31] The case arose out of a dispute between the plaintiff publican and the brewery Henninger, and turned on the legality of a beer supply agreement. Could a single agreement concluded by a local pub with a local brewery have an effect on intra-Union trade? The Court here decidedly placed the agreement within the network of agreements to which it belonged and held that 'the *cumulative effect of several similar agreements* constitutes one factor amongst others in ascertaining whether, by way of a possible alteration of competition, trade between Member States is capable of being affected'.[32] It was consequently necessary to analyse the effects of all beer supply agreements within the network to see if the single agreement contributed to a cumulative effect that had an interstate dimension.

Nonetheless, not all effects on interstate trade will lead to proceedings under Article 101. For the effects 'must not be insignificant';[33] and the Union will only police agreements that *appreciably* affect intra-Union trade.[34] According to its 'non-appreciably-affecting-trade' (NAAT) rule,[35] agreements will generally not fall within the jurisdictional scope of Article 101 if two cumulative conditions are met. First, '[t]he aggregate market share of the parties on any relevant market within the [Union] affected by the agreement does not exceed 5%'; and, second, 'the aggregate annual [Union] turnover of the undertakings concerned in the products covered by the agreement does not exceed 40 million euro'.[36]

2. Forms of Collusion between Undertakings

Article 101 covers anti-competitive collusions *between* undertakings. The prohibited action must thus be *multilateral*. But what types of multilateral collusions are covered by the prohibition? Article 101 refers to three types of collusions: 'agreements between undertakings, decisions by associations of undertakings and concerted practices'. Let us look at each collusive form in turn.

---

[31] *Delimitis v Henninger Bräu*, Case C-234/89 [1991] ECR I-9935.

[32] Ibid., para. 14 (emphasis added).

[33] *Javico International and Javico AG v Yves Saint Laurent Parfums SA (YSLP)*, Case C-306/96 [1998] ECR I-1983, para. 16 (with reference to *Völk v Vervaecke*, Case 5/69 [1969] ECR 295).

[34] The Commission makes a clear distinction between an appreciable effect on interstate *trade* on the one hand, and appreciable restrictions on *competition* on the other. The former will be discussed here, while the latter will be discussed later, in Section 3(d).

[35] 'Guidelines on the effect on trade concept contained in Articles [101 and 102] of the Treaty' (n. 25), para. 50.

[36] Ibid., para. 52.

(a) Agreements I: Horizontal and Vertical Agreements

The European concept of 'agreement' has been given an extremely wide conceptual scope.[37] The Union legal order is not interested in whether the agreement formally constitutes a 'contract' under national law. What counts is 'a concurrence of wills' between economic operators.[38] 'Gentlemen's agreements' have thus been classified as agreements under Article 101, as long as the parties consider them binding.[39]

One of the central concerns within the early Union legal order was the question of whether Article 101 covered only 'horizontal' or also 'vertical' agreements (see Figure 12.1). Horizontal agreements are agreements between undertakings that are competing against each other; that is: companies placed at the same commercial level. Vertical agreements, by contrast, are agreements between undertakings at different levels of the commercial chain; that is: agreements between companies *not* competing against each other. And since Article 101 prohibits anti-competitive agreements, would it not follow that only 'horizontal' agreements

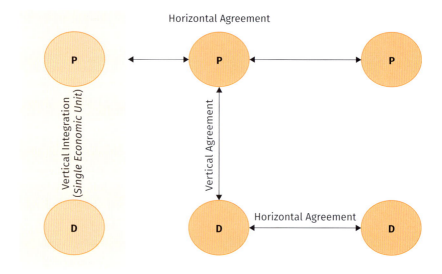

Figure 12.1 Horizontal and vertical agreements

[37] For an analysis of the concept of 'agreement', see J. Shaw, 'The Concept of Agreement in Article 85 EEC' (1991) 16 *European Law Review* 262.

[38] See *Bayer AG v Commission*, Case T-41/96 [2000] ECR II-3383, para. 69; and *Bundesverband der Arzneimittel-Importeure and Commission v Bayer*, Joined Cases C-2 and 3/01P [2004] ECR I-23, para. 97.

[39] See *ACF Chemiefarma v Commission*, Case 41/69 [1979] ECR 661, paras 106 et seq.

between *competitors* are covered? This logic is not without its problems. For while vertical agreements between a producer (P) and a distributor (D) may increase economic efficiency through a specialized division of labour,[40] they may also significantly harm the consumer through a restriction of price competition.[41]

Would vertical agreements fall within the jurisdictional scope of Article 101? The European Court has—famously and positively—answered this question in *Consten and Grundig v Commission*.[42] The German producer Grundig had concluded a distribution agreement for the French market with Consten. The Commission had claimed that the agreement breached European competition law. The applicants counterclaimed that the Union lacked jurisdiction under Article 101 as 'distributorship contracts do not constitute "agreements between undertakings" within the meaning of that provision, since the parties are not on a footing of equality'.[43] The Court disagreed:

> Article [101] refers in a general way to all agreements which distort competition within the common market and does not lay down any distinction between those agreements based on whether they are made between competitors operating at the same level in the economic process or between non-competing persons operating at different levels. In principle, no distinction can be made where the Treaty does not make any distinction.
>
> Furthermore, the possible application of Article [101] to a sole distributorship contract cannot be excluded merely because the grantor and the concessionaire are not competitors inter se and not on a footing of equality. Competition may be distorted within the meaning of Article [101(1)] not only by agreements which limit it as between the parties, but also by agreements which prevent or restrict competition which might take place between one of them and third parties. For this purpose, it is irrelevant whether the parties to the agreement are or are not on a footing of equality as regards their position and function in the economy. This applies all the more, since, by such an agreement, the parties might seek, by preventing or limiting the competition of third parties in respect of the products, to create or guarantee for their benefit an unjustified advantage at the expense of the consumer or user, contrary to the general aims of Article [101].[44]

---

[40] Lane, *EC Competition Law* (n. 10), 92: 'Their prime advantage is that they allow for net economic efficiency: they enable the producer to concentrate upon production and relieve it of the obligation of shifting the goods on the market, for that will be the concern of the (specialist) distributor who is better suited to the task.'

[41] Ibid., 97: 'Looking at the economics, it is not surprising: the factory gate value of goods is sometimes a fraction of their shop value[.]'

[42] *Consten and Grundig v Commission*, Joined Cases 56 and 58/64 (n. 24).

[43] Ibid., 339.   [44] Ibid.

The arguments in favour of including vertical agreements here were textual and teleological. Indeed, within its text Article 101 did not make a distinction between horizontal and vertical agreements, and it thus seemed to cover both types generically. Teleologically, moreover, Article 101 was said to not only protect against restrictions of competition imposed on the distributor, but also to protect third parties, namely: consumers and competitors. And since vertical agreements could create unjustified disadvantages for these third parties, they would have to be within the jurisdiction of European competition law.[45]

(b) Agreements II: 'Tacit Acquiescence' versus 'Unilateral Conduct'

Every agreement—whether horizontal or vertical—must be concluded through the consent of the parties. It must be formed by a concurrence of *two or more* wills. The idea of an 'agreement' will thus find a conceptual boundary where one party *unilaterally* imposes its will on the other. Yet there may sometimes be a fine line between tacit acceptance and unilateral imposition. And the European Courts have struggled to demarcate this line for the Union legal order.[46] The reason for this conceptual fuzziness lies in what the Courts call 'apparently unilateral' behaviour in continuous contractual relations between two parties.

A good illustration of such 'apparently unilateral behaviour' can be found in *Ford v Commission*.[47] The American car manufacturer had established a selective distribution system in Europe, and in particular in Britain and Germany, through a 'main dealer agreement'. That agreement appeared not to violate Article 101, and originally allowed German distributors to order right-hand as well as left-hand drive cars. However, as the prices for Ford cars on the British market suddenly increased significantly, British customers began buying from German dealers; and afraid that its British distributor would suffer the consequences, Ford notified its German dealers that it would no longer accept their orders for right-hand drive cars. These would henceforth be reserved for the British market.

---

[45] This second argument was an important one: vertical agreements would need to be within the scope of Art. 101 TFEU because they could have an anti-competitive effect both with regard to intra-brand competition—i.e. price competition between distributors—but also inter-brand competition between different producers. On the distinction between inter-brand and intra-brand competition, see Section 3(a).

[46] See *AEG v Commission*, Case 107/82 [1983] ECR 3151; *Ford-Werke AG and Ford of Europe Inc. v Commission*, Joined Cases 25 and 26/84 [1985] ECR 2725; and *BMW v ALD Auto-Leasing*, Case C-70/93 [1995] ECR I-3439.

[47] *Ford-Werke AG and Ford of Europe Inc. v Commission*, Joined Cases 25 and 26/84 (n. 46).

Was the decision to discontinue supplies to the German dealers an agreement? Ford claimed that the discontinuance decision was of a unilateral nature; and since 'a unilateral act cannot be included among agreements', it would fall outside the scope of Article 101.[48] The Court, however, held otherwise:

> Such a decision on the part of the manufacturer does not constitute, on the part of the undertaking, a unilateral act which, as the applicants claim, would be exempt from the prohibition contained in Article [101(1)] of the Treaty. On the contrary, *it forms part of the contractual relations between the undertaking and its dealers.*[49]

This extremely generous interpretation of 'consent' has nonetheless encountered some limits. In *Bayer v Commission*,[50] the German pharmaceutical company used its distribution system to market 'Adalat'—a medical product designed to treat cardiovascular disease. The price of the product within the internal market differed significantly as it was indirectly fixed by the respective national health authorities. The prices fixed by the Spanish and French health services were thereby on average 40 per cent lower than prices in the United Kingdom; and following commercial logic, Spanish and French wholesalers began exporting to the British market. With its British dealer registering an enormous loss of turnover, Bayer decided to stop delivering large orders to Spanish and French wholesalers. Instead, it provided them with the exact quantities that it thought would saturate their national markets.

Was this indirect export restriction based on a consensual agreement? The General Court rejected this view. While accepting that 'apparently unilateral conduct' can qualify as an agreement, the latter required—as a conceptual minimum—the '*existence of an acquiescence by the other partners, express or implied, in the attitude adopted by the manufacturer*'.[51] And in the present case, even tacit acquiescence was missing.[52] For the mere continuation of the business relationship could not as such be tacit acquiescence.

---

[48] Ibid., para. 15.

[49] Ibid., para. 21 (emphasis added).

[50] *Bayer AG v Commission*, Case T-41/96 (n. 38).

[51] Ibid., para. 72.

[52] Ibid., paras 151 et seq: 'Examination of the attitude and actual conduct of the wholesalers shows that the Commission has no foundation for claiming that they aligned themselves on the applicant's policy designed to reduce parallel imports . . . [T]he wholesalers continued to try to obtain packets of Adalat for export and persisted in that line of activity, even if, for that purpose, they considered it more productive to use different systems to obtain supplies, namely the system of distributing orders intended for export among the various agencies on the one hand, and that of placing orders indirectly through small wholesalers on the other.'

The judgment was confirmed on appeal,[53] where the European Court concisely clarified the situation as follows: 'The mere concomitant existence of an agreement which is in itself neutral and a measure restricting competition that has been imposed unilaterally does not amount to an agreement prohibited by that provision.'[54] Put the other way around, for an 'apparently unilateral' measure to become part of a continuous contractual relationship, the other party must—at the very least—tacitly acquiesce. And this tacit acquiescence must be shown through actual compliance with the 'apparently unilateral' measure.

(c) Concerted Practices and Parallel Conduct

The conclusion of an agreement is but one form of collusion between undertakings. Another form mentioned in Article 101(1) is 'concerted practices'. The concept was designed as a safety net to catch all forms of collusive behaviour falling short of an agreement.[55] This has been confirmed by the European Court, which has identified the aim behind the concept as follows:

> [T]he object is to bring within the prohibition of [Article 101(1)] a form of coordination between undertakings which, without having reached the stage where an agreement properly so-called has been concluded, knowingly substitutes practical cooperation between them for the risk of competition.[56]

The heart of a concerted practice is seen in a 'coordination' between undertakings 'which becomes apparent from the behaviour of the participants'.[57] Yet the Court was quick to point out that not all 'parallel behaviour' between undertakings—such as the parallel raising of prices—can be identified with a concerted practice.[58] Article 101 would 'not deprive economic operators of the right to adapt themselves intelligently to the existing and anticipated

---

[53] *Bundesverband der Arzneimittel-Importeure and Commission v Bayer*, Joined Cases C-2 and 3/01P (n. 38).

[54] Ibid., para. 141.

[55] For that reason, there may be no need for a categorical dividing line between an agreement and a concerted practice; see *Commission v Anic Partecipazioni*, Case C-49/92P [1999] ECR I-4125, para. 132: '[W]hilst the concepts of an agreement and of a concerted practice have particularly different elements, they are not mutually incompatible.'

[56] *Imperial Chemical Industries v Commission*, Case 48/69 [1972] ECR 619, para. 64.

[57] Ibid., para. 65.   [58] Ibid., para. 66.

conduct of their competitors'.[59] Parallel behaviour that follows from market forces would be beyond reproach. In the absence of any form of 'practical cooperation' through 'direct or indirect contact',[60] undertakings will thus be allowed to align their commercial behaviour to the 'logic' of the market.[61]

(d) Cartel Decisions Through Associations of Undertakings

This third category of collusion is designed to catch institutionalized cartels; and this may include professional bodies, such as the Bar Council.[62]

The inclusion of this form of collusion in Article 101 clarified that undertakings could not escape the scope of Article 101 by substituting *multilateral* collusion between them by establishing an association that would adopt *unilateral* decisions on their behalf. A cartel decision—even in the soft form of a 'recommendation'—may thus be caught as collusive behaviour under Article 101(1).[63]

3. Restriction of Competition: Anti-Competitive Object or Effect

In order for an agreement to violate the prohibition of Article 101(1), it must be anti-competitive; it must be a 'prevention, restriction or distortion of competition'.[64]

The meaning of 'restriction of competition' in this context has been very controversial. If it simply referred to a restriction of the *individual* freedom to trade, then all binding agreements would be anti-competitive. For '[t]o bind, to restrain, is of their very essence'.[65] This individualist definition

---

[59] *Coöperatieve Vereniging 'Suiker Unie' UA and others v Commission*, Joined Cases 4–8, 50, 54–6, 111, 113 and 114/73 [1975] ECR 1663, para. 174; as well as *Commission v Anic Partecipazioni*, Case C-49/92P (n. 55), para. 117.

[60] *'Suiker Unie' v Commission* (n. 59), paras 27 and 174.

[61] The evidentiary burden on the Commission is very high; see *Ahlstrom Osakeyhtiö and others v Commission*, Joined Cases C-89, 104, 114, 116, 117 and 125–9/85 [1993] ECR I-1307, para. 71: '[P]arallel conduct cannot be regarded as furnishing proof of concertation unless concertation is the only plausible explanation for such conduct.'

[62] See *Wouters et al. v Algemene Raad van de Nederlandse Orde van Advocaten*, Case C-309/99 (n. 13).

[63] See *Van Landewyck and others v Commission*, Joined Cases 209–15 and 218/78 [1980] ECR 3125, para. 89.

[64] This formulation covers hypothetical, quantitative, and qualitative limitations of competition. In this section, 'restriction' of competition will be employed as a generic term.

[65] See *Chicago Board of Trade v United States*, 246 US 231, 238 (1918).

of restriction has, however, never been dominant in the Union legal order. A second view has therefore argued that Article 101, while not protecting the individual freedom of a specific competitor, nonetheless protects the *structural* freedom offered by the market to—actual or potential—competitors. This view emphasizes the exclusionary effects of restrictions of competition and corresponds to the 'Harvard School'.[66] A third view has finally imported the 'Chicago School' into the debate on the scope of Article 101(1). It argues that the prohibition should exclusively outlaw 'exploitative effects' in the form of allocative inefficiencies to consumer welfare.[67] The case law of the European Courts has been closest to the second view—even if the European Commission has once tried hard to move towards the third view.[68]

This section analyses four aspects of what constitutes a restriction of competition in the Union legal order. We start by looking at the various dimensions of competition, before examining the two modes of violating Article 101(1)—restrictions by 'object or effect'. This includes an analysis of whether the 'ancillary restraints' doctrine represents a 'rule of reason' in disguise. A final subsection offers a brief encounter with the *de minimis* limitation on restrictions of competition.

(a) Two Dimensions: Inter-Brand and Intra-Brand Competition

A restriction of competition is primarily a restriction between competitors. Early on, the European Court had, however, confirmed that competition could be restricted by horizontal as well as vertical agreements.[69] But was this solely an admission that vertical agreements could restrict inter-brand competition; that is: competition between producers of different brands? Or did the inclusion of vertical agreements into the scope of Article 101(1) signal that *intra*-brand competition—competition between distributors of the same brand—was independently protected?

---

[66] The 'European' equivalent of the 'Harvard School' is the 'Freiburg School', which has become famous for its 'ordoliberalism'. For a concise overview of the philosophical positions of that school, see D. Gerber, 'Constitutionalizing the Economy: German Neo-Liberalism, Competition Law and the "New Europe"' (1994) 42 *American Journal of Comparative Law* 25.

[67] O. Odudu, *The Boundaries of EC Competition Law: The Scope of Article 81* (Oxford University Press, 2006), 102.

[68] See Commission, 'Guidelines on the application of Article 81(3) [now: Article 101(3)] of the Treaty', [2004] OJ C101/97. However, see also *GlaxoSmithKline and others v Commission*, Joined Cases C-501, 513, 515, and 519/06P [2009] ECR I-9291, where the Court rejected the 'Chicagoization' of European competition law.

[69] For a discussion of this point, see Section 2(a).

The European Court has preferred the second reading. The Union legal order consequently recognizes two independent dimensions of competition: *inter*-brand and *intra*-brand competition. In *Consten and Grundig*,[70] the Court thus rejected the plaintiffs' argument that there could be no restriction of competition through vertical agreements:

> The principle of freedom of competition concerns the various stages and manifestations of competition. Although competition between producers is generally more noticeable than that between distributors of products of the same make, it does not thereby follow that an agreement tending to restrict the latter kind of competition should escape the prohibition of Article [101(1)] merely because it might increase the former.[71]

Would every restriction of competition through vertical agreements violate Article 101(1)? In a later decision, the Court recognized that a pro-competitive effect in inter-brand competition might come at the price of a restriction of intra-brand competition. This holistic approach can be seen in *Société Technique Minière*,[72] where the Court found an exclusive distribution agreement *not* to violate Article 101 on the following grounds:

> The competition in question must be understood within the actual context in which it would occur in the absence of the agreement in dispute. In particular it may be doubted whether there is an interference with competition if the said agreement seems really necessary for the penetration of a new area by an undertaking. Therefore, in order to decide whether an agreement containing a clause 'granting an exclusive right of sale' is to be considered as prohibited by reason of its object or of its effect, it is appropriate to take into account in particular the nature and quantity, limited or otherwise, of the products covered by the agreement, [and] *the position and importance of the grantor and the concessionaire on the market for the products concerned*[.][73]

Whether there exists a restriction of competition will thus have to be evaluated alongside both 'brand' dimensions, and by balancing both dimensions.

---

[70] *Consten and Grundig v Commission*, Joined Cases 56 and 58/64 (n. 24).

[71] Ibid., 342. And at a later part of the judgment (ibid., 343), the Court provided the rationale for this choice: 'Because of the considerable impact of distribution costs on the aggregate cost price, it seems important that competition between dealers should also be stimulated. The efforts of the dealer are stimulated by competition between distributors of products of the same make.'

[72] *Société Technique Minière v Maschinenbau Ulm*, Case 56/65 (n. 26).

[73] Ibid., 250 (emphasis added).

(b) Restrictions by Object: European 'Per Se Rules'

An agreement may fall within Article 101(1) if it is anti-competitive by 'object or effect'. These are alternative conditions.[74] The fulfilment of one will fulfil Article 101(1).

The possibility of violating European competition law 'by object' will not mean that purely imaginary restrictions 'intended' in the future are covered. The reference to the purpose of an agreement must not be misunderstood as referring to the subjective intentions of the parties. On the contrary, it refers to the objective content of the agreement. It is designed to identify certain 'hardcore restrictions' within an agreement. These hardcore restrictions need not be subjected to a detailed analysis, as they can simply be presumed to be 'sufficiently deleterious' to competition.[75] In this sense, restrictions by object operate as 'per se rules'; that is: rules whose breach 'as such' constitutes a violation of EU competition law.

What are the hardcore restrictions that the Union considers restrictions by object? Various contractual clauses have been given this status—in both horizontal and vertical agreements. With regard to horizontal agreements, they have been said to include price-fixing clauses,[76] output-limiting clauses,[77] and market-sharing clauses.[78] With regard to vertical agreements, restrictions by object will be presumed to exist if the agreement contains a clause that imposes a fixed (minimum) resale price,[79] grants absolute territorial protection,[80] or is a 'restriction of active or passive sales to end users by members of a selective distribution system operating at the retail level of trade'.[81]

The most contentious type of hardcore restriction has been clauses that restrict parallel trade between States by means of granting territorial

---

[74] Ibid., 249.

[75] Ibid., 249. And see also *T-Mobile Netherlands and others v Raad van bestuur van de Nederlandse Mededingingsautoriteit*, Case C-8/08 [2009] ECR I-4529, para. 29: 'by their very nature, as being injurious to the proper functioning of normal competition'.

[76] See Art. 101(1)(a): 'directly or indirectly fix purchase or selling prices or any other trading conditions'; and see in particular *Imperial Chemical Industries v Commission*, Case 48/69 (n. 56).

[77] See Art. 101(1)(b): 'limit or control production, markets, technical development, or investment', and see in particular *Chemiefarma v Commission*, Case 41/69 (n. 39).

[78] See Art. 101(1)(c): 'share markets or sources of supply'; and see in particular *'Suiker Unie' v Commission* (n. 59).

[79] Commission Regulation 330/2010 on the application of Article 101(3) of the Treaty on the Functioning of the European Union to categories of vertical agreements and concerted practices, [2010] OJ L102/1, Art. 4(a).

[80] Ibid., Art. 4(b).   [81] Ibid., Art. 4(c).

protection to a distributor. And the classic case here is—once more—*Consten and Grundig*.[82] Grundig had appointed Consten its exclusive distributor in France. Consten had thereby promised to market and service the German products in France—a potentially costly commitment. In exchange, Grundig agreed not to deliver its goods to other traders on the French market, and it also agreed to contractually prohibit its German wholesalers from exporting goods into France. This level of territorial protection was still *relative*, since it solely applied to Grundig's own distribution system. Yet in order to prevent 'parallel traders'—third parties trading in parallel to the official distribution channel—from selling its products in France, Grundig had granted an intellectual property right to Consten. This intellectual property right, however, established *absolute* territorial protection for Consten: not a single trader within France could legally sell Grundig products without the official distributor's consent. In the eyes of the European Court, such an agreement establishing absolute territorial protection betrayed a clear wish of the parties 'to eliminate any possibility of competition at the wholesale level',[83] and thus constituted an agreement that had as its *object* the restriction of competition.[84]

(c) Restrictions by Effect: A European 'Rule of Reason'?

Where agreements do not contain clauses that are automatically deemed restrictions of competition per se, Article 101(1) requires detailed proof of the agreement's anti-competitive *effect*.[85]

The central question here is: Will the prohibition be triggered as soon as an agreement contains clauses that have *some* anti-competitive effects; or will it only apply to agreements that are *overall* anti-competitive? Put differently, should Article 101(1) catch agreements that limit—in absolute terms—production, yet which nevertheless enhance—in relative terms—competition

---

[82] *Consten and Grundig v Commission*, Joined Cases 56 and 58/64 (n. 24).

[83] Ibid., 343.

[84] For confirmation of this 'tough' view on restrictions of parallel trade as a restriction by object, see *GlaxoSmithKline and others v Commission*, Joined Cases C-501, 513, 515, and 519/06P (n. 68)—which overruled the General Court's attempt to soften that principle of European competition law in *GlaxoSmithKline Services v Commission*, Case T-168/01 [2006] ECR II-2969.

[85] In order to assess the effect of an individual agreement *on* the market, the Court will analyse the agreement's position *within* the market. It thereby applies a contextual approach that places an individual agreement within its economic context. Where an agreement forms part of a network of agreements, the Courts may thus look at the 'cumulative' effects within the market. On this 'economic' contextualism, see in particular *Delimitis v Henninger Bräu*, Case C-234/89 (n. 31).

through the development of a new product? The wording of Article 101(1) suggests an absolute test, but the argument has been made that an absolute test is over-inclusive and should be replaced by a relative test that weighs the anti-competitive effects of an agreement against its pro-competitive effects.

This debate on whether Article 101(1) follows an absolute or a relative test has been associated with the US doctrine of a 'rule of reason'. According to the latter, the prohibition of anti-competitive agreements will not apply to reasonable restrictions of trade. Should such an implied limitation also apply to Article 101(1)—even though the article already recognizes an express justification in Article 101(3)? The existence of a rule of reason doctrine has been hotly debated in European circles.[86] And the debate is not just theoretical: the constitutional choice concerning whether there exists a rule of reason in Article 101(1) may have significant practical consequences.[87]

What have the European Courts said? They have given ambivalent signals. For while the Courts—in theory—deny the existence of a rule of reason under Article 101(1),[88] there are some jurisprudential lines that come very close to a practical application of the doctrine. For example, did the European Court not insist that a restriction of competition was not anti-competitive if '*necessary* for the penetration of a new area by an undertaking'?[89] Was this balancing of anti-competitive effects against pro-competitive effects not a rule of reason in disguise? The European Courts have denied this, and have instead developed alternative doctrines to explain their reasoning.

The most famous doctrine in this respect is the doctrine of ancillary restraints. Three cases may explain this doctrine in more detail. In *Remia & Nutricia*,[90] the Court had to deal with the legality of a 'non-compete clause'. These clauses prevent the seller of a business from competing with the buyer within a period of time after the sale. This is undoubtedly a restriction of competition on the part of the seller; yet very few undertakings would be willing to purchase a business without a guarantee that its previous owner will temporarily stay out of the market. Finding that transfer agreements generally

---

[86]   See Odudu, *The Boundaries* (n. 67); as well as R. Nazzini, 'Article 81 EC between Time Present and Time Past: A Normative Critique of "Restrictions of Competition" in EU Law' (2006) 43 *Common Market Law Review* 497.

[87]   It will be seen later that Art. 101(3) is not a 'neutral' exemption for pro-competitive agreements, since it makes the exemption dependent on the fulfilment of four conditions.

[88]   See *Métropole Télévision (M6) and others v Commission*, Case T-112/99 [2001] ECR II-2459; as well as *O2 (Germany) v Commission*, Case T-328/03 [2006] ECR II-1231.

[89]   See *Société Technique Minière v Maschinenbau Ulm*, Case 56/65 (n. 26), 250 (emphasis added).

[90]   *Remia and others v Commission*, Case 42/84 [1985] ECR 2545.

'contribute to the promotion of competition because they lead to an increase in the number of undertakings in the market', the Court expressly recognized that without the non-compete clause, 'the agreement for the transfer of the undertaking could not be given effect'.[91] However, such ancillary restrictions within an overall pro-competitive agreement would fall outside the scope of Article 101(1).

This ancillary restraints doctrine was confirmed in *Pronuptia* in the context of a franchise agreement;[92] and it received its most elaborate form in *Métropole Télévision*.[93] The General Court here held as follows:

> In [European] competition law the concept of an 'ancillary restriction' covers any restriction which is directly related and necessary to the implementation of a main operation ... The condition that a restriction be necessary implies a two-fold examination. It is necessary to establish, first, whether the restriction is objectively necessary for the implementation of the main operation and, second, whether it is proportionate to it. As regards the objective necessity of a restriction, it must be observed that inasmuch as ... the existence of a rule of reason in [European] competition law cannot be upheld, it would be wrong, when classifying ancillary restrictions, to interpret the requirement for objective necessity as implying a need to weigh the pro- and anti-competitive effects of an agreement. Such an analysis can take place only in the specific framework of Article [101(3)] of the [TFEU].[94]

The (European) doctrine of ancillary restraints thus differs from the (American) rule of reason in that it does not involve a concrete balancing of the pro-competitive and anti-competitive effects of the agreement. The operation of the doctrine is, according to the Court, 'relatively abstract'.[95] It only tolerates contractual clauses restricting competition without which 'the main agreement is *difficult or even impossible to implement*'.[96] Thus, only *objectively necessary restrictions* of competition within an overall pro-competitive agreement will be accepted. These objectively necessary restrictions must moreover be 'ancillary'; that is: 'subordinate' to the object of the main agreement.[97]

---

[91] Ibid., para. 19.
[92] *Pronuptia de Paris v Pronuptia de Paris Irmgard Schillgallis*, Case 161/84 [1986] ECR 353.
[93] *Métropole Télévision (M6) v Commission*, Case T-112/99 (n. 88).
[94] Ibid., para. 104 (references omitted).
[95] Ibid., para. 109.
[96] Ibid.
[97] See Commission, 'Guidelines on Article [101](3)' (n. 68), paras 29 and 30.

(d) Non-Appreciable Restrictions: The *De Minimis* Rule

According to the legal principle *de minimis non curat lex*, the law should not concern itself with trifles. Translated into the present context, the European Court has declared that it will not use Article 101 to establish 'perfect competition' but only 'workable competition' within the internal market.[98] Minor market imperfections will thus be tolerated. Restrictions of competition will only fall within Article 101(1) where they do so 'to an appreciable extent'.[99] This is called the *de minimis* rule.

According to the Court, *de minimis* is measured not in quantitative or qualitative trade terms, but depends on the relevant market share. This view is supported by the Commission, which has offered guidance in its 'De Minimis Notice'.[100] With the exception of 'hardcore' restrictions,[101] the Commission considers that a 10 per cent aggregate market share for the parties to horizontal agreements and a 15 per cent aggregate market share for parties to vertical agreements will *not* appreciably restrict competition within the meaning of Article 101(1).[102] Importantly, the Commission and the Courts thereby investigate an individual agreement's overall economic context.[103]

4. Article 101(3): Exemptions Through Pro-Competitive Effects

Where an agreement has been found to be anti-competitive under Article 101(1), it will be void—unless it is justified and exempted under Article 101(3). Article 101(3) is designed to exempt anti-competitive agreements that have— overall—pro-competitive effects. The provision thereby applies to all agreements that violate Article 101(1)—and thus includes restrictions per object. It has direct effect and can therefore be invoked as a protective shield by any undertaking facing legal proceedings.[104] However, in an effort to enhance

---

[98]   *Metro SB-Großmärkte GmbH & Co. KG v Commission*, Case 26/76 [1977] ECR 1875, para. 20; and confirmed in *Metro SB-Großmärkte GmbH & Co. KG v Commission*, Case 75/84 [1986] ECR 3021, para. 65.

[99]   *Société Technique Minière v Maschinenbau Ulm*, Case 56/65 (n. 26), 249.

[100]   The exact title of the Notice is: 'Commission Notice on Agreements of Minor Importance which do not Appreciably Restrict Competition under Article 101(1) TFEU (de minimis)', [2014] OJ C 291/1.

[101]   Ibid., para. 13.

[102]   'Commission Notice on Agreements of Minor Importance' (n. 100), para. 8.

[103]   On this contextual examination of a single agreement, see text at n. 30.

[104]   The direct effect of Art. 101(3) had not always been the case. Indeed, it was one of the 'revolutionary' changes brought by Regulation 1/2003 on the implementation of the rules on competition laid down in Articles [101 and 102] of the Treaty, [2003] OJ L1/1.

legal certainty, the Union has adopted a variety of exemption regulations that provide detailed criteria when certain categories of agreements are exempted under Article 101(3).

(a) Direct Exemptions under Article 101(3)

Article 101(3) makes an exemption conditional on four cumulative criteria. The first two criteria are positive, the other two criteria negative in nature.[105]

Positively, Article 101(3) stipulates that the agreement must 'contribute[] to improving the production or distribution of goods or to promoting technical or economic progress, while allowing consumers a fair share of the resulting benefit'.[106] Where the agreement thus generates *productive* or *dynamic* efficiencies,[107] these efficiency gains might outweigh the economic inefficiencies identified in Article 101(1) but only under the—second—condition that consumers get a fair share in the resulting overall benefit. What is a 'fair share'? According to the Commission:

> The concept of 'fair share' implies that the pass-on of benefits must at least compensate consumers for any actual or likely negative impact caused to them by the restriction of competition found under Article [101(1)] ... If such consumers are worse off following the agreement, the second condition of Article [101(3)] is not fulfilled.[108]

---

[105] There has been a spirited debate on whether these criteria—all of which are 'economic' in nature—are exhaustive or not. The Commission considers them exhaustive (see Commission, 'Guidelines on Article [101](3)' (n. 68), para. 42): 'The four conditions of Article [101(3)] are also exhaustive. When they are met the exception is applicable and may not be made dependent on any other condition. Goals pursued by other Treaty provisions can be taken into account to the extent that they can be subsumed under the four conditions of Article [101(3)].' Nonetheless, it is important to note that the Treaties' competition rules cannot be completely isolated from other policies; and this is particularly true for those policies—like environmental policy—that contain an express horizontal clause (see Art. 11 TFEU (emphasis added): 'Environmental protection requirements must be integrated *into the definition and implementation of the Union's policies and activities*, in particular with a view to promoting sustainable development').

[106] Art. 101(3) TFEU.

[107] For an elaboration of this, see Commission, 'Guidelines on Article [101](3)' (n. 68), paras 48 et seq. The typical example of an agreement enhancing 'productive efficiency' is a 'specialization agreement'. A 'Research and Development' agreement is an example of an agreement that may enhance dynamic efficiency.

[108] Ibid., para. 85.

Yet, even if that is the case, Article 101(3) will not allow anti-competitive restrictions that are 'not indispensable' for the pro-competitive effects of the agreement; or agreements which 'eliminat[e] competition in respect of a substantial part of the products in question'.[109] A violation of either one of these negative conditions will mean that an agreement cannot benefit from an exemption.

With regard to the indispensability of a restriction, the Commission has developed a twofold test: 'First, the restrictive agreement as such must be reasonably necessary in order to achieve the efficiencies. Secondly, the individual restrictions of competition that flow from the agreement must also be reasonably necessary for the attainment of the efficiencies.'[110] The first test thereby requires 'that the efficiencies be specific to the agreement in question in the sense that there are no other economically practicable and less restrictive means of achieving the efficiencies'.[111] Once this global test has been passed, the Commission will then analyse the indispensability of each individual restriction of competition. Here, it will assess 'whether individual restrictions are reasonably necessary in order to produce the efficiencies'.[112]

Finally, a restriction—even if indispensable for the pro-competitive effects of the agreement—must, fourth, not substantially eliminate competition. This absolute limit on the exemptability of an agreement will be a function of the structure of the market.[113]

(b) Exemptions by Category: Block Exemption Regulations

In order to enhance legal certainty, Article 101(3) envisaged from the very beginning that an entire 'category of agreements' might be exempted. Article 103 thereby allowed the Council to 'lay down detailed rules for the

---

[109] Art. 101(3) TFEU.

[110] Commission, 'Guidelines on Article [101](3)' (n. 68), para. 73.

[111] Ibid., para. 75.

[112] Ibid., para. 78.

[113] Ibid., para. 107: 'Whether competition is being eliminated within the meaning of the last condition of Article [101(3)] depends on the degree of competition existing prior to the agreement and on the impact of the restrictive agreement on competition, i.e. the reduction in competition that the agreement brings about. The more competition is already weakened in the market concerned, the slighter the further reduction required for competition to be eliminated within the meaning of Article [101(3)].'

application of Article 101(3)'.[114] This legal base was used early on;[115] and in a way that delegated the power to exempt agreements 'en bloc' to the Commission. The Commission has adopted a variety of so-called 'block exemption regulations'.[116]

Many block exemption regulations originally followed a formal 'category' approach. They would contain a 'white list' of desirable clauses, and a 'black list' of hardcore restrictions for a type of agreement. This formal approach towards block exemptions has been overtaken by a more flexible and economic approach in the last decades. Absent any hardcore restrictions, modern block exemptions will thus generally make the exemption dependent on a market-share threshold. Importantly, even in the presence of a block exemption, the Commission always retains the power to withdraw the benefit of a block exemption from an individual agreement.[117]

The flagship illustration of the new approach to block exemption regulations is the regulation for vertical agreements.[118] The Regulation exempts all vertical agreements, provided that 'the market share held by the supplier does not exceed 30% of the relevant market on which it sells the contract goods or services and the market share held by the buyer does not exceed 30% of the relevant market on which it purchases the contract goods or services'.[119] The Regulation still contains a 'black list' of hardcore restrictions. Yet there no longer exists a white list of permissible contractual clauses, and the Regulation thus concentrates essentially on the economic effects of an agreement.

---

[114] Art. 103(2)(b) TFEU.

[115] Council Regulation 19/65 on application of Article 85(3) [now: Article 101(3)] of the Treaty to certain categories of agreements and concerted practices, [1965] OJ L36/533; and Council Regulation 2821/71 on application of Article 85(3) [now: Article 101(3)] of the Treaty to categories of agreements, decisions and concerted practices, [1971] OJ L285/46.

[116] See e.g. Commission Regulation 330/2010 on the application of Article 101(3) of the Treaty on the Functioning of the European Union to categories of vertical agreements and concerted practices, [2010] OJ L102/1.

[117] See Art. 29 of Regulation 1/2003 (Withdrawal in individual cases), [2003] OJ L1/1.

[118] See Commission Regulation 330/2010 (n. 116). For a discussion of this regulation, see R. Whish and D. Bailey, 'Regulation 330/2010: The Commission's New Block Exemption for Vertical Agreements' (2010) 47 *Common Market Law Review* 1757.

[119] Ibid., Arts 2 and 3(1).

Conclusion

EU competition law constitutes a cornerstone within the Union's internal policies. The Union is here entitled to 'regulate' and 'police' the internal market so as to ensure undistorted competition. EU competition law is thereby built on four pillars. The first pillar deals with anti-competitive cartels. The second pillar concerns situations where a dominant under-taking abuses its market power. The third pillar concerns the control of mergers. The fourth pillar, finally, deals with 'public' interference in free competition.

This chapter only looked at the first pillar of EU competition law: Article 101. The provision prohibits anti-competitive collusions between undertak-ings that distort competition and affect trade between Member States. We saw that the Union has given a wide jurisdictional scope to the provision (and EU competition law generally); yet that it tries to find an appropriate balance between pro- and anti-competitive considerations for every agreement. Due to the Union's historic task to create an internal market, vertical agreements have been of particular importance to the Union; and distribution agree-ments indeed continue to occupy a prominent place within the case law of the European Courts.

Epilogue
Brexit: Past, Present, Future

Introduction

The British exit from the European Union ('Brexit') has occupied the Union for much of the last four years. For the first time since its founding, a Member States decided to deliberately dissociate itself from European integration in an attempt to regain 'sovereignty' and 'independence'.[1]

Why and how did this happen; and may it happen to other Member States of the Union? With several severe crises afflicting the Union in the past decade—especially the financial and the migration crises—the question of whether Brexit constitutes an isolated case or a signal for an era of European disintegration has legitimately been posed.[2]

---

[1] For a critical view of the idea of national sovereignty in our 'global' times, see R. Schütze, *Globalisation and Governance: International Problems, European Solutions* (Cambridge University Press, 2018).

[2] S. Gänzle et al. (eds), *Differentiated Integration and Disintegration in a Post-Brexit Era* (Routledge, 2019).

This chapter, however, seeks to pursue a less ambitious task: it aims to explore the past, present, and future of the *British* exit decision. Section 1 begins by offering a brief historical overview of the past tensions between the United Kingdom and the European Union in an attempt to better explain the 'special' unease with which the United Kingdom viewed European integration. A former imperial and global power, its political self-understanding indeed differed from the very beginning from that of other Member States. Section 2 explores the 'present' withdrawal process under Article 50 TEU and the 'Withdrawal Agreement'. Section 3 tries to look into the future by analysing four possible EU–UK trade relationship options. Will both parties decide to create a common customs union or will they conclude a 'Canada Plus' agreement? A future trade deal is currently being negotiated; yet the option of a 'hard' Brexit remains. This option is discussed in Section 4.

1. Past: Britain as an 'Awkward Partner'?

The United Kingdom has never been too enthusiastic about European integration. When it came to choosing between the British Commonwealth and the 1957 European Economic Community, the British government unconditionally favoured its Commonwealth over Europe.[3] The reasons for this early rejection of European integration were economic and political in nature. Not only did the British economy believe itself more closely entwined with the British Commonwealth;[4] politically, doubts had arisen from the European insistence on 'supranationalism'—an idea that ran counter to the British ideal of national sovereignty.[5] To nevertheless contain the consequences of its choice *against* 'Europe', the British government quickly proposed a rival organization: the 1960 European Free Trade Association (EFTA). Set up as a non-'supranational' organization, it was meant to offer free trade without political integration.

And yet, in a spectacular move of reorientation, membership in the European Union suddenly became a British priority in the early 1960s. However, Britain's first application to join the Union was rejected by the Union. This

---

[3] For the classic analysis here, see G. St. J. Barclay, *Commonwealth or Europe* (University of Queensland Press, 1970).

[4] M. Camps, *Britain and the European Community, 1955–1963* (Oxford University Press, 1964), 3.

[5] Ibid., 4: 'Co-operation with Europe was desirable; integration with Europe was not.'

rejection came as a shock; and it was a shock to be repeated. Only the third membership application would finally succeed. This belated acceptance led to the signing of the 1972 UK Accession Treaty; and on 1 January 1973 Britain joined the European Union.

Ever since, however, Britain has not been the happiest of Member States. Doubts about European integration remained. One of the original core irritations here was the Union's budget. Britain believed it paid too much for what it got in return. And under Margaret Thatcher—the iconic British prime minister for all of the 1980s—the rebate issue was pursued with unbending zealousness: Britain wanted its 'own money back'![6] And in order to achieve this, Britain adopted a strategy of (un)civil disobedience by deliberately obstructing the Council in 1982.[7] This policy of obstructionism irritated France so much that it openly suggested that the United Kingdom should search for an alternative status to full Union membership—a suggestion that was instantly rejected. Progress on the British Budgetary Question, colloquially termed the 'Bloody British Question',[8] was finally made in 1984. Ironically, however, it was from this moment onwards that another major division between the 'British' and the 'continental' visions on Europe occurred.

(a) A Market Without A Government: The Thatcher Vision

What should be the aim of the European Union? For the (conservative) British governments of the past, the answer had always been this: European integration meant *economic* integration; that is: the creation of an internal market in which British businesses could benefit from frictionless trade and economies of scale and scope. This British vision was rooted in the historical origins of the European Union as an *economic* community whose primary task was the liberalization of trade. This exclusive trade-and-business vision had, however, never been shared by the other Member States. For the founding fathers of the Union, economic integration was only a first step towards further political and social integration and the internal market project was indeed conceived as a means to an end to achieve this broader—constitutional—aim.

The clash between these two visions of 'Europe' came to a fore when the Union underwent its first formal Treaty amendment: the Single European

---

[6] For the famous part of the Thatcher speech, see www.youtube.com/watch?v=pDqZdZ5iZdY.

[7] A similar episode of British obstructionism would recur in 1996 in response to the ban on British beef following the BSE crisis.

[8] R. Jenkins, *A Life at the Centre* (Pan Books, 1991), ch. 27.

Act (SEA). The SEA had, ironically, been inspired by a reform initiative close to Britain's heart: the completion of the EU internal market. This initiative had come from the 'British' European Commissioner Lord Cockfield—a close collaborator of Thatcher. It was seized upon by (then) Commission President Jacques Delors believing it to be the Union's best chance to reinvigorate European integration after a decade of 'Eurosclerosis'. However, and this is the important point, whereas for Britain 'the single market was an end in itself that could raise to a European stage the liberalizing and deregulatory elements of the Thatcherite project', for most continental European States, it was 'a means to an end, that end being deeper economic and political integration'.[9] And the other Member States had therefore pushed for a major institutional reform of the Union through the 1986 Single European Act.[10] Famously, the latter reintroduced qualified majority voting and with it the idea of European market regulation.

Yet the very idea that Europe could re-regulate markets and offer social rights to workers was anathema to the (then) British government. Furious to discover that the single market project was more that an exercise in deregulation, Thatcher set out her 'British' vision in 1988 in a famous speech at the College of Europe:

> We have not successfully rolled back the frontiers of the state in Britain only to see them reimposed at a European level, with a European superstate exercising a new dominance from Brussels. . . . [T]he Treaty of Rome itself was intended as a Charter for Economic Liberty. . . . By getting rid of barriers, by making it possible for companies to operate on a Europe-wide scale, we can best compete with the United States, Japan and the other new economic powers emerging in Asia and elsewhere. It means action to free markets, to widen choice and to produce greater economic convergence through reduced government intervention. Our aim should not be more and more detailed regulation from the centre: it should be to deregulate, to remove the constraints on trade and to open up[.][11]

---

[9] A. Geddes, *Britain and the European Union* ((Palgrave, 2013), 70.

[10] Yet far from being a surrender to continental views, British interests had predominantly found their way into the SEA, see S. George, *An Awkward Partner: Britain in the European Community* (Oxford University Press, 1998), 184: '[T]he British achieved real progress in areas that mattered to them. Majority voting was extended only in limited areas . . . [and] [s]pecifically excluded from the rules on majority voting were the areas of taxation, free movement of persons, health controls, and employees' rights. . . . The other clear victory for the British view was that no major increase was proposed in the powers of the European Parliament.'

[11] A. G. Harryvan and J. van der Harst, *Documents on European Union* (Macmillan, 1997), 244–5.

This speech articulated and reinforced the most crucial division between the British and the continental vision(s) for the European project. For Britain, 'Europe' was nothing but the 'common market' in which national regulation could be censored and in which re-regulation at the European level should not take place. By contrast, the continental vision insisted on re-regulating the common market by a common—supranational—government; and that would require more political integration. This further political integration to create 'an ever closer union' thereby meant two things in particular: an ever-growing move to qualified majority voting in the Council and the rise of the European Parliament as the most democratic institution of the Union. Both of these developments were opposed by the United Kingdom; and to escape their logic, a new strategy was soon applied: differential integration.

(b) From Differential Integration to Leaving the Union

The British insistence on a European market without a European government was not shared by many. And its rising opposition over the last three decades increasingly created 'a Europe of bits and pieces'.[12] The official starting point for differential integration is thereby the 1992 (Maastricht) Treaty on European Union. The latter marked 'a new stage in the process of European integration',[13] and for many British Eurosceptics, it became a bête noire that should never have been signed. For the Maastricht Treaty not only laid the foundations for 'Economic and Monetary Union' (EMU), but a significant push towards further political union had been made.

How did Britain react? With regard to EMU, it secured an opt-out;[14] and having vehemently opposed European integration on social matters too, it had also received an 'opt-out' here.[15] This was, however, only the beginning. For in rejecting the idea of an 'ever closer union' as such, the British response over the next decades was an ever critical attitude towards transfers of legislative powers to the European Union. When it thus came to the 1997 Treaty of

---

[12] The famous phrase comes from D. Curtin, 'The Constitutional Structure of the Union: A Europe of Bits and Pieces' (1993) 30 *Common Market Law Review* 17.

[13] Preamble to the 1992 TEU.

[14] See Protocol 'On certain Provisions relating to the United Kingdom of Great Britain and Northern Ireland', [1992] OJ C191/87, esp. Preamble 1: 'Recognizing that the United Kingdom shall not be obliged or committed to move to the third stage of Economic and Monetary Union without a separate decision to do so by its government and Parliament'. The opt-out can today be found in Protocol No. 15 to the EU Treaties.

[15] This second opt-out would eventually be dropped when a Labour government (Blair) returned to power in 1997.

Amsterdam, Britain not only decided to opt out of the supranationalization of the Schengen Agreement,[16] it also extrapolated itself from the Treaty title on 'Visas, Asylum, Immigration and other Policies related to the Free Movement of Persons'.[17] And the same strategy of 'differential' membership again surfaced with the 2007 Lisbon Treaty, where the United Kingdom obtained a partial opt-out from the EU Charter of Fundamental Rights as well as other things.[18]

By 2009, the United Kingdom was two-thirds in and one-third out of the European Union. While a full member in its formal rights, its opt-outs had gradually exempted it from some of its substantial obligations. 'No other country ha[d] the same special status in the EU.'[19] And yet, even this strategy of semi-detachedness stopped working when the country took a decidedly Eurosceptic turn in the last decade. The immediate result was the European Union Act 2011, which not only provided for a 'referendum lock' to any future competence transfers to the Union;[20] more dramatically, the Conservative Party leader David Cameron also promised a 'fundamental renegotiation' of the British terms of EU membership and an 'in–out' referendum.[21] This referendum was called for 23 June 2016; and a (slight) majority of voters in the United Kingdom here expressed their wish to leave the European Union.[22]

This Brexit referendum signalled the beginning of the end of British EU membership. This end was to be regulated by Article 50 TEU to which we must now turn.

---

[16] See Protocol 'On the Application of Certain Aspects of Article 7a of the Treaty Establishing the European Community to the United Kingdom and to Ireland', [1997] OJ C340/97. The provisions can today be found in Protocols 19 and 20 to the present EU Treaties.

[17] See Protocol 'On the Position of the United Kingdom and Ireland', [1997] OJ 340/99. The provisions can today be found in Protocol 21 to the present EU Treaties.

[18] See Protocol No. 30 'On the Application of the Charter of Fundamental Rights of the European Union to Poland and the United Kingdom'.

[19] HM Government, 'Alternatives to Membership: possible models for the United Kingdom outside the European Union' (March 2016), para. 2.10.

[20] For an analysis of the Act, see M. Gordon and M. Dougan, 'The United Kingdom's European Union Act 2011: "Who Won the Bloody War Anyway?"' (2012) 37 *European Law Review* 3.

[21] An informal promise was first made by David Cameron on 23 January 2013 in his 'Bloomberg Speech'; and a formal promise was made in the 2014 Tory Manifesto, which committed the party to holding a referendum by the end of 2017.

[22] With a turnout of 72 per cent of the electorate, 52 per cent decided to leave, while 48 per cent voted to remain.

2. Present: Withdrawing under Article 50 TEU

The European Union is not a sovereign State but a Union of States; and unlike sovereign States, it allows its Member States to withdraw or 'secede' from the Union. This right to withdraw has been expressly codified in Article 50 TEU. The provision states:

1. Any Member State may decide to withdraw from the Union in accordance with its own constitutional requirements.
2. A Member State which decides to withdraw shall notify the European Council of its intention. In the light of the guidelines provided by the European Council, the Union shall negotiate and conclude an agreement with that State, setting out the arrangements for its withdrawal, taking account of the framework for its future relationship with the Union. That agreement shall be negotiated in accordance with Article 218(3) of the Treaty on the Functioning of the European Union. It shall be concluded on behalf of the Union by the Council, acting by a qualified majority, after obtaining the consent of the European Parliament.
3. The Treaties shall cease to apply to the State in question from the date of entry into force of the withdrawal agreement or, failing that, two years after the notification referred to in paragraph 2, unless the European Council, in agreement with the Member State concerned, unanimously decides to extend this period ...

What is the nature of the provision? Within the European Union, the sovereign 'right' to withdraw had always been implicit in the Union legal order.[23] Article 50(1) TEU has now made this implicit right explicit. The provision thereby represents a compromise between a 'State-centred' and a 'Union-centred' version.[24] This compromise solution is nevertheless much closer to the former version. For the right to withdraw from the Union is *unconditional* and *unilateral*.

But, importantly, the right to withdraw is *not* automatic, because a State wishing to leave the Union must formally notify the European Council of its intention according to Article 50(2). For the United Kingdom, this happened on 29 March 2017, when the (then) British Prime Minister sent a letter to

---

[23] For the same view, see J. H. H. Weiler, 'Alternatives to Withdrawal from an International Organisation: The Case of the European Economic Community' (1985) 20 *Israel Law Review* 282.

[24] For a discussion of the drafting history of the provision, see R. Schütze, *European Union Law* (Cambridge University Press, 2018), 855–6.

the President of the European Council. This started the two-year negotiation period envisaged in Article 50(3) which had, however, been twice extended to 31 January 2020. During this period, Article 50 imposed a procedural obligation to try and reach a mutual understanding between the Union and the United Kingdom in the form of a 'withdrawal agreement'.[25] This agreement has been reached and it today governs the relationship between the European Union and the United Kingdom.

(a) Withdrawal Agreement I: Structure and Content

After a complex negotiation history, the Withdrawal Agreement was concluded in October 2019. The structure of the 2019 Withdrawal Agreement can be seen in Table 13.1. It entered into force on 1 February 2020.

This withdrawal agreement must—crucially—be distinguished from any future trade agreement between the United Kingdom and the European Union. It is merely designed to settle past commitments (even if it already contains a political declaration for a future relationship between the two parties).[26] Its material scope is limited to issues that arise from Brexit.

Table 13.1 Withdrawal Agreement: structure

2019 British Withdrawal Agreement
Part One: Common Provisions (Arts 1–8)
Part Two: Citizens' Rights (Arts 9–39)
Part Three: Separation Provisions (Arts 40–125)
Part Four: Transition (Arts 126–32)
Part Five: Financial Provisions (Arts 133–57)
Part Six: Institutional and Final Provisions (Arts 158–85)
Protocol on Ireland/Northern Ireland
Protocol on Sovereign Base Areas in Cyprus
Protocol on Gibraltar

---

[25] The wording of Art. 50 TEU only imposes an obligation to negotiate such an agreement on the Union; yet such a duty is equally imposed on the United Kingdom. This duty, while not directly based on Art. 50 TEU, derives from its (continued) status as a Member State of the Union and the duty of loyal cooperation under Art. 4(3) TEU.

[26] The Withdrawal Agreement therefore has an attached 'Political Declaration' on the future relationship between the two parties; yet this is a *political* declaration, which is, as such, not part of the *legal* Withdrawal Agreement.

From the very beginning, the three main problems caused by the withdrawal were: (1) the situation of European citizens (and businesses) that had exercised their free movement rights in the past; (2) a financial settlement between the United Kingdom and the Union had to be found; and, finally, there was (3) the 'Irish border question'.

The first issue appears to have been relatively straightforward. For while Brexit will eventually end the free movement of persons,[27] both sides agreed that the rights of EU citizens in the United Kingdom and of those British citizens in the EU-27 must be guaranteed so as to protect past life choices. This means, in particular, that those persons having legitimately exercised their free movement rights in the past, will *in principle* continue to enjoy these rights under Part II of the Withdrawal Agreement.[28]

The second issue also turned out to be easier than expected. For the Union had originally adopted a 'divorce model' and approached the outstanding financial commitments 'on the principle that the United Kingdom must honour its share of the financing of all the obligations undertaken while it was a member of the Union'.[29] This view sharply contrasted with a British opinion advocating a 'club model' and according to which 'Article 50 TEU allows the United Kingdom to leave the European Union without being liable for outstanding financial obligations under the EU budget or other financial instruments'.[30] Yet again, a detailed compromise was found that can today be found in Part V of the Withdrawal Agreement.

The third problem—the Irish border question—has proven to be the hardest. The problem stems from the complex legal arrangements governing (British) Northern Ireland and the Republic of Ireland. For after years of paramilitary conflict between the two sides (known as 'the Troubles'), the 1998 'Good Friday Agreement' had finally brought peace. Yet that agreement guarantees an open border between the northern and the southern island; and with Britain leaving the European Union, this open border was suddenly placed in jeopardy. Because once the United Kingdom leaves the European Union, the border between the Republic of Ireland and Northern Ireland

---

[27] For the constitutional principles here, see Chapter 11.

[28] This includes the right to residence (Withdrawal Agreement, Art. 11) and the right to non-discrimination (ibid., Art. 12).

[29] Council, 'Negotiating documents on Article 50 negotiations with the United Kingdom', at https://ec.europa.eu/commission/publications/negotiating-directives-article-50-negotiations_en, para.25.

[30] House of Lords, European Union Committee, 'Brexit and the EU Budget', at https://publications.parliament.uk/pa/ld201617/ldselect/ldeucom/125/125.pdf, para. 133.

becomes an *external* border of the European Union and that border will require border checks for goods entering the EU internal market.

The only—principled—future solution here seemed for the United Kingdom to remain permanently within the single market and the customs union. But what would happen in the absence of a future agreement to this effect? In order to prevent a 'hard' border from arising in the meantime, a pragmatic 'fudge' had to be devised. A first solution here invented the so-called 'Irish backstop'. Accordingly, all of the United Kingdom—including Northern Ireland—would have remained within the EU customs union *until a future trade agreement had solved the Irish border problem*. This semi-permanent solution, however, proved ultimately unacceptable to the United Kingdom and the 2019 Withdrawal Agreement has consequently selected another option instead. This option takes the United Kingdom out of the EU customs union (and the single market); yet it leaves Northern Ireland de facto within that customs union (and elements of the single market)—albeit its *de jure status* formally pretends otherwise.[31] De facto, then, a hard border between the Irish Republic and Northern Ireland has consequently been replaced by an invisible border in the Irish Sea (Figure 13.1).

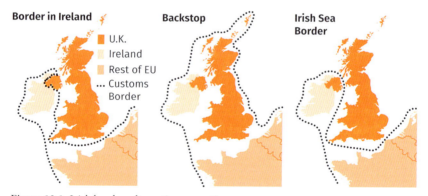

Figure 13.1 Irish border: alternative suggestions

Adapted from diagram in S. Fidler, 'Five Things to Know About Brexit Deal's Irish Border Issue', *The Wall Street Journal*, 10th December 2018

---

[31] See especially Withdrawal Agreement, Irish Protocol, Art. 4: 'Northern Ireland is part of the customs territory of the United Kingdom'; but see also Art. 5(5): 'Articles 30 and 110 TFEU shall apply to and in the United Kingdom in respect of Northern Ireland. Quantitative restrictions on exports and imports shall be prohibited between the Union and Northern Ireland.'

(b) Withdrawal Agreement II: Implementation and Governance

The most important decision with regard to the implementation of the With-drawal Agreement has been the introduction of a 'transition' or 'implementa-tion' period in Part IV of the agreement. Proposed by the British government itself, this period is meant to offer extra time for an *orderly* withdrawal. This period is set to expire on 31 December 2020; yet the Withdrawal Agreement— wisely— envisages the possibility of an extension.[32]

During the implementation period, the United Kingdom must apply (almost) all EU law.[33] It will thus, in particular, continue to be in the single market (with all four freedoms applying); and it will have to apply EU law *as EU law*.[34] By contrast, it will no longer be able to actively participate in the Union institu-tions. This period of 'passive' membership is not ideal in theoretical terms, but it is of utmost practical importance. For it is meant to offer legal certainty during a time in which the future trade relationship between the United Kingdom and the Union is discussed. The transition period was indeed conceived as a 'bridge' between (past) membership and (future) partnership; and, ideally, it should be as long as discussions between the United Kingdom and the European Union last in order to avoid a 'hard' Brexit.[35]

What happens after the transition period has elapsed? The United King-dom will then be fully outside the European Union; yet, for a period of time, this still means that the European Court of Justice can receive preliminary references on certain matters within the Withdrawal Agreement from British courts.[36] The main implementation of the agreement is, however, the task of a 'Joint Committee'.[37] It is to comprise representatives of the United Kingdom and the Union; and it will adopt its decisions by 'mutual consent'.[38] In the case of a disagreement between the United Kingdom and the European Union, a dispute settlement mechanism has been established that may ultimately lead to international arbitration between the two parties.

---

[32] Withdrawal Agreement, Art. 132 specifies that an extension for up to one or two years can be granted.

[33] Ibid., Art. 127(1).

[34] Ibid., Art. 127(3) as well as Art. 131.

[35] On this point, see Section 4 of this chapter.

[36] See esp. Withdrawal Agreement, Art. 158, with regard to references on matters falling within its Part II. The period set here is eight years.

[37] Ibid., Art. 164. The rules of procedure of the Joint Committee are set out in ibid., Annex VIII.

[38] Ibid., Art. 166(3).

The situation with regard to the Irish border question is, by contrast, more fragile and complex. For the status of Northern Ireland under the Withdrawal Agreement must be regularly confirmed by the majority of its people. Four years after the end of the transition period—and regularly thereafter—the Northern Irish Legislative Assembly must thus positively approve the status quo; and if the status quo were to be rejected, the 'Irish solution' would cease to apply two years later.[39] The result would be a hard border cutting through the island—endangering the fragile peace that has existed for the past twenty or so years.

3. Future I: (Possible) Trade Agreements with the Union

What types of alternative partnerships are presently available? While the United Kingdom will, of course, try to get a 'bespoke' agreement that works best for herself, what models has the European Union so far developed for States wishing to be closely associated with it? Three such models will be presented in this section: the EEA model ('Norway model'), the Customs Union model ('Turkey model'), and the Free Trade Agreement (FTA) model ('Canada model').

In terms of economic association, each of these models offers less than EU membership but more than World Trade Organization (WTO) membership with the three models ranging from the most associated 'Norway model' to the least integrated 'Canada model' (see Figure 13.2).

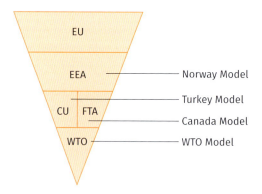

Figure 13.2 Declining levels of economic integration

---

[39] Irish Protocol, Art. 18.

(a) The European Economic Area: The 'Norway Model'

The Agreement on the European Economic Area (EEA) was signed in 1992 and entered into force on 1 January 1994.[40] It brings together the European Union (and its Member States) with the EFTA States except for Switzerland.[41]

The agreement aims to establish a 'homogenous' free trade area;[42] and thereby covers the free movement of goods (Part II); the free movement of persons, services, and capital (Part III); and competition law (Part IV); while it also regulates flanking policies that are relevant to the four freedoms (Part V).[43] The provisions in Parts I–V are (almost) identical to those in the EU Treaties. However, the EEA is not a customs union but a 'fundamentally improved free trade area';[44] and the EFTA States have consequently retained their freedom to negotiate commercial agreements with third States. The EEA Agreement equally leaves the EFTA States free to act autonomously in other important areas of EU competence (see Table 13.2). They will, however, have to contribute to the Union budget.

The central aim behind the EEA is 'to provide for the fullest possible realization of the free movement of goods, persons, services, and capital within

Table 13.2 EEA Agreement: coverage

EEA: Covered	EEA: Not Covered
Free Movement: Goods	Common Commercial Policy
Free Movement: Persons	Common Agricultural Policy
Free Movement: Services	Common Foreign and Security Policy
Free Movement: Capital	Area of Freedom, Security & Justice
Competition Law (and State Aid)	European Monetary Union

[40] Agreement on the European Economic Area ('EEA Agreement'), [1994] OJ L1/3.

[41] The EFTA comprises today four States: Iceland, Liechtenstein, Norway, and Switzerland. The latter is not part of the EEA, as the ratification of the EEA Agreement was rejected in a referendum. EU–Swiss relations are therefore based on a wide range and great number of bilateral agreements. The 'Swiss model' nevertheless comes substantively very close to the EEA model. The major 'institutional' difference relates to how regulatory homogeneity with Union legislation is achieved. The Union has been highly critical of the Swiss model, and it will therefore not be a viable option for the future relations between the Union and the United Kingdom.

[42] EEA Agreement (n. 40), Art. 1.

[43] Part V of the EEA Agreement contains rules on 'Social Policy', 'Consumer Protection', 'Environment', 'Statistics', and 'Company Law'.

[44] S. Norberg, 'The Agreement on a European Economic Area' (1992) 29 *Common Market Law Review* 1171 at 1173.

the whole European Economic Area, *so that the internal market established within the European Union is extended to the EFTA States*.[45] And in order to achieve that aim, the EEA Agreement not only duplicates the European Union's provision on 'negative integration'. On the contrary, a significant part of the agreement also deals with 'positive integration' within the EEA so as to ensure regulatory alignment between the EFTA Member States and the Union. Indeed, the idea of such a (dynamic) homogeneity 'is the key principle in the EEA'.[46]

This legislative alignment is principally achieved through an 'EEA Joint Committee', whose task it is to update the Agreement's annexes and protocols in the light of new legislative developments within the Union.[47] The EEA Joint Committee is composed of the representatives of the Union and the EFTA States and will act 'by agreement between the [Union], on the one hand, and the EFTA States speaking with one voice, on the other'.[48] In the past, and in (almost) all cases, the EEA Joint Committee has agreed to simply 'rubber-stamp' the relevant EU acts;[49] and the principle of legislative homogeneity has sometimes been identified with European 'hegemony'; or at least with a significant democratic deficit.

(b) A Customs Union: The 'Turkey Model'

The 1963 Association Agreement with Turkey ('Ankara Agreement') constitutes the oldest existing association agreement of the Union.[50] The purpose of the Ankara Agreement has been 'to promote the continuous and balanced strength of trade and economic relations between the parties'; and this aim of a closer economic partnership was to be primarily pursued through a

---

[45] *Ospelt and Schlössle Weissenberg Familienstiftung*, Case C-452/01 [2003] ECR I-9743, para. 29 (emphasis added).

[46] G. Baur, 'Decision-Making Procedure and Implementation of New Law' in C. Baudenbacher (ed.), *The Handbook of EEA Law* (Springer, 2016), 45 at 51.

[47] Union acts that are relevant for the EEA, are labelled as 'Text with EEA relevance'.

[48] EEA Agreement, Art. 93(2).

[49] Legislative exemptions and adaptations are nevertheless possible. If it were to come to a disagreement between the Union and the EFTA States, the disputed part of the EEA Agreement would be provisionally suspended (EEA Agreement, Art. 102(5)).

[50] Agreement establishing an Association between the European Economic [Union] and Turkey, signed at Ankara on 12 September 1963 by the Republic of Turkey, on the one hand, and by the Member States of the [EU] and the [Union], on the other, (1973) OJ C113/1. Many provisions in the Ankara Agreement are further clarified by an additional Protocol: Additional Protocol and Financial Protocol, [1972] OJ L293/4.

customs union between the contracting parties.[51] This customs union covers trade in goods and involves:

- the prohibition between Member States of the [Union] and Turkey, of customs duties on imports and exports and of all charges having equivalent effect, quantitative restrictions and all other measures having equivalent effect which are designed to protect national production in a manner contrary to the objectives of this Agreement;
- the adoption by Turkey of the Common Customs Tariff of the [Union] in its trade with third countries, and an approximation to the other [EU] rules on external trade.[52]

The implementation of the Ankara Agreement thereby heavily relies on a form of 'positive integration'; and the central decision-making body here is the 'Association Council'.[53] It consists of members of the Union (and its Member States), on the one hand, and Turkish representatives on the other. It adopts its decisions by unanimous agreement.[54]

With regard to the free movement of goods, the Association Council's most famous decision is Decision 1/95.[55] The latter establishes 'the rules for implementing the final phase of the Customs Union' by extending—almost always verbatim—the Union's own free movement of goods provisions to Turkey. In order to achieve this 'enlargement' of the internal market in goods, Turkey promised to harmonize and align Turkish legislation of direct relevance to the operation of the internal market 'as far as possible with [Union] legislation'.[56] And where there exists an—irresolvable—discrepancy of opinions, the Union or Turkey can both 'take the necessary protection measures'.[57]

[51] Ankara Agreement, Art. 2.

[52] Ibid., Art. 10(2).

[53] Ibid., Art. 22(1): 'In order to attain the objectives of this Agreement the Council of Association shall have the power to take decisions in the cases provided for therein. Each of the Parties shall take the measures necessary to implement the decisions taken.'

[54] Ibid., Art. 23, third indent.

[55] Decision No. 1/95 of the EC–Turkey Association Council of 22 December 1995 on implementing the final phase of the Customs Union, [1996] OJ L35/1.

[56] Ibid., Art. 54(1). These areas of direct relevance are defined as follows (ibid., para. 2): 'Areas of direct relevance to the operation of the Customs Union shall be commercial policy and agreements with third countries comprising a commercial dimension for industrial products, legislation on the abolition of technical barriers to trade in industrial products, competition and industrial and intellectual property law and customs legislation. The Association Council may decide to extend the list of areas where harmonization is to be achieved in the light of the Association's progress.'

[57] Ibid., Art. 58(2). These measures will subsequently be examined by the EU–Turkey Customs Union Joint Committee but ultimately they will be subject to international arbitration (ibid., Art. 61).

What is the substantive coverage of the EU–Turkey Customs Union? A customs union, unlike a free trade area, aims to abolish all customs-related barriers with regard to goods produced by the contracting parties but also third country goods 'in free circulation' within the customs union. In order to achieve this aim and so as to avoid deflections of trade,[58] the customs union will have a common commercial policy towards third States; and in the case of the EU–Turkish customs union, this 'common' policy is almost completely the European Union's commercial policy. Turkey has indeed promised to adopt 'substantially similar' commercial policy measures to those of the Union,[59] and in particular to 'align itself on the Common Customs Tariff'.[60] This means that the conclusion of international trade agreements between Turkey and other States is significantly restricted.

(c) A Free Trade Agreement: The 'Canada Model'

The European Union has established a wide net of bilateral trade agreements with third States. A good illustration of such a free trade agreement is 'CETA': the preferential trade agreement concluded in 2017 between the European Union and Canada.[61] With CETA, the two contracting parties '[f]urther strengthen their close economic relationship'; and while building on their respective rights and obligations under the WTO, CETA's principal aim is to create a free trade area in the form of 'an expanded and secure market for their goods and services through the reduction or elimination of barriers to trade and investment'.[62]

Having been negotiated over seven years, and filling over 1,000 pages, CETA has 30 chapters that cover diverse matters. And while in no way representing anything similar to the EEA or customs union arrangements, discussed earlier, CETA nevertheless also contains a chapter on 'regulatory cooperation'.[63] It has set up a 'CETA Joint Committee', composed of representatives of the EU and Canada, that can take decisions by mutual consent.[64]

---

[58] Deflections of trade occur when a third State choses that Member State within a customs union that offers it the easiest entry into the union.

[59] Decision No. 1/95 (n. 55), Art. 12.

[60] Ibid., Art. 13.

[61] CETA stands for 'Comprehensive Economic and Trade Agreement'. The text of CETA can be found at [2017] OJ L11/23.

[62] Ibid., Preamble 1 and 2.

[63] Ibid., Ch. 21.

[64] Ibid., Arts 26.1 and 26.3.

CETA's principal effect will be an (almost) total reduction of tariffs and it also promises to significantly reduce non-tariff barriers in goods. And going beyond the substantive scope of a customs union, it enhances the legal commitments with regard to the liberalization of services and investment and is also committed to a soft regulatory convergence. Finally, because CETA creates—like the EEA—a free trade area, the Canada model would allow the United Kingdom its own commercial policy vis-à-vis the rest of the world.

(d) Of Hard Choices and Red Lines

The three models presented offer three distinct partnership formats whose respective characteristics are summarized in Table 13.3.

Affiliation with the European Economic Area would undoubtedly represent the 'softest' form of Brexit. This option would not necessarily imply that the United Kingdom rejoins EFTA, yet it would mean that it principally accepts the free movement of persons while also committing itself to shadowing a significant proportion of EU legislation. These consequences could partly be avoided if the United Kingdom joined a customs union arrangement. Yet while it would here retain control over immigration, it would significantly reduce its capacity to conclude future international trade agreements with third States. What, then, about a Canada-style free trade agreement? In the light of the 'Political Declaration' attached to the Withdrawal Agreement, the latter seems today the most likely route.[65]

Table 13.3 Future relationship models: comparison

	EEA: 'Norway Model'	CU: 'Turkey Model'	FTA: 'Canada Model'
Free Movement of Goods	High	High	Medium
Free Movement of People	High	Low	Low
EU Competition Law	High	Medium	Low
Shadowing EU Legislation	High	Medium	Low
Freedom to Trade with Others	High	Medium	High

[65] Political Declaration setting out the Framework for the Future Relationship between the European Union and the United Kingdom (n. 26), para. 3.

Importantly, none of the three models offers full access to the EU internal market. Full 'membership' of the internal market can only be achieved though full membership of the Union; and all non-membership arrangements will consequently only offer partial access to the European market. The 'golden rule' of Union association is thereby this: the degree to which a third State is willing to accept positive integration via Union legislation will directly determine the degree to which it is entitled to enjoy the benefits of negative integration via the single market. This is the fundamental 'constitutional' principle behind all European integration, and if the Union were to give it up, the integrity of the Union would itself be endangered.[66]

Can the 'trade-offs' within each model described earlier be negotiated away? The United Kingdom hopes this can be done and has, optimistically, invoked the idea of a 'bespoke' agreement. And yet, there is a significant economic imbalance working *against* the United Kingdom: for whereas the EU is by far the largest trading partner for the United Kingdom with approximately 50 per cent (!) of all total trade; British trade only represents between 15–20 per cent of all trade conducted by the Union. So, even if the United Kingdom will be one of the most important trading partners of the EU, its relative bargaining power will be smaller when compared to that of the EU. And, legally, the Union is generally not an 'easy' negotiating partner. It is composed of various and diverse States that will need to find a compromise among themselves; and in the best-case scenario, this means a qualified majority in the Council under the Union's common commercial policy.[67]

4. Future II: A 'Hard' Brexit and the 'WTO Model'

What will happen if no trade agreement can be concluded before the end of the transition period? In this case, a 'hard' Brexit will occur in which the United Kingdom will fall back into the World Trade Organization and onto WTO terms. 'WTO terms' are the standard terms of international trade to which more than 150 States have signed up. And in the absence of a bilateral trade deal with the Union, the United Kingdom would, without the need to

---

[66] On the relationship between negative and positive integration, see R. Schütze, *From International to Federal Union: The Changing Structure of European Law* (in preparation).

[67] For a discussion of the (ordinary) treaty-making procedure, see Chapter 2, Section 4.

do anything else,[68] resume its independent membership in the World Trade Organization.

What is the structure and content of the WTO Agreement? The latter was concluded to 'provide the common institutional framework for the conduct of trade relations among its Members'.[69] Its substantive trade rules are thereby found in its various annexes, which integrate a number of sector-specific trade agreements into the WTO Agreement (see Table 13.4).

What are the fundamental principles governing world trade under the WTO Agreement? Its historical core lies in the 1947 GATT, which deals with the free movement of goods; but the WTO Agreement also partially covers trade in services (as well as other matters). The GATT thereby outlaws quantitative restrictions (and measures having equivalent effect) on imports and exports,[70] and it equally demands that imports 'be accorded treatment no less favourable than that accorded to like products of national origin in respect of all laws [and] regulations'.[71] This sounds very much like Article 34 TFEU; and yet, the interpretation given to the GATT is fundamentally different to the one given to the EU Treaties.[72]

Table 13.4 WTO Agreement: coverage

WTO Agreement Annexes (Selection)	
Annex 1A	General Agreement on Tariffs and Trade (GATT)
	Agreement on Agriculture
	Agreement on Sanitary and Phytosanitary Measures
	Agreement on Technical Barriers to Trade
	Agreement on Rules of Origin
Annex 1B	General Agreement on Trade in Services (GATS)

[68] That the United Kingdom will be a member of the WTO in its own right is confirmed in Art. XI(1) of the WTO Agreement. However, the exact nature of its rights and duties as a member are uncertain because its former status as a Member State of the European Union will be removed after Brexit. For a discussion of this point, see F. Baetens, '"No Deal is Better than a Bad Deal"? The Fallacy of the WTO Fall-Back Option as a Post-Brexit Safety Net' (2018) 55 *Common Market Law Review* 133.

[69] WTO Agreement, Art. II(1).

[70] Art. XI(1) GATT: 'No prohibitions or restrictions other than duties, taxes or other charges, whether made effective through quotas, import or export licences or other measures, shall be instituted or maintained by any contracting party on the importation of any product of the territory of any other contracting party or on the exportation or sale for export of any product destined for the territory of any other contracting party.'

[71] Art. III(4) GATT.

[72] R. Schütze, *From International to Federal Market: The Changing Structure of International Law* (Oxford University Press, 2017).

Importantly, and by contrast with the EU Treaties, the GATT expressly allows for customs duties as legitimate barriers to international trade. They are, however, subject to a famous WTO principle: the 'most-favoured-nation' (MFN) principle. According to the MFN principle, any customs advantage granted by one State to another must automatically be accorded to *any third State* trading in a like product.[73] What does that mean for trade between the United Kingdom and the European Union? It means that in the absence of a preferential free trade agreement, neither the United Kingdom nor the European Union can unilaterally decide to favour each other by not imposing any customs duties vis-à-vis the other. If the United Kingdom thus wanted to lower tariffs for goods coming from Europe, it would also have to do this for the rest of the world; and in the case of the European Union, such a move would be out of the question.

In the case of a 'hard' Brexit, the European Union will thus extend its 'normal' tariffs to the United Kingdom; and a selection of the most important tariff rates under its 'Common Customs Tariff' can be found in Figure 13.3.[74]

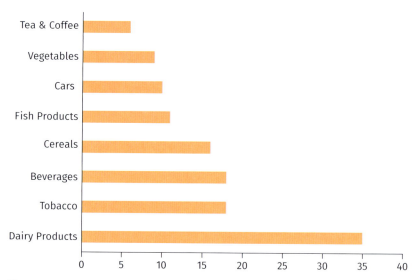

Figure 13.3 Average EU-bound tariff rates (selection)

[73] See Art. I(1) GATT: 'With respect to customs duties and charges of any kind imposed on or in connection with importation or exportation or imposed on the international transfer of payments for imports or exports, and with respect to the method of levying such duties and charges, and with respect to all rules and formalities in connection with importation and exportation, and with respect to all matters referred to in paragraphs 2 and 4 of Article III, any advantage, favour, privilege or immunity granted by any contracting party to any product originating in or destined for any other country shall be accorded immediately and unconditionally to the like product originating in or destined for the territories of all other contracting parties.'

[74] These figures are taken from House of Lords, European Union Committee, 'Brexit: trade in goods', at https://publications.parliament.uk/pa/ld201617/ldselect/ldeucom/129/129.pdf.

Conclusion

Is Brexit an isolated case or does it signal the beginning of an era of European disintegration? It is impossible to predict the future; and what this chapter has tried to do is to explore the specific reasons for Britain's departure from the European Union. Britain's interests in Europe were always predominantly of an economic nature; and its critical attitude towards 'political' integration had found numerous expressions in a wide range of 'opt-outs' in the EU Treaties. But even this halfway house 'inside' and 'outside' the European Union did not, sadly, prevent Brexit.

The Brexit process was governed by Article 50 TEU until 31 January 2020. Since then, it has been subject to the Withdrawal Agreement that was discussed in Section 2. This agreement is, however, only a first step. It solely delivers the British 'divorce' from the Union. Any future trade partnership still needs to be negotiated in a second agreement. The various 'standard' agreements were discussed in Section 3, and the likeliest option here is today a version of the EU–Canada agreement. In theory, this agreement will need to be concluded by 31 December 2020—unless the British transition period is extended. In the event that no agreement can be found, a 'hard' Brexit will occur, the consequences of which were discussed in Section 4.

Appendices

Appendix I
Academic Literature: Further Reading

The literature with regard to European Union law has exploded in the last 30 years. Today, there exists a forest of general EU law textbooks and journals. The list in Table 14.1 is therefore by no means comprehensive. It is meant to point the interested reader to a gateway for an in-depth study of a particular area of European Union law. The main pedagogical distinction, among English-language textbooks, is here between 'classic' textbooks and 'Cases and Materials' textbooks. For those readers who liked the approach taken in this *Introduction*, the easiest continuation would be my own *European Union Law*.

In order to provide the reader with some more specific literature suggestions, I have also listed between six and eight books and articles for each chapter of this book below. They could be considered 'essential reading' for a course on EU law. Yet the prior study of the relevant chapter in a bigger EU law textbook might still be useful before jumping to a particular journal article on a potentially (much more) specific aspect of EU law.

Table 14.1 General textbooks and journals

General Textbooks	General Journals
C. Barnard et al., *European Union Law* (Oxford University Press, 2020)	Cambridge Yearbook of European Legal Studies
D. Chalmers et al., *European Union Law* (Cambridge University Press, 2019)	Common Market Law Review
P. Craig and G. de Búrca, *EU Law: Text, Cases, and Materials* (Oxford University Press, 2020)	European Law Journal
R. Schütze, *European Union Law* (Oxford University Press, 2021)	European Law Review
S. Weatherill, *Cases & Materials on EU Law* (Oxford University Press, 2016)	Journal of Common Market Studies
M. Costa and S. Peers, *Steiner & Woods' EU Law* (Oxford University Press, 2020)	Yearbook of European Law

Introduction (History)

P. Craig, *The Lisbon Treaty: Law, Politics, and Treaty Reform* (Oxford University Press, 2010)

D. Curtin, 'The Constitutional Structure of the Union: A Europe of Bits and Pieces' (1993) 30 *Common Market Law Review* 17

P. D. Dinan, *Europe Recast: A History of European Union* (Palgrave, 2004)

P. Pescatore, 'Some Critical Remarks on the "Single European Act"' (1987) 24 *Common Market Law Review* 9

J.-C. Piris, *The Lisbon Treaty: A Legal and Political Analysis* (Cambridge University Press, 2010)

R. Schütze, *European Union Law* (Cambridge University Press, 2018), ch. 1

D. Urwin, *The Community of Europe: A History of European Integration Since 1945* (Longman, 1994)

Chapter 1: Union Institutions

R. Böttner, 'The Size and Structure of the European Commission: Legal Issues Surrounding Project Teams and a (future) reduced College' (2018) 14 *European Constitutional Law Review* 37

M. Chamon, 'The Institutional Balance, an Ill-Fated Principle of EU Law?' (2015) 21 *European Public Law* 371

R. Corbett et al., *The European Parliament* (Harper Publishing, 2016)

P. Dann, 'European Parliament and Executive Federalism: Approaching a Parliament in a Semi-Parliamentary Democracy' (2003) 9 *European Law Journal* 549

F. Hayes-Renshaw and H. Wallace, *The Council of Ministers* (Palgrave, 2006)

S. Novak, 'The Silence of Ministers: Consensus and Blame Avoidance in the Council of the European Union' (2013) 51 *Journal of Common Market Studies* 1091

N. Nugent and M. Rhinard, *The European Commission* (Palgrave, 2015)

R. Schütze and T. Tridimas (eds), *Oxford Principles of European Union Law*, Vol. I (Oxford University Press, 2018), chs 14 (Parliament), 16 (Council), 17 (Commission), and 18 (Court of Justice)

Chapter 2: Union Legislation

S. Hix and B. Høyland, *The Political System of the European Union* (Palgrave, 2011)

D. Jancic, 'The Game of Cards: National Parliaments in the EU and the Future of the Early Warning Mechanism and the Political Dialogue' (2015) 52 *Common Market Law Review* 939

B. Kohler-Koch and B. Rittberger, *Debating the Democratic Legitimacy of the European Union* (Rowman & Littlefield, 2007)

N. Nugent, *The Government and Politics of the European Union* (Palgrave, 2017)

C. Reh et al., 'The Informal Politics of Legislation: Explaining Secluded Decision Making in the European Union' (2013) 49 *Comparative Political Studies* 1112

C. Roederer-Rynning and J. Greenwood, 'The Culture of Trilogues' (2015) 22 *Journal of European Public Policy* 1148

A. Türk, 'Primary Legislation and Legislative Procedures' in R. Schütze et al. (eds), *Oxford Principles of European Union Law*, Vol. I (Oxford University Press, 2018), 689

Chapter 3: Union Competences

L. Azoulai (ed.), *The Question of Competence in the European Union* (Oxford University Press, 2014)

P. Craig, 'Competence: Clarity, Conferral, Containment and Consideration' (2004) 29 *European Law Review* 323

A. Dashwood, 'The Limits of European Community Powers' (1996) 21 *European Law Review* 113

S. Garben and I. Govaere, *The Division of Competences between the EU and the Member States: Reflections on the Past, the Present and the Future* (Hart, 2017)

T. Konstadinides, 'The Competences of the Union' in R. Schütze et al. (eds), *Oxford Principles of European Union Law*, Vol. I (Oxford University Press, 2018), 191

R. Schütze, 'Lisbon and the Federal Order of Competences: A Prospective Analysis' (2008) 33 *European Law Review* 709

S. Weatherill, 'Competence Creep and Competence Control' (2004) 23 *Yearbook of European Law* 1

Chapter 4: Fundamental Rights

L. Besselink, 'Entrapped by the Maximum Standard: On Fundamental Rights, Pluralism and Subsidiarity in the European Union' (1998) 35 *Common Market Law Review* 629

G. de Búrca, 'The Evolution of EU Human Rights Law' in P. Craig and G. de Búrca (eds), *The Evolution of EU Law* (Oxford University Press, 2011), 465

J. Coppel and A. O'Neill, 'The European Court of Justice: Taking Rights Seriously?' (1992) 29 *Common Market Law Review* 669

S. Douglas-Scott, 'The European Union and Fundamental Rights' in R. Schütze et al. (eds), *Oxford Principles of European Union Law*, Vol. I (Oxford University Press, 2018), 383

K. Lenaerts, 'Exploring the Limits of the EU Charter of Fundamental Rights' (2012) 8 *European Constitutional Law Review* 375

T. Lock, 'The Future of the European Union's Accession to the European Convention on Human Rights after *Opinion 2/13*: Is It Still Possible and Is It Still Desirable?' (2015) 11 *European Constitutional Law Review* 239

S. Peers et al. (eds), *The EU Charter of Fundamental Rights: A Commentary* (Hart, 2014)

Chapter 5: Direct Effect

P. Craig, 'Once Upon a Time in the West: Direct Effect and the Federalisation of EEC Law' (1992) 12 *Oxford Journal of Legal Studies* 453

A. Dashwood, 'From *Van Duyn* to *Mangold* via *Marshall*: Reducing Direct Effect to Absurdity' (2006/7) 9 *Cambridge Yearbook of European Legal Studies* 81

S. Drake, 'Twenty Years after *Von Colson*: the Impact of "Indirect Effect" on the Protection of the Individual's Community Rights' (2005) 30 *European Law Review* 329

P. Pescatore, 'The Doctrine of "Direct Effect": An Infant Disease of Community Law' (1983) 8 *European Law Review* 155

S. Prechal, *Directives in EC Law* (Oxford University Press, 2006)

R. Schütze, 'Direct Effects and Indirect Effects of Union Law' in R. Schütze et al. (eds), *Oxford Principles of European Union Law*, Vol. I (Oxford University Press, 2018), 265

J. Steiner, 'Direct Applicability in EEC Law—A Chameleon Concept' (1982) 98 *Law Quarterly Review* 229

Chapter 6: (Legal) Primacy

K. Alter, *Establishing the Supremacy of European Law: the Making of an International Rule of Law in Europe* (Oxford University Press, 2001)

B. Davies, *Resisting the European Court of Justice: West Germany's Confrontation with European Law, 1949–1979* (Cambridge University Press, 2014)

U. Everling, 'The Maastricht Judgment of the German Federal Constitutional Court and its Significance for the Development of the European Union' (1994) 14 *Yearbook of European Law* 1

R. Kovar, 'The Relationship between Community Law and National Law' in EC Commission (ed.), *Thirty Years of Community Law* (EC Commission, 1981), 109

M. Madsen, H. Olsen, and U. Šadl, 'Competing Supremacies and Clashing Institutional Rationalities: the Danish Supreme Court's Decision in the *Ajos* Case and the National Limits of Judicial Cooperation' (2017) 23 *European Law Journal* 140

W. Sadurski, '"*Solange*, Chapter 3": Constitutional Courts in Central Europe—Democracy—European Union' (2008) 14 *European Law Journal* 1

D. Thym, 'In the Name of Sovereign Statehood: A Critical Introduction to the *Lisbon* Judgment of the German Constitutional Court' (2009) 46 *Common Market Law Review* 1795

Chapter 7: National Actions

A. Arnull, 'Remedies before National Courts' in R. Schütze et al. (eds), *Oxford Principles of European Union Law*, Vol. I (Oxford University Press, 2018), 1011

M. Broberg, '*Acte Clair* Revisited' (2008) 45 *Common Market Law Review* 1383

M. Broberg and N. Fenger, *Preliminary References to the European Court of Justice* (Oxford University Press, 2014)

M. Claes, *The National Courts' Mandate in the European Constitution* (Hart, 2005)

M. Dougan, *National Remedies before the Court of Justice: Issues of Harmonisation and Differentiation* (Hart, 2004)

M. Dougan, 'The Vicissitudes of Life at the Coalface: Remedies and Procedures for Enforcing Union Law Before the National Courts' in P. Craig and G. de Búrca (eds), *The Evolution of EU Law* (Oxford University Press, 2011), 407

R. Lauwaars, 'The Application of Community Law by National Courts *Ex Officio*' (2007–8) 31 *Fordham International Law Journal* 1161

T. Tridimas, 'Liability for Breach of Community Law: Growing Up and Mellowing Down?' (2001) 38 *Common Market Law Review* 301

Chapter 8: European Actions

A. Albors-Llorens, 'Remedies against the EU Institutions after Lisbon: An Era of Opportunity' (2012) 71 *Cambridge Law Journal* 507

S. Andersen, *The Enforcement of EU Law* (Oxford University Press, 2012)

S. Balthasar, '*Locus Standi* Rules for Challenges to Regulatory Acts by Private Applicants: the New Article 263(4) TFEU' (2010) 35 *European Law Review* 542

K. Gutman, 'The Evolution of the Action for Damages against the European Union and its Place in the System of Judicial Protection' (2011) 48 *Common Market Law Review* 695

K. Lenaerts, I. Maselis, and K. Gutman, *EU Procedural Law* (Oxford University Press, 2014)

L. Prete and B. Smulders, 'The Coming of Age of Infringement Proceedings' (2010) 47 *Common Market Law Review* 9

A. Ward, *Judicial Review and the Rights of Private Parties in EU Law* (Oxford University Press, 2007)

Chapter 9: Internal Market: Goods I

C. Barnard, *The Substantive Law of the EU: The Four Freedoms* (Oxford University Press, 2019), chs 2–7

A. Easson, 'Cheaper Wine or Dearer Beer? Article 95 Again' (1984) 9 *European Law Review* 57

P. Oliver (ed.), *Oliver on Free Movement of Goods in the European Union* (Hart, 2010)

J. Snell, 'The Notion of Market Access: A Concept or a Slogan?' (2010) 47 *Common Market Law Review* 437

E. Spaventa, 'Leaving *Keck* Behind? The Free Movement of Goods after the Rulings in *Commission* v. *Italy* and *Mickelsson and Roos*' (2009) 34 *European Law Review* 914

M. Szydło, 'Export Restrictions within the Structure of Free Movement of Goods: Reconsideration of an Old Paradigm' (2010) 47 *Common Market Law Review* 753

F. Weiss and C. Kaupa, *European Union Internal Market Law* (Cambridge University Press, 2014), ch. 3

Chapter 10: Internal Market: Goods II

R. Barents, 'The Internal Market Unlimited: Some Observations on the Legal Basis of Community Legislation' (1993) 30 *Common Market Law Review* 85

G. Davies, 'Can Selling Arrangements be Harmonised?' (2005) 30 *European Law Review* 37

N. de Sadeleer, 'Procedures for Derogation from the Principle of Approximation of Laws under Article 95 EC' (2003) 40 *Common Market Law Review* 889

R. Schütze, *From Dual to Cooperative Federalism: The Changing Structure of European Law* (Oxford University Press, 2009)

P. J. Slot, 'Harmonisation' (1996) 21 *European Law Review* 378

S. Weatherill, *Law and Integration in the European Union* (Clarendon Press, 1995)

S. Weatherill, 'The Limits of Legislative Harmonization Ten Years after *Tobacco Advertising*: How the Court's Case Law has become a "Drafting Guide"' (2011) 12 *German Law Journal* 827

Chapter 11: Internal Market: Persons

C. Barnard, *The Substantive Law of the EU: The Four Freedoms* (Oxford University Press, 2019), chs 8–10 and 13

J. Borg-Barthet, *Governing Law of Companies in EU Law* (Hart, 2012)

L. Daniele, 'Non-Discriminatory Restrictions to the Free Movement of Persons' (1997) 22 *European Law Review* 191

M. Dougan, 'The Constitutional Dimension to the Case Law on Union Citizenship' (2006) 31 *European Law Review* 613

E. Spaventa, 'From "Gebhard" to "Carpenter": Towards a (Non-)Economic European Constitution' (2004) 41 *Common Market Law Review* 743

A. Tryfonidou, 'In Search of the Aim of the EC Free Movement of Persons Provisions: Has the Court of Justice Missed the Point?' (2009) 46 *Common Market Law Review* 1591

F. Weiss and C. Kaupa, *European Union Internal Market Law* (Cambridge University Press, 2014), chs 4–6

Chapter 12: Competition Law: Cartels

G. Amato, *Antitrust and the Bounds of Power: The Dilemma of Liberal Democracy in the History of the Market* (Hart, 1997)

J. Faull, 'Effect on Trade Between Member States' (1999) 26 *Fordham Corporate Law Institute* 481

A. Jones et al., *EU Competition Law: Text, Cases, and Materials* (Oxford University Press, 2019)

O. Odudu, 'The Meaning of Undertaking within Article 81 EC' (2006) 7 *Cambridge Yearbook of European Legal Studies* 211

A. Weitbrecht, 'From Freiburg to Chicago and Beyond: The First 50 Years of European Competition Law' (2008) 29 *European Competition Law Review* 81

R. Whish and D. Bailey, 'Regulation 330/2010: The Commission's New Block Exemption for Vertical Agreements' (2010) 47 *Common Market Law Review* 1757

R. Whish and D. Bailey, *Competition Law* (Oxford University Press, 2018)

Epilogue—Brexit: Past, Present, Future

P. Craig, 'Brexit: A Drama in Six Acts' (2016) 41 *European Law Review* 447

M. Dougan, *The UK After Brexit: Legal and Policy Challenges* (Intersentia, 2017)

F. Fabbrini (ed.), *The Law & Politics of Brexit* (Oxford University Press, 2017)

A. Geddes, *Britain and the European Union* (Palgrave, 2013)

L. Gormley, 'Brexit—Never Mind the Whys and Wherefores? Fog in the Channel, Continent Cut Off!' (2017) 40 *Fordham International Law Journal* 1175

A. Łazowski, 'Withdrawal from the European Union and Alternatives to Membership' (2012) 37 *European Law Review* 523

N. Neuwahl, 'CETA as a Potential Model for (Post-Brexit) UK–EU Relations' (2017) 22 *European Foreign Affairs Review* 279

How to Find (and Read) EU Judgments

All EU cases are identified by a number/year. Cases before the Court of Justice are preceded by a C-, while cases decided before the General Court are preceded by a T- (for the French 'Tribunal').[1] Following this unique combination, come the names of the parties to the case. A full case name would, for example, be: Case C-144/04, *Werner Mangold v Rüdiger Helm*. However, since no one can remember all the numbers or all the parties, EU cases are often simply abbreviated to the name of the main party—in our case '*Mangold*'.

In the past, judgments of all EU Courts were published in paper form in the purple-bound 'European Court Reports' (ECR). Cases decided by the Court of Justice were published in the ECR I series; while cases decided by the General Court were published in the ECR II series. However, as of 2012, the entire Court of Justice of the European Union decided to go 'paperless' and it now publishes its judgments only electronically.[2] The two principal websites here are the Court's own Curia website (http://curia.europa.eu/jcms/jcms/j_6/), and the Union's general EUR-Lex website (http://eur-lex.europa.eu/homepage.html). For the purposes of this book, the easiest way is, however, to go to www.schutze.eu, which contains the 'Lisbon' version of all classic EU Court judgments mentioned in this text (see Appendix III).

Once upon a time, judgments issued by the European Courts were—to paraphrase Hobbes—'nasty, brutish and short'. Their shortness was partly due to a structural division the Court made between 'Issues of Fact and of Law' (or, later: 'Report for the Hearing'), which set out the facts, procedures, and the arguments of the parties, on the one hand, and the 'Grounds of Judgment', on the other. Only the latter constituted the judgment *sensu stricto* and it was often very short indeed. For the Court originally followed the 'French' ideal of trying to put the entire judgment into a single 'sentence'! A judgment like *Van Gend en Loos* contains about 2,000 words—not more than an undergraduate essay.

This world of short judgments is—sadly or not—gone. A typical judgment issued today will, on average, be four to five times as long as *Van Gend*. (And in the worst case scenario, a judgment, especially in the area of EU competition law, may be as long as 100,000 words—the size of this book!)

The structure of a modern ECJ judgment given under the preliminary reference procedure may be studied by looking at *Mangold* (Figure 14.1).

---

[1] Importantly, cases decided before the creation of the General Court will have no prefix at all. For there was only one court: the Court of Justice.

[2] In the absence of a 'page number' in a printed book, the Union henceforth has recourse to a 'European Case Law Identifier'. This is composed of EU:C[T/F]:Year:Number.

JUDGMENT OF THE COURT (Grand Chamber)

22 November 2005

> This is a summary of the substantive issues involved.

(Directive 1999/70/EC , clauses 2, 5, and 8 of the Framework Agreement on fixed-term work—Directive 2000/78/EC, Article 6, Equal treatment as regards employment and occupation—Age discrimination)

> This is a C-case before the European Court of Justice. It is the 144th case registered in 2004.

In Case C-144/04,

> This is a summary of the procedural issues involved.

REFERENCE for a preliminary ruling under Article 234 EC from the Arbeitsgericht München (Germany), made by decision of 26 February 2004, registered at the Court on 17 March 2004, in the proceedings

> These are the names of the parties to the (national) proceedings.

Werner Mangold

v

Rüdiger Helm,

THE COURT (Grand Chamber),

> This indicates the composition of the ECJ in this specific case—here, the Grand Chamber. This is a collegiate judgment: all the judges sign the judgment and thus speak with a single voice for 'the' Court.

composed of P. Jann, President of the First Chamber, acting as President, C.W.A. Timmermans, A. Rosas and K. Schiemann, Presidents of Chambers, R. Schintgen (Rapporteur), S. von Bahr, J.N. Cunha Rodrigues, R. Silva de Lapuerta, K. Lenaerts, E. Juhász, G. Arestis, A. Borg Barthet and M. Ilešič, Judges,

> This is a reference to the Advocate General in the case. In the modern printed version, the Opinion of the Advocate General precedes the judgment.

Advocate General: A. Tizzano,

. . .

Judgment

1 This reference for a preliminary ruling concerns the interpretation of Clauses 2, 5 and 8 of the Framework Agreement on fixed-term contracts concluded on 18 March I - 10014 MANGOLD 1999 ('the Framework Agreement'), put into effect by Council Directive 1999/70/EC of 28 June 1999 concerning the framework agreement on fixed-term work concluded by ETUC, UNICE and CEEP (OJ 1999 L 175, p. 43), and of Article 6 of Council Directive 2000/78/EC of 27 November 2000 establishing a general framework for equal treatment in employment and occupation (OJ 2000 L 303, p. 16).

2 The reference has been made in the course of proceedings brought by Mr Mangold against Mr Helm concerning a fixed-term contract by which the former was employed by the latter ('the contract').

> Having given a brief synopsis of the issues involved, the Court starts by presenting the legal context; that is, the relevant norms of European and national law.

Legal context

The relevant provisions of Community law

The Framework Agreement

3 According to Clause 1, '[t]he purpose of this Framework Agreement is to:

(a) improve the quality of fixed-term work by ensuring the application of the principle of non-discrimination;

(b) establish a framework to prevent abuse arising from the use of successive fixed-term employment contracts or relationships'.

. . .

The relevant provisions of national law

14 Paragraph 1 of the Beschäftigungsförderungsgesetz (Law to promote employment), as amended by the law of 25 September 1996 (BGBl. 1996 I, p. 1476) ('the BeschFG 1996'), provided:

Figure 14.1 *Mangold* judgment: structure

...

The main proceedings and the questions referred for a preliminary ruling

20 On 26 June 2003 Mr Mangold, then 56 years old, concluded with Mr Helm, who practises as a lawyer, a contract that took effect on 1 July 2003.

21 Article 5 of that contract provided that:

'1. The employment relationship shall start on 1 July 2003 and last until 28 February 2004.

2. The duration of the contract shall be based on the statutory provision which is intended to make it easier to conclude fixed-term contracts of employment with older workers (the provisions of the fourth sentence, in conjunction with those of the fourth sentence, of Paragraph 14(3) of the TzBfG ...), since the employee is more than 52 years old. ...'

...

31 Those were the circumstances in which the Arbeitsgericht München decided to stay proceedings and to refer the following questions to the Court of Justice for a preliminary ruling:

'1 (a) Is Clause 8(3) of the Framework Agreement ... to be interpreted, when transposed into domestic law, as prohibiting a reduction of protection following from the lowering of the age limit from 60 to 58? ...'

...

Admissibility of the reference for a preliminary ruling

32 At the hearing the admissibility of the reference for a preliminary ruling was challenged by the Federal Republic of Germany, on the grounds that the dispute in the main proceedings was fictitious or contrived. Indeed, in the past Mr Helm has publicly argued a case identical to Mr Mangold's, to the effect that Paragraph 14(3) of the TzBfG is unlawful.

...

Concerning the questions referred for a preliminary ruling

On Question 1(b)

40 In Question 1(b), which it is appropriate to consider first, the national court asks whether, on a proper construction of Clause 5 of the Framework Agreement, it is contrary to that provision for rules of domestic law such as those at issue in the main proceedings to contain none of the restrictions provided for by that clause in respect of the use of fixed-term contracts of employment.

...

On those grounds, the Court (Grand Chamber) hereby rules:

1. **On a proper construction of Clause 8(3) of the Framework Agreement on fixed-term contracts concluded on 18 March 1999, put into effect by Council Directive 1999/70/EC of 28 June 1999 concerning the framework agreement on fixed-term work concluded by ETUC, UNICE and CEEP, domestic legislation such as that at issue in the main proceedings, which for reasons connected with the need to encourage employment and irrespective of the implementation of that agreement, has lowered the age above which fixed-term contracts of employment may be concluded without restrictions, is not contrary to that provision.**

...

This is one of the most important sections for the reader of a judgment. The Court here presents the facts and the procedure(s) of the specific case.

The Court quotes the preliminary questions referred to by the national court.

We saw in Chapter 7, Section 4(b) that the Court will check if the national court was entitled to use the preliminary procedure under Article 267 TFEU.

In the main part of the judgment, the Court will answer each of the preliminary questions, one by one. Sometimes, it may change their order—as in this case; or it may decide that one question was not admissible, or that the answer to one question makes its response to another unnecessary. (In many direct actions, the Court has come to clearly separate the 'Arguments of the Parties' from the 'Findings of the Court' for each of the legal points raised.)

This is the core 'ratio decidendi' of the judgment.

How to Use the Author's Companion Website

The author's companion website for this textbook can be found at www.schutze.eu. Its principal aim is to allow readers to have all the EU cases as well as the recommended readings and some extra materials at their fingertips (see Figure 14.2).

To that effect, each online chapter contains full-text versions of all the cases dealt with specifically in that chapter (see Figure 14.3); and, where these cases were decided prior to the Lisbon Treaty, they have been 'Lisbonized' and renumbered. In this way, students will be able to read *Costa v ENEL* or *Cassis de Dijon* as if they were decided under the TEU/TFEU today (see Figure 14.4).

The 'Further Readings' tab will direct the reader to the publisher's website for a specific book or article; and, if you are on campus and your university has online access to a publisher, you should be able to read and/or download the specific article or chapter directly.

The companion website also contains a range of extra learning materials for each chapter and there are also some general revision materials—including some revision slides and case summaries. And for those who cannot get enough of European Union law, there is also an additional online chapter on EU competition law dealing with Article 102 TFEU.

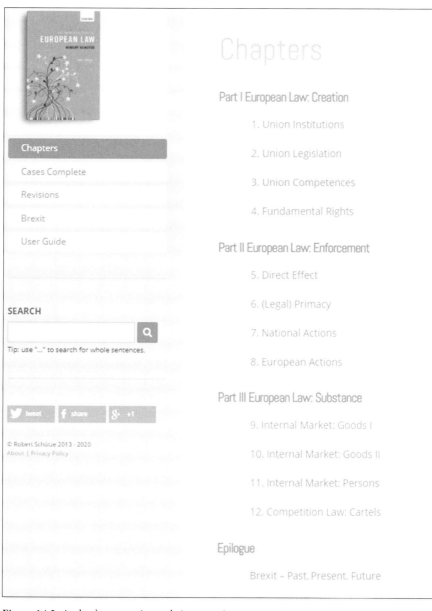

Figure 14.2 Author's companion website: overview

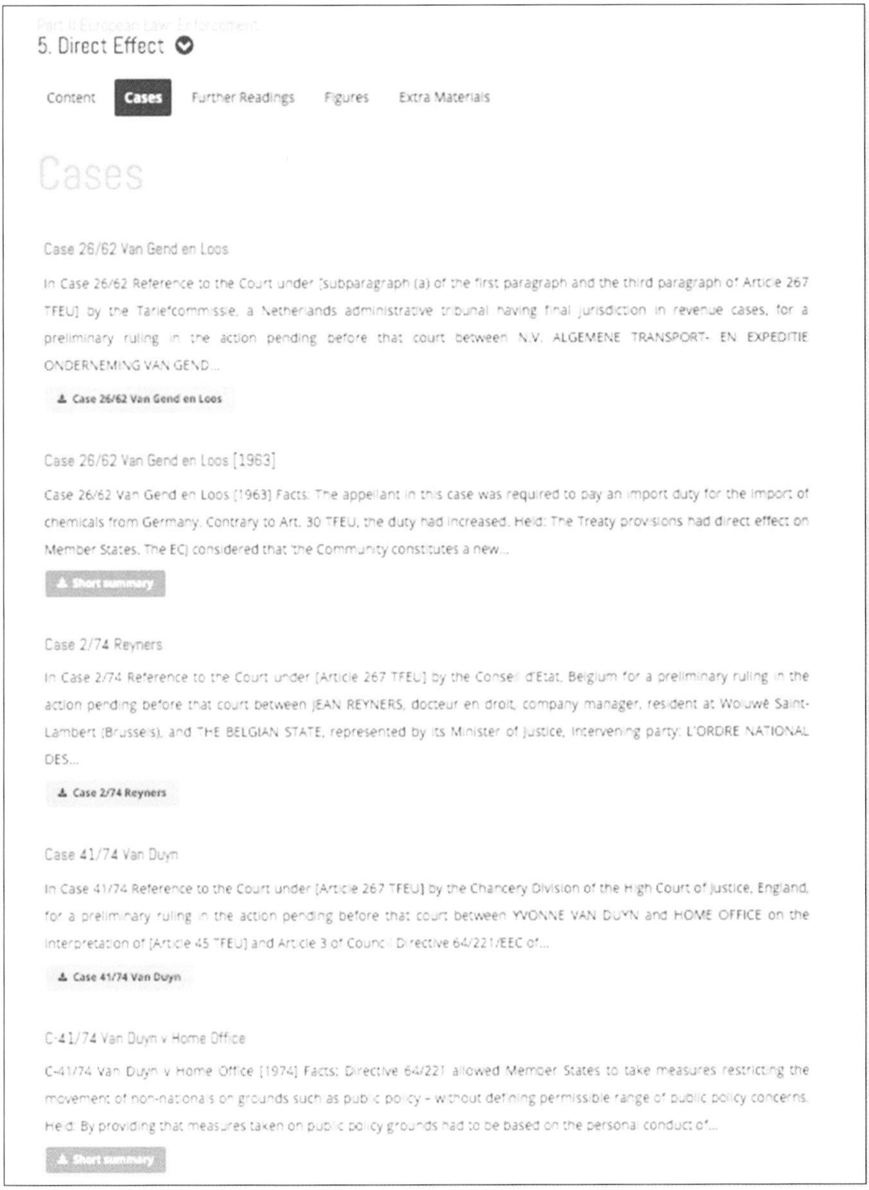

Part II European Law: Enforcement

5. Direct Effect ⊘

Content   **Cases**   Further Readings   Figures   Extra Materials

Cases

Case 26/62 Van Gend en Loos

In Case 26/62 Reference to the Court under [subparagraph (a) of the first paragraph and the third paragraph of Article 267 TFEU] by the Tariefcommissie, a Netherlands administrative tribunal having final jurisdiction in revenue cases, for a preliminary ruling in the action pending before that court between N.V. ALGEMENE TRANSPORT- EN EXPEDITIE ONDERNEMING VAN GEND...

⬇ **Case 26/62 Van Gend en Loos**

Case 26/62 Van Gend en Loos [1963]

Case 26/62 Van Gend en Loos [1963] Facts: The appellant in this case was required to pay an import duty for the import of chemicals from Germany. Contrary to Art. 30 TFEU, the duty had increased. Held: The Treaty provisions had direct effect on Member States. The ECJ considered that the Community constitutes a new...

⬇ **Short summary**

Case 2/74 Reyners

In Case 2/74 Reference to the Court under [Article 267 TFEU] by the Conseil d'Etat, Belgium for a preliminary ruling in the action pending before that court between JEAN REYNERS, docteur en droit, company manager, resident at Woluwé Saint-Lambert (Brussels), and THE BELGIAN STATE, represented by its Minister of Justice, intervening party: L'ORDRE NATIONAL DES...

⬇ **Case 2/74 Reyners**

Case 41/74 Van Duyn

In Case 41/74 Reference to the Court under [Article 267 TFEU] by the Chancery Division of the High Court of Justice, England, for a preliminary ruling in the action pending before that court between YVONNE VAN DUYN and HOME OFFICE on the interpretation of [Article 45 TFEU] and Article 3 of Council Directive 64/221/EEC of...

⬇ **Case 41/74 Van Duyn**

C-41/74 Van Duyn v Home Office

C-41/74 Van Duyn v Home Office [1974] Facts: Directive 64/221 allowed Member States to take measures restricting the movement of non-nationals on grounds such as public policy – without defining permissible range of public policy concerns. Held: By providing that measures taken on public policy grounds had to be based on the personal conduct of...

⬇ **Short summary**

Figure 14.3 Author's companion website: cases and summaries

In Case 26/62

Reference to the Court under [subparagraph (a) of the first paragraph and the third paragraph of Article 267 TFEU] by the Tariefcommissie, a Netherlands administrative tribunal having final jurisdiction in revenue cases, for a preliminary ruling in the action pending before that court between

N.V. ALGEMENE TRANSPORT- EN EXPEDITIE ONDERNEMING VAN GEND & Loos, having its registered office at Utrecht, represented by H.G. Stibbe and L.F.D. ter Kuile, both Advocates of Amsterdam, with an address for service in Luxembourg at the Consulate-General of the Kingdom of the Netherlands

and

NEDERLANDSE ADMINISTRATIE DER BELASTINGEN (NETHERLANDS INLAND REVENUE ADMINISTRATION), represented by the Inspector of Customs and Excise at Zaandam, with an address for service in Luxembourg at the Netherlands Embassy,

on the following questions:

1. Whether [Article 30 TFEU] has direct application within the territory of a Member State, in other words, whether nationals of such a State can, on the basis of the Article in question, lay claim to individual rights which the courts must protect;

2. In the event of an affirmative reply, whether the application of an import duty of 83 to the import into the Netherlands by the applicant in the main action of ureaformaldehyde originating in the Federal Republic of Germany represented an unlawful increase within the meaning of [Article 30 TFEU] or whether it was in this case a reasonable alteration of the duty applicable before 1 March 1960, an alteration which, although amounting to an increase from the arithmetical point of view, is nevertheless not to be regarded as prohibited under the terms of [Article 30 TFEU];

Figure 14.4 (Lisbonized) *Van Gend en Loos*

Index

F